Off Mike

Introduction

I WAS MAD FOR LITERATURE. Drunk to be steeped in it, interpreting it, creating it. I, the would-be younger brother or surrogate son or even poor cousin to Saul Bellow—he being the kind of writer, as that writer's writer Cynthia Ozick once told me, who comes to us every thousand years or so, if we are in luck. If I couldn't be Bellow's younger brother or surrogate son or even his poor cousin, then I would earn the authorship mantle from whatever talent I might hold and wherever drive would lead. This book, in part, is about that quest.

I didn't make it as a writer, but it wasn't for lack of trying. I was as driven to write as any writer I know, as willing to put in the hours alone pushing out words and turning them around. I also worked hard to become a well-read man, a man of letters. For some reason I came to believe that feeding the hungry mind would make me a better person, and I wanted to live a life that could answer Bellow's primary question: How should a good man live?

"Goodness is achieved not in a vacuum, but in the company of other men, attended by love." That was how Bellow defined being good in his first novel, *Dangling Man*. But the demonic can be magnetic. When I was young, I was a miscreant, a would-be tough guy with a slight and wavering moral compass. In Bellow's ouevre, goodness is tied to idealism and social conscience, to a kind heart and giving meaning to life's chaos. I felt as a young man in metamorphosis from high school that I would find it, this goodness—like his character Augie March—by going at things as I taught myself and as I learned, free-style.

But my drive to write did not grant me success. Stymied as a writer, I developed as an educator, a classroom teacher and, later, accidentally, as an interviewer.

My first interview, a baptism of fire, happened by fluke: in 1976, the AudioVisual head at San Francisco State University asked if I might be interested in interviewing Gore Vidal on the campus's new-at-the-time intracampus television network. I jumped at what seemed like a serendipitous opportunity. It was an interview that would cast me as nervous, deferential neophyte and Vidal as sour, condescending, inebriated and mean.

Heading into the interview, I was sure—both of us being literary types with left-wing politics—that we would become fast friends. I wanted to do a professional job and ask good, thoughtful, intelligent questions. I read as much as I could on Vidal and reread early works of his like *Myra Breckinridge* and *The City and the Pillar*, as well as his newest novel at the time, *Kalki*. More impressed by Vidal's essays than his fiction, I still felt certain that the two of us would have much to talk about and would get on well.

When we met briefly before going to the television studio set to begin the interview, Vidal seemed world weary, as if afflicted with terminal weltschmerz, but more important, he smelled of liquor and his voice was thick with booze. I noticed a copy next to him of James Atlas's biography of Delmore Schwartz. I asked what he thought of the book, hoping to initiate a bit of literary conversation before we went on the set. What did he think about Schwartz, a gifted Jewish writer and lifetime friend of Saul Bellow, the prototype for Bellow's novel *Humboldt's Gift*? Vidal's response shocked me and felt like a blow. "Schwartz thought he was better than we *goyim*," Vidal replied acidly. Then he added offhandedly, "The Jews really think they run New York."

Was Vidal baiting me, sensing my Jewishness and trying to gore me with it? How could one with such radical sympathies sound like such a rank, bloody anti-Semite? He must not have meant what he said. How could he? Well, I did know a few Jews who acted like they thought they ran New York, and I shunted Vidal's remarks aside. I was on my maiden voyage. I had a job to do.

Now the amazing thing about the interview was that once we were on the air, Vidal was "on" in a way that took me as much by surprise as his prior world-weariness, condescension and anti-Semitism. The lights and cameras rolled, and he was a different man: he sounded sober and was all performer. I gave him a short but flattering introduction that I had memorized, mentioning that I was an English professor and that Vidal's real name was Eugene Luther Gore Vidal. He quickly ripped into me for bringing up what he archly called "my Christian name," adding that, unlike our born-again president, Jimmy Carter, he, Vidal, was a born-again atheist.

In the first part of our interview Vidal made me squirm by derogating English professors as a pack of pedants who wanted nothing more than to write reams of useless criticism that no one but other English professors would ever want to read. We were all a bunch of Dryasdusts who longed to create something as obscure as endless annotations of *Finnegan's Wake*. Before the interview, I had felt as though I needed to defend my tribe. Now it was my profession.

Vidal was animated and electrified, palpably alive as he proceeded to skewer his favorite targets—*The New York Times*, Republicans, corporations, Reagan, Nixon, President Jimmy Carter. Some of it was clever stuff, refined and caustic humor that I might have enjoyed were it not for the anti-Semitic cracks and the invective against English profs.

I was trying to hang on during the interview, to keep the dialogue flowing without losing my temper or cool, without being cowed by the realization that I was conversing with the larger than life, literary Gore Vidal. As the interview moved into politics and I asked Vidal about his social concerns, another self emerged. Vidal was suddenly benign, casting himself in the role of munificent socialist. When the interview ended and the cameras were off, he once again became world-weary, cold and aloof, the man I had met before the interview, as sterile as I'd found his apocalyptic novel *Kalki*.

There was not, I felt, anything particularly distinguished about my performance that afternoon, though I knew that I was professional. Anyway, how was one supposed to measure performance in something as difficult to judge as interviewing?

It was, however, quite a performance on Vidal's part, and it was the sort of interview that might have turned someone else away from interviewing, especially since he lit out without so much as a *thank you* or *nice talking to you*. But other things later converged that drew me to interviewing and set me on a path. Trying to meld life into art, as I read and interpreted and taught and wrote about writers, I went on to talk and talk and talk with writers until I had interviewed more writers, perhaps, than anyone ever has or will or should. I was on the road, my own road to literary Damascus.

I am in some ways what I wanted to be. I am a learned man and a literary figure of sorts. I am also a public intellectual and a maestro for educated radio listeners who prefer their discourse high and civil. I am a writer's interviewer. Publishers vie for a slot for their authors because we sell more books than any local radio program in the country. I am a broadcaster who has been on both the commercial and public sides of the radio and television dials, as different as the moon's two sides. A babbling bibliophile. I'm the inverse of Saul Bellow, who said he was a bird and not an ornithologist. But does all of it make me a better human being? It has taught me how little I know.

1   A Lust for Lit

I BEGAN TO REALIZE IN COLLEGE at Ohio University that I wanted to be a good boy, a *mensch*, with a reputation to counteract the bad boy reputation I had managed to build in high school. And I wanted to study literature, though literature did not seem masculine, and wasn't I, like all smart boys in my cultural world, supposed to find an occupation more in keeping with aspirations to higher income and greater status? My father, blighted by a life of hard labor in Cleveland, had impressed upon me the importance of being a white-collar professional. Medicine was the calling that I felt should have called me to please my father. It called him until quotas against Jews kept him out of medical school and he wound up with a blue collar wrapped around his occupational neck for the rest of his adult life. Or law. Quite a few of the guys in my fraternity were studying law, business, accounting or marketing, and most appeared on their way toward career tracks of money making. Who made money studying literature?

I enjoyed friendships with a number of guys in the fraternity who, by my standards, came from money. One invited me to his home in Cincinnati, a sprawling suburban house complete with a live-in black maid. When I told his mother I was thinking of majoring in English, she gave me a sad but sympathetic look and said consolingly, "You can't make money with English, Mike." What could you do with literature? Impress girls, sure. Augment knowledge and maybe wisdom. Adore the aesthetics. But what could you really *do* with it?

As a sophomore I began, in a nascent but earnest way, to realize that what I wanted to do with literature was create it. To do what great authors have always done, fashion stories in language and make my language enable others to see, feel, be moved. I secretly made a pact with myself to find my way to hallowed literary ground.

But because I began to fancy becoming a writer did not mean I had it in me—the gift, the drive, the discipline. I had been writing poetry since high school. Most seemed puerile and putrid to me, even though girls sometimes seemed impressed. I began to write stories and read them to friends. Those who liked me were generous, at times even unsparing in praise, which made me doubt their perspicacity. Who knew if I had the makings?

Digger, my closest friend, could not understand why I was drawn to literature. The summer before our junior year, he informed me he was abandoning the idea of law school and becoming a botanist.

"How do you make a living working with plants?"

"Research. You'd be surprised. There's money in it. Too bad, because I love studying government, but botany's what I really want."

It seemed senseless to him to interpret poetry or to do useless scholarship on made-up stories. What advantage was there to figuring out meaning in the work of a bunch of dead authors whom no one but other people who liked literature could possibly care about? It wasn't like botany, where you could do research and come up with concrete applications that had to do with health, disease and food, nor was it like law, where you could alter the course of innocence or guilt, affect legislation and commerce. To Digger, literature was a waste of time but, he reasoned with me, as long as I liked it so much, maybe I should teach it. "You're a natural teacher—good with people, great at public speaking. Why not?"

We argued as we did in high school over Cuba under Castro, whom he scorned as a Communist, over his love of Barry Goldwater and over my liberal ideology drawn from thinkers like Thoreau, Bertrand Russell, C. Wright Mills and Erich Fromm. But what he said about me and teaching made sense. Teaching had the earmarks of a noble calling. And, besides, wasn't literature a portal to all areas of knowledge? I was ravenous for knowledge. It was what I was after. Knowledge could advance me, better me, enlighten me. Knowledge could bring wisdom, perhaps even virtue.

I read all of Saul Bellow during my summer vacation. I became caught up in *The Adventures of Augie March*, drawn to the bildungsroman form and the voice of erudition and street smarts. I began imagining a sprawling novel like *Augie March* scaffolded from the life experiences behind and ahead of me.

I had, since childhood, felt neglected by my father and, like the orphan Augie March, longed for other men to adopt me. It wasn't because I lacked respect or love for my old man. It was more his limitations—he was not the attentive, love- and approval-giving father that I craved. The father who took his son to ball games or played catch with him or put his arm around him and told him that he loved him and was proud of him. That was the father I longed for and imagined while missing for years the kind of father that he was, one of a generation that put family first, who worked long hours as a laborer at a job he hated so that he could earn and provide.

We were the poor cousins. We were supposed to have money. I remember the excitement and buzz in the neighborhood when an item appeared in the afternoon *Cleveland News* about my great Aunt Eva's estate—including in it fifty thousand dollars, a grand sum, willed to my parents, Zaz and Betty Krasny, but never received. Great Aunt Eva—or Tant, as we called her, from the Yiddish word for aunt, *tanta*—was a rich woman. She would come to visit us in a chauffeur-driven limousine and hand each of us—my brother Vic, my sister Lois, and me—a couple of tens or twenties, bills we would never have even seen were it not for her.

Tant's house was in front of the ice cream factory where Dad worked, off Cedar Avenue, in what was then and still is Cleveland's black ghetto. Tant had a loaded gun and a German shepherd because of her fear of "the *shvartzas*," Yiddish for blacks. Thieving of all kinds in that neighborhood was commonplace.

Tant had ownership of the ice cream plant as part of her divorce settlement decree from Jake Fisher. Why my father—an educated man with a degree from Ohio State in bacteriology and a love of medicine—went to work for Jake Fisher in the first place remained a family mystery, but it was clear to me that it was tied to failure. Whatever his reasons for working at the factory, rather than going into dentistry or pharmacy or some other medically related field, my father was never the man he wanted to be. He was, to the world outside our home, an ordinary man. He was easy to like—a man with an intellect, a good sense of humor, sweetness and charm, who cared about the good opinion of others. He was a good guy. Decent. Capable. Kind. Honorable. Stoic. He was also a seeker of knowledge, an autodidact who never seemed to tire of the pleasure and stimulation he derived from educating himself about medicine, theology, language, anthropology, history or the game of bridge, in which he had once been state champion.

Dad's cousin Mike was the prime mover at the ice cream plant. There were stories throughout my boyhood about how charming and brilliant Mike was. My father idolized him and named me in his honor—though I was also named, as is the tradition in Jewish families, for a dead relation, my great grandfather, who was a cantor in Russia. As a boy I thought I would be a cantor: I loved leading services and using my singing voice. But since I was named in honor of Mike, I began to think, in my adolescence, of trying to model myself after what I thought of as his image—a confabulated one from my own imaginings and lore that I had heard about him. Fay Rose, the vivacious woman who ran Heights Pharmacy, was in love with cousin Mike. Women supposedly found him irresistible. More important was that he was supposed to have been remarkably well read, highly knowledgeable in nearly every field of study.

After Tant's death, Mike felt that he alone deserved ownership and control of the business, and my dad didn't have the fight or the *sechel*, Yiddish for business cunning, to stop him. Mike took over the major share of the plant's operation, and my father wound up working for him and later, after Mike died, for his widow.

Mike was just one of the relatives on my father's side who was economically a lot better off. My father had three sisters, and one of them, Gea, married a man named Willy Miller, who owned another ice cream plant. I worked in my Uncle Willy's plant on the assembly line and the loading docks, often with Negroes, as they were called back then. The status of being the boss's nephew didn't translate to my blood aunt, who everyone in the family adored and who yelled at me one afternoon for stacking ice cream gallon baskets the wrong way. I found it difficult to understand how my own aunt could yell at me, and I brooded over it to my mother—who quickly informed me pithily, "It's business." That was the ethos for many who came through the Depression. Blood was secondary, like nearly everything else, to making money. The idea of putting business or money first, ahead even of blood, was something I learned morally to reject early in my adolescence. Mike might have been my dad's cousin, and he may have once felt brotherly toward my dad in their younger years, but not when it came to business. And my Aunt Gea would be kind and familial toward me, send me money for birthdays and Chanukah, but in the plant all that dissolved. I was just another worker subject to her reprimand. If those were the ways of business, give me literature!

Though we were the poor cousins, we were in many ways in a kind of limbo because we did not think of ourselves as working class. My dad, for a number of years, had had a lot of responsibilities running things at the plant, and he was a part owner on paper, though without any draw except a worker's salary. He put in eighty-five- to ninety-hour weeks, including weekends and not including time with emergency problems that frequently occurred when plant machinery broke down, often in the middle of the night. In summers he could work as much as a one-hundred-twenty-hour week. Exploited? In many ways I thought of the way he worked as a form of slave labor. Ambition never seemed to cross the threshold of his designs.

I, on the other hand, began to feel ambition stir. Like Augie March, I liked kids—we all did in my family—and I liked the idea of teaching them. Somehow, I figured, I'd make a living. Speaking talent I knew I possessed. Since I was a boy I had repeatedly heard how well I spoke, how intelligent I sounded, how impressive my vocabulary was. I had also learned by high school's end, out of self-preservation and innate curiosity, to be a good listener, to follow my mother's rule about always being polite, allowing others to talk instead of trying verbally to dominate and be the center of attention. Nearly everyone seemed to like being a storyteller, even normally non-talkative types like the hoods I ingratiated myself with in high school, asking them to hold forth on things they knew about—how they combed their hair or customized their cars or built a zip gun or street fought or got girls. Everyone, I felt, had something to teach me. I was learning how to take control of conversation with well-paced questions and responses and an attentive tone. I was learning, too, how being smart without being smart-ass was the way to win good will—how to be a nice guy rather than someone running at the mouth and ready to duke it out, as I had been in high school.

Still, I took speaking well for granted and considered it not worth valuing because it came naturally, and becoming a teacher or a scholar hardly matched my ambition. I was turning more and more literary, identifying more with authors and their characters. I began to believe I could create someone like Bellow's fictive Augie March, a textual faux representation of self, life's adventures interwoven, both real and imagined. As Isaac Babel said, "Passion rules the universe." I would go where my passion for literature led.

I hoped it would lead me to becoming a writer. I hoped the more reading I ingested, the more it would propel me. Bellow was the lodestar. To have his style, his erudition. To have people feel about reading me the way I felt about reading him. Plus, it sounded pretty cool to say I was going to be a writer, and I began not only to say it but to believe it.

In my sophomore year I took a creative writing course from a novelist named Cecil Hemley—a shloompy, kindly Jewish man who always seemed to have a cigarette dangling from his lower lip and who had done translations of the great Yiddish writer Isaac Bashevis Singer. Hemley read our stories aloud in class and asked what we thought, then followed with his own critique. I waited weeks before he read my first story, and the waiting and excitement and fear mounted in me as he went through most others before getting to mine. Mine was a story about an old, pious Jew who had lost his way and encountered random anti-Semitic violence. The class made respectful remarks about the story, and one of the students, Stan Plumly—who would later become a distinguished poet—said particularly favorable things. My heart was beating wildly, and I was thinking, "You are a writer. You are a writer." Then Cecil Hemley talked, and what he said was not pretty. The story had no real conflict. It was just an old man getting beaten up. It was only a sketch. Its language was stilted, too formal sounding, too sesquipedalian, meaning too prone to big words. It was, in comparison to some of the other stories which he had praised, "pedestrian."

What a word to be labeled with. Pedestrian. Could he be correct? Somehow I believed he was, but how could he be when I loved language?

Loved telling jokes and tales and using my oral skills? Was I merely fooling myself thinking I had it in me to be a writer, when the truth was I was pedestrian? Was Hemley one of those self-hating Jews who disliked my story because its Jewish content embarrassed him? Or did he dislike it because he disliked me? If the story was pedestrian, did that make me pedestrian?

How could I be pedestrian, I asked myself, when I was a budding intellectual? In my last year in high school, I fell out with my fellow members in PDG, a club founded by guys like me, from the working-class sections of Cleveland Heights. Nearly everybody who was anybody then had to be in a club. Initially, I was glad to be a PDG. I felt like I belonged to something important. I wore a PDG pendant on a chain around my neck and hung out with the guys in the club in the front hall in the mornings, trying to look cool and hoping I'd be seen by girls. Most of the older guys in PDG were the athletes or would-be cool guys and girl chasers who gave short shrift to schoolwork and did wild things that were new and unbelievable to me. They instigated a panty raid on an all-girls school called Hathaway Brown. Scaled the fence at the municipal swimming pool in University Heights for night-time nude swims. Drank liquor. Went to whore houses. A few of them even smoked marijuana. The PDGs had a violent ethos, a credo based on saying and acting out every impulse.

I, too, liked a good fight. I could work myself up for the slightest slight or feeling that would well in me when someone acted rude to me or didn't treat me properly. I knew by that time how to box and street fight, and I knew that I was naturally strong like my father and my brother, even if, unlike them, I was verbal and sensitive—effeminized, I feared, by emotionality and interest in things like poetry. I cottoned to the image of being a strong and violent, thuggish guy who could kick ass—even though I still had a constant fear of certain hoods that made me feel, deep down, that I was really a sissy.

What did that band of miscreants of my youth have to do with the person I was trying to become? They were lodged in a small ventricle of my heart, ensconced in some mythic, visceral Cooperstown, shrouded by the tenderness and nostalgia I felt for them and our feral boyhood. But I was moving on. I had discovered the world of books and the fact that I had an intellect. As a senior in high school, I took courses in international relations and Russian and started hanging out with the bookish set.

I had neither the cumulative grades nor the resources to go to any other than a state school but I was determined to stay on track and do well as a college student at Ohio University. At Ohio U. I would also find a path to doing good. In my second year, I seemed wedded already, at nineteen, to wanting to live an outwardly bourgeois life of respectability. I wanted a future that would mean security against the blue-collar insecurity of my boyhood. I wanted to be someone, to gain recognition, which seemed to accrue mostly to bourgeois merit. I wanted to impress, especially girls, with what a good guy and *mensch* I could be, despite intermittent boilings in my blood. Middle-class virtues of sobriety and good character beckoned, if only I could keep my impulses, urges and feral instincts at bay. Of course, I was only a sophomore. A sophomoric sophomore. Too self-reflective for someone who had joined a fraternity and was hungry for recognition and girls. I was inventing myself.

Like most of my contemporaries, I had been influenced by Salinger's Holden Caulfield, who disdained all varieties of phoniness. I had a few black friends, one with the improbable name of Steve Allen, and I felt sympathy for civil rights and the still embryonic struggle for racial equality. I invited Steve to come to my home over one of the vacation breaks, only to hear him respond, I WOULDN'T WANNA BE IN YOUR NEIGH-BORHOOD ANY MORE THAN YOU'D WANNA BE IN MINE. But the church bombing in Birmingham in 1963 that killed four young black girls sickened and angered me, and I wanted, somehow, to do my part. I wanted to help the black cause and earn respect from blacks as one who stood in solidarity with them against prejudice, which was all too prevalent at Ohio University in 1963. This was an era when nearly every fraternity and sorority had covenants prohibiting Jews and blacks. No wonder I began to feel emotionally allied and increasingly empathic with blacks. Jewish identification with victimhood, perhaps.

During rush week I was required to go to all the fraternity houses on campus—including Phi Kappa Sigma, a frat known as the Skulls. The Skulls had a huge Nazi flag draped on a wall, and every Christmas when fraternity members went caroling at sororities and girl's dorms, they reportedly sang to the tune of Jingle Bells:

> Dashing through the Reich
> In my Mercedes-Benz
> Killing all the Jews
> Saving all my friends
> Rat-Tat-Tat-Tat-Tat
> Mow the bastards down
> Oh what fun it is to kill
> Hitler's back in town

Bigotry, back then, was rampant in Greek life. I remained mute one night when I heard a Sigma Chi drunkenly singing, "There'll never be a nigger who will be a Sigma Chi." And I remained silent when my fellow Jewish fraternity brothers in Phi Sigma Delta, Alpha Delta chapter, joked about *shvartzas*. I remained silent because I was not sure what to say or how to say it, and I remained silent for fear of not being liked. I overheard some of the local good ole boys in the barber shop in Athens talking about how hard it was to cut nigger hair, and I wanted to tell them that the word was offensive and that they should abstain from using it, but I felt my words would have little or no effect and would simply sound self-righteous or target me as another nigger-loving Jewboy.

Could words change attitudes? If I was going to be good, I was going to have to speak up or take action even, put myself on the line like the freedom riders did or like Cleveland Rabbi Arthur Lelyveld, who went South to protest segregation and was photographed in *The Cleveland Plain Dealer*, badly bloodied by segregationist crackers. How could I not show moral courage and not speak up? I was nineteen years old, and I brooded and beat myself up about allowing racially bigoted remarks to pass without a response from my pedestrian self.

Then George Lincoln Rockwell came to Ohio U. Rockwell was leader of the American Nazi party. I believed in free speech, but I was upset that he was invited to speak, even though it was in the name of civil liberties and hearing views from all sides, even the most extreme.

I decided that with George Lincoln Rockwell, I could do something. I could take action against a minister of bigotry and hate. I could jettison my own sinful acts of silence with silence. Civil disobedience could be effective. It surely had been for Gandhi and Martin Luther King. I admired them and Thoreau. I convinced friends and fraternity brothers to distribute a leaflet I wrote up urging everyone who planned to attend Rockwell's lecture to protest him and his ideas by wearing a white shirt and dark pants. I urged that no one applaud or respond in any way to Rockwell's hateful and prejudiced speech, that all simply sit in silence throughout the entire talk with arms folded. As soon as the speech was over, I added, everyone should immediately leave the auditorium single file, without noise or incident.

At Rockwell's talk the crowd of people in white shirts and dark slacks, sitting with their arms folded, was impressive. I had accomplished something, though I didn't know exactly what or whether Rockwell, who looked over the audience with furtive, darting eyes, even knew that he was being protested. Still, it made me realize that solidarity can bring results.

I was becoming increasingly political. International relations and current events held great interest for me, and I kept up. When one of our profs came in and announced one afternoon that we were at war with Red China, there were shrieks. "I just wanted to see if you guys are up on what's going on in the news," he gloated. "Most of you don't even read the papers." I did. Even *Pravda*, which my high-school Russian enabled me to get through and which showed dramatic disparities in the way the U.S.S.R. and the U.S. reported news.

I was convinced that the United States had no business in Indochina and South Vietnam, at a time when most students on my campus had no idea of what went on there. I got into a slightly heated discussion with a guy named Gunther, a Sigma Chi who lived in my dorm and wanted to go "fight gooks."

"I believe in what we're doing there, Mike," he told me. Gunther and I also argued about civil rights, and he said, " I got nothin' against the coloreds, so long as they know their place."

Though I was firm and sure about my own beliefs on civil rights and Vietnam, I was still reluctant to get into arguing, to appear too aggressive or liberal, for fear I wouldn't be liked or that popular gentile guys like Gunther, who appeared to like me, would disapprove of me and other Jews. It would take more time for me to develop greater confidence and to stand more firmly, even aggressively, behind what I believed, to know there was little to be proud of if you did not speak up or stand up. I possessed a democracy-bred notion about being open and polite to varying viewpoints, but when a slightly intoxicated male, gentile adviser to the Sigma Kappa sorority told me that fraternities and sororities should never " let jungle bunnies or Yids in," I said to him, turning and walking away with a touch of histrionics, "I'm one of those Yids."

Lyndon Johnson came to Ohio University. I waded into a large crowd just to have a look at him as he spoke. I was sympathetic with a lot of his social and racial programs, the idea of the Great Society. I was impressed by seeing a living president and having the memory with me for life. I soon saw more icons. Digger and a few other friends and I went to see Bob Dylan, and I went with Digger to see The Mamas and The Papas. Digger and I and Catfish and Rich Kritchman, both now dead, went backstage after a concert and met Peter, Paul and Mary. The folk-singing trio was my first really close encounter with celebrities, and it was thrilling. Mary Travers took a shine to Digger and they corresponded for a while. I thought that was cool. When Digger's father Harry died of a brain tumor, our friend Catfish wrote to Mary and told her. She called Digger from Minnesota. Now that was really cool! She was married to a Jewish photographer, but all of us figured Digger could probably have nailed her.

I also went to see John Ciardi, who appeared on campus in what was billed as a literary talk, which was enough to draw me in. Then editor of *The Saturday Review*, Ciardi had translated Dante's *Inferno* and published a number of volumes of poetry, in addition to writing a respected critical book called *How a Poem Means*. A man of charm and good looks and wit, Ciardi became an instant role model for me. Maybe I couldn't be John Ciardi or Saul Bellow, but I could become a man of letters, a literary man, a learned man, a good man with charm and wit and vitality. Damn right I could!

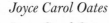 *Joyce Carol Oates*
    Joyce Carol Oates is telling me that she and I are like brother and sister because we are of the same generation and from similar places. She has written about Shaker Heights, which I like to call

the other side of the tracks from the Cleveland Heights neighborhood I grew up in. Shaker Heights, she says, is like Birmingham, Michigan, or Princeton, New Jersey. She knows places like that like she knows the tougher places. We are both working-class bookish intellectuals.

Oates was a dutiful daughter. When she wrote her parents from college, the letters were sunny, good-daughter letters. She didn't really know her parents. Her mother took care of her and her brother and father and, like so many mothers including my own, was a server, a quintessential homemaker, unheralded and uncelebrated and then mourned by her few loved ones.

Every time I talk to Oates, I wonder what fires her imagination. She links it to daydreaming, fantasizing, dreaming while asleep. "The psychological is what I am interested in," she tells me. "It's what is close to my heart." She calls Nietzsche the greatest psychologist and talks about how he uses his aphorisms like a scalpel. She appears fragile, vulnerable and owl-like with a trill, high but dulcet voice that hides those secret places in her heart that push her imagination into darker realms.

Calling her Sister Joyce, I remember our talk about her novel *Foxfire*, feeling we were connected then, too, by our shared love in adolescence of the wild kids, our attraction to those who fed on impulse and roughness and yet had kindness and heart. I remember cradling her in my arms as she went speechless on air at the conclusion of one interview when I mentioned the name of her beloved deceased literary agent, and I recall water welling in her eyes as she spoke in another interview of her parents, comparing her mother, both beautiful and lost, to Marilyn Monroe. She tried writing *Missing Mom*, her forty-fourth novel—about a murdered mother—for mothers like her own, who had only an eighth-grade education. I remember, too, the flash of anger at me on stage when I said others view her work as depressing. Brecht's words, "the man who laughs has not yet been told the terrible news," could be hers. When I remark how her descriptions of place are often filled with urban decay and grotesque imagery and ugliness she quickly self-defends, "Yes. But I also have lots of beauty too. Landscapes. Trees."

Oates says she has "a realistic vision." She compares herself in literary lineage to Poe, Hawthorne and Kafka. She speaks more freely with age now about her own life and her parents and their lives, as if she is trying to stab out her past, understand how it fits with this lionized and award-winning writer and poet, this Princeton professor she has become.

I try to understand how she is so attuned to the violence in America's underbellies and secret ravines. Her father's grandfather killed himself with a shotgun after trying to kill his wife. Her mother's father was killed. These became legends and myths never spoken of—but she was aware of them without knowing anything. Her mother knew few of the facts and only talked about any of them when she turned eighty. Jimmy Carter told me that both his grandfather and great-grandfather were murdered. That may explain a lot about brother Billy and sister Ruth, I joke, but it doesn't explain Jimmy.

A caller phones to say Joyce Carol should write a book exploring the lives of slaughterhouse workers, and she responds, "Wow! That would be interesting!" My own father's father was a butcher who took my dad, then still young, to a slaughterhouse and said, "Here's life." "Life is a slaughterhouse" is a worthwhile scalpel of an aphorism, but it never really stuck to my insides.

Oates is haunted by real violence. Where do the stories come from? Like the famous one, "Where Are You Going, Where Have You Been?" of young Connie, trapped into leaving her family lest they be killed by a man posing as a teen, or the rich teen in a Grosse Point set story, a girl who steals for the thrill of stealing and is whored out in the Detroit slums and violently abused by a pimp who makes her feel alive.

This is life as Oates sees it, and what she congeals from the news and her own haunted imagination into narrative. She tells me about watching films of Joe Louis boxing. She is a boxing aficionado. Boxing is primitive she admits—based on hurt and a science of pain. She says she prefers to watch fights in black and white rather than color.

Perhaps, she adds, it is because history interests her more than the violence. But she speaks with girlish wonder about the quickness of Ali, and sticks up for Mike Tyson with remarks about how exploited he and other boxers have been by their managers. Her fear of violence is also her attraction to it. It is the haunting that has given much of her writing its form and life.

Russell Banks

I'm thinking of Robert Lowell as Russell Banks strides into the studio—the line from "Skunk Hour": "I myself am hell;/ nobody's here—." But Banks doesn't wear any of his New England despair. The suffering in his work is nowhere on him. The proletarian kid is a man in a fine suit. He looks like one of those distinguished silver fox types.

This is not our first encounter. Banks has done book flogging many times, and the book tours, along with years of classroom teaching, may account at least in part for his ease at the microphone. As the E Channel says about the famous, it is good to be Russell Banks. Invariably heralded as one of the country's best writers of fiction, he also has a happy marriage with wife number four. Going through three divorces was, he assures me, a rough learning curve. But now, with this wife, he has it right at last. She is a poet. They understand each other's drive to write, to move away from one another into their shared world of archeologic solitude.

Banks is personable. Voluble. Well-spoken. Yet I know what lies underneath the mask. I know the despair and horror and cruelty he sees. I see it in his work. But it is nowhere in his face, speech or demeanor.

All his books, Banks says, are about good-intention-paved roads to hell. His questions are moral ones. I tell him I see links between him and Hawthorne, and Banks assures me that is no stretch because of their New England regional heritage and their wrestling with moral questions. Though, he adds, unlike Hawthorne, he is no fabulist.

I had talked a few weeks before to Oates. I knew she and Banks were friends. I talked with him about the affinity both have for violence. Both propel characters into the woods, like Hawthorne's "Young Goodman Brown." Into the horror, the afflictions, the misery of lives that usher gloom.

Many writers of stature are brewed in political radicalism. Banks is. He is angry about racial injustice. Angry over all that colonialism has wrought. In the aftermath of Bush's reelection, Banks speaks of how bleakly pessimistic he feels. He says that, at age sixty-four, he has never felt so alienated or depressed. Quite a statement from a writer whose work is dark and laced with catastrophe. But, if he is feeling the weight of the words he speaks, it does not peek out at me from his public writer's talk-show-guest mask. A caller, asking for wisdom on how to act in the face of what prevails in the culture, is simply told, soberly, "we just have to engage."

Banks talks about his life. About how he stole a car at sixteen, soon after getting his license, and wound up homeless for a while. Blue-collar blood runs in his veins, and he says that for years he had disdain for, even prejudice against, the blue-blooded and the privileged. Since his mid-thirties he has himself led a privileged life, as a tenured professor. You can take the boy, like Banks, or me, his interlocutor, out of the prol life, but you can't take the prol life out of us. Or, for that matter, out of a girl like Oates.

Banks talks about *Rule of the Bone*, about how he imagined that narrative voice from boyhood talks with his brother as they lay in their bedroom on their cots. Cots! The word hits me with my own past. My brother Vic and I slept on cots. Cots, I fancy, give us class kinship.

Banks speaks of living well off his writing and of being reasonably successful, but he makes a sharp distinction between being a well-selling author and a best-selling one. Does Banks wish he were a best-selling author? Does it bother him that his novels are not mass sellers? I'm testing a hypothesis. Saul Bellow once confessed to me—while also asking me if he should marry the much younger graduate student who would become his final wife—how gratifying it would be if he could sell more books in mass numbers and reach a wider audience.

"Doesn't bother me in the slightest," Banks says. " It wouldn't change my life to write best sellers. What would I buy? A kidney-shaped pool? A Lear jet?"

Even with four marriages and four daughters, money doesn't drive Banks or concern him, as it does many writers I know. What he needs far more than money is the solitude to go within to find the stories and the characters and the language. He claims he can see horror, terrible cruelty and human fallibility without being overwhelmed. He does what artists have to do . . . and he does it with traditional forms and a realistic vision that sometimes compels him to pull away with a trembling that can last for days. Still, he has to engage.

E. L. Doctorow

Doctorow has trouble hearing. I am nearly shouting questions at him on stage, unlike the easy flow of conversation we had when I was seated close to him at dinner before the event. He is sweet-tempered, boyish, kind and a lifer leftist. His softness and charm make me feel at ease, as if I am with a colleague or pal.

We discuss, on stage, his early life. It was his father's idea, Doctorow says, to name him Edgar. "He liked a lot of bad writers," he tells me, "and Poe was our greatest bad writer." Like most serious authors, he has stock ways of talking about how he began writing; he claims that, since he was nine, he had the idea of being a writer lodged in his mind, though he wrote nothing. Not having television until he was seventeen helped him turn into a writer, because there was only radio and the public library. For a time, he thought of becoming an aeronautical engineer, but only, his brother divined, because he liked the sound of the words. It began, the thrust, the fever, the climb up to major writer stature, with a voice saying, "How is this done?"

At the Bronx School of Science, Doctorow "drifted" to the school literary magazine. He wrote a portrait of a doorman, a holocaust survivor, for an English class. Doctorow got into trouble with the teacher because the piece was supposed to be based on truth, and the teacher discovered the doorman did not exist. "No one," he says, "realized what a portent this was or that it was what journalists have always done."

Doctorow became known as the novelist who blended history and fiction. Real historic characters were allowed into his novels in meetings that never took place, with words they never uttered. William Shawn of *The New Yorker* thought *Ragtime* immoral and refused to review it. Doctorow shrugs his shoulders and asks, "What did I do wrong? As a boy I read Dumas and Tolstoy, and Richelieu and Napoleon would appear. I opened the sluice gates and wound up getting blamed for Oliver Stone's JFK movie."

Writing begins for him with an image. He saw a tugboat with *Billy Bathgate*, a gangster, having his feet set in cement, and Doctorow brought in Dutch Schultz because Schultz was from the Bronx. He passed a sign in the Adirondacks that said "Loon Lake" and liked the words. It is not a rational process.

Doctorow tells how his mother's only comment after reading *World's Fair* was that he said she had fat calves. He handed his wife a draft of *The Book of Daniel*, his novel based on the sons of Julius and Ethel Rosenberg, then returned from a long walk to find her weeping—which made him realize he had told the story right.

The tales of how and why he became a writer soon lead him to political talk that comes, it seems, from a deeper place. Doctorow calls the Bush Administration "the most frightening I can remember," and he gets applause when he denounces it for "secrecy, stupidity and arrogance." Weeks after our dinner and on-stage conversation I will read of him being booed and hissed at Hofstra for saying similar things in a commencement speech. But this audience, of course, is a San Francisco one, and it is close to the reelection of George W. Bush. Doctorow's tone has shifted and so has his rhetoric, and he is suddenly letting out indignation at the Bush Administration for being "hateful to the environment" and "ruinous to the economy." Yet his voice is steady and measured, calm covering rage. "They are scary . . . to civil liberties . . . and they are disgracing this country in foreign policy. They're obsolete. It's a tragedy. The key word is obsolete. They're throwbacks to nineteenth-century thinking when we now have the opportunity, with our power and principles, to build concordance of civilizations versus old imperial ways." When he comes on air nearly two years later, in a far more taciturn mood, to discuss *The March*, he is still molten with anger at Bush, Cheney and Rumsfeld and their Iraq war.

I steer him back in our stage interview to writing, and he talks of how he learned from Dickens and Twain that a writer can express wonder and awe through a child's voice. "It's diction," he tells me. "You fall into it as an ear. You either have it or you don't." Then he gives me one of his wide, sweet smiles and adds, as if in the burst of an afterthought, "The last people in the world who know anything about the creative process are those who do it."

 Gay Talese

At seventy-four Gay Talese is still what my father-in-law would have called a vision of sartorial splendor. Natty as a show model. I tell him right off that from my experience with authors, only Tom Wolfe, wearing a powder blue suit, compares.

This is the man David Halberstam called the most important nonfiction writer of his generation. Those of that generation who recall Talese's work, above all, connect it with the mafia and sex in America and, of course, New Journalism—the term Tom Wolfe glorified him with, which, like the word memoir, he now hates. He wouldn't want to be associated with Hunter Thompson, who was dazzling and interesting but couldn't be believed, who was "just having fun."

Nonfiction requires a great deal of research. You have to discard about 70 percent of it, and a lot of it is a waste of time. The work takes time. It's difficult. You need pride and commitment, seeking not to be prolific but to achieve the highest level possible, so when it's done, you can feel you've done your best. But there is too much sloppiness and lying going on in nonfiction. They deliberately make it up and get into the paper like Jason Blair in *The New York Times*. "My dear wife believed James Frey. You can't trust the nonfiction writer."

Talese was reared in the Catholic church, and the tenets of life after death and good works while living stayed with him in his writing. As a young reporter, he felt he was a foot soldier for the historians. The presumptuousness, no doubt, of a young, naïve man. It still may be. But it's what motivated him. *The New York Times* was like the Vatican to him. He thought of himself as a scribe in a monastery and thought about redemption and restoration. His mission all along, he says, has been to tell the stories of America that historians ignore.

Talese, a Jersey boy, spent a lot of time in Selma, Alabama. He wasn't doing well in school. He wasn't a particularly ambitious kid. There was no grade given out for curiosity. A doctor his father knew suggested the University of Alabama for him, a segregated school then with a few Italians like him, a few Greeks and a few Jews. Alabama was a second shot at life. He felt it reflected America more broadly. In 1938 and 1939, he saw the Klan in full regalia on his South Jersey home turf. The northern press singled out the South and forgot about New York and New Jersey. When Martin Luther King marched from Selma, Talese's life changed. He never saw such bravery. Young people put their lives on the line for what eventually would bring about the Voting Rights Act. Curiosity drove him back to Selma decades later. He wanted to see how much had changed.

Talese at age nine, ten and eleven eavesdropped at his mother's dress shop. That was where his writing career really began. He heard common, ordinary life stories, Willy Loman type stories that he says are in all of us. "This was news. Not in the newspapers, but news. It gave me a larger sense of the world. It became my school of writing. It was my beginning." His first book was about the bridge construction people who built the Verrazano-Narrows. His book on *The New York Times* was about those who produced the newspaper, not about the celebrated. Even his famous piece on Frank Sinatra was about the people around Sinatra. Talese continues to talk to the people around his home in South Jersey, to measure America by his home there. He stays in touch with who he is and was and isn't insulated at Elaine's or with the Manhattan cognoscenti. He writes about atmosphere like a moviemaker works with scenes, so he can work it into a story.

"How do you get to the story? Writers often don't tell how they write, how they go about writing what they've written. Tolstoy. Baudelaire. Zola. Hemingway. Fitzgerald. The act of writing for each was different. Tolstoy's wife typed all his work. Hemingway achieved so much, including the Nobel, but was so despairing of life he took his own. Styron went into a depression."

Talese tells me his publisher wife says it sometimes seems there are more writers than readers. Many may have stories, but telling them takes craft, learning and apprenticeship. It's hard work. Talese says he is very careful with facts, writes well, is proud but modest and is "not an egomaniac." He is also one of the few Italians who makes a living writing in English. The Italian tradition is not one of solitude. Italians are visual artists. Like Renaissance painters. Scorsese. Coppola. Italian writers are few in number, and those who are, often write about antisocial behavior, like the mafia.

I tell Talese the story about Mario Puzo and Sinatra. I'm surprised he doesn't know it. Supposedly, Sinatra saw Puzo in a restaurant after he had seen the film of *The Godfather* and Old Blue Eyes told Puzo he disliked the portrait of Johnny Fontaine, the singing idol alleged to have been drawn from his own life. Sinatra, so the story goes, was somewhat threatening with Puzo, and Puzo supposedly said, "You are a northern Italian and you're threatening me, a southern Italian?" Talese laughs at this, then offers that his people came from the impoverished south of Italy, the toe of the boot, Calabria. They were like poor American Southerners after the Civil War. They were driven to find a better place economically. His father arrived in 1920 and by 1926 was an American citizen. Gay Talese is seventy-four and is still as driven as he was as a boy to tell stories of America.

2   The Noble Path

S ENIOR YEAR. I was convinced that writing was my calling. I lived in a trailer out in the woods, adding to the allure and self-created image of being literary, fobbing myself off as a writer-in-the-making, while still wondering inwardly if I had it in me. Salinger said writing stories was like being a dash man, but the novel—that was the loneliness of the long-distance runner. Did I have the stamina? The grit? The drive? The talent? The wind?

I took another creative writing course, this time from Walter Tevis, author of *The Hustler* and a teacher who gave me encouragement. Tevis had the reputation of being a heavy drinker, but I saw him as a devoted and dedicated teacher who was generous to me. There was a cachet and coolness to pool playing, and I loved the idea that the man who not only wrote *The Hustler* as a novel but also its screenplay was my teacher and mentor. I even learned inside stuff from him about how Jackie Gleason was selected to play the role of Minnesota Fats. How pocket billiards master Willy Moscone took shots for Gleason and Paul Newman. How Tevis made up the character of Minnesota Fats on what he described as a cold, rainy morning, despite the fact that a fat guy who had been on the Johnny Carson show a number of times repeatedly claimed to be the real Minnesota Fats. Tevis never knew whether or not to go after the fake Minnesota, who sold pool cues and other pool paraphernalia under that signature. Tevis was a gentle man and a bit of a philo-Semite, even confessing to me once that he wished he had been born Jewish. He took to me, at least in part, because it was clear how much I admired him. I suspected Cecil Hemley, who was Jewish, didn't like my work because of the Jewishness in it, and I suspected Walter Tevis, who wasn't Jewish, liked it because of its Jewishness.

Tevis was a great storyteller and entertainer, and he taught me that good teaching could be made more lively with amusing anecdotes and animated personal ways of relating to literature. When we read Faulkner, he told us about how he had driven through Oxford, Faulkner's hometown, one day and thought to himself how he might actually see his idol, the great progenitor of Yoknapatawpha County. He told us how he mused about going to local bars to look for Faulkner, but it was a Sunday, and they had blue laws then in Mississippi prohibiting the purchase of spirits on the Lord's day. While Tevis was thinking about the fact that he was actually on Faulkner's home turf and could even stay in Oxford and hunt around for Faulkner, a man stumbled drunkenly in front of his car and slammed his hand down on the hood. Tevis swore that it was Faulkner.

I enrolled in the honors college and did an honors project on Saul Bellow with a professor named Lester Marks. I got the notion that I might somehow interview Bellow. Doctor Marks had taken me under his wing and, along with Mr. Tevis, had become my main mentor and a role model for me to take in as I was taking in writers and literary characters. The son of a New York State Supreme Court judge, Lester Marks had an appealing boyish charm and was considered cool by many students because he drove a motor scooter to classes. He was quick-witted, likeable and handsome. I became his grader and even got to know his wife, a kind, prematurely gray Polish American who was a psychiatric nurse. I also met their two small daughters; it was unusual for a student in those far more formal days to get to know a prof's family. Lester and I would become friends (though he was still for many years Dr. Marks), and we sat around in his office exchanging jokes or discussing authors or thrashing around topics both serious and frivolous, often with a genial pal and colleague of his who headed up the English composition program. I did a lot of listening as they smoked and gossiped about the university president, whom neither liked, or we talked about academic politics or politics in general—and such conversations, with good bright men, professors who loved humor and the life of the mind, were, I realized, where I felt at home, what I wanted out of college and missed in dorm and fraternity life. What I had there was a lot of camaraderie and tail chasing, the frat boy stuff, which was now seeming more puerile, though some of it was still appealing. But I had new, heady appetites—for literature and writing and ideas and the kinds of conversations that could lead to deeper levels of thought. Underneath I was still a proletarian, a peasant who made a fist around a fork and who spat loogies and was at ease with boyish impulsivity and vulgar animality. But I was also learning more, by reading and observing men like Walter Tevis and Les Marks, how to act and behave like a *mensch* and, how cool, to be intellectual. I was learning, too, the music of good conversation and to camouflage myself as bourgeois. Bourgeois respectability and conformity meant self-control and keeping the bad boy at bay, feral instincts sheathed.

I wanted to be manly and tough and unemotional. That, too, meant being cool. Even more than being an intellectual, being cool beckoned. Emotion was weak and female. The challenge was to make myself not feel. To be good and kind without being vulnerable or suffering—as I had in high school, like Goethe's Young Werther—the despair and ecstatic torture of what felt then like unrequited love. I admired Camus's character Mersault in *The Stranger*—a man so removed from feeling that he felt not even his mother's death or the visceral effects of the blinding Algerian sun that induced him to kill an Arab. That was the kind of existential numbness that I sought. It wasn't only about being cool. If I kept feelings at bay, I couldn't be hurt. I could stay clear of pain. I wanted to be the Don Juan who seduced without being vulnerable or suffering like Romeo with fair Rosaline before he met Juliet. I was secretly contemptuous of those seeking permanent relationships, all the fraternity guys I knew who were already lavaliered or pinned, even planning weddings. Better dead than wed, I thought, playing on the better-dead-than-red slogan of the times.

By senior year I was known as a lady's man, and I liked being thought of in that way. I finally had my own place, my unapproved off-campus trailer, for seductions (my literary identities even included fragments of a few rakes, like the infamous Lovelace in Samuel Richardson's eighteenth-century classic *Clarissa*). Feminist shibboleths about not objectifying women were notions that inhabited the future. I was taking mostly literature and creative writing classes and proctoring and grading for Dr. Marks. I felt I had it made. But I still really had no idea where I was headed or what I was going to do with a life led by literature except, like Bellow, to follow the novelist's discipline of nobility.

Les Marks suggested I do a masters degree in English. Was I really grist for the scholarly mill? Was teaching literature really to be fate for my character? I felt comfortable enough to stay where I was, at Ohio University. The English department had a number of good, solid teachers as well as potent and highly respected writers who would be coming aboard, like Gregory Corso and Lawrence Durrell, and by this time I knew my way around and even semi-taught a composition class and had acquired a, wow cool, faculty key to the elevator. I say semi-taught, because my role involved going into the classroom and turning on a television set, with cathoded lectures, then answering student questions in the last few minutes. But I relished the give and take, the short performances required of me and the role I began to feel destined to play. Teaching writing, even in this marginal way, seemed to help some students, and I wanted to help.

I was suddenly on a path toward grad school. I allowed Les Marks to guide me as I allowed Digger to guide me into doing an honor's thesis. Digger revealed to me: "Get this. You sign up for the honors college and you do a thesis and you get to graduate with honors. Pretty good deal."

Digger was ridiculed as my follower, but the truth was he gave me the idea to follow a more scholarly bent, and he gave me the idea to join the honors college. I asked Lester Marks to direct my proposed honors thesis on Saul Bellow.

By this time, Bellow was the darling of most literary critics. Not only had he established the original voice of *Augie March*, celebrated by many as the greatest innovation in the American novel since *Huckleberry Finn*, he had breathed new life into post-World War II American literature with his fusion of great erudition and Jewish-boy urban street smarts. I wrote a fawning letter to him, care of where he taught—the University of Chicago's Department of Social Thought—telling him how much I admired his work and mentioning, too, that my friend Rich Kritchman knew his oldest son, Greg. I got back a form letter from the secretary of the department informing me of Mr. Bellow's office hours, and that was all I needed to take off and hitch from Athens to Chicago to interview Saul Bellow. It was whimsy and the desire to please Les Marks. But I was smitten with Bellow's prose, his narrative powers, the literary world he had created. I had no idea that the strange pilgrimage I made to Chicago in 1966 to meet Saul Bellow would be the first interview of a writer in what eventually would become virtually a career.

Meeting Saul Bellow was both less and more than I expected. By today's standards I would likely be viewed as a stalker. I went to his office—alluded to in the terse, formal response I had received from the Department of Social Thought—and got a look of bewilderment from Bellow as he saw me standing there and listened to me, haltingly and deferentially, speak of writing to him and receiving the letter from the department secretary. I tossed in Rich Kritchman's name and the at-best tenuous connection to his son, Greg. It was clear he had no idea who I was or who Rich was and no expectation of giving me an interview. But something—perhaps my awe of him or my youth, or the mention of his son—caught him, and he invited me into his office.

He was wearing a large winter coat and one of those Russian hats that made him look slight. His office was austere. I expected to see writing awards, framed photos or other evidence of his achievements, but there was only a single bookshelf and the kind of utilitarian look one might associate more with an Eastern European professor's office. Bellow was cordial, if a bit formal, and as I threw out questions, I kept reminding myself that this was the same man whose prose had wildly ignited my imagination, who had managed to meld great learning with great humanity, humor, ebullience and vitality into crisp, fluid, often soaring lyricism. I wanted him somehow, magically, to see in me someone he would like to adopt, to make me a son, Stephen Dedalus to his Leopold Bloom. Dr. Marks had remarked to me that writers were no different than the rest of us. Even the greatest writer smelled of mortality. In the meantime, I was a twenty-one-year-old father seeker who was managing to keep a conversation going with a great writer and trying to connect the man who was offering measured and serious responses to my questions with the writer I had come to know well from *The Dangling Man* on through *The Victim, Seize the Day, Augie March* and *Henderson the Rain King.*

Les Marks had asked me to find out about something that had piqued his curiosity in a mild way—whether or not there was any relationship between Kirby Albee, a character in Bellow's *The Victim*, a novel about anti-Semitism, and Melville's *Bartleby the Scrivener*. Les thought the names sounded alike, and so I asked Bellow, adding that it was a question that my thesis director wanted an answer to. I received a surprisingly stern-sounding caveat from him about foolish questions posed by literary critics.

"They attempt to find meaning through names. What red herrings! As if names unlock the mystery of a work of literature and provide a key." I remembered Walter Tevis telling me how he had taken names randomly for his novels, *The Hustler* and *The Man Who Fell to Earth*, from a phone directory. Yet names certainly often did suggest meaning. Why else had Henry James named his protagonist Newman in *The American*? And, of course, there was Arthur Miller's Loman in *Death of a Salesman*. But I was there to listen, and I listened with rapt attentiveness as Bellow went into a surprising mini-tirade against literary critics, calling up a metaphor of how they were like men in boats in mid-ocean, all alone but for their idea of what was right. It seemed to me ungrateful for him to be branding all critics with such a broad brush. He, after all, had received effusive, nearly universal praise and acclaim from them. Plus, I was an aspiring critic. Only later, when I read *Herzog* and learned more about his life at the time of our interview, would I understand how his animus against critics may have been personal and tied to having been cuckolded by Jack Ludwig. Over thirty years later he would as much as admit this to me privately. But even when he then referred to critics as parasites, I remained composed and agreeable and rapt and simply threw him another question. It was a bit, I thought, like being a pitcher. You serve up pitches, and you hope you get them over the plate. I was nervous and likely more than a tad sycophantic, but I was also having fun. I was interviewing Saul Bellow!

"When I wrote *Henderson the Rain King* they said I had written a Nietzschean novel. Or some said Reichean. Or Hegelian. Or Freudian. What do they know really?" Suddenly he broke into a boyish, nearly furtive-looking grin and added, "Me? I'm not telling."

Bellow spoke to me the entire hour, softly but firmly, about writing with what I was impressed to recognize as deep intellectual conviction—freely sprinkling his short recitations with names like Malraux, Gide and Proust, writers I had only heard of but not yet read, inwardly, silently vowing I would. Reading Bellow helped to create a kind of nascent desire in me to be as well read as he was, but meeting him and listening to him made me hungrier for the voluminous knowledge he had acquired from a lifetime of serious reading. Literature would be my métier.

I followed Bellow out of his office and down the hall until he abruptly stopped. He had on his Russian hat and long coat again, and it was suddenly clear to me that he was bidding me goodbye. "Well," he said. "I must go." And I realized that we were standing in front of the men's room. The writer as mortal! He extended his hand, and I took it and shook it gratefully, thanking him repeatedly, sounding, I'm sure, both foolish and too effusive. But I was grateful. Truly grateful. Though I realize now it had no doubt been the office-hour time he set aside to talk with whomever came by. It was my dumb luck that no one else did. But I had come all the way from Hellenistic sounding Athens to Carl Sandburg's city of hog butchers, Dreiser's city and James T. Farrell's and Nelson Algren's, and I had met my hero.

When I returned to Ohio from Chicago, Les Marks told me there was a National Defense Education Act Fellowship available to the English department, and he and others in the department strongly felt I was the most deserving candidate. The NDEA would pay tuition and fees and a stipend of $2,500. If I got the fellowship, I thought, it would seal my pursuit of a masters degree at Ohio U., and that would not be a bad deal. As long as I had books and girls, I would abide.

So in my fifth year at Ohio University, I finished an M.A. degree as a National Defense Fellow. I still toyed loosely with the idea of going to law school but knew that it wasn't something I really wanted—only something that sounded, like medicine, more impressively bourgeois and prestigious than becoming a scholar and a teacher. Or even a writer. More than conventional monetary success, I still wanted bourgeois respectability, though I was increasingly critical of the pursuit of money and what I saw as the hold of a material culture on spirits and psyches. I continued to feel split between aspirations tied to literature and scholarship and writing and ones linked to the outer trappings and pursuits of a good, material life. The struggle of trying to get stories down on paper pleased me, even as most of the vignettes and self-involved episodes I tried turning into tales turned into rejection slips. "You can paper your walls with those," Walter Tevis counseled. "I had plenty of them too. But then, when you get an acceptance or even a few scrawled lines of response, it will matter all that much more."

I was actually discovering that I liked graduate studies, even courses that a couple of years before would have seemed a stretch to me, like Chaucer and Victorian Literature, Renaissance Poetry and Literary Theory. I had fashioned a schedule that involved being up late, even into bird-chirping morning hours, and sleeping late or until my first class, which met twice a week in the late afternoon. That was the kind of sleep pattern I believed a writer was supposed to have; in between reading and studying and trying to play the satyr, I churned out stories and sent them to magazines like *Playboy, Esquire,* and *Oui,* habitually getting form rejections.

Walter Tevis proffered another piece of advice that stayed with me when he told me that—notwithstanding his monetary success with *The Hustler* as both a book and a movie—he would have been better off writing work of more distinguished literary merit, since that could have meant Guggenheims and other fellowships and grants as well as an easier, better paying, higher-status teaching position than the one he had at Ohio U. I absorbed from Tevis, too, an even greater contempt for buck chasing; he spoke disparagingly to me of cynical advertising men who might have been worthy writers or dedicated teachers.

I already knew I would be a dedicated teacher. I studied Buddhism in a comparative religion undergraduate course and was smitten with the idea of finding a noble path and sticking to it. Teaching and writing. Both noble paths. "Your work is to discover your work and then with all your heart to give yourself to it." The Buddha also spoke wisdom about compassion and service, and I was doing regular volunteer work at the local orphanage and the state mental hospital—where my weird psychologist friend Mike Rothburd had trained his adolescent charges to repeat my name over and over spookily in unison when I walked past them. Was I also a serious writer who had a novel in me? Hell, I was getting a trail of rejection slips! No one wanted to publish me! Yet

I believed that the fiction within me was raw and inchoate. Latent and submerged gifts of mesmeric storytelling would rise from me. If bad came to worse perhaps I could even be a shlockmeister and turn out trash novels like Harold Robbins, Jacqueline Susann or Irving Wallace if that was what was needed to pay the bills. But somehow I would one day make my name as a serious writer. I would learn the writer's trade.

When I began to get offers of acceptance to Ph.D. programs I went to everyone I respected for advice, including Calvin Thayer, my Elizabethan poetry professor—who had surprised me earlier in the year by writing in the margins of a paper I did on Robert Herrick's sensual poetry, next to my misspelling of phallus (sic phallas): "Krasny: If you can't spell phallus correctly write prick." When I went to him for advice on where to go for a Ph.D. and told him I had a fellowship offer from the University of Massachusetts, he said, " I think you'd like those U. Mass. aristocratic broads." I even called Les Marks, in Norway on a Fulbright, for advice. Finally, based on the amount of the stipend and the school's reputation, I chose the University of Wisconsin. I finished my M.A. over the summer, still getting money from Uncle Sam, and made an overly ambitious reading list for a three-unit independent study course with the department chair. He laughed, assuring me it would be a major feat if I could read half the books on the list. Out of honor, desire and drive I read them all.

I taught my first course in the spring at Ohio U., working with students in as dedicated a way as possible, even more so with the academically challenged. I felt flush because the English department offered me $750 to teach the class in composition, which was $750 in addition to my fellowship money. I was at ease in front of students, despite the fact that I showed up to teach in the customary tie and jacket and was called Mr. Krasny, while I in turn called my students Mr. or Miss. Things were still formal, but I was able to communicate the passion I felt about literature and help students feel more able and confident about putting thoughts into language. I also acted in a couple of ways that avoided the *dukkas*, the Buddhist word for desires, in ways that seemed right and morally enhancing.

One attractive young woman came to see me about her grade and was apparently quivering with a physical attraction that my girlfriend, Susan—who was doing homework at the desk next to mine—observed to me later. Miss F. had marked all her essays in the upper right-hand corner with the initials JMJ, which I found out, after asking her, stood for Jesus, Mary and Joseph. From her own Catholic background, Susan understood this. At Susan's convent school, girls couldn't wear patent leather shoes that might reflect their underpants, and they were told by one of the priests never to go to a drive-in movie or to eat pizza since both could jostle their hormones. Susan observed to me: "The poor girl is right out of the convent, and she has a terrible crush on you." Whatever Miss F. had, she was in a serious crisis of faith that I wanted to empathize with and be properly teacher-like about. She refused to accept the argument that Hamlet could have contemplated suicide because, she parroted from her Catholic school teachings, Shakespeare had a Catholic worldview.

Miss F was pretty and sexually repressed, but I felt instinctively that any kind of flirtation, let alone seduction, was absolutely verboten when it comes to a student. Nor would I push Susan, who longed to stay a virgin until marriage, to consummate. Despite seeing myself as a seducer, I considered myself honorable. And though strapped badly for cash and willing to write papers for money for not-too-bright fraternity brothers, I soon discovered that I had qualms—a brand of ethics linked to fear—about continuing to do such hired ghost work now that I was a teacher. A rich Greek-American guy approached me to fix him up with an A in the class that I was teaching and offered me $1,000. He was trying to keep his grades high enough to ensure a student deferment since, like all of us, he was starting to sweat being drafted. I felt good about resolutely turning him down.

I later found out that he got someone in the registrar's office to alter all his grades, so he was able to maintain enough of an average to avoid flunking out and preserve his student deferment. But I felt, with him and with Miss F., that I was learning how to be good and how to checkmate deceptively easy temptations like fast money or innocent flesh.

David Mamet

David Mamet knows he's getting older. It has led him back to Judaism. "I became what I am," he tells me, "what is mine by proclivity and heredity." Funny word to use, proclivity. He says words with

Ts in them with a bite that sounds syllabic and affected—pro-cliv-ity, act-tor, wri-ting. He is pleasant and chipper and polite. It is his first time in San Francisco. He tells me he loves the weather and the wine and that everyone he has met so far is "peachy." He also tells me that, as he grows older, his thoughts tend to the past. There is little that is really useful about writing. One's interests change. One should steal from anybody but oneself. He wrote *American Buffalo* over a quarter of a century ago. Many refrigerators don't last that long. He would rather change.

Mamet was a nice middle-class Jewish boy. He felt fortunate to have been born in Chicago, the son of a labor lawyer in a town full of unions and writers. He wanted to escape, and he did. He did "everything in the world to support myself and loved it all." He thought at first he'd become an actor but his "affections did not in that way tend." He became a playwright instead, and a director, and then went on to what he called the big casino and wrote for the screen. He tried once to teach creative writing at Yale. All one needed to learn about writing, he decided, was pencil and paper and to write well. Academics were teaching the opposite of art. In the academy, students wrote to please superiors. In art, the self struggles with the expression of inchoate opposites and unrest.

Mamet answers callers with near military-sounding precision and cheeriness, after saying that he will crumple paper and pretend to know the answer to any questions he cannot answer.

> Caller: "WELCOME TO SAN FRANCISCO, DAVID."
>
> Mamet (heartily): "THANK YOU, SIR."
>
> Caller: "HELLO, MR. MAMET."
>
> Mamet (vigorously): "GOOD MORNING, SIR."

He is cheerful about the breakfast he had that morning and about pizza night at the Rainbow Suites off Route 2 in Vermont, where he sees other famous writers. He is thrilled to be part of a Torah-reading community and thinks Jewish renewal is great. He calls tracking a deer one of the greatest experiences of his life. Can he really be so upbeat about so many things? I remember that Mamet was so pleased that a journalist for *Esquire* was coming to interview him in Vermont that he said, "goody goody gumdrops from the gumdrop tree." Yet Mamet went years without giving interviews. He wouldn't crack even a wisp of a smile and looked a bit grim years later—when I interviewed him on stage for a theater fundraiser and mentioned the famous *New Yorker* cartoon that featured a well-dressed man telling a street beggar "Neither a borrower nor a lender be—Shakespeare" and the street beggar answering, "Fuck you—David Mamet."

Mamet says that maybe the audiences didn't understand what he was trying to do in *Oleanna* because it was a bad play. Perhaps his script about Jimmy Hoffa, which he wrote for his father, didn't do as well as he thought it would because the script was no good. Is this feigned modesty? He blithely says he sits in an office by himself and naps all day long. The word discipline, he says, makes his blood run cold.

He deludes himself into thinking he writes when the spirit moves him. Perhaps inability to concentrate has been responsible for his success, since as soon as he completes something, he has to move on to something else. Writing is like poker. You play the cards dealt and then they're dead. He has no intention to go home or to stop.

Paul Auster

Paul Auster is telling me how he knew Marc Rudd, the radical Columbia student leader of SDS in the sixties. They went to high school together in New Jersey, and Rudd lived down the hall from him at Columbia. "I'm for Mao and you're for King Lear," Rudd told Auster.

Growing up in New Jersey and studying French in junior high, Auster never could have predicted becoming a seaman on an oil tanker or a French translator, let alone an internationally acclaimed novelist. He never could have predicted working in film. He wrote a Chistmas story for *The New York Times*, and film director Wayne Wang read it. It was a fluke. Wang's *San Francisco Chronicle* didn't get delivered that morning, so he went out and bought *The Times*. Auster liked collaborating on a film after working so long alone in a room. It was his chance to learn another language and tell a story in a different way. He taught writing at Princeton and kept asking himself, how do you teach writing? He felt honored when the University of Chicago offered him a teaching position, but he had just gone to a film wrap party, which felt to him a lot like a circus, and he decided that that kind of experience was a lot more fun than being with academics.

Auster tells me that plumbers do more valuable work than writers. A book can't change someone in any direct or immediate way, but a plumber patching up a leak or fixing a stopped-up toilet performs a necessary and valuable service. You write because you want to write or because you need to write. Writers work hard and often get no response, but forget too often that the world doesn't owe them any. Auster says his work comes from intensely emotional states and is about spirit more than mind. I mention that the author David Foster Wallace told me he avoids sentimentality, and Auster responds by saying he avoids cynicism. Cynicism, he says, is the dominant approach to the worlds of business, art and politics, because it stems from fear of emotion or feeling. It is much easier to make fun of things, though cynicism can distort reality as much as sentimentality does. Auster thinks the cynicism of our era eventually will be laughed at as much as we now laugh at Victorian sentimentality.

Auster has a fervent interest in Kafka. Many compare him to Kafka. I tell Auster they look alike. "Big ears and probably the same racial stock," he says with a laugh. Though certain things from Kafka may have seeped into Auster's work, he declares, "Kafka is Kafka. Why would anyone try to write like him?" A caller compares an item in Auster to Beckett's work, and Auster reflects that he admires Beckett above all mid-twentieth-century writers but doesn't see any parallels between their work. Another caller asks about his work and the work of Borges. Auster says he once "read Borges assiduously." But, Auster adds, "Borges is much smarter than I am. I feel more grounded than Borges." Auster talks about being in Buenos Aires and seeing tributes and affection everywhere for Borges. Plaques and streets named after him. Never had Auster seen more evidence of a writer more beloved in a major city. "Borges," he says, "is a scholar. I'm not. I'm doing it more intuitively."

When Auster writes, he is in a different state. The core of a novel for him is everything he didn't know that comes bubbling up in him without any map or science. Writing memoir is different. Memory, rather than the unconscious, is the source, and it feels like a different part of the brain. You can find things you thought were lost.

Auster works six to eight hours a day but never produces more than a single page. He can write a single paragraph up to fifteen times before typing it up. I try free, unedited associations with him. I'll say a word

and he can respond with the first word that comes to his mind. Fate
brings death. Destiny future. Caprice whim.

At the end of our interview, Auster says to me, "You are really good
at what you do." My immediate unedited response: "I would much prefer
being really good at what you do."

T. C. Boyle

T. C. Boyle was a punk who grew up with a group
he describes as "terminal wise guys." He says they were all low lives and
degenerates, but there was joy with them. Like the old pal of his who
showed up at a reading he gave and asked, during the Q & A, if Boyle's
hair was real and how old he really was.

Boyle is an upbeat, high-energy, amicable guy who has the look of an
older neopunk. I tell him he looks like a motorcycle gang member or a
rock and roller, with his black leather jacket, earring and skull ring that
he tells me is his memento-mori. "It lets me know where I'm headed."
He explains that he's in traveling clothes. But he also tells a story about
being on stage for a reading in Central Park with Patti Smith, during
a New York heat wave, and wearing an old t-shirt. After the show, he
headed off in his sweaty, stinking t-shirt to do Charley Rose.

Boyle is on air with me to plug his newest book, a novel called *Riven
Rock*. It's based on the real story of Stanley McCormick, the schizophrenic son of Cyrus McCormick, right out of Kraft-Ebbing's *Psycho-
pathia Sexualis*—known for being what they called back then, near
the twentieth century's turn, a sex maniac. I also talk with him about
his next book, *The Inner Circle*, a novel about Kinsey and sex research.
Boyle wants to shape real stories into myth. Michiko Kakutani's reviews
of both his books were not so favorable, and Boyle says she doesn't get
him. He claims she wants him to write straightforward, compassionate,
realistic tales that he has no interest in writing. He sees his contribution
to American literature in the wild stuff. She liked his story "If the River
Was Whiskey," which he says anyone could have written. He wants
readers to be taken by surprise and moved. He wants sex on the page to
be powerful in reader's minds. He wants emotional resonance, with sat-
ire and naturalism coming at readers together. "I'm always attracted to
hyperbole, to the ridiculous, to over the top. I'm Irish after all." Which

is probably why he says he will shoot himself in the movie theater if they use broken accents rather than Spanish in a film being made of *The Tortilla Curtain.*

He admits his drive to write may well be the sublimation of his drive to drink, a way to distract the depression and alcoholism that runs in his family. But he concedes all this in a flurry of bold statements that come out with only slight hints of irony. "I've never written a bad story," he exults. "I want to be the country's dictator. In the classroom I am more like Jesus before they nailed him to the cross . . . No one ever told me what to do in my whole life. I can do anything I want. I am a monster of ego." He proposes a solution for the Middle East. Move all Iraqis to Vermont and put them on welfare and build them houses. Then pave over Iraq. Of course all the hyperbolic declarations are uttered in ways that are likeable, touched by Irish charm. It is clear, above all, that Boyle loves what he does. "Writing is an obsessive-compulsive disorder. A kind of miracle. Something out of nothing. Out of you. Only you can write it, whether it's good or bad."

Boyle wants above all to be good at his craft. Entertaining. Getting in the minds and bodies of his characters, even if it's an immigrant Mexican woman, as in *The Tortilla Curtain.* He relishes once having been compared to Faulkner and Marquez because he created his own postage stamp of reality out of Petersville, New York. They are his literary antecedents, his mentors, his heroes. When he runs out of steam or falls flat, he reads Faulkner. He wants readers to confront their prejudices and ethnic stereotypes, to show them both sides, to entertain them and make them realize literature is fun. He wants readers to feel bad and admit their worst intentions. "I believe in literature," he says with a wisp of solemnity. "I resent the fact that it has to take a backseat to soap opera, movies, rock and roll and everything else."

Boyle makes me curious about his marriage, after he refers to himself as his wife's twenty-five year slave and says he bought the first California house that Frank Lloyd Wright built in Santa Barbara for her. She takes care of him, he says, and he "licks the floor with his tongue" for her in return. He wanted to give her a life of ease second only to that of Princess Grace before the accident.

Boyle says he loves to read science and biology and strongly believes the planet is too overpopulated, that if you're a real environmentalist you'll cover yourself with mulch right up to your neck and then shoot yourself in the head. It's all you can do.

 ### *Joan Didion*

Joan Didion still says she is from California even though she lives in Manhattan and has for over a decade. Her identity is linked to California. It's everything she is. She would never describe herself as a New Yorker. Yet the memoir she has come on air to discuss with me, before the tragedy that produced *The Year of Magical Thinking*, is called *Where I Was From*. But then California is not really a geographical place to her any more than it is the enchanted home of her *Was*. California is a state of mind. She needs to tell her story to live, and to tell it in memoir.

What, I wonder, is under her halting and stammering, her nervousness and her pauses and her girlish, nearly flirtatious laughter? What is under the woman who writes such fastidious and precise and poetic prose, who one woman caller breathlessly says changed her life and another rhapsodizes over as "our greatest American writer?" In response to the praise she quotes Robert Penn Warren. "Only the writer knows where the rot is."

When her adopted daughter, Quintana Roo, was quite small, the enchantment over California roots dropped away. The former Goldwater Republican saw the rot too clearly; she saw what was under the California dream that began in elevated prose from the gleaming in Josiah Royce's eyes. She hated high school. Couldn't wait to leave and told me they wanted to get rid of her. Regimentation. Hall passes. It felt punitive to her, but she was still certain then that the dream that was California, the California she would try and fail to define her relationship with, was no dream at all. It was a there that was still there, and then suddenly it became a different there, and that there changed for a lifetime who she was and who she would become and turned her writing toward greatness.

Then came the deaths of John Gregory and Quintana. She talks this time with me of *The Year of Magical Thinking*, her book on John's death, about how she went crazy after he died, how she was giving the impersonation of a sane person. She could see the thin thread to death in her novels but not in her personal life, not until her husband keeled over at the dinner table from cardiac arrest and died. It simply wasn't in her vision. She speaks haltingly about the breaking of her own illusion that we can control events in our personal lives. "I always thought I had a degree of control over events and could make things happen. I gave up a lot of stuff. The need for control. The need to be hidden." She tells me she has dropped a mask or two in her writing. She is, she says, more open. She responds more directly and listens as she has never done.

I ask her if she knows a Pirandello story, "War." She doesn't. I explain. A man meets another man who has just lost his son in the war. The father whose son was killed speaks of the higher cause his son has died for and the importance of his son's life being sacrificed for country. The other man asks: "Then is your son really dead?" The father, with sudden recognition of the realness of death beyond his brave-sounding words, loses control, weeping.

Didion has stayed the course. She went on tour and talked about the book even after her daughter died. Does the touring help, I ask? "Not necessarily," she replies. "But it doesn't not help." She has had to move on to work. A screenplay and then the book and now the tour. She has had to survive herself.

3   Marrying Up

I RENTED A SMALL EFFICIENCY on West Main Street in Madison, Wisconsin. My landlord was a bald-headed fellow named Epstein, the name Philip Roth gave to a crass, vulgar but sympathetic Jewish character in his first story collection, *Goodbye, Columbus*. I had my nice Jewish *mensch* boy act down; despite finding Epstein coarse and brusque, like Roth's character, I behaved courteously. I was glad to have an off-campus place that I could afford, at $110 a month, so I could live alone as I had done the past couple of years at Ohio U. Epstein confided to me as I signed the lease, "A mixed couple lived here before you."

"A Jewish guy and a *shiksa*?"

"Boy are you from another world! No. A Jewish girl and a *shvartza*."

Again, I thought I should speak out. But what, exactly, should I say? That the word *shvartza* was a word Epstein dare not use? My own father used the word—and when I called him on it, he quickly answered that it meant black. "What's wrong with calling them what they are? Negro is Spanish for black. Shvartz is Yiddish. What's the difference?"

.   .   .

MY WORDS at least were registering with students. Teaching Edith Wharton's *House of Mirth* to a football player who wrote at a third-grade level proved as futile as trying to change Epstein's or my dad's vocabulary, but I found the role of classroom teacher gratifying, and I felt wedded to teaching, grading and tutorials. I also felt alive in the classroom. More importantly, I felt like I was making a difference.

Considering how much I felt for Susan, I was quick enough to move back to the aspiring lothario role. I had held Susan, that summer before going off to Madison, both of us naked, while she sobbed convulsively in my arms. It was our last night together, and she had made up her mind that it was over. She would have to distance herself and put me behind her. There could be no other option. I didn't want to let go. I couldn't imagine I'd find someone as lovely or as bright again, someone for whom I had undeniably strong feelings that felt like love and who had felt attached enough to me that she could sob uncontrollably as I held her on our last night together, our first and only night as lovers. In many ways we were alike, I realized, both wanting to be artists and intellectuals, both thinking ourselves nonconformists, both locked into conformity and expectations that we believed others had for us and we had for ourselves.

In my new digs, I decided to put up a poster of a thermonuclear explosion, complete with a huge mushroom cloud. No one woman would claim title to or possession of me. I would, as the Beat poet Ferlinghetti put it, scatter my seed across the landscape. I was a lover and a writer.

I pursued girls with vigor and tried, once more, to numb feelings, to protect myself from either falling into unrequited love, as I had experienced for years as a teen in love with love, or into love requited but ultimately lost, as with Susan. The trick, I thought, was to keep young women moving along an assembly line of sexual adventures and, in that way, protect my heart.

After only a few weeks in Madison I was back in the hunt, with names of numerous prospects to pursue. I aimed high. One young woman had been a Wisconsin homecoming queen, another had been in *Playboy*. In my own playboy-of-the-Midwest mindset, I would go after all of them. I wound up with a small town doctor's daughter who was a Jewish virgin.

Nancy's name had been given to me by a guy at Ohio U. who knew her and extolled her looks and wildness. She was quite pretty, the daughter of a southern Ohio Jewish doctor, a senior who drove a Vespa and smoked a lot of pot. I liked her, and we had fun together, but I was shocked to discover when we first had sex that she was a virgin. The huge red spot on my bed sheet was the ocular proof, along with her confession. "Yes. You're the first," she confided. "I was a virgin. I was pretty hung up about it too. My father is studying psychiatry now and he's been pushing me to find someone, preferably a nice guy like you, and get past the virgin stuff. I'm glad I did."

"Your father wanted you to get laid?"

"Not exactly. Well, maybe. Sort of. I guess so. He thought I was becoming neurotic about it and he was probably right. I was." Whereupon she jumped out of bed and went to my phone and placed a collect call to her father. I lay there listening to her explain to him that she had just had her first "coitus," as she actually called it. I was stunned. "Yes," I heard her say. "He's very nice. You'd like him. He's a lot like you." (Pause) "You want to talk to him?"

At this point I thought the call must be a hoax. Yet I knew it wasn't. I was being asked to come to the phone to talk to the father of a girl I had just deflowered. I did not want to talk to him.

"Come on," Nancy urged me. "It's okay. He won't bite you." I finally, reluctantly, did as she asked, and her father was cordial. He told me he hoped we would meet soon.

Nancy had a friend whose name was also Nancy—a blonde Scandanavian-looking girl who had a boyfriend in medical school. A Greek American named George, he was bookish and liked, as I did, discussing philosophy, politics and intellectual matters in general; we became friends. I liked the idea of dating a doctor's daughter and hanging out with a future doctor since, as the son of a man who spent his adult life grieving over not becoming a physician and idolizing many who were, doctors had special status with me. George was a guy of wide girth who had read a lot of existentialism and, like me, was enamored of Camus. Like many future docs, and docs I would later become friends with, he saw himself as a Spencerian or Renaissance sort of man—wanting to marry his readings in the humanities, philosophy and the arts with his formal training in science and medicine. We decided to co-teach a course in Madison's Open University—a student and faculty-run university without walls or fees, which was a reaction against the institutionalized type of learning that radicals increasingly came to view as too elitist and too costly, hence part of a closed university. Our course was based on our musings about Camus's notion of the absurd, which I titled "After the Absurd: Where Do We Go from Here?"

I was one of well over one hundred English Teaching Assistants at U. of W. Most of them were radical or had radical sympathies. One of them, a very pretty woman named Pauline, worshipped Rosa Luxemborg but dressed like a show model. She was always spouting Rosa or quoting Emma Goldman and yet showed up at one big Bascom Hall demonstration in a taxi. Lynn Cheney, the conservative wife of Vice President Dick Cheney, was one of us, but not politically. I did not learn until meeting her years later, in a conversation that rapidly turned into a rip-snorting argument that we were both at the U. of W. as English T.A. Ph.D. students. There was a lot of talk among my fellow T.A.s and across campus at the time about taking radical action. The U. of W. was allowing recruiters on campus from multinationals like Dow Chemical, a napalm manufacturer, and many saw it as complicit in the Vietnam war. This was a view that eventually led to the bombing of the campus math research center and the death of a young father—a math graduate student working there late at night—who was blown up by a detonation targeting sins somehow linked, in the minds of the perps, to the murder of Che Guevera. Still, a lot of the ideas of my fellow radical grad students made sense to me. They were talking about equality, peace, justice, a better world and bringing an end to a war that I detested. I made friends with many of them. But ideas infiltrating from the Weathermen and the Black Panther Party—about using bombs and fighting the hegemonic power of capitalism by breaking shop windows and going after all cops, whom they saw as pigs—were ugly to me. I still believed in civil disobedience. Many of the campus radicals I knew were from bourgeois backgrounds. They came from the kind of comfortable lives I had aspired to. I liked many of them, and sympathized with what they sympathized with, what they stood for. But I wondered why they had such rage against authority when their lives, by my lights, had been so damned good and comfortable. Of course, I didn't yet understand the nature of Oedipal rage or how leading a gilded life could intensify guilt and rebellion and the wish for revolutionary, even violent change.

Radicalism was bubbling on nearly every front, including the pedagogic. We English T.A.s had a meeting early in the year to discuss what to do about ineffectual profs. One of the more radical among us, who would later become a labor organizer, suggested placing a tape recorder in the lecture hall of one of the professors who listlessly read each year's lectures from the same yellowed, weathered notes. "Let him lecture to an empty room with no one in it. Let him talk to a tape recorder." It made some of us laugh aloud until another T.A. explained that this prof was a sick man whose wife had just died. Every one of the profs we talked about targeting for bad teaching had problems that made it impossibly uncompassionate to go after them. What kind of revolutionaries, I wondered, did that make us?

I personally wanted to be a different kind of teacher, an antifascist pedagogue who conducted—no, who co-taught—with students in classes that were student-centered rather than run by or, worse, dominated by me as an authority figure, whose power of the grade could send young men off to combat and death. Having read an essay by Jerry Farber called "The Student as Nigger" and books like *Teaching as a Subversive Activity, Summerhill* and *Death at an Early Age*, I reasoned that students had as much or more to teach me. I wanted to make my classes flow in a collective, equitable spirit.

The Madison culture I moved in made politics and The Movement central. Herman Hesse's *Siddhartha* and writers like Herbert Marcuse and Norman O. Brown were must-reads. I wanted to read everything that was important to read including Franz Fanon's *The Wretched of the Earth* and *The Autobiography of Malcolm X* and a lot of Marx and other radical and anarchistic stuff like Bakunin, Kropotkin, Rosa Luxemborg and Emma Goldman that I loved discussing. I wanted to read everything that everyone else was reading or recommending. I wanted to outread all my mostly bourgeois-born contemporaries, to speak on everything with authority without being authoritarian or, heaven forfend, fascist-sounding. Revolution, like fascism, was a much-used word with different meanings, and many used it promiscuously. But the notion many of us shared was that revolution was imminent, would come, would cleanse, change and purify our world. I teetered on the brink of embracing revolutionary zeal, but I was conscious of being working-class while all the would-be revolutionaries I knew were from the bourgeoisie.

When protests erupted across the campus against Dow recruiters, I asked my class to discuss those issues instead of the assigned material. Teaching had to be relevant to life and politics. There I was, in Bascom

Hall, leading a discussion about what was happening on campus, when the smell of tear gas began filling the classroom. Police were racing after protestors, invading the building and ordering everyone out by bullhorn. I saw that the door to the classroom was blocked by baton-wielding riot police. One of my students cried out: "Mr. Krasny we can't get out of here." I made a quick decision—written up in Pulitzer Prize winning journalist David Maraniss's account of the Dow protests and the war, *They Marched into the Sunlight*. I led my class of some twenty-five out the window.

Despite the radicalism of its T.A.s, U. of W.'s English department was fairly dry and old-fashioned. Its reputation for excellence was based largely on the scholarship of older members of the department, including the professor with the yellowed notes. Some faculty members were trying to make changes to fit the new radical zeitgeist, and that included, to my relief, switching the traditional Ph.D. requirement of Old and Middle English to two semesters of Linguistics. They also allowed one T.A. to be on the curriculum committee that decided which texts would be adopted for all freshman and sophomore English classes. I had enough friends, after just a couple of months, that I campaigned for the position and won, becoming the first Ph.D. student ever to serve on a text-selection committee.

I was amazed to discover how much the book representatives wanted to wine and dine me. Decisions about which texts would be adopted meant lots of dollars for the publisher. One day, I imagined, publishers would also be coming after me, plying me with food and drink to get me to sign a book contract.

I did something regrettable, linked in my mind then to the spirit of what we self-proclaimed radicals preached. As a member of the curriculum committee I wrote publishers requesting an enormous number of books, many of which had little relationship to the two English courses—English Composition and Introduction to Literature—whose texts I was responsible for selecting. I became, like Augie March after all, a book thief—though I was not swiping them from bookstores, and I rationalized that some of the books might possibly be relevant or could be relevant to those classes. But essentially I was a pirate, building a library for myself and winning the admiration of a couple of grad school cronies who thought ripping off publishers was cool, right in step with the anarchic spirit of the times. Famed radical street artist, yippie and Chicago Seven member Abbie Hoffman did, in fact, write a book titled, *Steal This Book*. But I felt ashamed and mortified when Bill Lenehan, a fellow text committee member of mine and head of English Comp, confronted me with a letter he had received from a publisher enclosing a copy of my request for a spate of books. I realized that I had behaved badly and vowed to sin no more in the name of radicalism.

I was still seeing Nancy, and when she and the other Nancy went to Milwaukee over the weekend, I hung out with George. I had a small record player, and George had Jimi Hendrix and Vanilla Fudge albums, and we got stoned together in my apartment on some of what he claimed was Acapulco Gold; everyone in those days claimed to have Acapulco Gold, the gold standard for marijuana smokers, just as Cuban cigars were for cigar smokers. As I got higher, I became convinced that George was making a move on me. He was a big guy, and I felt certain that he wanted to pull me into an embrace. I liked smoking dope. I liked doing watercolors while high, or writing poetry that seemed extraordinary until I looked at it with sobriety in the morning. But I had had an incident earlier that year when I was at a party with a raven-haired undergraduate from Los Angeles, who was with me in the bedroom of the house. A guy came into the bedroom, naked to the waist, and began leaping up and down, shouting "I'm the Wizard of Oz." I asked him if he could give us some privacy, and he answered, "Who says you get privacy? I'm the wizard, and you two are sex-crazed dope smokers." I hustled the girl out of the house and into the street and told her I thought the guy was a narc. "A narc?" she said incredulously. "Where'd you get that? He's no narc. He's a jerk."

Well, maybe he wasn't a narc. And maybe, too, George wasn't a reefer-driven would-be gay rapist. But I was not taking chances. I made up some lame story about needing to see a friend in trouble. "I gotta go now," I exclaimed, and moved swiftly to the door. George was still on my floor, toking, but he got up, hearing the urgency of my voice, and quickly followed me out into the street. "See you," I said to him, trying to sound nonchalant and waving at him as I walked away, only to circle around the block and reenter the apartment building. But I didn't want to return to my apartment, the scene of the high.

Instead, I went down to the basement efficiency apartment of a young, somewhat reclusive nurse named Denise. I had had my eye on her for a while, and we had exchanged hellos. But my anxiety kicked my sexual desire into libidinal overdrive, and soon, after describing what I had experienced or thought I had experienced with George, I was putting moves on her.

Was George really sexually after me, I wondered later? Or was it paranoia or some kind of homoerotic panic brought on by the grass? Was the kid in the house who was calling himself the Wizard of Oz really a narc or was that, too, a result of the dope?

I had read enough Freud that I questioned whether or not I was projecting feelings I had for George onto him while under the influence of cannabis. I started thinking about times I would goose friends of mine when we were boys, grab their crotches as part of adolescent horseplay, no different than mooning them or breathing on them when I knew that I had sour breath. But the incident with George suddenly put everything into a different psychological frame. What if I had been proving my heterosexuality by conquests, trying to show I wasn't a guy who wanted other guys?

Being literary seemed, deep down, a bit suspect to me as far as masculinity went. It was true that I had masculine models like Les Marks or Calvin Thayer, the prof who had told me I'd like the aristocratic broads at U. Mass. or Frank Fieler, another Ohio U. English prof who had been a semi-pro football player. I had manly teaching assistant colleagues. And, of course, there was Papa Hemingway, the ultimate man's man writer—though his overcompensatory masculine behavior had Freudian suspicions written all over it, especially when one considered the pressure under Grace, his mother, who dressed him as a child to look like a girl. I was still holding my fork with a fist and had a violent streak in me that spoke of maleness, but I was also soft, tender, afraid, craved and wanted closeness and intimacy, loved good poetry. How manly was I?

．　．　．

CHASING GIRLS and reading and studying and teaching and being on a curriculum committee didn't allow a lot of time for writing, but I knew this was all just a waystation until I could get to the serious business of

writing the fiction that I thought was in me. Every interesting or unusual episode or adventure in my life and every distinctive character I
met and all the prodigious learning I was bent on amassing would all
be crystallized and distilled into a potent literary brew. People would
read and respect me. So I believed.

I got to know the famed and eventual Nobel Prize winning Yiddish
writer Isaac Bashevis Singer. He had come to the U. of W. for one year
as a visiting professor. Cecil Hemley, my creative writing prof, had been
one of Singer's translators, so I approached him and told him I had been
a student of Mr. Hemley's. I felt elevated simply by being in Singer's
presence, doing small errands for him. Perhaps some of his writerly
luster would rub off. Though if he should ever speak to Mr. Hemley
and happen to mention me by name, he might be told how pedestrian
a writer I was.

I made time to do errands for Isaac Singer. I envied his gifts, the
fleetness of his translated Yiddish and the ways it evoked in me the
shtetl world or bore in on the deeper motives and secret passions of Jews,
including Jews who lived in the Shoa or came out of it, but never escaped.
There was everything in Singer one could want in a fiction writer—the
range of human emotion, lively and credible characters. He wrote, too,
with a mystic's eye, and was smitten with interest in the occult and the
supernatural. I often felt, in reading him, that I was being transported
back to the world of Polish Jewry. I felt that some of his stories spoke
directly to my blood, even though my ancestors all came from Russia.
It was his Jewishness that spoke to me most of all. After the lightning
victory of the Israelis in the Six Day War, I remember thinking to myself that I was young and Jewish, and that it was good to be Jewish.
Suddenly, being Jewish did not carry with it shame of sheeplike, non-
resistant walks to gas chambers and ovens. Jews had one-eyed Moishe
Dayan and a blitzkrieg-like victory over a more powerful foe.

Singer and I became friends at U.W., and once again, as with Bellow,
I played the role of thoughtful and sensible young reader who admired
the great writer. How remarkably humble and sweet an old man he appeared to be to me, with his angular, birdlike face and white hair. I was
useful to him, since he was incapable of doing many things like getting
to the bus (he didn't drive) or making reservations on a train (he refused

to fly) or even reserving a hotel room. I was glad to do these things for him just so I could hang around and bask in knowing him. There was something about his *shtetl* mentality, his helplessness and reliance on the kindness of others, that I saw in myself, though I would later see steelier and lecherous sides of his character. Singer seemed a lot like me, too, in that he cared little about much aside from reading, writing and ideas, and, of course, women.

One day I took him to the Greyhound station to get him on a bus to Chicago for a speaking engagement. There were many young people wearing University of Wisconsin sweatshirts, and Singer asked why they wore shirts with the school name. I was unsure how to answer and felt I was being tested, but I suggested that students might want to show off where they went to school. Singer, with a smile, said, in his thick, broken, accented English: "You tink I should get vun fur me mit says Farrar, Straus and Giroux?"

I still seemed to see the world very much divided into Jews and gentiles. I wanted Jewish role models and Jewish friends, yet I also feared being too parochial or too open about my Jewishness, since I believed it might inspire dislike or make people see me differently. Not that the University of Wisconsin was a hotbed of anti-Semitism. Radicalism, yes, but not anti-Semitism, though I did have intense discussions with friends about the justness of the Palestinian cause. I was not unsympathetic, and I understood and empathized with many of their grievances. With men like my Uncle Martin, my father's sometimes ardent Zionist brother, I became verbally more of a supporter than I actually was, just so that I could argue with him. I argued, too, with my radical friends; if the Palestinians were a dispossessed people, what were those who survived the jaws of German annihilation?

I was nondenominational in my selection of girls. If I fell for someone, it would likely not be a Jewish girl, since the odds were much more in favor of meeting and falling for a Christian girl, as I had for Susan. By mid-November, I hit a low point in my philandering when I met up with a Northwest Orient flight attendant, who had been urged to call me by an O.U. crony. A redhead, she used more hair spray on her bouffant hairdo than I ever imagined could be sprayed on to a human scalp. I found it difficult, after a one-night stand in my small efficiency apartment, even to inhale without taking in the smell of hairspray. She babbled vacuous gibberish, and seemed to have at best the attention span of a small mammal. There was a lot of screwing the one night she spent with me but, I thought, all that screwing was not worth all of the hairspray or jabbering. I felt, after she left, that I needed to fumigate. After saying goodbye to her, even as I gritted my teeth, I began to feel depressed at the thought that I would never find anyone of Susan's caliber. I would just have to go on shedding my lust. I soon found otherwise. I found HER.

.   .   .

IN THE LATE 1960s Madison had little if any industry or manufacturing. Just Oscar Meyer Wiener and Gisholt. There was something still nearly bucolic about Wisconsin's capital city with its verdant campus and its setting on a number of lakes. Its domelike capitol building, at the center of the city's circular drive gave it the appearance of a strangely surreal and miniaturized District of Columbia. By winter everything was laden with blankets of snow, visible breaths of air streamed out of mouths, and cars refused to ignite. In the winter of 1967, when the air breathed by leftist students was charged with political fervor, even the most radical of campus radicals hibernated out of the cold, looking for warmth.

I went out of the cold into the library one night. Libraries for many years had been refuges for me, where there was quiet and books and I could browse or read or study, though invariably I was also furtively prowling. For what? An attractive face? Sexual prey? Companionship? Love? Wherever I happened to be, I was looking. I was always looking. But looking was the passive part, the easy part. One had, too, to make the move. One had to act.

I first saw Leslie sitting in the library. I thought she was beautiful. To describe a woman as beautiful is like hearing someone described as interesting. Describing a woman as beautiful only reveals the paucity of language, its subjectivity and the need for poetry.

She was reading an organic chemistry book.

I considered myself smooth with girls, at ease initiating small talk and playing the role of someone interested and interesting, making conversation without visible motive. With Leslie I was initially ill at ease with making small talk, thinking she was too classy, too lovely.

But wasn't I, a natural talker, able to talk to anyone? Hadn't I had Susan and Nancy and many others who at first seemed above me? I had a master's degree. I was a Ph.D. candidate. I was the first grad student to be on a curriculum committee.

So I approached her with what I felt were feeble and unimaginative questions about the organic chemistry book she was reading, though I did glean information. She was a premed student. A future doctor! I dropped the name of a handsome and popular medical student I had met casually and briefly with George, someone who might give me, by association, some credibility.

"He's my friend," she brightened.

We talked, awkwardly—since it was, after all, the library—but I managed to get her name and left the library holding it in my mind like a winning poker hand. I ran out into the cold and headed immediately to the student union, where I knew there was a list available of addresses and phone numbers of every undergrad.

I called her. I asked her out. She put me off a number of times, but I was persistent. I took her to my West Main efficiency. I cooked for her. The would-be playboy bachelor trying to win over the beauty with his nonexistent suaveness and no real culinary skill—only suddenly, incomprehensibly, I was besieged by the runs. In so small an apartment I could not, would not, use the bathroom for fear of audible, frightful flatulence. "Oh. I left something in the car," I explained breezily, then ran downstairs to the small, private, basement bathroom outside Denise the nurse's apartment. Ten minutes later I was back in the kitchen cooking, and then I was suddenly under attack again. "I'm sorry. I need to make a phone call." Another race down the stairs and into the refuge stall in the basement where all my human sounds went unheard, wondering, why, God, do you give me diarrhea now? Why, when I have in my apartment a beautiful, classy, brainy Jewish girl—the kind my parents, especially my mother, dream about for me—do you make me have to race out repeatedly to flush out my guts? What an impression I must have made, inventing excuses and, over and over again, darting out of the apartment, barely able to hold in my load, my body betraying me.

It was a miracle. We became a couple. I soon discovered that her most recent boyfriend had been a college student drug dealer who had left the state in a deal with prosecutors; his illicit dealings were a total shock to her, as she had never even tried drugs. The idea that this wonderful girl with integrity had been with a guy who peddled drugs permanently shifted my sense of reality.

Leslie was impressive in every way. I thought the odds were against me falling for a Jewish girl—but was it, I wondered, an accident that I gravitated to her dark, Old Testament beauty when I first saw her there in the library? Was I more programmed to fall for a Jew? My mother had told me since I was a small boy about how *shiksas*, gentile girls, wanted Jewish husbands because Jewish men didn't drink and treated their wives well. The great *shiksa* conspiracy, I called my mother's homilies, though I must have bought my mother's sales pitch that we nice Jewboys were catches who ultimately needed to be caught by nice, deserving Jewish girls.

The Schoenberg story was the most instructive cautionary tale from my mother's arsenal. Schoenberg had lived a few blocks from us in Cleveland. He was planning to marry out of the faith. His parents treated him as if he had died and lit *yahrtzeit*, mourner's, candles. This was not unusual then, especially among Orthodox Jews, but my mother had her own confabulated version of the story. Schoenberg's mother couldn't stand that she wasn't going to witness her son's marriage, so she went to the church and stood silently and quietly in the shadows, in the back, behind all the pews. She saw her beloved son kneeling to kiss the priest's ring—as if any Catholic cleric other than the Pontiff wears a ring that others kneel to and kiss—and the sight of her son with the priest caused her immediate, fatal cardiac arrest. This story was related to me with all the conviction of truth, and its message couldn't have been clearer. Marry a *shiksa* and you kill your mother.

Yet my brother, Vic, had eloped earlier that year with a Russian Orthodox girl named Marina, who had no intention of converting to Judaism. When I started realizing that I had serious feelings about Leslie, I also realized that she was just the sort of girl I could bring home to please my mother, the kind I could marry if I were the marrying kind. Her father was a regional counsel for the IRS in New York City, and her mother was a social worker—a pedigree that was certainly more impressive than my own frustrated, factory-working dad and my housewife mom who never completed high school. Moreover, Leslie had been a musical talent who played both violin and piano and had studied ballet and modern dance and taken physics at Harvard's summer school. Should these things matter? Should her beauty matter? Perhaps not. But all of it did matter to me, though what mattered most was that I was mad about a sensible young woman with spirit and brains and integrity who, miraculously enough, was in love with me.

When I brought Leslie home and introduced her to my family, including my materially better off cousins, I could tell that I had hit the jackpot with so lovely, well-mannered and intelligent a young woman. She was not only Jewish but had the refinement and the bourgeois impressiveness of great looks, fashionable dress and a pleasant, outgoing demeanor. I went back with Leslie to New York and met her family and I, too, was impressed. Contradicting all my old prejudgments about New York Jews, her family and their friends were decent, respectable, with all the staid bourgeois virtues I wanted for myself. Staten Island, her home—ever associated with a nickel ferry ride—seemed an enclave different in every way from the kind of shallow materialist culture I had come stereotypically to identify with Long Island Jews. Her father, known for his many manifold acts of charity and kindness, became another role model for me. I saw a dignity and rectitude in him that I could emulate. And, I realized to my surprise, her family was impressed with me. Maybe I had managed to shed my plebeian, feral ways and become the nice intellectual *mensch* I had been striving to be. As Kurt Vonnegut said, you are who you pretend to be.

But wasn't I destined, even as I fell harder for Leslie, to be a Don Juan, a Casanova, a Lawrentian man who could not be tied to one woman? All such inner conflict would one day be grist for the novelist's mill, transformed to narrative art.

.   .   .

1968. The would-be playboy of the Midwest world had settled down with Leslie. For all purposes we were living together, albeit in separate apartments, since she was still too young and middle-class to tell her parents. I felt deeper in love than I ever thought I could be. We argued a great deal, but I felt incomplete without her. When we were even briefly separated, I yearned for her like a sick pup. I found myself thinking of the unthinkable, of marriage, even though I fought it. How could a man who loved women think of settling down with only one and looking, as they said, at the same face every morning?

We adopted a mutt from the Humane Society, whom we named Rimsky. She chewed the carpet of my West Main apartment and caused Epstein to come after me with threats of a lawsuit until a lawyer cousin of one of my father's bridge partners worked out a deal for me to pay for the damage. Leslie and I worked for Gene McCarthy but would have supported Bobby Kennedy since he, too, was opposed to the war. Hubert Humphrey, President Johnson's VP and a social reformer, had called Vietnam a great adventure and supported LBJ's war.

Digger and I argued constantly over the phone, as we had always done, about politics—ever since high school, when he was taken with Barry Goldwater's *Conscience of a Conservative*, and I wrote letters to Cleveland newspapers defending Castro or opining on the Sino-Soviet rift and felt excited, even flushed, to see my name in print. Now, a more moderate Digger lived in Goldwater's state, and it was his and my first presidential election. Digger argued that my support for McCarthy would ensure the election of Richard Nixon, and more people would be hurt by cutbacks of social programs. It was the same argument Gore supporters would use against Nader supporters over three decades later. But I was firm in my dump-the-hump position. I was immoderately angry at Humphrey for supporting a war I hated and was drawn to McCarthy because of his opposition to the war and his sympathy with the student movement. I was charmed by his intellect and taken with the fact that he was a poet and a philosopher, an intellectual and a humanist. He was one of the *us* that I had chosen to be.

Digger would taunt me for years after the 1968 election, as if my work and support for McCarthy personally helped ensure the election of Nixon, who managed to get us deeper into the morass of the war in Southeast Asia.

I felt boxed in by the war. I simply wanted it to end. It was apparent to me that neither of the leading presidential candidates would lead us out. I was prepared, if drafted, to go to Canada and live among my mother's relatives in Ontario.

The war raged in Asia and protest grew as those of us in the so-called Movement learned more about the real nature of our country's involvement and chose to march, as Leslie and I did, or to follow a more violent revolutionary path. There was a kind of more-radical-than-thou attitude among many on the left. Since action was the litmus test of radicalism and revolution the rallying cry, many argued that protest, too, had to be violent, as if to match the deeds of the war makers, as if only blood could alter the tide of history.

The personal was supposed to be political, but I still had to sort the two. The war was personal for me since I could be drafted, but the violence of my fellow lefties against the war seemed blind to me, excessive and futile. Marc Rudd of Columbia and other radicals of his ilk built bombs with which they could blow up themselves as well as innocent bystanders. They seemed to me a bunch of overindulged rich kids. Yet I, too, felt the war merited more than marching, distributing leaflets or canvassing for Gene McCarthy's improbable presidential candidacy.

Bobby Kennedy was murdered. So was Martin Luther King. The two political causes I felt most deeply about, the two that cut the deepest inside me, were opposition to the war and advancement of civil rights. Dr. King, the great champion of the latter, was increasingly becoming a spokesman against the war when he was gunned down. A number of us gathered up on Bascom Hill the day after his murder. We were unclear why he was killed or whom to blame. It was easy to hold government officials responsible for the war, but we could not do that with the killing of Dr. King. Even when James Earl Ray—a poor redneck who somehow mysteriously found the money to flee to Europe—was fingered as the alleged assassin, many of us felt there had to have been greater, more political and nefarious forces at work. We were a racially mixed, though mostly white, throng of sympathizers on Bascom Hill, mourning Dr. King and stunned by his murder but not knowing how to protest—groping, really, for some sense of what to do or how to act as we came together on that rainy morning in a spontaneous sharing of loss. A young black student, with horn-rimmed glasses, walked past us, muttering to another black student, "Ahm gonna get me a gun."

King's death convinced me that if I was going to become a scholar I ought to become a black scholar and make a contribution to the greater righteous cause of black scholarship. I even had a writer in mind, the light-skinned black poet Jean Toomer, who had published a book about black life called *Cane* in 1923. Though richly praised by a number of highly regarded literary figures of his day, the book sold only five hundred copies, and Toomer disappeared into obscurity. I loved the book's soaring lyricism, its romanticized but earthy portraits of black southern characters who lived close to the red soil and the pines, as well as its tortured, neurotic struggle with identity that mirrored Toomer's profound confusion about who he was. The Jean Toomer who wrote *Cane* was a young man who felt black and white and neither, who felt strongly masculine as well as feminine. Caught between different races, genders, cultures and classes, he set out for Georgia with another young writer, Waldo Frank, to discover people and a land he could paint with his lyrical poet's eye. He spent a lifetime after *Cane* seeking ways to define himself, to spiritualize his life and give it higher meaning. Toward the end of his life, he even took up Dianetics, the Ron Hubbard blueprint for Scientology.

Walter Rideout, one of the nation's leading American literature scholars, chaired the University of Wisconsin's English department and would later become president of the Modern Language Association. He was the author of a highly regarded critical work called *The Radical Novel in America* but was decidedly no radical. The reputation he had acquired among my leftist fellow T.A.s was, in fact, that of a fascist, since most of the more radical nontenured professors had been purged under his watch as chair. I went in with trepidation to talk to him about the possibility of his directing a dissertation on Toomer since I had become, despite my politically nonviolent stance, strongly identified with radical protest and The Movement. Plus I had written away for all those books from publishers and didn't know if he had heard anything of that caper. Despite his reputation for political conservatism, I wanted him to take me on.

I found Rideout to be a good liberal-minded humanist who had been inaccurately branded a fascist. At the time, that label was applied to anyone perceived as old guard, who resisted change or saw excess in The Movement. He was, in truth, a decent, affable and likeable man with whom I established a rapport based on shared scholarly interest. He took me on because he appeared to like me and was interested in Toomer. I felt grateful. Even after he saw me, months later, marching on a picket line in protest against poor wages and lack of health care for T.A.s and came up to me with a sour look, asking if I was trying to shut down the university (I wasn't)—even after that, we somehow managed to maintain rapport.

Darwin Turner, an African American who had written more on Jean Toomer than anyone, came to Wisconsin later that year as a visiting professor. I got him to agree to be my second reader. My third was a politically radical white guy named John Sullivan, a much-admired teacher of American literature who had been to Harvard to study African-American writers. I had an impressive dissertation committee. I had a beautiful girlfriend. But the year was one of great loss and great change. Robert Kennedy and Martin Luther King were in the ground. Richard Nixon was president.

Later on in the summer a number of my friends became grooms and brides, and so did I. A few had lavish nuptials that made me think of the East Coast Jewish wedding captured by Philip Roth in his early collection, *Goodbye, Columbus*. Roth managed to do a good, satiric, cartoon-like but realistic rendering. Every Jew I knew or had ever met from around the Newark area, where *Goodbye, Columbus* was set, saw themselves or someone they knew in the novel or the movie. That was the kind of literary creator I wanted to be. To write not exactly a roman a clef, but a novel's version of my own Cleveland roots, of my life—what Faulkner called his postage stamp. To bring Cleveland Jewish lives, including my own, into focus the way Bellow did with Montreal and Chicago, Roth did with Newark and Singer did with Polish Jews. To create literature that was artful, visionary, aesthetic and wise, distilled from ravenously acquired knowledge, with characters who cast shadows. I was more than a guy writing a dissertation on an African-American writer. Like Bellow and Singer and Roth, I was, or soon enough would be, a Jewish novelist. I would work my way through a Ph.D. degree, sure, until I got my union card. Then I would find a teaching job, and after that, at last, embark on my real calling as a novelist. I was taking in experience, watching people, stashing anecdotes and personal episodes, filing it all away in my mental craw, storing stories and fragments of life's hues for my novelist's palette. I was, as Fitzgerald's Nick Carraway said of himself, simultaneously within and without. And I was passing myself·off as a writer. Without having sold or published a single story, I had sold myself on the notion that I was destined to be a novelist. I talked openly, expressively, credibly of writerly ambitions, so even people I didn't know began to see me as a writer.

Leslie spent a few months after an early graduation working in virology research at the Sloan-Kettering Cancer Research Institute in New York. I realized I missed her, so much that I couldn't return to my would-be Lothario ways. I went from thinking that I had to be alone to the realization that I did not want to be. We married in the summer of 1969 in a small, elegant wedding planned by my tasteful mother-in-law, at the Croyden Hotel in Manhattan. I was in love. In my mind there was no other reason to marry. I wanted to be with Leslie because I could not abide being without her.

"Listen, your woman is part of your glory," my old pal Blackie told me that summer, right before my wedding—soon after he married a wealthy girl from the Cleveland suburb of Beachwood and met Leslie and gave his hearty approval. Many years later, after Blackie made millions, he would throw incredibly extravagant wedding receptions for all four of his daughters, reveling in the fact that his wife still looked great, with new boobs.

My in-laws were smart, decent and attractive. My mother-in-law could be assertive, in the New York style I had been prejudiced against, but she had vivacity, charm and a good heart. My father-in-law was a distinguished, white-haired, Cornell-educated attorney, whom friends and relations called Ira the Good because of his habitual kind deeds. Both were active and prominent in charitable and community work. Both made me proud—as Leslie and her younger sister, Louise, did—that I was joining my life to theirs. I was doing what a good Jewish boy did who wanted to make his parents proud. Leslie's family took pride as well. Her mother had put the engagement announcement in the local paper, *The Staten Island Advance*, heralding the fact that Leslie Tilzer was to become the bride of a doctoral candidate. Her family and their friends and relatives were nice people. My parents and their friends and most of our relatives were nice people. I was a nice Jewish boy marrying a nice Jewish girl. "It's nice to be nice," in fact, was on a wooden plaque that the mother of a friend of Leslie's had on a wall above her kitchen sink.

Nice could be dull and unexciting, as were most bourgeois virtues, but nice was safe and where I had been heading since leaving high school. Mine was not the true path of the nonconformist, the bohemian or the radical, although I had elements of all of those inside me. Good, kind and nice seemed more the path for me than Joyce's Stephen's fervid, artistic path of silence, exile and cunning. I wanted to be the nice Jewish boy who made his family proud, who proved we were as good as others in our family who, I felt, had done us wrong. My parents felt none of this. I felt I needed to feel it for them.

My wedding reception, though small, was impressive. And the fact that Siri, the wife of my friend John Boereske, showed up braless was probably even more impressive to my Uncle Joe and my dad's brother, Martin. But thanks to the classy quality of the wedding and reception, all my wealthier relatives were impressed by my bride and her family. I wanted my brother Vic, who lived in San Francisco with his Russian Orthodox wife, Marina, to be my best man, but he offered lame excuses and didn't show. Everyone thought he must have been mad at me, but he simply didn't care enough or didn't want to pay the cost, even though my parents offered to pay, or was inhibited by his wife. Whatever his reasons or lack of them, his absence caused me great hurt and a rupture that lasted for years until we both somehow managed to become brothers again.

.   .   .

AFTER THE WEDDING, HONEYMOONLESS, I stopped with Leslie in Doylestown, Pennsylvania, to visit Jean Toomer's widow. Marjorie Content Toomer was a photographer, the daughter of a Wall Street speculator and a close friend of the artist Georgia O'Keefe. We stopped to see her as Leslie and I hauled back to Madison from New York with a rented U-Haul. I was hoping to interview Marjorie Toomer and find out as much as I could about her husband as well as the mystery of his racial identity. In New York, I had managed to dig up a personal questionnaire that Toomer had filled out when he was briefly a student at CCNY. When asked on the form about his racial origins, he wrote "cosmopolitan."

Marjorie Toomer took to us, especially to Leslie, and I thought it highly auspicious to my marriage that Toomer's widow had just that morning come across some of Toomer's autobiographical writings and other unpublished work, lying around in the attic. It was a treasure trove of material that she simply handed over to me. Though I soon enough discovered that none of it had much literary merit or relevance to the puzzle of Toomer's racial identity, it was useful material and ensured my place as a Toomer scholar (which sounded, I joked, like an oncology researcher). Within that year, Toomer's major work, *Cane*, would be brought back into print. It would soon be republished by Harper's as a perennial classic, then as a critical edition by Norton that included essays of mine. But, before all that, I took prelims. Years later I discovered that a cadre of my more lefty, radical T.A. friends had broken into Bascom Hall at night and stolen, reproduced and distributed copies of the exam. It was doubtless, to them, a revolutionary, antiestablishment act that I was happy to have missed. I had, after all, married into the bourgeoisie.

Michael Chabon

I've told Michael Chabon a number of times that he is who I wanted to be. Just to have a novel like *The Amazing Adventures of Kavalier and Clay*. He also has a Pulitzer, but when *People* magazine wanted him to be one of the year's best-looking men, he declined the request, asking "Why would you want a nebbish like me?"

Michael does have an inner nebbish. You can see it in him and occasionally hear it in his voice. He was the archetypal comic-book-reading fiend, a Jewish kid whose parents divorced when he was twelve. He wound up leaving Baltimore to be with his father in Pittsburgh and managed to tie some of his Jewish identity to the Jews who created Superman, Batman, Captain America, and Spiderman. Talk about your Jew conspiracies.

Chabon wanted to reenter that glory age of comic books, to find a way in and to time travel back. He loved magic too. The figure of the magician is, he tells me, a seductive one to writers because magicians try to create illusions and distractions and keep us from seeing what they are really trying to pull off. Comic books and magic and the golem all helped him pull off the magic of *Kavalier and Clay*. He took the Pulitzer home to Berkeley, where he and his Harvard lawyer-author-wife, Ayelet, live with their four kids.

Chabon loved *Mambo Kings* by Oscar Hijuelos. He thought, as he flipped television channels, that he would see the two brothers meeting Ricky Ricardo on one of the black-and-white repeats of "I Love Lucy" because Oscar created doubt in his mind—even though Michael knew the novel's scene of the brothers meeting Ricky was fictitious. "Fiction can confer more reality," he says, quoting Walker Percy to me from *The Moviegoer.*

A caller asks him if all the research he does ever interferes with his fiction, and he says he has felt hampered by facts. Library research is much more tempting to him than writing. If he can't find documentation for something, he feels compelled to search for it until he has to give up, and then he feels forced to make it up. People who know will tell him after he makes something up that he got it right. By the time he got to *Kavalier and Clay* he could write what he wanted to write, and he no longer felt frustrated about his own abilities as he had when he started writing *Mysteries of Pittsburgh* when he was twenty-four.

For Chabon, the essential pleasure of writing is in use of language. It is, he claims, as if he is the receiver and the language outside him a radio broadcast he has tuned in. It happened to him a lot when he was writing *Wonder Boys*. I feel no reason to tell him how unexcited I was about *Wonder Boys* compared to *Kavalier and Clay*. As Twain said—that's what makes horse races.

In *Wonder Boys* he tapped into Grady's voice, and he felt as though he were transcribing. He catches the rhythms of sentences before the words come or before the sense of the sentence arrives, and he can simultaneously feel the next sentence coming, with its beats and its nouns and its dependent clause and few syllables, and then the words pour in. It's irritating to have to come up with technical matters like plot and character. The craft, the storytelling, does not come easily to him as it does to born storytellers. It is language that comes mystically to him.

Jonathan Safran Foer

When Jonathan Safran Foer walks in for our interview, I immediately think how much more natty he looks than the first time I met him. His clothes are well-tailored. Though he still seems like a kid to

me, because he still is a kid, he wears a new look of confidence, the air of
the successful writer that he also is. He has what we used to call a presence,
something I don't recall from our previous meeting, when he was on with
me discussing *Everything Is Illuminated.* His new novel, *Extremely Loud and
Incredibly Close,* his post 9-11 novel, is no sophomore jinx. Updike, no less,
reviewed it in *The New Yorker.* But it isn't as good as his first novel. A nine-
year-old protagonist in this one, but too much post-modern would-be vir-
tuosity. Give him high marks for boldness and risk taking.

Until a *New York Times* interviewer asked him a question about his
life at age nine, he never talked about the chemical explosion that took
place in a public school summer camp chemistry class he was in. There
were serious injuries. It affected him. He repeatedly peed in his pants.
But the memory didn't come back to him for years until that interview.
Life is like that. A dark hallway and then light. You see who you are and
what life is like after the fact.

Jonathan says he intentionally writes, but not necessarily with intention. He opens himself up. It is intuitive. The editing is intentional. Writing books is like singing in the shower. "I like the way the voice sounds,
and I enjoy it. You choose your tunes and the key knowing your voice
range." Writing is intimate. He writes in cafes, libraries, subways, lying
down. Just him and the words. It can become an intimate reflection, but
he is glad when writing inspires more writing. "There aren't enough
writers," he says, making me think of Flannery O'Connor's crack about
there being too many bad ones or Salman Rushdie commenting that
there are too many. Jonathan gets heady thinking of Rushdie, who gave
him a good blurb, initially reading Foer's newest book on an airplane.
"It's too much. I read *Midnight's Children* and *The Moor's Last Sigh* before
I even became a writer. When it was still a dream." He adds: " I wrote
books I wanted to read rather than wanted to write."

Though he has become to many a young literary star, with a highly
thought of, pretty writer wife, he is still star-struck for star readers. He
desperately wanted Stephen Hawking to read his novel. He sent three
letters, wrangled Hawking's phone number and called him, but never got
a response.

He still likes games, the kind he might have played himself as a
precocious nine-year-old. Did I know that polish is the only word that

changes both meaning and pronunciation when capitalized? A listener quickly faxes in—"What about lima bean and Lima, Peru?" Foer seems taken off guard, but allows that the caller is right. Then he quickly asks, like a quiz master, if I know the only word with three consecutive pairs of letters. Answer: Bookkeeper.

Francine Prose thinks he is hilarious. Does he consider himself a comic writer? "I don't consider myself anything. I think, have I peed in the last three hours or do I need to?"

"There's that motif again," I say "of holding it in or going in your pants."

He quickly shifts away from my wise-ass remark and speaks with aphoristic-sounding wisdom. "Self-consciousness is the enemy of creativity. It's very hard to let go."

 ## Ian McEwan

Ian McEwan has copped the Booker Prize for *Amsterdam*. I warmly offer congratulations as we sit down and prepare to talk for an hour. Clinton and Monica Lewinsky are still being blabbed about in the news, so we start off talking about sex scandals. "Ours explode and aren't so monumental," he says. "The standards are Edwardian. Set moral standards are not those by which the rest of the country lives."

Novelists like to talk politics. McEwan says politics and journalistic culture have become intermeshed in the U.K. Tabloidization has triumphed. Novels are higher gossip.

McEwan also likes discussing his characters, analyzing them, philosophizing about who and what they are as real people of his creation. Clive and Vernon in *Amsterdam* have fatal moral slips that they don't see in themselves but manage to see in other people. "We're all great self-dissuaders," McEwan observes, "lining up the evidence in our own favor." If two characters like Clive and Vernon have a falling out, the falling out will bring rearrangements of the past.

McEwan brings up an offbeat point. Why, he wonders, does he invariably say he was not sleeping when someone calls, wakes him from a sound sleep and asks, "Did I wake you?" Why does he say "no"? He wonders: "Is it our ridiculous work ethic?"

McEwan is a great admirer of Bellow. Years later, he will write a stirring tribute to Bellow in *The New York Times*, a panegyric to his impact on the novel and literature. Funny how so many leading British novelists wildly admire Bellow. McEwan speaks of how no Brits have in their work the democratic width of a Bellow novel—which perhaps, the British author offers, English social structure cannot admit. No towering singular figures for the Brits except Lessing and maybe Naipaul. No combining of street and intellect as in Bellow or the sweep and formal ambition, the intelligence and sensuality and brilliant way with a sentence of Bellow, Updike or Roth. Still, McEwan acknowledges a ceiling he believes all novelists face, even the most political of novelists. "If you want to change the world," he says, "don't be a novelist."

David Lodge

I'm trying to concentrate on David Lodge without associations—with Karen Armstrong, because she was recently on, and both she and Lodge are Catholic Brits. Or with Mike Leigh, because Leigh, too, was recently on, and he and Lodge are both from Birmingham. Or with me, since both Lodge and I are English professors—though Lodge is now emeritus and retired. He already noted to me how quickly he got out of what he calls the ongoing academic conversation; in his case, he says, getting out was not quick enough.

A lot of our conversation orbits around questions of consciousness. He has just written a book called *Thinks*, which plays with questions of whether consciousness is outside us, like matter or energy, and can't be explained, or is simply subjective. He even talks about consciousness and quantum physics, though he admits to understanding little about quantum physics and cites the line that anyone who claims to understand quantum physics is mad or a liar He is soon talking about NeoDarwinians. About how—excepting Richard Dawkins, a devout atheist who doth protest much and vehemently against God—NeoDarwinians ply us with purely materialistic explanations, often overshadowed by repressed desire for the spiritual, which reemerges following loss of a beloved. So many, Lodge says, wistfully hope in bereavement for spiritual truth. Even Darwin's proliferation of symptoms after *The Origin of Species*, may have been psychosomatic, caused by his having brought down the linchpin of orthodox belief in creation. There is a stubborn belief in the spiritual that clings to us, says Lodge. I wonder if this is his boyhood

Catholicism speaking out, or whether he is projecting against the secular shibboleth that we all are machine and no ghost.

Lodge taught at Berkeley and wound up gaining an American audience through his academic satires, which included a character named Morris Zapp—partly based on English literature scholar Stanley Fish, a friend of Lodge's. Lodge tells me Fish "glories in the identification and rather exaggerates it." He adds, "There are a lot of other sources for Morris Zapp, including Groucho Marx." Lodge says he "carnivalized" his profession, the desires and appetites of the flesh of people who have high-minded aspirations to truth and beauty and who fight bodily desires that run counter to intellect and the authoritative mechanisms of their profession and its institutions. He could never have become a campus novelist in the U.K. To undermine the profession would have been unthinkable. There was too much majesty in being a professor. Which prompts me to ask him if Prince Charles really talks to his geraniums. Lodge confirms it.

The interview with Lodge strikes me as that fine balance between serious, even highbrow intellectual discussion splayed with fun and not so serious digressive asides. In the spirit of the asides, a caller phones in, an academic who knew Lodge during his Berkeley days, reminding him that the hero of his novel *Changing Places* gets a call while on a radio talk show.

Lodge tells me how he has a brain split between being a novelist and being a literary critic, each side feeding the other, and that he is self-conscious as a novelist because he is also a literary critic. He is thinking of his reader all the time when he writes, of friends or peers, of an ideal reader who is ever alert, responsive to the messages he is sending, but critical and ready to jump on sloppiness or error. "Writing is always directed."

4   Slouching Towards Tenure

I STAYED FRIENDLY with many from the so-called Movement during my last year in Madison, though my closest
friend was a Jewish guy from Maine named Eliot Rich who was more
a teacher and scholar than a radical. Eliot wanted to teach Shakespeare
and acted like an adoring older brother to me—the older brother I felt
I had lost since my brother Vic was inexplicably absent from my wedding. Unlike my brother and father, Eliot was a man of great warmth—a
tactile, extroverted, hail-fellow sort of man. He was the first man I was
friends with who hugged me and told me that he loved me. He didn't
make me feel that I needed to recoil or feel homoerotically threatened
by that, though, truth be told, I was never exactly at ease about it.

The year 1969 was a major turning point, or tipping point, for me and
Eliot and others like us. As a teenager I had thought sixty-nine would
be an exciting year because it was, after all, the number connected with
so many oral sex jokes. That summer, while I prepared for my prelims,
Sharon Tate and her friends were slaughtered in their home by the
Manson family, driven by mad helter skelter race war visions from the
warped mind of would-be song writer and aspiring musician Charles
Manson. And there was another killing by the Manson tribe—that of
a couple named LaBianca, who were mistakenly slain because Manson's
gang had gone to the wrong house across the street from Sharon Tate's.
I always had a difficult time with preachments of violence from the far
left, but Bernadine Dohrn's reaction to the LaBianca killings irretrievably turned something around inside me. Dohrn was the attractive
Weatherwoman, a darling and icon of many on the left for her ferocious

opposition to the Vietnam War and her outspoken denunciations of an ever-growing list of reprehensible government actions, many of which were finally coming into the light—like the bloody murder in Chicago of Black Panther leader Fred Hampton or the horrible My Lai massacre led by Captain Medina and Lieutenant Calley. Dohrn had earned great respect for her radicalism, but her reported response to the LaBianca murders was to gush at the fact that one of the victims—whom she called bourgeois pigs—had had a fork plunged in her. I never forgave her those remarks, even decades later when she had reinvented herself as a warrior of nonviolence.

I still thought of myself as a lefty. But the truth was, if becoming bourgeois meant developing a bourgeois state of mind, I was becoming more bourgeois by the day, and secretly not displeased about it. I still despised materialism and the pursuit of money. Leslie and I still looked and dressed like hippies. But in 1969 my mind was less on protest and revolt than, like any good bourgeois husband, on getting a good job.

Denver was where the Modern Language Association was having its annual convention that year, and as far as jobs went it was a buyer's market. Eliot and I went together in search of teaching jobs. Had it not been for my dumb luck in having Marjorie Toomer turn over a cache of unpublished manuscripts and the fact that, as Langston Hughes once put it, the Negro was once again in vogue, I doubt I would have managed to find a job. But with unpublished manuscripts of a soon-to-be leading black writer (who probably never truly thought of himself as black) and letters of recommendation from scholars like Walter Rideout and Darwin Turner, I was marketable. Black was in vogue in 1969, just as in future years New Historicism or Deconstruction or Queer Theory would be.

The MLA convention was a meat market—full of people desperately seeking tenure-track professorships, looking to establish scholarly footholds, planning to meet up with old friends, hoping to catch sight of big name literary critics of that era like Leslie Fiedler or Wayne Booth, or just looking to get laid. There was a great deal of grist here for the novelist I would become, the sort of material that British novelist David Lodge was able, years later, to turn into fiction. Two incidents were prime material for the novel I would someday write.

The first story took place after the MLA. I interviewed with a group of professors from Southern Illinois University at the conference; they were keen on my Toomer manuscript coup and invited me to Carbondale to interview. So I take a couple of flights to get to Carbondale. The travel agent tells me it would have been easier to schedule me to fly to Hong Kong. The second leg of the flight, on Ozark Air, is choppy. After drinking on the plane and being driven to Carbondale from a nearby town called Edwardsville, I have a few more drinks and begin to realize what life in Carbondale would mean. Drinking. As well as working on books to publish with the university's press and canvassing for the Democratic Party. Harry T. Moore, a D. H. Lawrence biographer and critic of British lit, is the God-like figure at S.I.U. Gossiping about Harry T. and drinking and canvassing for Democrats and publishing in the press and Carbondale itself all add up in my mind to dreariness. I know I don't want the job. Yet at that time, hot as I believed I was in Denver, Southern Illinois is the only prospect immediately following a number of interviews I had at the MLA convention.

The Southern Illinois hiring committee takes me to what they considered to be the best eating place in town, an Italian restaurant in the local Carbondale Holiday Inn. I feed on what I later described to Leslie, Eliot and others as rancid-tasting lasagna and then proceed with the hiring committee to the home of the English department chair, Howard Webb.

Seated around a fireplace, with burning logs, Howard Webb informs me in a serious, nearly pious way that the committee wants to hire me as an assistant professor, wants me to join the department. I tell him I am grateful and humbled by the offer. "Will you accept?" he asks, with great solemnity, as if offering me a throne, and after a few seconds of silence, I bolt.

The flight, the drinks, the lasagna—all of it is doing its work on me. I am throwing up in Chairman Webb's toilet, retching and vomiting while Chairman Webb and his colleagues wait by the fireplace with no clue as to why I ran off after his tendered offer. I am a bit woozy, but I feel I am ready to go back and explain to them why I dashed off and inform them that I am grateful for the offer but would need time to think about it. The truth is I have no inclination to accept the offer unless no other offers come through. I flush the toilet. To my horror, it overflows.

A question I pose. What does one do in such a situation? What would you do? You've puked your guts into the toilet while a group of serious academics are waiting for you to return after they'd just offered you a tenure-track professorship. All your vomit is coming up from the toilet and is swimming around in the water like small minnows just below your ankles, and the water is even starting to seep out from under the closed door of the small bathroom. So what do you do? Well, here's what I do. I tell myself that it's best to tell the truth, and armed with that thought, I go out and hastily explain to Howard Webb and his fellow English profs what happened, how I had been taken suddenly ill, had thrown up and watched in horror as the toilet overflowed. Chairman Webb quickly calls for his son and instructs him to get a mop and to go to work in the bathroom cleaning up my vomit but I, grateful to the department for wanting to hire me, will not hear of Webb's kid cleaning up my puke. I go to wrest the mop away from the son, only to hear the father shout at him that he should do the mopping up and not let me—while I am insisting that it is my mess and I should clean it.

So that was my first academic job offer—me fighting with a kid over a mop to get at my vomit and able, finally, to yank it away from him and do the cleaning myself while the Chairman brought the bucket. Fortunately, I did get other job interviews on other campuses that led to other offers, and one was from San Francisco State. I had my initial interview with S.F. State in Denver because of the second incident that seemed promising to the blossoming novelist in me—a chance encounter in an elevator with San Francisco State's English Department Vice Chair, Ed Nierenberg. I thought I had sent S.F. State a letter of inquiry about a job opening prior to the Denver convention, but if I did I never heard back. I honestly wasn't sure one way or the other. But when I saw Ed Nierenberg's nametag with San Francisco State on it, I initiated a conversation with him and was able to say that I had not received a response from his department. Ed had the sort of essential decency that compelled him to want to make up for the mistake, which may have been my mistake. As we conversed and I informed him of the scholarship I was doing on Toomer, he became interested and told me, to my surprise, that he would see if he could get the committee to interview me. He asked that I call him later on, and when I did he said that, yes, the committee would like to see me. A few days after my return from Carbondale, Caroline Shrodes, the department Chair at S.F. State—who sat during my entire Denver interview reading the Who's Who at the MLA Directory—called me to say how great the weather was in San Francisco and to ask if I wanted to come to work there. I accepted. I learned something valuable as a budding novelist about the vagaries of destiny that would take me to San Francisco. If I had not gotten into that elevator with Ed Nierenberg, I would not have gone to teach there and would have had a different fate, just as I would have if I hadn't ducked into the library on that cold and wintry Madison night that I first met Leslie.

When I went to San Francisco to live and teach I took in its beauty—the mountains, the ocean and the skyline that emerge as you move across the wide girders of the Golden Gate Bridge—and I saw how really lovely, as Theodore Roethke wrote of a beautiful woman, how lovely in the bones the whole area seemed. High atop the bay, on the deck of Chair Caroline Shrodes's beautiful home in Sausalito, I stood nursing a cocktail, drinking in the vista of mountains and the Golden Gate Bridge embraced by stray clouds and drifts of rising fog. I was at the annual ritual of a party in which the chair feted the department faculty each year so the newly hired like myself could mingle and be welcomed.

Caroline Shrodes, I was told, bought her impressive home from profits earned by co-editing a widely used composition anthology, *Reading for Rhetoric*, one of the texts I voted to adopt during my run on the text selection committee. She was a husky-voiced lesbian who had earned a scholarly reputation from work in a field called bibliotherapy, and she had established a firm and, some said, despotic hand as chair—drawing to the department an assortment of lively and engaging faculty, many of whom were young and attractive and some who were refused tenure at other universities and, in at least two cases, teachers who had left other positions because of sex scandals. She had nearly single-handedly built a department where teaching was given great weight, as were courses and scholarship in literature and psychology, and young professors like me were allowed to teach pretty much whatever we wanted to teach and offer all kinds of experimental courses. I was meeting my colleagues and feeling proud to be part of this department, though uncertain about whether I could curry favor with Caroline, who had acquired a number of telling sobriquets such as Catherine the Great and Elizabeth the First. A cadre of gay male profs buzzed around her for approval, and a few were known as her Earls of Essex. Many of the young and not-much-older-than-I colleagues had been hired a year or two before. They had been through the throes of the 1969 San Francisco State student strike, in which many of the faculty had gone out on picket lines to support black student demands for courses and a Black Studies Department. The strike had been a defining moment for many who were forced to decide, in Eldridge Cleaver's famous words, if they were part of the problem or part of the solution. There was deep bitterness over the strike that would last for decades and irony in the lack of interest and precipitous drop in student enrollment in black studies courses and curriculum just a few years afterward. I was glad I had arrived the year after it ended.

There was still much talk about the strike, however, and about S. I. "Don" Hayakawa, the Japanese-American semanticist and former S. F. State president who turned himself into a folk hero by grabbing a bull-horn, screaming at protesting students and then moving against them with what appeared to be a stern hand. Hayakawa went on to become a Republican California Senator in a career more associated with bouts of narcolepsy than with the authoring of any significant legislation. Many of my new colleagues loved telling war stories from the strike, and I listened and learned their sentiments, who their heroes and villains were. My bona fides as a black literature scholar with a lefty rep carried weight with the mainly white, liberal, strike-activist profs, who were nearly uniformly sympathetic to the black student cause—though I soon discovered that a couple of them had been surreptitiously holding classes off-campus and collecting paychecks when they were supposed to be out on strike without pay. The strike's leaders were mainly black students or came from the faculty, like the black sociologist Nathan Hare, but my new English department colleague, Eric Solomon, a Boston-bred Jew who was the Harvard-educated son of a psychiatrist, had been the strike's titular leader from the Caucasian side. Some of my colleagues had already begun describing me as a young Eric Solomon, largely because of a certain facial resemblance and the fact that we were both seen as fluent, smart Jewish guys who were politically left. I admired Eric. So did most of my colleagues, even ones who had stood with Hayakawa.

Eric was a lot smarter and more learned than me, but I was pleased that others thought me like him.

Race was still a sensitive issue following the strike of the year before, and I elected to teach a course in black literature even though I feared the wrath of militant black students, who would no doubt see me as a white boy trying to teach them about their own writers. I hunkered down for—who knew—perhaps violence. I figured I might be targeted as a honky Jew who had to be taught to stay in his own literary white hood.

But it didn't go down as I had feared. Quite the contrary. I established rapport with nearly all the numerous black students who signed up for the class, and I think I managed it by being openly honest. I told them right off that I was an outsider who had no claim on the black experience, no desire to be what in today's lexicon would be termed a wigger, a white boy trying to be or talk or act black. Then I started talking about African-American writing. I talked as a man who had learned a lot and could show it with performance skills honed from three years of classroom teaching at the University of Wisconsin. I talked as a man who respected the literature and felt passionate about communicating the ideas in it.

There was an older black man in the class with Medusa-like hair who, I couldn't help notice, was glaring at me during the first class with a kind of brash malevolence. I sensed as I lectured about black writers and their importance, with animation heightened by fear, that his attitude was thawing—revealed by the way he initially sat with his arms folded across his chest, then dropped to his sides. I heard him whisper to the young black man sitting next to him, audibly, "This white boy knows his shit."

James Washington Blake was a Watts-born former house painter and poet who went back to school in 1968 and headed up a student strike similar to SF State's at Contra Costa Junior College, with nonnegotiable demands for more black courses and more black faculty. Jim was one of the most vital people I have ever known, and he had a quick-to-trigger range of emotions that made an impact on nearly anyone with whom he came in contact. Many of the other black students admired him, and he admired me, more as time went on. I think, aside from his respect for

my scholarship and ease with language, it was because I gave him a wide
berth and attentively let him prattle on in class, even in occasional dia-
tribes. I still wanted to be a somewhat student-centered teacher and to
learn from my students, and Jim was a natural educator who loved being
the center of attention. He also loved the fact that I gave importance to
what he had to say and that I was amused by his humor and won over by
his warmth and vitality. I also had to keep him in line and maintain my
teacher's role. But he took to calling me his little brother even though
I was his teacher. He was about six-five and very imposing. A number
of my colleagues found it amusing to hear that he confronted Caroline
Shrodes in the hall one day and scared her with a sudden, impetuous
rush of emotion, insisting that she keep his little brother on the faculty. A
frightened Caroline was perplexed until he mentioned the little brother's
name, Dr. Krasny. She thought Jim delusional and initially wondered if
he actually believed that I was his younger sibling. I told her that I had
no hand in the hallway confrontation, but I'm not sure she believed me.

Jim had a way of intimidating people, especially gays and lesbians,
and despite my affection for him, such behavior disturbed me. He had
no censoring devices, and in one class he started fulminating about how
"faggotry" would bring down Western civilization. One of my homosexual
students, a Chicano who had written love poems to me in what I considered my introduction to San Francisco, left class in a huff. I sensed that
was the effect Jim wanted, and I scolded him and lectured him about
homophobia, but I knew that it was futile. I found myself feeling—with
black students like Jim and a number of others who openly spoke garbage about "fags and sissies"—like I felt with southern Ohio good ole
boys who talked disparaging rot about "the niggers." Still, I had built
up enough of a following among black students that I could try at least
to point out to them the inhumanity of homophobia.

I was feeling a growing sympathy not only for gays and lesbians but
also Native Americans and other groups who were outsiders or marginal.
I felt growing ties, too, to my own Jewish identity. I had begun to read
much Jewish history and literature, especially about the Shoa, seeking
knowledge about those who fought back and gaining increased familiarity with Jewish mysticism and a whole range of other Judaic topics. I
signed up as a Sunday school teacher—in part because I needed extra

money, but also because it gave me an easy way to explore and learn more about my own identity and roots and seemed like a possible path to being good, knowing what it meant to be good. Teaching college and Sunday school. Working for prison reform. I told myself I was doing good things. But I needed to do more, to learn what goodness was and how to translate it into life without being a sap or a fool.

Roots were in. A major television series, based on the novel *Roots* by Alex Haley, became explosively popular, a saga of the search by a black man for his forbears out of Africa. I was in the curious role of guiding black students back to the literary roots of their own racial and cultural heritage.

But my being Jewish was tricky. Blacks were accusing many Jews of being cultural vampires, active too long in leadership and policy-shaping roles in civil rights organizations and as teachers of blacks. Even Jewish scholars I had come to admire—like Melville Herskovitz and Herbert Aptheker or the Berkeley historian Leon Litwack, who had made major contributions to black scholarship, or radical attorney William Kunstler, who defended the most politically violent blacks from alleged injustices of the American justice system—were being beat up in print by culturally radical blacks or taken on by black orators who wanted to free black people from any tinge of outside influence. A number of the black students who seemed to accept me as one of their own also held some rather vicious and ignorant stereotypes about Jews. I had established a reputation as the white prof who taught black. My office swam with black students. "Like the black student union," one of my colleagues described it. I may have been, as one of my black students called me, "a palefaced nigger," but I was also a Jew.

I was able to joke about being Jewish with some students who seemed prejudiced, yet most were respectful. Anti-Semitism was not as intemperate a force or as out of control in northern California as it seemed to be on the East Coast. There Jews and blacks had a very different dynamic, and the Jewish population was much less assimilated than in northern California, where wealthier Jews had roman numerals after their names and worshipped in synagogues that no one would call shuls. I probably endured a few of the kinds of remarks that I should not have from some of my students, though when I called any of them on sounding anti-Jewish, I invariably felt bad because they felt bad. Blake once went into a harangue about being "sick of the damn holocaust when millions more niggers died comin over in slave ships." I asked him if we needed to play a numbers comparison game with such large-scale tragedies. But there was also hostility against Israel that I let slide, telling myself that one could be critical of Israel or pro-Palestinian without being anti-Semitic. Some outrageous remarks I parlayed with humor. Buriel Clay—who would become a respected playwright and black expo organizer for whom the Western Addition, a black urban neighborhood in San Francisco, named its local theater—noticed a copy in my office of Michael Gold's proletarian novel, *Jews without Money*. Not knowing I was Jewish, he quipped, "What is this shit, man? There ain't no Jews without money." I simply laughed and said, "You're looking at one." I tried to be the educator, plying Clay with stories of my own confabulated Dickensian Jewish youth and tales of Jewish penury, but, hell, a number of my students seemed to have problems not so much with Jews but more with the white race, which Jews were part of. Two of my students, Ed Bullins and Reginald Lockett, had published militant anti-white writing and had already achieved, as Clay eventually would as a playwright, a kind of literary stature. The fire in their work against the white race did not connect in any way to the courteous, and respectful and warm way they interacted with me. They seemed to me to be just students looking to learn and humping for a grade and a sheepskin that would allow them to do what I was doing, earn money teaching so they could write. But here was the real rub. They were writing, a number of them, and getting their work into print. Jim Blake published a volume of poetry that included a poem about Jewish ghetto store owners and their exploitation of blacks. The last line in the poem, to my embarrassment, sang out praise "to the Sanhedrin of Schwerner, Goodman and Krasny." I had students who were more established as writers than I was!

As to why I was successful in building up a black following, I realized it likely had a lot to do with my youth, the appeal of someone young who could joke in hip ways and who cared about the black cultural and literary heritage and had passion in teaching it. I was, truth be told, generous and probably even indulgent, but never patronizing. I was willing to give them and their writing attention, to read and critique their work which often was finding its way into print, while I was still trying to figure out exactly where and how to find my own voice.

. . .

I SPENT MY FIRST FEW YEARS as a college teacher getting articles of scholarship into print and forging good collegial relations and close ties with many students, not just black ones. San Francisco State was still a college; it would become a university when Governor Ronald Reagan proclaimed it one a few years later. It was an institution I liked being part of. I liked my colleagues and my students. I enjoyed the fact that many of the students were older and working-class, taking courses at State because it was conveniently right off the trolley car line outside the downtown area, but still within the urban core of San Francisco. Tenure was my goal, the carrot and the stick.

Job security was the reason that I coveted tenure. Other untenured assistant professors were getting cut loose, and I felt fortunate. One of the untenured who was not rehired allegedly had his students meet with him naked in a hot tub and dispensed them tablets of LSD. Unlike the untenured at Berkeley or Stanford, I could probably get tenure without having to publish a book or two that was approved of by my senior colleagues. Tenure would mean academic security and provide me with a living from teaching, something I enjoyed, while I pursued the writer's life.

The problem was that the reality of becoming a writer was not any closer. It wasn't for lack of trying. I had some of the outer trappings. I was driven, up all hours trying to bang out tales. I was a professor of literature who knew a lot about writers and writing and had begun to know a lot of writers. I was seen by many as a writer, even though I had a diminutive portfolio of sketches that I had published only in small and unsung literary rags. Yet I could not, in truth, take ownership of being a writer. If celebrated authorship was to be my destiny, I had better get on with producing literary art worth celebrating.

I was ravenous to read and learn and write, and I started spinning tales based on a mélange of characters from my boyhood. Theodore Solatoroff, then editor of *The American Review*, wrote me kind and encouraging notes, one which said he thought he had read everything there was to read about the Jewish-American experience, until he read my sketches of characters like Blackie and Jake the Thief and other guys from around my old neighborhood, like Pissy and Frog and Sig the Sprayer. But he wasn't publishing me. I needed, he advised, to move more from sketch to tale. I knew what was needed but I was not doing it. If it was lying like buried treasure inside me, I did not seem to have found the proper gear to get at it. I needed more expansive scenes, a sharper eye for detail, conflict that would show the edges and crannies of deeper humanity. I needed to dramatize rather than summarize.

I finished my dissertation, published articles from it and went on, in the summer of 1971, to finish a short novel about a character I affectedly named Swann, with Proust in mind, threading narration from my own experiences with a neurotic voice that both was and wasn't me. I let a lot of the hidden and darker me on to the page, as if writing in a fury of primary process. How else to get at truth? One must expose and bare oneself and do what Sylvia Plath called the big striptease, so long as readers were engaged. Didn't Lionel Trilling see neurosis as the pulley that lifted art? Leo Litwak, a colleague and first-rate novelist, read the novel and loved it. Eric Solomon read it and encouraged me, but clearly thought Leo's praise inflated. Leo gave me the name of a New York agent. I sent it to her and received a letter back full of so much praise that it made me tear up. But the novel was so personal that I began to dread the possibility of its being published; it filled me with a surprising terror unlike any I felt since boyhood. I was soon having inexplicable urges to drive into oncoming traffic, even though the literary agent was unwilling to try selling the novel in its original form. Writing too close to the viscera of my own past and childhood brought out psychic gargoyles. My self-destructive urges hit a low point when I stopped driving the car in the middle of the Golden Gate Bridge and asked Leslie to take over.

Still, I wanted desperately to be a writer.

I turned temporarily away from trying to create literary art and spent the bulk of the summer torturing myself with books by Jackie Susann and Harold Robbins, Sidney Sheldon and Judith Krantz, looking for some form that would move me from the painful, dark, hidden, hurtful terrain of my early years, though soon enough I realized that I didn't have the DNA required to write potboiling schlock. Like the old cliché, I wasn't bad enough or good enough. I lusted for literary art and was unable to consummate.

My labor at writing also affected my marriage. On weekends, Leslie wanted to go to a museum or a movie or take a walk on the mountain with me, and I would decline. My work took precedence—and my real work, aside from class preparation and paper grading, was sitting at a typewriter and, as Philip Roth would later write in *Ghost Story*, turning sentences around and then turning them around again. I had a full life, but I also had the sort of work ethic that allowed no life if I was summoned by higher creative or professional duties. I sat at the typewriter for hours, waiting for words that often would not come. And when words did come, they often were not the kind of words I had hoped would come—not exquisite or passionate or engaging or even particularly illuminating. I needed narrative conflict, stories worth telling, characters who cast shadows. I was a literary prospector looking for gold amidst dross, panning with hope of El Dorado.

Could I write anything that was more than pedestrian? Anything that had real life in it? How, when I felt so often like a bloody hack just clearing brush? Or when I delved so deeply into my own unconscious that it nearly drove me to drive into oncoming cars? But when rare and precious bursts of language and insight came, it could quicken all that was in me.

Writing was lonely and solitary. But, truth be told, I was more stimulated by the liveliness of discussing ideas in the classroom or my university office. To sit for hour after hour trying to create out of nothing, out of the vastness of everything, without any likelihood of reward—that was the real test, the true mettle of being a writer. One of my heroes, Kafka, would have accepted the fate of sitting alone with only his work, like the hunger artist in perhaps his most famous story aside from "The Metamorphosis"—no reward but the performance, giving up life even, starving to death, because starving is the art, and it doesn't even matter if starving has gone out of style or audiences are no longer interested; the artist has to go on. Or, as Beckett said, "I can't go, I must go on." Not because you want to be a writer, as Rilke told the young poet, but because you had to be and would die for not being. That was the truth of what drove great art, and I refused to believe it wasn't in me. Refused to accept that the pedagogic or fleeting talk that won me approbation could ever possibly give me what writing could give. So I continued to write under the practical cover of positioning myself for tenure, and I went on fighting demons like those aroused at Montgomery Ward after writing *Swann*.

Leslie and I were there to buy a vacuum cleaner, and we were waiting for what seemed an excessive amount of time for assistance. I politely asked the salesman, a hulking character, if he would help us, and he told me, brusquely, that we would have to wait. The longer we waited, the angrier I became. But instead of leaving the store, I luxuriated in my anger and aggressively announced to another salesperson that I wanted the rude vacuum cleaner salesman's name—whereupon he came over to me, menacingly, a twisted smirk on his face. "You want my name. I want your name." An unblinking stand-off of staring and heavy breathing followed, until Leslie grabbed me by the elbow and said, "Let's get out of here. Now!"

She told the therapist we went to see weeks later that she had to pull me away, but the truth is I was scared of the guy, and though I didn't blink, I certainly didn't have the courage that I wanted. I felt as if I should have bloodied the salesman, and I felt diminished. Perhaps I hadn't acted with violence because it was my own verbal, reactive aggression that had started the trouble. It really didn't matter. My brooding went on well after the incident. Something had impeded my violence, and I walked off willingly with my wife. Was it his hulk? Her insistence? My prudence? I knew that walking away was the right, smart thing to do. Was I going to beat someone bloody or, more likely, get mauled and hospitalized over bad service and bad manners? No matter. I wanted to hurt the guy. Or if not hurt, then at least call in a complaint to the Montgomery Ward service department. Why, Leslie asked in the therapist's office, was I carrying on to her about such loony macho bullshit, about manhood? What did that mean? Had my street boyhood returned, as Nietzsche says all eternally returns? Or had it never left? Or had I read one too many black novels and works of black militancy? Or maybe stared too much into the flames of holocaust literature and felt, moronically, that I had to respond for all those Jews who went like sheep to showers and ovens by assaulting a rude Montgomery Ward vacuum cleaner salesman. It was, in many ways, a black thing, a guy thing, a prol thing, maybe a Jewish thing, but it was also me inwardly screaming to prove myself violent and tough and a man. Did good men want to punch out menacing salesmen?

Herb Gold, a respected writer who had also taught at San Francisco State, understood the male aggression I was struggling with. He told me a story of how Norman Mailer had challenged him to a fight the first time the two had met, and his response was to say okay—whereupon Mailer made friends with him. Which was a funny side to the whole Montgomery Ward episode; as much as I wanted to beat up the salesman, I also would have liked—preferred, in fact—to have made friends with him, to have shown him what a good guy I really was under the aggression that had surfaced with my impatience.

I clearly had a problem, and therapy was in order. But it took one other incident to convince me I really needed to get my irrational, reactive rage under control. We went, Leslie and I, to see a movie in Mill Valley, a rather sleepy Marin town south of where we lived. Mill Valley wasn't the sort of place one identified with roughnecks, but when Leslie and I walked out of the movie theater we saw a group of four delinquent-looking characters who could have been anywhere from seventeen to their early twenties. I heard loud noises, and at first I had no idea what they were; then I saw Leslie leap in fright as a cherry bomb exploded close to those of us exiting the building. The young punks were laughing. I heard my wife mutter "jerks." Things went into super speed after that. I raced away from her to our car, opened the trunk and took out a baseball bat. My heart was stomping in my chest. I was possessed. I felt alive. I came at them, waving the bat over my head, shouting, "Come on."

"You crazy, mister?"

"Damn right. You throw cherry bombs at people. You think that's funny? You think that's cool? Come on. Let's see what you got. Come on."

Leslie was screaming at me. "Michael! Michael! Leave it alone! Come on! Please!"

But I didn't want to leave it alone. I wanted them to come at me. Fury coursed through me. It scared then thrilled me as they scattered and ran off calling me crazy, and observers broke out in spontaneous applause. I was a filmic hero to everyone except my wife.

"You could have really hurt someone," she shrieked at me once we were in the car. "You could have gotten us killed. You're lucky you aren't in jail." I was defending her, I defended myself. "Did I ask you to defend me? I don't need you to fight assholes for me. What kind of fool are you?" I spoke of manhood. "Manhood? Bullshit!"

So I went to see a therapist, this being before the invention of anger management classes. I knew I had to learn to stave off my anger. Leslie was taming me, teaching me proper table manners—how to use a fork and knife properly and eat with my mouth closed. I was fighting her, but I was really fighting me.

I was no fighter. I was a writer. From my reading of Buddhist writings, I believed passivity was tied to goodness. It was good to be pacific because peace was good. But the world was full of assholes. One wanted aggression. The blood craved aggression. Aggression, I told my students, could be a virtue—think of aggressively grabbing a child out of the path of a speeding car or hoisting someone off of a suicide ledge. But how much aggression could you have and still be good? Even Bellow's sweet, brilliant Moses Herzog took out a gun while staring through the window at Gersbach, his cuckholder, who was giving a bath to Herzog's beloved daughter.

I took up karate and it helped me. I studied goju-ryo with an eighth-belt don named Yamaguchi, who led classes at S. F. State and had his own dojo in San Francisco. I loved the ritual of martial arts, the robes and the bowing and the moves and the take-downs and punches and kicks and the sense it gave me of greater power combined with the potential for inner peace. I had much aggression. Couldn't this, too, be part of my art?

· · ·

1972. Leslie and I rented a small home in Ross, one of wealthy Marin County's wealthiest towns—a small, pastoral place of insular affluence and charm with an auto repair shop in the center of town right down the street from us. I liked to say I lived in the slum of Ross because all around our small cottage and the auto repair—which would later be demolished and transformed into a fashionable, upscale set of stores—was beauty and wealth and stately, arboreal homes that would be owned, more than two decades later, by the likes of film stars Sean

Penn and Robin Wright Penn and movie director Barry Levinson. Ross had a countrified, nearly serene, rural quality. Each day I walked to the small post office with our two dogs past Ross Common, a verdant field next to Ross school. Francis Ford Coppola had shot a scene in *The Godfather* there, in which the young Michael Corleone went to meet Kay (Diane Keaton) at the school in New England where she taught. Ross Common became—astonishingly, no doubt, to the white, affluent residents who lived near it—an occasional scene of softball games I organized that included colleagues; students, a good number of them black.

I was doing what I could, politically, with prisoners and ex-prisoners for the amorphous cause of social justice—motivated by the desire to do good and to serve. But it was difficult, and not simply because of scary looking thugs who wore looks on their faces like ads for recidivism. I hadn't really believed in the revolution for years, and my work with prisoners, including Jewish prisoners at San Quentin, had been rewarding in many ways but also disillusioning. The Jewish cons, a small group, were mostly gentile by birth, including a stammering black man who quoted Martin Buber and Abraham Joshua Heschel. A Jewish guy from New York named Sid said to me, of murdering his wife: "I didn't mean to. I honest to God didn't. I wouldn't have, just for my kids' sake. But the bitch had it coming."

Every time I went inside the walls of San Quentin, a maximum-security prison right in the heart of Marin County, it depressed me. It also made me realize that many of the men I saw probably belonged exactly where they were, even though many protested their innocence. I realized that it was no secret why they were called cons. Every time I went in, I was worked on by a number of them to do things for them and send things to them. Maybe next time, they pleaded, I could sneak or smuggle in what they wanted—usually simple items like cigarettes, candy, money or books. But I didn't like them working me, and I didn't like having to say no. A black con whom I was helping, by reading and editing his manuscript about his life on the streets, called me one day while I was in my office at S.F. State and informed me that he had broken away from a work detail and was on the lam. Could he come see me and hide out with me, and could I help him publish his manuscript so he could send money to his kids? Playing the role of pal to prisoners, I realized, carried risks. I was a teacher and a scholar, not a reformer.

When it came to fighting for social change, my heart was much more in working for George McGovern's presidential candidacy, even though I knew it was a lost cause. Leslie and I went out and canvassed through the Ross neighborhoods door to door and came face to face with people who felt Nixon was the one or, worse, that even he was not conservative enough. McGovern, with his epicene, Liberace-like voice, promised he would end the war and help the poor and the downtrodden. But the possibility of him getting elected was hopeless.

I had become a stereotype, an intellectual, liberal, hippie Jewish professor. I was appalled to discover, when I returned to Cleveland and got together with Pissy and Horse, my old neighborhood cronies, that they were both ardent Nixon supporters. So was my mother's sister Esther, who defended her choice to me even after Watergate by saying, "At least I picked a winner." So was my father's brother, Marty, who still hid his copies of *Playboy* under the bed. So was Leslie's sister Louise's beau, Harvey, a wealthy stuffed-toy manufacturer who defended Nixon to me on Vietnam: "I'm the boss of my company. I make the decisions. If people who work for me don't like my decisions, they can leave. The president is our boss."

I was angry with those who supported Nixon. I was invited by a rabbi in Marin to give a sermon at a Friday night service, and I chose as my topic why Jews should not support Nixon. It made many of the congregants adore me, while others were indignant, even furious, and not all of them because of their support for Nixon. Some felt politics had no place in a synagogue. To me, raised as a conservative Jew, guitars had no place in a synagogue, but there they were, accompanying the Friday night service.

I was becoming more active as a Jew—teaching Sunday school and leading reading groups, lecturing and writing. I was also still the young twenty-eight-year-old, driven careerist. "You look like a damn professor," Pissy said with a gruff laugh upon seeing me in Cleveland for the first time in five years—and with my tweed sport coat and long, hippie hair and mustache, I did indeed look like I was out of central casting. I was beginning to get more of my work into print—articles and reviews on black, Jewish and Native American writers, literary criticism on U.S. writers, fiction in small obscure quarterlies and essays in local newspapers. The sheer number of publications, I hoped, would provide me with enough capital to get me through the professorial goal post, the gates of tenure.

I was a popular teacher, and not just with black students. When I began at S.F. State, everything, in my mind, had to be student-centered. Me facilitator. You students. You talk. I listen. I guide. But I learned early on, by teaching black literature to black students, that I was much more respected for the learning I possessed and my showmanship in lecturing, drawing out student responses and leading animated discussions. I had turned more toward performance in my classroom teaching. If only I could write like I could teach!

I was now mainly teaching courses in the modern American novel and twentieth-century American literature, and all that I read and taught was affecting my voice and style as a would-be writer of fiction. I abandoned *Swann* and began working on a new novel, *The Rossman Odyssey*, named for the fact that I lived in Ross and for Kafka's *Amerika* protagonist, Karl Rossman.

Harold Pinter, a Kafka acolyte, was another writer to whom I was strongly drawn. There was something in Kafka's brooding spirit and paranoia and cockeyed vision of the world, with its scabrous and painful humor, that appealed to me. Pinter, too, was in that mold, and so it was no surprise that five years later I would chase around Hampstead Heath in London trying to meet Pinter with Leslie, the barrister brother of a Brit colleague of mine and his BBC archivist pal. It would be a romping good, fun night of going to pubs, getting snookered and hearing from the two Brits, who both played cricket with Pinter, that he was a pleasant enough chap, damn good dresser and mad about cricket but, when you got down to it, not really all that interesting.

I also wanted to meet Philip Roth. Soon after the election, when Nixon crushed McGovern and Leslie cried when we heard the news over our car radio, we were on our way back to Cleveland and New York to visit our families. I had sent notes ahead to Roth, Norman Mailer, Jerzy Kosinski and another writer popular at the time named Alan Lelchuck, author of *American Mischief,* inviting them all to a Park Avenue soiree at the Manhattan home of one of my English students.

Nicole, who took an erotic literature class I was teaching (remember we could teach pretty much whatever we wanted to teach then at S.F. State), was a young woman from a wealthy European and Australian background. She was rich, tall and lovely and, even for that period of free and rampant promiscuity, was doing an amazing amount of screwing. We became friends, and when she confided that she "fancied" me, I fixed her up with Digger. It was a damn good deal for him, since he was a penniless Cal Tech post doc living on crackers and peanut butter. He loved her good looks and her lustiness and, though he complained that it wasn't manly or part of his code, he tolerated her insistence on paying for trips for the two of them to New York, Maui and Tahiti.

Nicole's father had a hideaway in Manhattan off Park Avenue, a pied a terre, redolent of riches, that included a full-time, uniformed maid and a butler. Digger saw it when he was there with her and marveled to me about it. When I knew Leslie and I were headed to New York, and that Digger and Nicole would also be there, I suggested a party and said I would try to provide literary star power. I got Roth's address from someone who knew someone and Mailer's from a woman colleague of mine he used to sleep with and with whom he had kept in contact. Klinkowitz, a Wisconsin chum of mine, had come to know Kosinski. My sister was also in New York and said she would come with her friend Caroline, and I invited the literary agent who was so high on my novel, *Swann*.

I was excited. I had written warm, engaging letters to each of the writers and told them there would be wine, women and great food in this mogul's opulent Manhattan digs. The address alone would surely impress them. I imagined I would form indelible friendships with each of them, and they, in turn, would welcome me into the writer's club, help promote my work, write lofty, praiseful blurbs and give me entrée to the literary world I so badly wanted to be part of. Perhaps, more realistically, they might simply agree to read my fiction and help me find a publisher.

The agent came first. She went into raptures over the furnishings and decor, the paintings and other assorted wall hangings. My sister and Leslie's sister and my sister's friend were all equally impressed. It was impossible not to be. But none of the writers showed. Not even Lelchuck. Caroline kept asking me, "Where's Philip, Michael?" until it began to sound to me like an annoying mantra. Nor did I get to meet Pinter in

London. But a few years later, Nicole would be living in London and sleeping with Ted Hughes, Britain's poet laureate and the widower of the head-in-the-oven feminist martyr Sylvia Plath.

. . .

LATER THAT SUMMER, my sister Lois's world crashed in. Her husband, David, was arrested by a joint task force at one of my niece's dance recitals; the charge was arson conspiracy. Though Dave had all the outer trappings of a successful businessman, he had been buying properties, heavily insuring them and hiring a torch to burn them. He would wind up being sent to the penitentiary. My old crony Mike Levine would also be sent away to a criminally insane institution for shooting and killing supermarket magnate Jules Kravitz and wounding Kravitz's wife with the intent to kill her. Another Heights High classmate of mine got in trouble that same summer for threatening to kill Nixon—claiming the president was trying to shut down his cult, which, according to news reports, had no other members in it. In high school we called this boy the Zapper because he frightened girls with his crazed stares. He got his ass kicked by a bunch of Italian hoods for writing and circulating a pamphlet proclaiming Mary, mother of Jesus, the whore of Bethlehem.

I tussled mentally with what these three criminal cases meant as I prepared for two big events—my ten-year high school reunion and a reunion of guys who were in PDG, my high school club. Its letters supposedly stood for pretty damn good but were actually just chosen at random. Was there a nature/nurture equation of some kind that might help me understand Dave, the Zapper and Levine?

The aspiring novelist in me wanted to understand or show all of this writ large—emphasis being on show, since good novelists, as I told my students, show rather than tell, though telling seemed to be my proclivity. Perhaps that was my problem as a writer, aside from lack of talent or true artistic fuel. Yet I was grappling with big questions that seemed like they could lend themselves well to the large, canvassed novel I hoped to write. Questions such as what motivated my brother-in-law and Mike Levine and how much of that motivation, or even the Zapper's, connected itself to the Cleveland prol Jewish world we grew up in, and how much any of it was universal and buried deep in me too. I could never burn down buildings or murder for money or threaten to kill a president, but I believed I understood my brother-in-law's need to act out of impulse and desperation and to set aside moral sense. Money wasn't my demon; it didn't drive me. But in the cloistered and connubial Jewish suburban world of Cleveland, men and their wives were judged by what men made and the homes they owned and the cars they drove and the country club that they belonged to. One Jewish country club, Oakmont, took in only German Jews and allowed no Russian Jews for years until Al Rosen, the great third baseman for the Cleveland Indians, applied. My memories were fresh of gold-plated, name-engraved seats at Park Synagogue, up in front at the house of prayer, reserved exclusively for congregants who were the largest contributors. There were also booklets that the Jewish Welfare Federation published at the end of each year—until howls of protest caused them to stop—listing amounts pledged along with names of the would-be donors and the amounts they actually contributed. I understood, too, the hostility against Nixon.

Levine had always been a guy who kept himself on a short leash. Would I have initiated a scheme to get money as he did? No. But I could fathom his anger. I could also imagine what it must have been like for the poor Kravitzes. Levine picking them up at the airport with his black sidekick, pretending to be there at their son's behest, then pulling his gun and driving around aimlessly. The black accomplice also pulled a gun and pointed it at them. He would get sent off to life without parole and Levine, schemer and shooter, got sent to Lima State for the criminally insane. The story all came out in the trials and news reports. Levine demanded money in a sum that Kravitz said he could not get; he thought Kravitz was playing him by claiming such a large amount wasn't accessible, offering him only a measly few grand in cash to be set free. All this while the supermarket tycoon was concerned primarily for his terrified wife, as she pleaded with Levine to let them go—Levine feeling his head was going to burst, then shooting them both and tossing their bloody bodies out of the same car he would take the following day to get cleaned at AlPaul carwash at Cedar Center. Leaving them for dead. Not knowing Mrs. Kravitz was still breathing.

Good material for a novelist, no? To murder or create, T. S. Eliot's Harry says in *The Cocktail Party*, as if those are the choices. Norman

Mailer and Truman Capote—both tried to find out why we have a murderer inside us, like an inner child, lurking, caged in the soul's cellar or under the false mask of politeness, like LeRoi Jones's masked Dutchman, Clay. Like the failed artist and house painter Adolf Schicklegruber, the lousy poet bin Laden or the would-be playwright Saddam Hussein? Like Jones's Clay, who said that art, jazz and the blues were all that kept Charlie Parker and Bessie Smith from murder? If I couldn't create, what did that mean? Could I succeed, as I appeared to be doing, at jettisoning aggression and rage and being the good, dull, accomplished, make-your-parents-and-in-laws proud Jewish boy who sat on the Jewish Welfare Federation board? Maybe all I was really destined for was quiet desperation and bourgeois respectability, both possible murderers of the would-be artist.

Most of those who attended my ten-year reunion had become nice bourgeois types. They were people who came from the same time and place as I did but were not like me. Where were the hoods in their high school lives, the hoods who had played such a central role in mine? None showed up at the reunion. Most of the nice Jewish kids probably had no contact with them and were free of the range and color of experiences I had had. I wanted to be normal, as so many of them appeared to be, but I also wanted to be more.

Both Digger and I were still proving ourselves. We wanted to show them, all of them, whoever "them" was, and even though "them" likely did not care. We went together to the reunion with an outward charm and polish and self-control. Those we had formerly made fun of we greeted with benevolence, and to those who made fun of us, or who never could have imagined either of us amounting to anything, we tried to show off our best and most dignified selves. With no small thanks to Leslie I looked hip, well-attired and pretty good. I had worked at getting svelte and muscular, and I had a tan. I wanted to prove to those who thought the worst of me that I was somebody. I was Janis Joplin going back to Port Arthur Texas to strut her stuff to all who had once thought little of her or made fun of her.

Blackie picked me up for the PDG reunion in a limo. He had a Vidal Sassoon haircut and couldn't stop talking about me living in San Francisco with fags. He also wanted me to know that he was making more money than Sheldon, another club member a couple of years older who, like Blackie, was now very rich, though from family wealth.

Blackie talked mainly of money and provided me with low-downs on the other guys. He told me he knew that he thought and talked too much about money. It made him think he should see a psychiatrist. "Why don't you?" I asked. "What," he answered, "do you think I'm crazy?"

He was, as usual, full of stories that spoke to the degeneracy of our former high school club brothers. One insisted on bringing a hired whore into his marriage bed. Another listened on the other end of the phone, eavesdropping as his wife described in detail what she was going to do to another guy's *shvantz*. One caught his mother being boinked in the back seat of some guy's car. His mother! Another was headed for the Ohio Pen in a few days for selling cocaine. Again, nature or nurture?

"What do you teach out there, Kraz?" he suddenly asked me.

"Literature. In fact I'm doing a new course this semester on transatlantic drama."

"Drama, eh? Should I call you Bruce?"

"Don't be an idiot. We're talking playwrights like Harold Pinter and David Mamet."

Blackie snorted. "Fag stuff, Kraz. You're teaching fag stuff."

Things were pretty sedate poolside at the hotel where the reunion was being held. I was trying to act dignified and thinking, strangely enough, about the stuffy old Anglophile Eliot and his metaphysical verse in "Burnt Norton" on time present and time past. How much had I left my time past behind? How much was still in me? I may have been teaching the works of Eliot and Pinter, but how much of this Cleveland world I grew up in and these club guys—once mostly jocks, lowlifes and would-be ass-men—were still in my blood?

Inside, when the food fight began at dinner—started by a younger club member whom we used to call Chuck the Schmuck—I felt a bread roll hit the side of my head, and I leapt to action, ready to kick ass. Java Man was there, and he too jumped up and yelled, "I'm going to piss on the head of the next asshole who throws food."

After the food fight settled down, guys stood up and gave little spiels. Blackie, The Duke, Trapezoid and Duck Miller all talked about how the PDG years were the best days of their lives. Then Stag walked in. The place went wild. Stag was a guy who had hair on his chest at fourteen and was nearly mythic in the eyes of the guys because of his Herculean strength. They called him Posie, too, because of his bad body odor, but he was now an Encino businessman with a white shirt and a clean, powdered, courteous look. They were begging Stag to sing Stagger Lee. Blackie was laughing so hard tears were cascading down his cheeks. He and Duke and Java Man and Duck were all pleading with Stag to sing. But Stag would not sing.

Later the guys went upstairs to play poker, and a tomato showed up—that's what Sheldon, who brought her, called her—and she offered services for hire. She was a stew who worked part-time as a hooker, and she told me, "Sheldon says I didn't do him, but I did. I wonder what his wife would think if she knew." Jerry B., who had just left a girl at the altar in Vegas and flown back to the reunion on a stolen credit card, and Duck Miller—the guy who had thrown the young girl we called Porkchop over the side of a boat for not putting out to him on the first and only annual PDG boat ride—both had sex with the stew hooker, who complained that the hundred bucks they ponied up together was supposed to be a hundred each.

"You not getting in on this action, Kraz?" Var the Star asked me as I sat on the bed nursing a stomach ache and a case of the runs.

"No."

"Good, Kraz. Good for you." This said by a guy who had the reputation of screwing any female with protoplasm. He once initiated an ugly party, where the guy who showed up with the ugliest girl was guaranteed a cash prize. I can proudly say I did not participate in that. But quite a few of the guys did. Var had brought with him a creature he called The Poopsie, who had the body of a fire hydrant and the face of a sow. I am not trying to be mean. The point is, he was screwing her.

Afterward we went to a dance place, and a half-drunk Java Man burned my pants with his cigarette. "You burned Krasny's pants," Blackie scolded. "Fuck Krasny's pants," Java said.

Blackie was pointing to a thin, pretty, scraggly haired girl who was shaking it up on the dance floor. "Didn't she screw you in high school, Kraz?"

What was it about these guys? What still connected me to them and linked me to my brother-in-law, Mike Levine or the Zapper? Could all that shared past be effaced, transmogrified, tempered by volition, wisdom, age, diminished like the aggression that still could sieze me? I told myself I was a Ph.D. and no longer a PDG, but I still had no idea, really, who I was or who I was going to be.

Alice Walker

I have wondered if there is something about my Jewishness that reminds Alice Walker of her ex-husband, Mel Leventhal, the young New York Jewish attorney whom she married in defiance of Mississippi laws against miscegenation and lived with as wife and man, the state's only interracial couple, in an Ole Miss then full of Klansmen and nigger haters. She and her husband moved there after three civil rights workers were killed, before their bodies were found. A force of nature was at work, pulling them to each other against man-made law, Mel bidding her to take a lick from his chocolate ice cream cone in that Jim Crow time. Mel's mother sat *shiva* for him when he married Walker, but her feelings changed when she discovered that others would kill her son because of his wife. Walker believes people can change.

She has a reputation for being prickly with interviewers and acting like a diva—though she has always been warm and even slightly girlish and flirtatious with me. When I look at her, I sometimes see a young, pigtailed colored girl, as she would have been called back then, younger even than the girl who fell in love with the Jewish civil rights lawyer. She laughs a lot with me, feels at ease.

Walker says she learned in Mississippi how bright and fearless the human spirit can be. Her love of writers like Jean Toomer and Langston Hughes and the Indian lore that is also part of her heritage—and, also, the Buddhist teachings and meditations she has absorbed—all make her celebrate and honor the sanctity of humanness, make her heaven bent on teaching compassion and love. Her mother was a teacher and a healer, and that is what Walker has become. Literature and literary art have come to mean much less to her now, dwarfed in her mind by the necessity to heal the ancestors, enshrine the human spirit and root out and speak out against violence and depravity.

Walker didn't think she would write again—though poetry, to her surprise, continued to flow from her, and so did a way too didactic novel—since she cared only for her role as a sojourner of truth, a medium for beneficent power. She speaks about the source, creator and spirit, and she speaks, with force, for the indigenous, the dispossessed and all earthlings, and she has come to speak against genital mutilation and oppression. But where is the gifted storyteller, whom Muriel Rukeyser knew had narrative power and whose storytelling gifts eventually earned her a Pulitzer Prize and an American Book Award? The storyteller is now a former avatar. Walker now calls herself "an apprentice elder."

She has followed the pattern of the poet we both love, Jean Toomer, who poured the black part of his soul and his literary passion into one book, *Cane*, then turned to mentoring Gurdjieff and Ouspensky, to spirituality and cosmic consciousness. How can storytelling be important when there is suffering to combat, higher consciousness to attain and the need to teach human transformation?

I listen attentively as Walker talks to me of how we all need darkness and shadows as well as brightness and light. How the only thing she is addicted to is solitude. How the earth is God, how youth are looking for connection to the divine but without shamans or elders. Many, she says, choose drugs, looking for ecstatic, religious, spiritual experiences they cannot find in the culture. She says Marx was right about private property being theft. How indigenous people knew that the land belonged to no one because, collectively, we are all of the earth.

"Democracy?" Walker asks. "It's always been run by white men with money. What kind of democracy is that?"

August Wilson

August Wilson tells me why being black is more important to him than being an American or being a playwright or even being male. It is because he was black in his mother's womb before he had any other identity. African Americans must direct his plays, and he has to have African Americans in charge of all the artistic elements, including music. Perhaps especially music, since the blues are his primary influence and the bedrock of everything he does. Baraka and Borges have been important, too, and so has the painter Romare Bearden, but the blues reign supreme.

Wilson has tried to make his plays the equal of Bearden canvases. I think about how light-skinned Wilson is, but Bearden was even more so. Bearden could have passed for white, but like Wilson, the painter put blackness first. Remembering my experiences teaching black literature, I ask him about a white man directing one of his plays since one could argue, as I did, that someone white has the advantage of being an outsider. He sounds peeved: should Coppola have directed *Schindler's List* or Spielberg *The Godfather?* he asks. "I don't buy an outsider having more insight into my culture than I do." His concern, he says, is artistic. Black people know black culture best.

Wilson tells me he doesn't know dramatic literature. He rarely goes to the theater or movies. Blues are the best literature black Americans have, the best response to the world they find themselves in and to their history; the blues are life-affirming and carry ideas and attitudes of oral tradition. The music has emotional reference. Many critics compared *Fences* to *Death of a Salesman*, but Wilson knew nothing of Miller's play. There were, he says, human aspects of culture that both keyed on.

Wilson has two Pulitzers. The big prizes are impressive. But his case is special. He left school in the ninth grade in a story he tells that is the stuff of myth. He had done a twenty-page report on Napoleon that one of his sisters typed for him on a ten-dollar-a-month rented typewriter. The teacher insinuated that one of his older sisters wrote the paper. "I wrote their papers," Wilson said. The teacher didn't believe him. Wilson tore up the paper, walked out and "never looked back." It freed him from restraints. He hid out at the library to hide from his mother, but he read what he wanted to read there, and the world opened up. Years of library reading, then out to the streets of Pittsburgh's Hill District.

Wilson gets calls on air from people who lived in the Hill District or knew it, including a white cab driver who picked up fares there, even though the big cab companies like Yellow wouldn't go into the area. One woman caller says that her mother, who was Jewish, lived there in racial harmony, and Wilson concurs. It was a delightful place to grow up, he says. "We were a neighborhood. We were integrated. All of us got along well. Everyone was a social parent to all of the children. By the early sixties it was all black."

Wilson started the Black Horizon theater, when he was twenty-three,

as a tool to politicize and raise community consciousness. Black anger
was the hot stage commodity then. Ed Bullins, who wrote *The Electronic
Nigger* and some of the angriest black plays, was my student, a reticent
and gentle, soft spoken man. Wilson, not nearly as angry in his plays as
young Bullins, seems to me a tougher type. Straight-talking, biting out
words with no BS, but also pleasant, nostalgic about the past and at least
outwardly hopeful of life affirmation, despite a tragic vision that has
been mounted on stages across America. The idea of covering black life
in America through the decades came to him after he wrote *Jitney, Fences,*
and *Ma Rainey.* He realized he had plays from different decades, so why
not continue? "It gave me something larger," he explains.

Wilson started out in the theater as a director and not a playwright.
He tried to write dialogue and only came up with "What's happenin?"
followed by "Nothin." Two years later he came to write plays. He says
you only write what you know and you write yourself and then it's all
unconscious. Early on people suggested he write comedy, but comedy
for him was just normal humor that came out of natural situations. Melodrama? If a play has melodrama let it be what it is. Characters can take
over plays, but he remains the boss. He can kick them out at will. He
wants them to maintain their dignity.

He started out writing poetry, and he concludes by telling me he
has a plan to write a novel and perform a one-man show called *I'm Not
Spaulding Grey*.

This, of course, was before Spaulding Grey, in mental and physical agony, leaped Hart Crane–like to death. Wilson doesn't know Grey's
work, but that, he says, doesn't matter.

 Maya Angelou

Before I interviewed Maya Angelou for the first time,
I saw her one evening walking toward a limo driver in the Los Angeles
airport. He was holding a sign that said "Dr. Angelou." The title is hon-
orific. Yet why shouldn't she buoy herself with it? There are people who
like to tell you they have a Ph.D. in life or in living on the street. My dad
used to say that plumbers deserved to be called doctors because of how
much it cost to hire them. When I completed my Ph.D., my wife's blunt,
rich uncle Manny said to me, "Why don't you become a real doctor?"

Dr. Angelou had been a hooker in San Francisco before she wrote *I Know Why the Caged Bird Sings*, a book that frightens parents still because of the sexual abuse. Many wanted it kept away from their children. Shielding innocence? Perhaps, too, a fear of a melanin-induced contagion linked to sex molestation, as in Alice Walker's *The Color Purple* or Toni Morrison's *The Bluest Eye*.

Caged Bird made Angelou famous. It gave school kids all over America who were allowed to read it a way of seeing suffering and hearing lyricism and feeling hope. Francine Prose hated it and said so in print. She couldn't understand how anyone could use it as a teaching tool because of its rotten syntax and poor grammar. People have wanted to ban the book, Angelou tells me. People who feel they are without skeletons or closets (let them cast the first stones), people who think nothing bad ever happens to them. I cite Hawthorne to her—our Puritan conscience who believed in the negative path, believed we grow, like Hester Prynne, from moral error. "Yes," she says with her mellifluous, rich, hymnal voice that comes from Arkansas poverty but has in it the black church and Africa.

Angelou was the poet who read "Good Morning" to begin President Clinton's inauguration and what liberals hoped would be a new chapter for America. The narrow prejudices of Arkansas were broken down in her, she tells me, by the books she read. Her beloved brother Bailey was only fifteen, a year older than she, when he introduced her to Kenneth Patchen, Thomas Wolfe, Virginia Woolf and Philip Wylie.

The first time she came on the air with me, her novelist son, Guy, phoned in. I asked him how it felt to be in her shadow. He told me he had always felt within her light.

She tells me a story about almost dying in a car wreck with a man who called himself a mean and crazy nigger. She told him he was better than that. But he was reckless and nearly killed her. "People tell you who they are," she says. "A woman I know in New York recently said to me 'I'm selfish.' She was telling the truth."

Angelou has the weakness I have had of wanting to be identified with greatness. She calls James Baldwin her brother, as if he were Bailey, and she assures me she never would have written *Caged Bird* if not for Jimmy. She talks as if she had been an intimate and close friend to both Malcolm X and Martin Luther King. Perhaps she was. She says that they were both men of great humor. She says she loved them both. She mentions connections she has to Yale and Harvard. She mentions her Grammies and gifts of scholarships to women of all colors. It is hard not to admire her even though, as I see it, she is not the great writer many believe her to be. She wants to be regal and nearly manages to bring it off. One big-hearted public radio supporter, who stood watching her outside the glass during our most recent interview, came up to me after the interview and nearly swooned over seeing her. She has acted, danced, composed, written scads of verse and drama and six autobiographies, but she will be remembered for the first autobiography, *Caged Bird*, which was the one book she never intended to write, the creation that flowed from her self and gave her all her stature and fame.

Edward P. Jones

Jones appears as ordinary as the folk he writes about. He says he is still the person he was ten years ago before he had a Pulitzer, a National Book Critic's Circle Award and stories in *The New Yorker*. Still no car nor cell phone and no desire for either. No furniture since he decided to chuck it all years ago and has remained so busy and on the road that he simply hasn't replaced any of it. "I'm content in many ways," he tells me.

Four or five years out of college, Jones was homeless for about a week, with both parents dead. He had no idea what would become of him. It was a desperate situation, and the taste of homelessness made him live on two dollars a day once he got a job, the job of writing dreary tax news summaries for those in tax-related vocations.

He had published a volume of stories, *Lost in the City*, but with a ten-year plan in his head, he knew he had to write a novel. He had heard in college about black slave owners, and it was something he wanted to do research on, but he put it off for those ten years in which he composed the book in his head and lived with the characters. After ten years, he concluded that working out the book in his head was really writing. Henry Townsend, his wealthy young black slave owner, was on his deathbed, and Jones had to find out how Henry got there and what happened after he died. Imagination had to be played out, and when it did, it worked. Jones was fascinated with how his own mind operated and how good he felt about coming to resolutions at the end of the novel. People couldn't believe he made it all up, but he relied on nothing from life—though he built on people from the world he came from in Washington, D.C. "You have to be true to those people, true to their experience." Jones knows his characters thoroughly because, he says, he is like God, their creator. He is always in control of his people, "doomed to worry" about his characters. It is hard because you have to build them out of nothing. But only the what if truly matters. Every step of the way must be imagined so the reader will be pulled in. It's a lot of sweat. Storytellers must go down roads other storytellers have not gone down before and must strike out on their own. "That's what I did," Jones says. "I built my own house."

He built his stories and his novel out of the ordinary people he grew up with who affect his imagination—good, hard-working people, and some not so good. He had to explain each as fully as he could, including the white characters. Jones believes in storytelling and that characters come first. If you have a cause, you need to write an essay, not a tale.

"If you're black," Jones says, "there is a legacy of slavery. Though many think we've gone a million miles, it's cast a long, long shadow. For one-hundred-and-fifty-plus years, blacks were not given their proper place in society. People suffered because of it. People suffered in New Orleans as a result of the floods because they were black. The South won the Civil War."

Jones's own mother suffered. She was illiterate and abandoned by her husband when Jones was an infant. Jones saw her working hard all of the time, early to late, suffering indignities nearly every day. She had a series of strokes and then lung cancer. "If she'd lived for the joy of life, a good-time girl, I could have accepted that. But she suffered."

Jones is a solitary man. He doesn't hang around with writers. He reads them and tries to determine how they take in the world. He expresses a strong interest in Irish writers and a special appreciation for Mary Lavin. He tapes all the TV judge shows and watches them at night. "I go out with friends to dinner, lunch, movies. I visit and talk with friends. But I am not out and about in the world. I live in my imagination. It is always for me a question of what if."

Young love. Michael Krasny and his
girlfriend, Leslie Tilzer, in a photo booth
in Madison, Wisconsin. 1967.

At Ohio University graduation with Les Marks (Left) who
directed Michael's honor's thesis on Saul Bellow. 1966.

Digger (Left) and Michael on their way out west following
graduation from Ohio University. 1966.

A rare photo of teacher, author and Michael Krasny mentor
Walter Tevis at home in Athens, Ohio. 1967.

Michael with parents and siblings in Cleveland, Ohio. 1986.

KGO publicity photo of Michael Krasny.

Leslie, Lauren, Michael and Alexa Krasny in Greenbrae, California 2007.

5   Expanding Identity

W HEN THE COUNTRY TURNED two hundred, Leslie
and I got pregnant. What kinds of new shifts in
identity would I reap from taking on the new identity of fatherhood?
Much of my intellectual and scholarly energy had been drawn toward
questions of identity, whether trying to fathom what Jean Toomer's
mixed racial bloodlines meant to him, trying to excavate the nature of
black or Jewish identity or figure out my own. Munich and the slay-
ing of the Jewish Olympic athletes opened a vein in me, and I began,
after that tragedy, to search out my own Jewish identity with greater
intensity and to increase my role as a lecturer and educator on Jewish
subjects. I liked Alfred North Whitehead's definition of a Jew as someone who continues to ask himself, what is a Jew? I read everything I
could on identity and went out of my way to meet the psychoanalytic
identity sage Erik Erikson, who was then living in Marin and lecturing each year on Ingmar Bergman's *Wild Strawberries*. This was the
decade that Christopher Lasch, Tom Wolfe and others linked to nar-
cissism and me-ness. My brand of existentialism had taught me that
the self is protean and fluid, slippery, perhaps impossible to define.
Multiple selves exist simultaneously within us. I tended to connect my
own identity to masculinity, even though I was becoming more willing
to accept what D. H. Lawrence called the hidden lady in me or what
Adrienne Rich so fittingly revealed in her great poem "Diving into the
Wreck" as androgyny—and to Jewishness, even though a part of me
still felt black. I identified self, too, with what I professionally did as
an academic, with whom I had married, and with whom I associated

and identified. Even though all helped identify who and what I was, it often felt as if none truly did.

I was now a tenured professor. That, too, was an identity. Caroline Shrodes had retired as chair, and the seemingly ever smiling, Jesus-loving Jimmy "I'll never lie to you" Carter was the nation's president. Nixon had been forced out over the debacle of Watergate—which I watched greedily and religiously as it was televised each day, hoping to see The Trickster and his entourage of bad guys get their comeuppance. Ford pardoning Nixon was not a happy day for me.

But getting pregnant and getting tenure made me happy. I celebrated tenure with Leslie by buying a bottle of champagne for the two of us, though being pregnant, she was loath to imbibe. It wasn't only liquor that worried her. She worked as a biochemist at the U. C. Medical Center following completion of a Master's in molecular biology and worried about handling radioactive isotopes like P32 and Iodine 131 every day. We both feared our child-to-be might be affected and emerge damaged from the womb. And both pregnancy and tenure created new kinds of anxieties with new identities.

I was still not an established or recognized writer. That was the main narrative of my identity script. The life of the academician, the life of the mind, of the scholar and teacher—those were merely props to provide me the living and economic necessities for the writer's life. Bellow taught at a university, and so did many other contemporary novelists. Now that I had tenure, I could concentrate on the real goal, the one that mattered most and defined my deeper self.

But how could fatherhood not interfere? I would not have the luxury that my father's generation did of leaving all or most of the custodial care of children to my wife. Leslie worked a far less flexible schedule. Moreover, she had made it clear, and I had agreed, that bringing-up-baby labor would be shared.

What possible good was it that I had spent so many hours alone trying to push out a tale or a novel, with nothing to show except a few short stories that were more like sketches or shards printed in small, barely read literary journals and magazines? Just as in my boyhood, when I imagined myself a great athlete and fell off to sleep dreaming of glories that would never come, I had become an adult with dreams of becoming a respected and valued author, and none of that had borne fruit. I was a failure of a writer. That felt like my real identity, my secret Clark Kent identity, more of what Bellow would have called the abiding self.

Jeff Klein, a Columbia-trained journalist who would later edit *Mother Jones* magazine and become a friend, proclaimed to me that he and I were both, as far as establishing ourselves as writers of fiction, one Jew too late. We had witnessed the literary triumph of Bellow, Malamud and Roth, the triumvirate that Bellow once wisecracked had begun to sound like Hart-Shaffner-Marx, and we'd seen the ascendancy in American novel writing and literary criticism of what Truman Capote had petulantly called the literary Jewish mafia. But it wasn't Jewishness that was keeping me out, as it had kept my father out of medical school.

I'm not certain when I began to see myself, really see myself, as an interviewer. There was a moment when I realized that it was something that I could do and, I believed, do well. Perhaps, I thought, I could temporarily set aside my novelist's ambitions and see if I could take on a new identity as an interviewer. Could I possibly use the skillfulness I had developed as an educator and classroom teacher to draw others out as an interlocutor? It would require less reliance on lecturing and a different style of performance, but I suddenly believed it was something I ought to look into. I had experimented one evening, performing a stand-up comedy routine at San Francisco's Holy City Zoo, on its amateur comedy night. The boozed-up audience had already thinned by the time I went on stage, following a run of pretty lame and not funny would-be comics. It was hardly an auspicious debut into the world of live performance, but I wrote and published a piece about the experience, emphasizing how difficult it was to be out there without a net, facing a bored and alcohol-lubricated audience.

It was soon after that when serendipity intervened and I did my first interview with Gore Vidal. I might have taken it as a warning to stay out of the interviewing arena but, though the experience left a bad taste, I still wanted to forge ahead. I met Jane Fonda briefly at San Francisco State soon after the Vidal interview, when she appeared on campus in support of an anti-nuke rally that I helped organize. Soon after, I read that Lenny Michaels, then a U.C. Berkeley literature prof and the talented author of *Going Places*, had led an on-stage conversation with the movie actress Tuesday Weld. Here, I thought, was something that would really be fun—to interview a movie star like Jane Fonda or Tuesday Weld. I saw an item in the local paper mentioning that the San Francisco International Film Festival would be honoring the Swedish-born movie beauty Ann-Margret. She had done many song and dance films, including a few with Elvis, but more recently had launched a career as a serious film actress with *Carnal Knowledge*, a film directed by Mike Nichols, and in a riveting performance as Blanche DuBois in *Streetcar Named Desire*.

Though I had never met him, I called Peter Scarlett, the film festival head. I told him I was a lit prof who had just done a televised interview with Gore Vidal and that I wanted to put my hat in to interview Ann-Margret. I expected to be rebuffed, but he suggested that we meet, and we did so a few days later in his office. As was the case with Vidal, I felt that if I were going to interview Ann-Margret, I had to be as fully knowledgeable about her as possible. There were some, I knew, who managed to wing interviews, to propel themselves along by sheer improvisation. I considered myself fast on my feet, but I needed to show Peter Scarlett that I could be a bear at preparation.

All the prepping I did before meeting Scarlett proved unnecessary. We hit it off because I was a bit of a film buff, but also because, from the start, I was interviewing him—letting him tell me all about the festival's history and what films were planned and how they had managed to get Ann-Margret, and I was lobbing a slew of other questions that simply flowed from my curiosity and ability to keep conversation moving. I was hired! No fee, but that didn't matter. I was jazzed just to be interviewing Ann-Margret.

Before the event there was a gathering to meet Ann-Margret and her husband, Roger Smith, at the home of a rich Pacific Heights film festival patron. I noticed how gushy and even sycophantic many acted around her. When Peter Scarlett introduced me as the man who would be interviewing her, I made eye contact and firmly shook her hand, then turned to her husband, Roger Smith, as Peter introduced me to him. I was surprised to hear Ann-Margret say to me with a throaty laugh, "You'll be gentle with me, won't you?" I came back with some cheesy, faux charming line about how I could never be anything but gentle with a woman like her, especially with her husband there. But I

was once again surprised, as I had been by Gore Vidal, by the woman
I met backstage later that evening, before the interview. Ann-Margret
seemed nervous. "This is not like acting," she said to me in a voice laced
with fear. "I'm going to be out there with no role. Just me." It was hard
for me to believe that this woman, who had not only starred in many
films and done stage work, but had also gone all sequined up onto Las
Vegas stages on a motorcycle, was experiencing a kind of performance
anxiety. I spoke soothingly, reassuring her that we would have a fine
conversation and that she would be terrific.

Though I hadn't been gushy with her when we met, I was in my introduction. A local film critic told me later that you would have thought
I was introducing Lillian Gish. She came out, looking radiantly at the
audience as I settled into one of the large on-stage armchairs—only to
realize, as she came over to sit in the other one, that I had seated myself
in the chair that Peter Scarlett had told me was to be hers. I was facing
the audience square on while she was turned toward me, as though she
was the interviewer and I the interviewee. I felt like a major fuck-up, but
I told myself the show must go on and my job was to continue to make
her feel at ease, so I extended a warm welcome to her and began with a
question about her metamorphosis into serious acting.

H. G. Welles and Henry James had a once-famous saturation-selec-
tion debate about the novel—Welles speaking out in favor of a kind of
large and sprawling, put-everything-on-the-canvas style versus James's
idea of the figure in the carpet, with all Is dotted and Ts crossed. You
can throw everything into an interview and cut the broadest swath or
focus and pare it down. An interviewer can concentrate completely on
the person being interviewed and be as removed as possible, much like
the narrative voice in a novel that guides everything but is unobtru-
sive. Then there is the interviewer who brings in knowledge and self. A
good interviewer can make a dull subject a lot more interesting by self-
performance but runs the risk of sounding self-involved, and it isn't the
interviewer that the audience has come to see or hear. I approached my
first couple of interviews as I had early on approached teaching. My interviews were subject-centered, just as I had wanted my classroom to be
student-centered. Jim Lehrer of the "News Hour" would tell me many
years later that a really good interviewer ought to be invisible.

By those standards, I was a really good interviewer with Ann-Margret, though my style inevitably evolved, morphed, changed over the years. I would become unfettered and more confident, like in the classroom, trying to weave in my own comments and perceptions. Being polite was always an imperative, as was being thoughtful and intelligent without trying to be showy (though, I would later discover, showiness was not beyond me). I kept the questions coming with Ann-Margret, kept my eyes locked on her, listened raptly to her as I had to Bellow and Vidal, despite his anti-Semitic cracks. When I mentioned Elvis and she spoke wistfully of "that gentleman," I remarked that she could be Blanche DuBois describing ex-beau Shep Huntleigh or Belle Reve before it was sold. When she said her marriage to Roger Smith was one of the longest ones in Hollywood, I pushed her to "tell us why" and got her to muse about how two people so close knew how to push each other's buttons, and how the two of them had learned not to push. I got her to tell me about her husband's struggle with myasthenia gravis and how she got so heavily into the character of Blanche that she nearly lost her mind—which led us to a discussion of acting, which led to a conversation about her early beginnings in show business and where she came from, and then back to the differences in her acting career now. A full interview. A lot of information, personal and professional. Nothing spectacular, but engaging, especially to anyone interested in Ann-Margret. When we finished, she swept me in her arms and kissed me on the lips—prompting my brother, Vic, who was in the audience, to remark that it was the only time he felt sibling rivalry.

I felt good about the interview, but apologized profusely to Peter Scarlett and the others involved for having plunked myself down in the wrong chair. I felt stupid about it, but I also felt I had accomplished something. I believed it went well, but how does one truly know? Part of me felt like a grand success and part of me like a fuck-up over the chair, and part of me had no idea how I really did.

. . .

MY DAUGHTER, Lauren Brett, was born in San Francisco's Kaiser Hospital on March 17, 1977. Seeing life that Leslie and I made was my life's greatest thrill to date, and we were both deeply relieved to have a healthy baby.

I think having a child did a lot, too, to help curb some of the more toxic physical aggression I had been warring with. Not that therapy and karate hadn't also helped, and not that a big part of me didn't inwardly, secretly continue to revel in, even celebrate, the idea of masculine strength and if necessary, violence. But now I was a dad, and I wanted to keep my child protected and safe, and those feelings gave me greater caution about my own aggression.

I had a pretty good life. We had purchased our first home, in San Anselmo. My friend Phil Bronstein—who would later take over as editor of a local newspaper, the *San Francisco Examiner*, and marry Sharon Stone—visited me in our new digs and said to me, "You have it all. You have everything I could ever want." Jim Ragan, one of my cronies from Ohio U., who was by now a poet and a U.S.C. film prof and who, coincidentally, also paired off with movie stars, living *in seriatim* with Dyan Cannon and Susan Blakeley—came to visit from Southern California and echoed Phil's sentiments, telling me, "You have the life I want." But a guy like Ragan, living with movie stars, had himself a pretty desirable life, too. I jokingly offered him a year's exchange, but with marriage and now fatherhood, those kinds of fantasies, like my aggressions, had receded into a greater sense of domesticity or perhaps—as Gore Vidal once claimed of married men, especially those with progeny—greater docility.

When we brought Lauren home, I put on the stereo, and Leslie and I looked at our newborn; in all her tininess and sweetness and utter helplessness and fragility, she filled me with the need to protect and the certainty that I would love her with the fullness and bounty of a lifetime. When Stevie Wonder came on singing "Isn't She Lovely," Leslie, who stood holding and cradling her, got emotional.

I was a tenured professor, and tenure—as I joked to my students by echoing the famous Erich Segal line about love from *Love Story*—was never having to say you're sorry. I was now a homeowner and the father of a lovely infant girl, as well as the husband of a beautiful scientist who loved fine music and played violin and piano. But even with the exhilaration of fatherhood, and despite all I had to be thankful for, I lamented inwardly that at thirty-three, the age Christ was when they nailed him to the cross, I still was not the writer I thought I would be. I soon enough realized, too, that in agreeing with Leslie to share childcare, I had set up another impediment to reaching that goal.

It was important to me to be like Phil Donahue or Alan Alda, paradigmatic men of the era who had managed to set themselves apart as good, sensitive, feminist men, presumably without losing maleness. I was evolving. It was all part of the zeitgeist, but I felt good, liberated, by accepting new rules that said men can be sensitive and emotional, that fathers and mothers need to share childcare. I wore my daughter on my back, in the pack I toted her in, like a badge of honor.

But another world was opening too. Sydney Goldstein, who would later run San Francisco's City Arts and Lectures, a premiere venue for cultural, art and entertainment figures—was in charge of the public speaking program at the College of Marin. Knowing my history with Saul Bellow, she asked if I would interview him. I agreed. On the day of the interview, Sydney told me Bellow had been moody and expressed a preference not to be interviewed. I wound up, instead, merely introducing him and did so lavishly, as I did with Ann-Margret, doting on his achievements and also on how kind he had been to me on that cold, snowy Chicago day when I took the El out to surprise him in his office. He seemed smaller to me this time, more delicate really, and I sat there with all the others in the audience as he read a story of his that had just appeared in *The New Yorker* called "A Silver Dish." It was my first exposure to writers getting fat fees simply for reading their work, and a number of those in the audience expressed displeasure to me about it afterward.

Soon after, I did an interview for Sydney with the socialist writer Michael Harrington, author of a book about poverty, *The Other America*, which I read and was influenced by as an undergraduate. It was part of my early education as a young, would-be radical. To prepare, I read essays by Harrington and reread *The Other America* as well as his other, more recent work, and we had an enlivening and satisfying on-stage conversation. It gave me a rush to bring ideas on stage, as I loved bringing them out in the classroom—getting Harrington to open up in front of an audience mostly disposed to being in his corner and lapping up what he had to say, making him look good. The process, the dynamic, whatever you want to call it, excited me, and I was high on the pleasure and felt natural. Then Sydney asked me, weeks later, to introduce Susan Sontag.

My role as a public intellectual was being launched.

By now head of City Arts and Lectures, Sydney asked me soon after to interview Isaac Bashevis Singer, who had won the Nobel Prize for Literature and whom I had gophered for in Madison. When I began the interview, I asked him what it was like to win the Nobel. He answered, in his soft voice and Yiddish accent, with a keen sense of comic timing: "The first man who asked me how did I feel to vin the Nobel Prize, I told him I felt surprised. I felt delighted. Then others asked me. All these nice people from the newspapers and radio stations. How did I feel? I kept telling them. I felt surprised. I felt delighted. I ask you. [Pause] How many times can a man feel surprised and delighted?" I kept plying Singer with questions. I asked him so many questions that he paused and remarked on it in a way that sounded a tad crotchety. Then I asked him what I thought was the real money question, and his answer brought down the house.

Me: "Do you believe in free will?"

Singer: "I have no choice."

It wasn't until over a year later that I read in a literary journal the transcript of an interview in which he offered the same, identical quip. Like Vidal's line about being a born-again atheist, it was boilerplate. So I learned to avoid asking too many questions and not to flatter myself that I was inspiring great zinger lines.

I had applied for and was awarded a one-semester sabbatical, since the traditional automatic year-long sabbaticals were things of the past. I did some scholarly writing, which had always come easily, but my intention was to work on fiction. I soon learned how difficult it was with a baby to look after. Lauren was pretty easy, but when she wasn't napping, she had to be fed and changed and cared for. I found the time I spent taking care of her to be increasingly difficult. Leslie came home from work, and I would sound off like a martyr about how hard it was to go for hours doing nothing but childcare, how it made it impossible for me to find consistent blocks of writing time and do the work I felt mattered. I felt empathy for women who cared for children and pushed aside what restlessness or spirit of adventure they might possess. I realized, too, something that Singer said to me in our on-stage interview about the need to write. He compared it to the sex drive and declared, in his broken English, that if you wanted to do it, you would somehow find the time.

I couldn't seem to find the time, and the place, our new home, was full of distractions. I felt the only way I would get serious writing done would be to find a work space or a room of my own. Since I couldn't afford to rent a place, I hired first an older woman and then a young girl to come in at an hourly rate and care for Lauren while I tried to write. Then I joined up with two other women writers who also had small children and hired a woman who, coincidentally, was once the wife of an accomplished contemporary fiction writer whose work I admired. Martha had a sunny disposition and seemed intelligent and refined, and the three of us felt lucky to have found someone of her caliber to care for our kids. Until I came back after a few hours of trying to grind out prose to find my darling Lauren with a huge bite on her cheek that one of the other children had inflicted. "She's a biter," Martha explained with flat equanimity, as she pointed to the child who left her teeth imprinted in my daughter's cheek. I held Lauren in my arms and felt like I might faint from the helplessness I felt at seeing the ugly bite mark on her face. Then Martha said to me: "Lauren cried a lot and wanted me to hold her. I didn't think that was a very good idea, because she has to learn to deal with adversity, but I did. I held her briefly." That, for the rest of the sabbatical, was the end of handing my daughter over to another's care.

After the sabbatical, it was even harder to write. I was still a full-time classroom teacher, and at S.F. State that meant a four-course load. It galled me that Ivy League profs or those at U.C. Berkeley and Stanford never taught more than one or two classes, and most never even deigned to do their own grading. Of course, their classes were often enormous, especially introductory ones, but the fact that I did all my own grading was a point of pride. Good men work hard and remain stoic about it. Tenure had not changed or withered my intention of being a fully committed teacher and spending lots of time with students. I remembered a book called *Academic Gamesmanship*, which presented the professoriate as good pay and perquisites for little work—quite the deal for those slick enough to get in the club. I felt, by contrast, that I worked hard, gave much to my students and put a lot of time into teaching for what seemed meager pay compared to remuneration in the private sector. I had a Ph.D., tenure and a modicum of prestige and status, but I felt vaguely penurious.

We had taken out a second loan to buy our home, and with Leslie not working and seeking a new career, I was paying bills at month's end and realizing that my monthly expenses often exceeded what I earned. It had been another source of pride to me that I was not caught up in the pursuit of money, and I still talked a great sixties rhetoric, both in and out of the classroom, about anti-materialism, money being the root of too much pain and misery. But I had difficulty managing it. Like Bellow's Herzog, I often felt I was money's medium rather than the reverse. The notion of being a provider of child care to my daughter was considerably less threatening to my sense of masculinity than the idea that I was not a good enough earner for her. I had made many friends outside the academy, a lot of them successful professionals. I seemed to be drawn especially to doctors, usually specialists with wives who either didn't work or worked for piddling wages. My wife, on the other hand, felt she needed to work, but decided to go to law school. I had profound doubts that we could make it solely on my salary. It seemed terribly unfair to me that I had come so far to make so little, especially compared to my doctor friends and other successful men I knew. By this time Blackie was a multimillionaire. But then I berated myself for being concerned about money, given how lucky I was compared to the multitudes out of work, the undercompensated and those doing jobs they loathed. I was fortunate to have a job I liked with the security of tenure and a steady income that was decent, by broader standards.

I had a metaphoric money moment when I went to see Mel Swig, a leader in the San Francisco Jewish community and head of the world famous Fairmont Hotel, which his family owned. Mel was also head of the advisory board of the local Jewish newspaper, and I went to see him to plead on behalf of my friend Phil Bronstein, who was then assistant editor of the Jewish paper and craved the editor's job. Herb Gold and I had tried to convince Phil's boss, the editor of the paper and a former hockey reporter, to include a literary supplement, but we soon realized that we were dealing with a man who had no interest in anything literary. When I asked Mel to make Phil the editor, Mel exclaimed about the ex-hockey reporter: "Do you know what he makes? I can't even imagine how he lives on it." The figure he threw out was considerably higher than my professor's salary.

It was, at least in part, the gnawing sense that there was not enough money, and that I was an inadequate provider, that set me off on a job search. Writing was bringing no worthy creative results and, except for an occasional book review or journalistic piece that I cranked out, it was bringing no income. Interviewing, however, was something I knew by then that I could do. My strengths were in leading conversations and building rapport. I had humor and natural verbal skills. I had some erudition. Some got paid for doing interviewing. So why not see what possibilities were out there? A perfect sideline gig, I felt, would provide extra income but not take away from my academic life. And it would only be a temporary career. The creation of great literary art was still my priority. I would cold call people in power.

Television seemed like territory I ought to explore—in part because I interviewed Vidal for television, but also because I grew up watching talk and interview programs on TV. Phil Donahue, with his liberalism and feminist sympathies, seemed like a good role model. Couldn't I, on a local level, be Donahue? It was worth investigating. I thought of those I watched on television as a youngster, like Merv Griffin and Mike Douglas, and I felt that I could do as good a job.

I needed a ruse to get to meet some of the big shots. I decided to use the journalist's role and see them under the pretext of writing an article on people who run television stations. Why not? It might be an article worth writing. The first interview I lined up was with Russ Coughlin, the tall, white-haired general manager of the local ABC-TV affiliate station, KGO. A major figure in San Francisco, where he was born and raised, he had high visibility as a political commentator and was generally considered, at least by San Francisco standards, a right-winger. Years later Russ and I would become friends, but at this juncture, I was just a would-be journalist interviewing a powerful man, with a hidden agenda of finding some way into the clubhouse he ran.

Not everyone likes being interviewed, but it can be flattering. It allows the person being questioned to hold forth, to feel important, to play educator, enlightener and storyteller and assume the role of a kind of performer. Even men of power, perhaps especially men of power, have their own needs to put on masks and give narratives. People often want to make you feel they are important, and they can find ego gratification in the curiosity about and interest that you show in them, the questions that you ask, the attention. The interviewer's art involves being a bit of the courtesan.

I learned a lot from talking with Coughlin—about him and about the industry, even about some of his political views—but I didn't have the nerve to break role and ask him if he wanted to employ an aspiring would-be talk show host. I made similar appointments with Fran Martin, then the head of the local NBC affiliate, and Zev Putterman, program director for the public television station KQED. Martin—patrician scion of the rich San Francisco newspaper clan that then owned the *San Francisco Chronicle* as well as the TV station—seemed impressed by my academic title. But when I haltingly inquired about the possibility of doing work for the station, his demeanor changed, as if a shade came down. "Talk to Jim Shock, " he said. So I did. I talked to Jim Shock, who produced the local midday show. I could see myself hosting "Midday," but I knew that I needed to start modestly. I hesitantly broached the subject of doing one-on-one interviews with serious-minded guests on the show, which mainly had lighter fare geared for stay-at-home moms. Jim Shock told me he could use a film reviewer. Well, that would be a start. A foot in the TV door. Then he asked if I wanted to join him at a nearby joint for a beer.

Shock seemed to get chummy with me in the bar, though I sized him up as one of those guys who talks and talks at you without really making a connection, who mainly likes to spend time in the bar with darts and yakking and plenty to drink. I was grateful to him that he gave me a shot. Except that after that day I made call after call to him without getting a call back.

If I had a shot, it seemed to me, public TV was a more likely fit. KQED broadcast my interview with Gore Vidal and a eulogy I had written for Buriel Clay. Zev Putterman, who headed up programming, was the son of a rabbi. He had a personal history that included drug addiction and Synanon, the rehab program that turned out to be a dangerous cult. Synanon made headlines when a former member—whom its leader, Chuck Dederich, viewed as an enemy turncoat—found a rattlesnake in his mailbox.

"You think I would hire you to be a talk show host? Are you out of your mind?" That was Zev Putterman's response to my gentle inquiry about possibly hosting a show on public television. "I'm supposed to put on a guy who has zero experience except for interviewing that freak Gore Vidal?"

"No. No," I backpedaled with some embarrassment. "I wasn't talking seriously about hosting a show, really. That's more a long-term goal. I need seasoning. But I'm interested in breaking into television. Doing interviews or political commentary."

"Then learn about it. You think because you teach English to college students you can come into television with no experience? Do production. Learn things from the bottom up. This is no mickey-mouse industry."

I felt humiliated. It was nearly enough to make me give it all up. Then, to my surprise, to my shock, so to speak, Shock called me and said he wanted to test me as film reviewer for the midday show.

I had seen *Saturday Night Fever*, and I decided it would be a great film for me to review. I loved the music, the dancing, the portrayal of lives going nowhere that were a lot like lives I knew growing up in Cleveland. I remembered Leo Litwak, exclaiming to me about *Saturday Night Fever*, "The sexuality. I was blown away by the sexuality." I went to see it three more times, and I had lots to say about it and, I felt, the energy to say it well and convincingly.

I handed the producer a neatly typed copy of the film review I'd written. As soon as it was replicated and fed into the teleprompter I was seated in a comfortable chair behind a small table on a studio set with potted plants and a screen of plain black behind me. I read my lines and tried to project enthusiasm, excitement, ease. I was, in fact, consciously trying to perform. The producer and crew were pleasant and professional as they filmed me. I made certain to thank each one of them. But I could glean no real reaction from them either positive or negative. I waited for a call back from Shock. It never came.

I went to see another television big-shot, Fred Zehender, news director of the local Oakland-based TV station KTVU. Zehender had a reputation as a good guy. When I came clean and told him I wanted to work in television, he said, "We're going to be doing some news editorials. Let me talk to our news director, and we'll see if we can find a place for you."

This seemed to me like it might lead to something. But I was wounded by the way things went with Shock, and I wanted to know what happened with the test, my review of *Saturday Night Fever*. I continued to call him, but he never called me back. It was humiliating. I decided to try once more but this time, instead of giving my name to the receptionist when she asked for it, I simply said: "This is someone referred to him by Fran Martin." That, of course, was true, though the original referral had occurred months before. It got Shock on the line.

I decided to be direct. I asked what he thought of my film review. "I loved it and I hated it," was his cryptic answer. "I'll call you if I need you," he abruptly added, then hung up.

When I did my first editorial for Fred Zehender, I learned directly from him what Shock might have hated. My language. Too cerebral. Too academic. Too sesquipedalian, as Cecil Hemley pointed out years ago. Zehender gave me my first big lesson in language control. "You're writing for a wide audience. You have to be easy for viewers to understand, precise, concrete. Simple even." He was telling me the kinds of things I had told English composition students for years, but that I had to hear now for myself. I wanted to please Fred, and so as I began doing commentaries—alternating weekly with Reg Murphy, then publisher of the *San Francisco Examiner*—I took pains to craft pieces that would be readily understood by as wide an audience as possible. It wasn't easy. I had been speaking for too long in academese, and I joked with friends that people called in to say they knew Murphy, but who was the other schmuck doing commentaries?

I learned quickly the power of television by the number of people who mentioned they had seen me. I also learned how much television depended on the visual. Fred would send a guy out with a minicam, and we'd do an editorial on the Bay Bridge or Treasure Island or some place—it didn't seem to matter where so long as it had a high visual component. I had ideas to communicate, but the content was of much less interest than the visual backdrop. When we went on a shoot, it was just me and the minicam guy, no cue cards or teleprompters. I felt more like an actor or a political candidate than a news commentator, but once I joined AFTRA—the American Federation of Television and Radio Artists—and my first checks began to arrive, I felt I was embarking on a new career that was exciting and would help pay for our mounting bills. That is until Rich Hall, who ran the Channel 2 newsroom, decided to pull the plug on the Reg Murphy and Michael Krasny editorials. It taught me how swiftly things can be deep-sixed in television. It set me off once again on a search.

.   .   .

I WAS PUSHING AWAY the desire to write. Writing had become like being long hours with a lover who barely acknowledges you or lies immobile while you pant ardently. I had a rap down about how good, quality fiction writers, like my colleagues Leo Litwak or Herb Wilner, couldn't find a publisher, how the cartels, with their bottom-line mentality, had taken over the publishing industry. The old-guard, established novelists, like Bellow and Updike and Roth, would inevitably have readers, but if you were trying to break into novel writing and you had a literary sensibility and a book that didn't have mass selling power or the potential link to television or film, you were out. Jerzy Kosinski's *Steps*, which won a National Book Award, had been sent over the transom to a slew of publishers by a writer for *California* magazine. No one recognized the book, and no one wanted to publish it. Only one editor noted that the style reminded him of Kosinski. The industry was changing and moving toward celebrity books and blockbusters, with an occasional literary success story that was mass marketed, like John Irving's *The World According to Garp*.

Leo Litwak had praised *The Rossman Odyssey*, my novel about a guy who lusts after the dream of being a rock star. "So many first novels, despite promising moments," he wrote, "are labored and unbalanced. Krasny's novel is different. I am impressed. It is not merely promising; it is realized. The achievement is of the order of Roth's *Portnoy's Complaint*. The language is supple. He almost immediately hits a nerve and doesn't let up. It is painful comedy. The only difficulty he may have in publishing it is the pain it might cause. I, nonetheless, expect it to be published, expect that Krasny will achieve some celebrity from its publication, and that this book may initiate a distinguished career as a novelist." Still, *Rossman* languished as a closet novel. It was easier to blame my ongoing failure as a writer on the changing publishing industry.

But the country was also different, less literary, more commercial. The gloom from long gas lines and Americans held hostage in Teheran had overshadowed, for the majority of Americans at the polls, the accomplishments of Jimmy Carter's presidency, the attempted high road he'd taken on human rights and the peace accord he helped broker at Camp David. Seeing Egyptian leader Anwar Sadat get off a plane and step on Israeli soil caused me to cry, something I could do now since I had embraced my emotions and transformed myself into the new-style, sensitive male. Carter's brokered peace between Sadat and Israel's Menachem Begin would inevitably lead to the murder of Sadat by Islamic fanatics and greater bloodletting between Arab and Jew. And I was not optimistic about Reagan's presidency. I had seen how tight-fisted and skinflintish he had been as governor of California, especially when it came to funding social programs and higher education. He was, unlike Nixon, a likeable character who knew how to play the role of nice guy and who could make you like him with his aw-shucks boyishness and self-deprecation. But I felt certain he would never demonstrate compassion for those in dire need, since he'd slashed funds for the blind and the disabled while he was governor. As a professor, I resented his unwillingness to approve raises for us and his loose talk when students rioted in Berkeley about how he would do whatever was needed even "if it takes a bloodbath."

The Democrats, though, seemed weak. Carter seemed especially so in dealing with the Khomeini regime's invasion of the U.S. embassy and taking of America hostages. But Republicans seemed to care mainly about saving money on entitlements and cutting back tax expenditures, even though they were perfectly willing to spend huge sums on defense programs like Star Wars instead of on social programs.

My need for a more suitable presidential candidate than Carter or Reagan led me to Illinois congressman John Anderson. And my need for more personal income and a political platform for my views led me to KTIM, a small radio station in my home county of Marin. The station was very alternative rock and roll, what used to be called free-form—the sort of place where you might, as I did on my first visit, run into a group like the way offbeat Plasmatics. Though owned by the conservative local newspaper *The Independent Journal,* it was essentially run by hippies. I went in to talk to the station manager, with tapes in hand of my interview with Vidal and political commentaries I did on Channel 2. My proposal was simple. I would do a once-a-week interview program focusing on profiling people who lived in Marin. There were many artists, writers, filmmakers and rock and rollers living in the county, and I proposed that I would do an hour interview with a different personality each week. Cody Ryan, the station manager, was enthusiastic and agreeable. The station was being sold, he told me, and could use a program with some local and public affairs merit to it. The only problem was that his enthusiasm was based on the assumption that I was offering my services for free. I told him that I didn't expect much, perhaps a hundred dollars a show, but that I should be compensated since I intended to do all the leg work in finding and booking guests and doing the interviewing.

"A hundred a show? One hundred? One C note? You gotta be out of your tree. You have any idea what kind of budget we're operating with here? The DJs work for close to nothing. Like four or five bucks an hour. They'd skin you and me alive if I paid you a hundred bucks for a one-hour show." I knew this wasn't exactly big-time radio, and the shabby office I was in above *The Independent Journal* spoke volumes about how much of a shoestring budget the station must have been trying to get by on, but I wanted some kind of compensation. I told Cody that, as a member of AFTRA, I had been getting over twice the impossibly high C-note mark for two-to-three-minute television commentaries. I also told him that I knew they were a small radio station, but since they were both AM and FM, they could simulcast me. I really wanted to do the program, and I did not want money to be the stumbling block. I went down to $75 per show and he countered with $50, adding, "that's going to be a bitch, and it's as high as I can go." I assessed things and figured I was not coming out too badly. I'd have an extra two hundred a month to help pay our seemingly insurmountable bills while Leslie continued on in law school. More important, I would have my own show. The tricky part was what to do with it.

I began my radio program at KTIM with Rollin Post, the premiere political commentator in Northern California and someone with whom I knew I would enjoy talking politics. Rollin showed up for my first

9 A M. Sunday broadcast in tennis togs. He was a great talker and I enjoyed spurring him on—sharing ideas, analysis and quips and generally letting him do most of the talking, serving up questions like a softball pitcher who wants the batter to hit for distance. I learned even more how important it is to engage, listen and keep the person you are interviewing interested, to make the conversation a genuine give and take of ideas. Rollin had strong political views and, like me, was a good liberal. He refrained, though, from fully expressing his personal views about Reagan, just as I had done in my televised political commentaries to give myself an aura of journalistic objectivity—something I would later realize is probably oxymoronic.

Some of the skills I had honed in the classroom were useful. Talking on the radio felt natural. I liked it. I was at ease with it. Which doubtless was why it seemed of much less value to me than words in print, than literature. My kind of talk with Vidal or Ann-Margret, Michael Harrington or Rollin Post, took work and preparation but went out into the air and felt more perishable to me than anything on the page. Writing, by contrast, was arduous, done in solitude and moored to struggle. The high I got during the flow of the interview with Rollin Post was tempered by my knowledge that it was heard by only a small sliver of a small radio station's audience.

That year, Marin was skewered in an NBC-TV special called "I Want It All Now," as a too-affluent enclave of hedonism. Hot tubs and peacock feathers were the operative symbols that became associated with life in Marin County, and those images, of wealth and self-indulgence, were multiplied by the publication of a book by Cyra McFadden called *The Serial.* It was really a comic book, a satiric spoof of the excesses of Marin County's "lifestyle." I liked the fact that Cyra ridiculed all the weird kinds of human-potential manias that were rife in Marin. The county was too rich, too materialistic and too inundated by human-potential seekers and human-potential gurus like Werner Erhard and their acolytes. But I wanted to counter the stereotypes people had of Marin and Marinites, just as I had wanted, throughout my boyhood and young manhood, to counter stereotypes I believed people had of cheap or overly aggressive Jews. There were, I knew, many talented people living in Marin who were making significant social contributions. They were the ones, along with the famous, whom I wanted to get on the air, and I decided to call my program—to my eventual embarrassment at the cheesiness that nonetheless made people smile—"Beyond the Hot Tub." If you wanted to do radio, I rationalized, you had to risk being cheesy. After all, Barbara Boxer, who would later become a congresswoman and then a United States senator, vied for a place doing political commentaries on KTIM that she wanted to call "Boxer Shorts."

The easy part for me was the interviewing. Getting guests, especially more celebrated guests, turned out to be the far greater challenge. Sally Stanford was my second interview. A famous Marinite who had been the madam of a house of prostitution, Stanford had published a book about her life, made into a film starring Dyan Cannon called *A House Is Not a Home.* She owned a restaurant in Sausalito, called Valhalla, and held forth there every night, seated in a huge chair that looked like a throne, spinning stories to whomever listened about the cat house she ran and the figures she knew, like legendary San Francisco mayor Sunny Jim Rolfe. I picked Stanford up at the Valhalla and drove her over to KTIM for the interview, and I was both amused and appalled on the drive over. Appalled by what turned out to be her racism. Amused because the local paper had been running articles about prostitutes hitchhiking in Sausalito by Highway 101 and giving drivers quick blowjobs. The newspaper called them hitch hookers.

"What do you think about these hitch hookers I've been reading about, Sally?" I asked her as we drove to the studio. Stanford had no clue what I was talking about, so I explained, noting that one article reported that a hitch hooker allegedly did six guys in less than twenty minutes. Without a beat Stanford fired, "Good business woman."

Then, somehow, we got to talking in the car about some of the Bay Area old timers, including Mel Wax, a public broadcaster who worked for many years with Rollin Post. "He's a nigger," Stanford blurted. I thought I was hearing things. "What?" I asked in disbelief.

"Mel Wax. He's a nigger." Well, Mel Wax was pretty dark, all right, although I don't know if he was black. As one of my black students said of Sadat, Wax might not have been able to get served in the South during the Jim Crow years. But here I was confronted by the awful "N" word again, not knowing how to respond. It was hard for me even to say the word. When I was teaching black students James Weldon Johnson's *Autobiography of an Ex-Colored Man,* a sweet young black woman named Sandra laughingly said, "Why don't you just say it, Doctor K? Go ahead." So I said it. Right in class, in front of some thirty to forty black students; I shook my head and gulped and said it, before Richard Pryor went on to repudiate it and Kramer of Seinfeld flailed hecklers with it during a stand-up comedy routine. It was a pedagogical imperative—no different, I had decided, than talking about Mark Twain's Nigger Jim. The students laughed their asses off.

"Mel Wax isn't . . . what you called him. And that's an awful word."

"He's a nigger," Stanford stated flatly. Should I have taken her back to the Valhalla and refused to interview her? No, the show had to go on, and I, above all, had to be a pro, a cardinal rule. I would go ahead with the interview, just as I had with Vidal. Yet I felt compelled at least to speak out, and I decided to do so as I pulled up with her into the parking lot of *The Independent Journal.*

I put the car into park and turned to her with a serious look, so she would know that what I had to say mattered. What I wanted to say was something with real feeling like, "I don't want to have this interview get off on the wrong foot, but I need to tell you that nigger is an ugly and hurtful word." I was looking her right in the eye, about to say the words, but I saw the overly made-up face of an ignorant old woman and realized that, whatever I said, it would not only be futile, but it would be more for me than for Sally Stanford. So I stayed mum and told myself I would speak up after the interview ended. But, after talking with her for an hour, politely asking her one question after another for the live broadcast, it was difficult to break role. By what passes today for good broadcasting, I should have been immediately confrontational, asking as my first question: "Tell me why you still use that ugly, racist 'N' word." But this was then.

I continued plucking people out of Marin who were worth interviewing, though the biggest names were the hardest to nail down. George Lucas, the filmmaker who created *Star Wars,* turned me down flat, and so did his wife at the time, Marcia, who had worked as his film editor and responded in effect, "No. I will not do the show. Never. Ever." I called Bill Graham, the famous rock entrepreneur, asking him to appear, and his response was, "What's in it for me? What do I get out of it?" I stumbled for a suitable reply, and our dialogue continued as I heard strange, chaotic sounds on the other end. "You hear that noise?" Graham suddenly exploded. "That's the kinda crap I gotta deal with. There's a whole rock band right here in my office now, and they've got the combined emotional maturity of one six-year-old. Now tell me why I should give you an hour of my time?"

An attractive young woman who worked with me at the station tried to get a famous playwright on the show by pitching him in a Mill Valley bar he hung out in. The playwright showed more interest in her than in being interviewed, and he wound up going off with her, somewhat drunk, to her apartment, where he sat down, lit a cigarette and asked her for sex. "Are you kidding?" she responded. "I don't even know you. Why would I want to have sex with you?" He looked down and said, "You don't want to have sex with me?" She said, "No. I definitely do not want to have sex with you." He said, "Okay," and then got up, casually sauntered out the window of her apartment and let himself down.

I called Rollo May, the famed psychoanalyst who lived in Tiburon, and he agreed to do the show if I would pick him up and drive him to the studio, like Sally Stanford. I respected Rollo May. I had read his work and found compelling his amalgam of myth and existential humanism and his grappling with big ontological questions. Out of respect I called him Dr. May and he, after asking me about myself and discovering that I had a Ph.D., called me Dr. Krasny. That set the tone for a formal-sounding interview, with Dr. May speaking haltingly, but intensely, in response to a range of questions. I took pride in the high level of our exchange, pleased by the erudite tone of the conversation. I believe, after all these years, now that the once weighty name of Rollo May is receding in memory, that my interview with him was a benchmark.

Cody decided to switch my broadcast time to Sunday evening, a much better fit. We agreed that we might even liven things up by taking phone calls. One night I had on Pierre Mornell, a Mill Valley psychiatrist who wrote a book about needy, suburban, stay-at-home women who went batty waiting for their uncommunicative husbands to return home from work. The book was called *Passive Men, Wild Women*, and its title prompted a call from a man who said he liked playing the passive role in sex and wondered why his girlfriend wasn't more agreeable to his infrequent requests that she whip him. Whereupon a woman's voice could be heard in the background shrieking, "Its not infrequent! It's not infrequent!"

By that time, I was managing to attract publicity. With so much attention on Marin, a local journalist picked up the "Beyond the Hot Tub" motif and profiled me, emphasizing the Marin-based personalities I interviewed and the fact that I was an English professor. I also mentioned in that profile that I was from Cleveland. The interviewer asked me if I knew Joe Esterhaz, the highly successful screenwriter of *Basic Instinct* and *Flashdance*, who then lived in Marin. "Yes, I knew Joe. He edited the school paper at Ohio University and took a class with me from Walter Tevis." I added that Tevis asked one day if anyone in the class knew Esterhaz. I raised my hand. Tevis then said, "Tell Mr. Esterhaz that there is a tradition at Harvard that allows the editor of the school paper not to come to class. That tradition does not hold in my class. Inform Mister Esterhaz that he is failing my class." Joe called me after the interview and made light of the incident to me over lunch, telling me that he had to admit to his kids that the story was true as I had told it. A few years later I was jolted when I went to see a movie of his called *Jagged Edge* featuring a lead character—a Machiavellian but astute prosecutor, played by Marin's Peter Coyote—whose name was Krasny.

Ronn Owens was then the host of a late nighttime radio program on KGO radio, the local ABC affiliate. I knew little about commercial radio, but I knew KGO was the most successful station in the Northern California market, one of the most successful in the country, and it had 50,000 watts of power. Owens struck me as what we would have, in my boyhood, called a fast-talking New York sharpie type, but I liked him, and we both had been drawn to the unlikely Anderson campaign. When I told him I worked in radio, and what kind of show I did, he said, "We've got a great starting team but our bench is weak. Why don't you send me a tape, and I'll pass it on to the P.D. Maybe we can get some fill in work for you." I didn't even know then what a P.D. (program director) was, but I figured, what the hell. I took his address and sent him a tape of the interview with Pierre Mornell.

. . .

KTIM WAS PURCHASED from *The Independent Journal* by a Los Angeles-based group of investors. That meant moving to classy new studios in another part of San Rafael and outraging the more faithful KTIM listeners by going more mainstream and no longer playing music on the cutting edge. In some ways the changes represented what would happen to the music radio industry as well as the book industry—increased homogenization that would drive out the experimental and innovative.

At KTIM, there was a white guy named Doug Wendt who did an all-reggae show, at 11:00 P.M. on Sundays, after I went off the air. When we were still a free-form station, above the old I.J. building, he would bring in Rasta characters nearly every week. The smell of marijuana was enough to give you a contact high. Doug had complained about what he called apartheid radio and was thankful for an hour at the experimentally inclined KTIM. One night he introduced me to a tall black man with dreadlocks. " Mike Krasny, meet the king of reggae. This is Bob Marley." We shook hands, and that was about it. But I remember thinking, as the station changed over, that moments like that one were unlikely to occur again. Sure enough, Wendt and his reggae show were sent packing.

Before we moved over to the new studios, I managed to get members of the Grateful Dead on air. Rock Sculley, the band's manager, showed up with Mickey Hart and Jerry Garcia, and there were deadheads swarming out into the street—as if they had the kind of magic, underground communication Thomas Pynchon wrote about in his novel about hippie precomputer communicating, *The Crying of Lot 49.* I knew little about the Grateful Dead or their music, but I had prepped and was pleased with how well the interview was going and how teddy-bear gentle Garcia seemed—until he suddenly startled me by taking a small gold spoon out of his pocket and a tightly wound, rubber-banded napkin; he casually opened it and started spilling white contents onto the spoon. I frantically signaled the engineer to go to a station break and public service announcement and said, firmly but kindly, to Garcia, "You can't snort coke here." As I said, marijuana was pretty common around the old KTIM, and not just when Doug Wendt and the Rastas were around. But cocaine made me concerned, especially with all the deadheads hovering around outside; the police could have flown in at any moment, and

I could have been tossed behind bars as some sort of accessory. Garcia smiled and simply said, "You can't?" and then methodically put everything back into his pockets.

In the new studio we had on Marty Balin, lead singer of Jefferson Starship, and his band. They passed a bottle of hooch around, swigged from it and got pie-eyed. I was concerned that the moment would get out of hand. But then Trish Robbins, a D.J. at KTIM and an ex-girlfriend of Balin's, came in, and everyone spontaneously began to sing the great Sam Cooke song "Having a Party." It was like the moment in Cameron Crowe's film *Almost Famous* when the rockers are on a bus and everyone starts singing the Elton John song "Tiny Dancer." Music takes over and everything else dissolves.

I interviewed Daniel Ellsberg, the presidential adviser and former war hawk, who had turned over the Pentagon Papers to *The New York Times*. I met with him at the new studios and saw the excitement his presence stirred among those who happened to be at the station that evening. Ellsberg struck me as tough-minded and deadly serious, humorless really, intense and dour, but I felt good about the interview, and I was glad I had on the air someone with such passionate opposition to war and nuclear weaponry. Important to me, personally, was the fact that, even though Ellsberg was a brilliant military tactician with an arcane understanding of the details of sophisticated armaments and nuances of foreign policy, I held my own with him. I realized something I had known since interviewing Saul Bellow—the bigger the name of the interviewee, the greater the heft of intellect, the more I wanted to rise to the challenge.

A wide variety of rock personalities lived in Marin: Janis Joplin, Journey, Santana, Maria Muldaur, Sammy Hagar, Van Morrison and a host of others. Grace Slick of Jefferson Starship was fun to talk to, though her speaking voice was surprisingly raspy, as if it had been battered—which it no doubt had been—by nicotine and booze. She had, in fact, positive things to say about booze and recreational drug use and the way both had made her feel—even as she spoke to me of the importance and necessity of breaking the hold they had had on her. I ended the interview, telling her what a pleasure it had been talking with her, and she whooped in response, then gave me a hug and left. Kissed by Ann-Margret and hugged by Grace Slick! Life, I thought, was changing in curious ways.

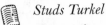 *Studs Turkel*

Chicago-born Studs Turkel is nearly deaf. We try different sets of headphones on him, including one set that looks like a pair of giant earmuffs. He's spent a lifetime listening in order to compile oral histories, and now he can hardly listen at all. His impairment leads him to boilerplate humor about hearing higher truths—in bed with instead of embedded journalists in Iraq, Scarpia instead of Scalia.

Studs is a klutz. Inept. Mechanically dumb. He's been that way his entire life. Never learned how to drive a car or use a word processor or do anything on a computer. It's not just his age or the Luddite excuse. He goofs up. He often forgot to press the tape recorder button or pressed the wrong button. He lost Martha Graham and Michael Redgrave and almost lost Bertrand Russell. The fact that he's a screw up and mechanically helpless probably gave him more drive, more of a need to prove himself. May have even kept him curious and pushed him on to a Pulitzer as he talked to people and—when he didn't screw up—recorded all they had to say about the Great Depression, work, religion, hope. At ninety he's still curious, still pushing himself. Punching, really. The way he talks has always reminded me of a boxer. He jabs away at ideas bare-knuckled and throws an occasional haymaker. He knows his epitaph. It will be, "curiosity did not kill this cat."

He invented himself as Studs in 1935, after reading James Farrell's *Studs Lonigan*. He calls himself an agnostic and says that's another way of saying he's a cowardly atheist. But his real roots are Jewish, overshadowed by a radical, secular brand of American idealism and activism that made him become more an American archetype than a man of any breed or tribe. Thomas Paine and Sam Adams are his heroes, and he is a hero to those who have honored labor and the union movement, championed civil rights and single-payer health plans, condemned capital punishment or preemptive war in Iraq or war in Indo-China or war in Grenada or war against the Sandinistas or war against pock-marked Noriega in Panama. He signed petitions for nearly every good, brave cause—petitions against Jim Crow, against the poll tax, against lynchings and against McCarthy—but he refused to sign a loyalty oath and was branded a Commie. He assures me he was no hero. He was scared as hell.

But being a part of causes greater than himself makes him feel greater than himself. He held on for decades to faith in the Marx-spawned notion of the sacred masses. "We need," says Studs, "to get over our national Alzheimers and recover our memory for the sake of our American spirit." The Democratic Party, he says—once the party of FDR and JFK and his own party—ought to dissolve if they don't find their testes, their gonads. Bush seems to him right out of W. C. Fields. Schwarzenegger, too. Yet he is convinced that the people know and that the people are still ahead of the game.

Don DeLillo

I'm trying unsuccessfully to get a laugh out of Don DeLillo. I've brought up déjà vu, which appears as a symptom from the toxic event in his novel *White Noise*, and he excitedly begins to tell me that something has just occurred to him concerning déjà vu. I ask if he feels we have had this conversation before, but he doesn't crack a smile, and he starts to talk about how time—past, present and future—may all be operating simultaneously. Could déjà vu simply be future time's leakage into our present?

Then we are on to *Libra*, his novel of the Kennedy assassination—sparked, years after that America-altering tragedy, when he learned that Lee Harvey Oswald had lived within a few blocks of him in the Bronx. DeLillo wouldn't have written the novel had he not discovered that, though Oswald was three years younger. They heard and saw the same things and, he learned, both had played hooky from school at the Bronx Zoo. All of which, he felt, gave him entrance into Oswald's mind. DeLillo is as much of New York and his generation, I tell myself, as I am of Cleveland and mine, but he has made what his senses took in come alive in print, captured the past from an embedded memory that may, who knows, be part of the same single continuum of time.

DeLillo is always pleasant at first with me, until seriousness begins to override the initial amenities. Now that we are old hands at on-air conversation, he seems especially felicitous and glad to see me before this sit down, displaying a wide smile. He holds gratuitous emotion in check and answers each of my questions with a kind of clenched seriousness. We are in each other's company for an hour every few years, and I wonder to myself what it would be like to be buddies with him, the way he characterizes his friendship with Paul Auster. "We're pals," he tells me when I ask why he dedicated his most recent book, *Cosmopolis*, to Auster.

He inscribed my copy of *Underworld* "To Michael: A Co-Conspirator," and recalling the inscription makes me mention paranoia, which entered his work in the seventies and eighties. DeLillo says it comes for him more out of the culture than out of his consciousness. In the nineties it moved out of the culture and more into cyberspace. It simply isn't as noticeable to him now as it once was. The word was overused and misused. People were saying they were paranoid about minor fears like mosquito bites. Paranoia moved off into the culture's dark corners.

My parents, unlike DeLillo's, did not come from overseas, from Italy, but I find my most human link with him when I start asking about his Italian heritage. I reference an article that Gay Talese once wrote about not understanding how the great tradition of Italian storytelling fits with the dearth of great Italian-American storytellers in fiction, as opposed to film and as opposed to the abundance of Jewish-American and African-American storytellers. DeLillo says that he, and probably any of his fellow Italian-American authors, want to be seen as American storytellers. Speaking in a way, rare for him, that sounds personal, he tells me his parents came from Italy to America and found a different world. He was born here but duplicated what they had done.

Margaret Atwood

I picture Margaret Atwood looking under rocks for bugs with her brother. I see her as the little girl she was, with wild, wiry hair. We both laugh when I start the interview by telling her she looks younger with her feral hair. "Hair is an important motif," she tells me. "There's nothing I can do about it."

I have a picture of her in the Canadian woods, where her entymologist father hunted for insects. She talks about loving *Robinson Crusoe* as a girl and being able to start fires with two sticks. "I was a Brownie," she says, and then asks me if I was a boy scout. I tell her I was, and she tells me that me being a boy scout beams out of me.

I'm crazy about Atwood. Her intelligence and thoughtfulness and girlishness charm me.

She talks bluntly about gender differences. Men's images of their loved ones, she says, are all shot through with gauze. Women are harder and more practical. "It's the guy's wallet that's shot through. I didn't say that. Strike it. I give you Petrarch and Laura, Dante and Beatrice. Guys love at first sight more. They're visual. Appearance to them is more important." She will tell me in another interview that some fellow once told her that she had risen above being a woman. How feminism to her means three words. Separate bank accounts. She adds: "I take no stand on cosmetics."

Atwood was on a science track in high school. She wasn't good with numbers, though she was better with algebra because she found it a little more like literature. She grew up with scientists, which made her skeptical of science. She became a writer in the 1950s. *Cat's Eye* was "somewhat autobiographical" of her childhood years—the games she played, the schools she went to and the kind of people she knew. Writers take their own experiences, she says, and extend them outward. Her father would shake his head and decry what a loss to botany it was when she became a writer. She was a black sheep because she became a writer and not a scientist. Now she has a Booker Prize and international literary fame.

In the United States she is cast as American. In England they ask her what part of America she comes from. She never felt any particular hostility about being a Canadian. It's just not a very big category.

Critics and reviewers, Atwood says, have a hard time and can burn out quickly. "It's a hard job. Maybe they should spell each other off in tag teams." She adds that she writes reviews and serves as a judge for literary prizes. "It's hard, but someone has to do it. It's like giving blood or volunteering for your local fire department. It's a duty that one should do every once in a while."

She has a message of hope for a caller worried about the Patriot Act and government repression. She mentions Studs Turkel's book on hope and reassures the caller with words of advice. "Don't panic. Hold the line. Find calming activities. Breathing helps. Do a lot of yoga. The world has seen worse. It's still a democracy with congressmen who want to keep your civil liberties."

When I interview her again on stage a couple of years later, we hug warmly beforehand like a pair of old dancing partners. She is Scotch Presbyterian from the rural cold of Nova Scotia, but I regale her nevertheless with a Jewish joke. She is talking at dinner, before our on-stage conversation, about the parrot in her newly published dystopian novel, *Oryx and Crake*, and about linguistic experiments with parrots to teach language to autistic children. I tell her the one about the female parrot that repeatedly says one word and one word only. Horny. That's the only word the parrot knows. Its owner is told, by a friend, of a man with two parrots that chant Hebrew prayers. The owner and his friend decide to take the female parrot to the man with the two male parrots and put her in with them while they pray, hoping she'll learn holy words from them rather than continuing just to say the one word. So they do it. They take the female parrot and drive over to where the other male parrots are perched in a cage wearing small parrot prayer shawls and yarmulkes and davening, repeatedly bending back and forth in prayer. They put the female parrot in the cage with the male parrots. Immediately she squawks. "Horny." The two male parrots cease davening. They shout: "Our prayers have been answered!"

I remember when I interviewed her years before in her home near the University of Toronto for *Mother Jones* magazine. I can still see a strange assortment of flickerings in my mind—her cat resting near the kitchen walkthrough, a plate full of vitamins she took, slowly, one by one, as she popped each in her mouth. Vague, dimmed-by-time memory traces of her husband and her daughter. She had introduced Salman Rushdie the night before to a large crowd, and I told her I remembered her being tough and stoic, even though he was under the fatwa and she, too, had been threatened. She admits that it was "a bit nervous making." She smiles. "The tension is less now, but you never know. None of us do."

Grace Paley

Amazing Grace Paley is gracing my studio, seated across from me with a smile after our warm hug. It's hard not to think of her as a spark plug—short and squat, gray-haired, her vitality still intact and optimistic good nature on display. Considered by many to be our greatest living woman short-story writer, she sees herself more these days as a poet, though she is shy and nearly self-effacing when she mentions that Vermont has made her its poet laureate. After World War II, hers were the nation's first drops in the first wave of feminist writing. She wrote stories, kitchen dramas she called them, during the masculine fifties. She thought no one would ever read them, but she couldn't write anything else. She couldn't write a novel. At eighty, she tells me she would still write one if she could figure out how to do it, but her efforts have been, she insists, a waste of time, "all wrong," "pedestrian," "pedantic." Yet her stories continue to delight, especially those early stories that include voices of men and of an Irish housewife mother whose husband abandons her, and of Faith, who Grace likes to say, "works for me." She tells me she had to speak in other voices before she could speak in her own. But what do her stories do, I ask? She lets out one of her robust New York laughs. "I'll be damned if I know," she replies.

I ask her that question because her life has also been about politics. Protest. Gentle anarchic pushing. Organizing. Marching. She stammers when she speaks of her activism, but she finds the words to say what she needs to say—like her characters who, she tells me, speak well when they need to. "I hear people talk," she says. "When they're really speaking truthful, they speak well and I hear that. They somehow find the words. Of course I help them." She admits she writes better than she talks. Writing tells her what she doesn't know and not what she knows. But the real spark in her is the political, indefatigable radicalism forged in a Jewish world that is no more. A father who was the neighborhood doctor and who filled the house with classical music from the only Victrola on the block. He bullied his wife, yet Grace adored him, though she also stood up to him in the fifties since, as she put it, "I was living in Greenwich Village then." She believes there is still a Movement. Believes that the people in this country will never allow fascism, though she adds, "It's up to them." Believes in the fight for women's reproductive rights and the fights against racism, militarism, the arms trade and environmental despoilment. She sees all the dots connected. At eighty, it's difficult to say how many years are ahead of her. Maybe none, though she quickly adds that her brother lived to ninety-three. She is a perennial icon to politically conscious and literary women. She is a grandmother of biracial children. She is modest and sweet and girlish and shy. I thank her for the hour. She says, "Thank you for putting up with me."

6   The Big Show

WHEN YOU HAVE THE ACHE TO WRITE, the itch to
write, the desire that makes you believe you ought
to or need to write and you aren't writing, there is an empty place inside
you that you have to fill. I was filling it with teaching, radio, my wife,
my kid and lots of other people. I liked the stimulation I got talking to
others, establishing rapport. Yet writing, except for imagined or eventual readers, precluded interaction with others and was pretty much a
one-way street; it demanded enforced isolation.

"Whatever gives you a rush," was the philosophy of my English department crony Mike Gregory, and radio was giving me a rush, though
it seemed a poor substitute for the plodding, tough, solitary work of
novel writing and I still felt, on some level, that I was biding my time. I
was doing programs that focused on matters that I felt were important.
Hospice care. Homelessness. Environmental hazards. Citizenship. The
new KTIM studios were pleasant and clean, with new equipment and
a general manager who, though not unpleasant, reminded me of an in-
souciant bank branch manager.

In the meantime, there was KGO. Ronn Owens had taken the tape of
the interview I did with Pierre Mornell and passed it on to the station's
program director, who invited me to come in and talk with him about
doing fill-in work on the huge ABC station. The P.D. was a fairly low-
key guy, a former minister who later would run into trouble as a result
of an alleged affair with one of the station's few on-air women, a talk
psychologist. He was quick to inform me, when we met, that he considered Marin a small demographic of the station's overall listenership.

The subtext message was "don't be too Marin." He suggested I watch Ronn do his nighttime show and then perhaps I could do fill in. When out of courtesy I told David T.—the pony-tailed music P.D. at KTIM—I was going to be doing fill-in for KGO, he looked at me with wide-eyed wonder, as if I just told him I had won the lottery.

When I went to KGO to talk with the station's program director, I was struck by how impersonal, professional and bare it seemed compared to the small, new, youth-filled KTIM studios—where the walls were plastered with posters of contemporary rock groups and there was only one occasional news anchor instead of a beehive of news people, reporters in the field, and traffic copters. A combination of news and talk, KGO had become dominant in the Bay Area market, evolving from the early days of Ira Blue, a nasal voiced New York Jew who claimed to be the nation's first radio talk show host. Radio talk would continue to rise in popularity, and KGO would continue to be the number-one radio station in the market for decades to come. The station would, in fact, become one of the country's greatest radio success stories ever, and talk radio would keep its steady climb upward in listeners throughout the United States until over a quarter of all Americans would get most of their news and information from radio talk programs.

Being a good and forthright educator of the airwaves was my mission—mixing, as I did at KTIM, engaging, informative and celebrated people with topics that fulfilled the ideals of public service. Stations were even required, at this time, to air a quota of public affairs community programming, though that would be abolished under Ronald Reagan. Instead, a growing, festering and eventually insatiable demand for controversy would take flight and fill the airwaves. I was not even thinking of controversy when I first made my way through the KGO newsroom to the P.D.'s office, though I was aware enough of controversial and sensational television talk programs featuring shock figures like Joe Pyne and Wally George. Both used confrontation and verbal attacks on liberals and the counterculture as staples until, later on, Morton Downey and Bill O'Reilly took conservative, combative style to new levels of vulgarity and bullying. A calm and seemingly imperturbable former liberal, Cincinnati's Democratic mayor Jerry Springer, eventually would ratchet up ratings in television even more by getting willing guests to confront and assault each other. In radio there was Alan Berg, the liberal Denver-based talk host who had built a career on 50,000-watt KOA confronting right wingers, bigots, assorted Klansmen and white supremacists until a Neo-Nazi group called The Order gunned him down in 1984.

Talk radio at KGO was mild by contrast. Some controversy erupt-ed from hosts' takes on topics in the news and their interaction with callers, but there was mainly a wide assortment of interviews with news-makers, politicians, entertainers and even, in the case of the morning host Owen Spann, an occasional guest psychic like Sylvia Brown. Spann was deft and capable but a little bland and hardly what you would call a personality. He wasn't looking for controversy. He mainly got people to talk. Controversy for its own sake had not yet infected this leading talk station.

Before I went on air at KGO for the first time, I was scared. I was afraid of being exposed to so many people, making a fool of myself or getting facts wrong or just sounding stupid. Public speaking never frightened me. I joked that though it was supposedly the number-one fear of most Americans, it was probably one of the few things I did not fear. I'd get a slight tremor of nervousness before a new semester's opening class or prior to doing interviews on stage or at KTIM, but this was different. This was the big show—tens of thousands of listeners.

I was stepping into a vast, unknown new world, and *that* frightened me. Who knew, despite the general level of civility, who or what you might set off with so large an audience? Only a few years before, some lunatic had entered KGO's studios with a gun and shot one of the en-gineers dead while firing at the morning talk host, Jim Dunbar, who sounded a bit like a fumbling college prof. Jim had been popular as a morning host and was Mr. Nice Guy both on and off the air, a one-time station manager who turned himself from a morning talk host into a morning anchor and would be inducted into the radio hall of fame. The shooter thought Dunbar's mild and non-confrontational voice transmis-sions were wresting hold of his brain.

I observed Ronn Owens before doing my own first KGO broadcast. I saw a guy who liked working the phones without having studio guests, just taking one call after another, many from out of state, on topics he had introduced at the top of the hour. Ronn was revved up, jacked with

adrenalin and keen to engender controversy. There was serious arguing going on with one listener about abortion. Ronn was literally on the
edge of his seat, hunched over the microphone in a near oral embrace
of it. He turned off his live mike with a push of his finger, then turned
to me and said, "I've got him now. Now I've really got him." Then he
verbally ploughed into the caller's defense of fetal life and clicked him
off the phone bank with another flip of his finger and went to the break.
He leaned over to me and said, confidentially, "Abortion debates are like
gun control. They're talk show 101. But they get people stirred up. Last
time we talked about abortion on my show, some guy was waiting for
me outside the studio with a gun." He grinned, then added, "Of course
I'm not too damn controversial." Ronn, who was Jewish, also argued
the Israeli cause on air with a fervent loyalist's zealous support; he was
articulate and, I felt, brave in his naked, unbridled defense of Israel. Jewishness, or at least unbridled Zionism, could get you killed, as it would
Alan Berg. Though, to be sure, a big part of Berg's modus operandi
was to bait racists by getting them to call in and verbally make fools of
themselves, then caustically ridicule them.

I thought to myself, "This is crazy." I knew from listening that, with
the exception of the all-night weekday guy—a light-skinned black man
named Ray Taliaferro who verbally pistol-whipped callers who disagreed
with him—the KGO talkers were not out to stir controversy, as Ronn
was trying to do that night. When Ronn eventually morphed into a
morning host, replacing Owen Spann, he would take pride in presenting himself as a reasonable, moderate centrist who, more often than not,
interviewed the famous or near famous, with guests on a wide range
of subjects. The afternoon guy, Jim Eason, was a North Carolina good
old boy who was amusing and easy to listen to. He called himself Jim
Easy. Eason was a kind of cracker-barrel wit who on occasion would
criticize student protestors and welfare cheats but was more identified
with show-biz personalities who passed through San Francisco, eager
for promotion on his program. This was still an era of moderate civility and reasonable talk, rather than the contentiousness and more heat
than light that was to come.

The staple for KGO was a mix of guests and open phone lines on
what they called newstalk—subjects in the news or current topics that

people wanted to phone in and talk about. They started me modestly doing fill-in in a near dead zone, the 1:00 to 5:00 A.M. shift on Sunday morning. The regular all-night host on weekdays 1:00 to 5:00 was the rabble rouser Ray Taliaferro; by contrast, the 1:00 to 5:00 weekend guy was Al Jazzbeau Collins, a sweet, nonconfrontational beloved San Francisco personality. People connected Jazzbeau—a gremlin-faced character with a deep, warm, pleasing voice—with jazz from the days when he played jazz on another station. I would learn that he actually knew little about jazz, but it was easy to like Jazzbeau. He had a cult of loyal listeners up and down the West Coast including truck drivers, a group he played to as they wended their rigs and got off at truck stops to call him and talk about whatever was in their skulls. Jazzbeau talked, really, about nothing. He came up with no topics. He knew little, cared almost nothing about issues, yakked it up with listeners and did no prepping.

Compared to Jazzbeau, I was from the other side of the prep continuum. I was not in a state of overdrive, eager for confrontation—as Ronn Owens seemed the night I observed him—but as I set out to do fill-in for the first time, I was well-prepared, overprepared really. I wanted to interact with listeners and provide top-drawer news analysis along with good, solid interviewing, though I would need to book guests on my own, and 1:00 A.M. on a weekend wasn't exactly prime time. Still, I could reach a mass audience from this platform, help shape or reshape or inspire thought, be an educator of the airwaves, a bringer of light into the darkness. I pushed myself to read eight to ten newspapers and every news magazine I could. I wanted to be thoughtful, one who moved good, civil conversation to a high level. With the sudden chance to reach thousands of people, I also wanted to be a voice of reason. KTIM had two on-air phone lines and, depending on who the guest was, the lines might not blink. But here was a phone bank with lines from all different parts of the Bay Area, and my voice might ignite all of them! It was exciting. And as any talk host will tell you, it can be addictive.

Notwithstanding the lofty notions I had of higher discourse and humane conversation, it could be humbling sitting alone in the middle of the night in a small, glassed-in studio with only a phone bank and, on the other side in the control room, an engineer and lone call screener. Things moved along fairly well with plenty of calls, until I started moving into the stone dead zone around 4:00 A.M. Then it was suddenly a desert, except for a drunk, an insomniac or a trucker who would phone in to ask where Jazzbeau was. It was one of those times, as when Marty Balin and his band were carousing in the KTIM studio, when I asked myself why I was doing this. It's the question stand-up comics must ask when they're playing to a near empty room or a bunch of heckling sots. Fortunately, I did so much preparation that I could fill time—do what Jim Eason liked to call tap dancing—and avoid dead air. I did Jazzbeau's shift on a number of occasions, and I always came in loaded with subjects to talk about, in fear of that dreaded 4:00 to 5:00 hour dead zone, when the phones weren't blinking and I had the feeling that no one was out there—though I soon learned that listeners were up at all hours. Hit a particular nerve or hot topic, and the phones instantly lit up, no matter what time, even at the weirdest hour of the night. Only about 10 percent of all listeners, I was informed early on, would ever call. But they were out there.

Talk radio is like a roulette wheel in that you never know what will come up or who will call about what. I began with a well-focused topic, and the callers took the talk in directions I never imagined. My inner mantra was, keep the discourse up and the bar high and the level of callers will stay up. It was not necessarily the case. There were moments when I felt like the guy in the *Saturday Night Live* skit who threw out one ludicrous idea and heinous statement after another, but still got no one to phone in. Then some offhand comment by me or a listener, a question about a historical fact or an old song or film, and the phones went wild. I tried a little of everything in those fill-ins from 1:00 to 5:00, even inviting late night stand-up comics to come on air straight from their nighttime gigs and once even agreeing, because of Owen Spann and my own curiosity, to have on a psychic. Put a psychic on commercial radio and you'll never need to worry about getting phone calls, no matter what time of day or night.

In these days of talk radio, it wasn't unusual to hear Jim Eason with Dotty and Ginny, two women who ran an outfit called Share the Wealth, which was essentially a newsletter of recommendations on all kinds of buys, from *chotchkies* to fine linen. Doctors of all specialties were regularly featured guests. Noah Griffin, a late-night black talk host who would sue KGO and lose over not getting a permanent slot, even had on his insurance agent. Anything that could sustain an hour—only forty-two minutes, really, with ads and news. Of course the all-night hours I was subbing in had far fewer ads, and I had to read ones that weren't prerecorded.

People heard me on air and they commented—including a student, who said he was driving up from Monterey and heard this voice that sounded familiar and thought to himself, "That sounds like my English professor." Then, upon hearing more, he thought, "That is my English professor . . . and he's reading a Safeway advertisement!" All of us who worked on air for KGO had to read ads. From the start, I had a creepy feeling about reading cheap overnight ads for car places and greasy spoon restaurants. I asked myself—why was I doing this? The only person who did not read ads, because he was a physician, was Dr. Dean Edell, a popular advice-giving medico. I didn't want to appear as if I had airs or thought myself too good to do what all the others did, except Edell. I figured I would need to win some spurs before I could ask for ad-reading exemption. But I really had no idea how I sounded or came across. They kept calling me to do fill-in, but I worried that it might have had more to do with the fact that I was available and got the job done. I sometimes got called on Sunday night, while I was still on the air at KTIM, to come in to work for Jazzbeau. Leslie would call the KTIM hotline, tell me they wanted me at KGO, and I would leave KTIM at 11:00 and drive to San Francisco, about forty minutes away, to do the live 1:00 to 5:00 broadcast. A trenchant West Coast hippie who called himself Travis T Hipp was then on KTIM as a talk host. His rambles were a jumble of right-wing, libertarian, gun-owner-rights rhetoric and blasting caps leveled at U.S. foreign policy and drug enforcement. He told me one night that he heard me on KGO and was in a state of incredulity—not so much because I had made it to the big show, which I heard he had been trying to do for years, but because it was only an hour or so after I had left KTIM. "Are you nuts?" he asked me. "No. I love radio." "Well," said Travis. "So do I. And I'd love doing KGO. But I don't love it that much."

Like so many performers, I was insecure and unsure of myself, and not exactly getting flooded with responses from listeners. The few letters I did receive were mostly about an issue I discussed; a few were complimentary, a few cranky—one in crayon, even—and a couple were Jew-baiting and anti-Semitic. Was I making a difference, creating any kind of an impact? The measure of performance, as far as management was concerned, was how many letters you generated, regardless of whether you were praised or damned. By that criterion, I was not making my-self stand out. But I was becoming increasingly more at ease with the work, and I knew, despite my insecurities, that I was learning the craft, finding my radio voice, making myself highly informed and adding to my general knowledge with the intense prepping I did for every show. I wanted to use my skills as an educator in my broadcasts, to be a man with a microphone working for enlightenment and the common good.

KGO management continued to give me more work, including filling in for Eason and Owens, the two hosts with the biggest listenerships. The station was located right on Golden Gate Avenue, near where Leslie was completing law school at U.C. Hastings, and one afternoon, when I filled in for Jim Eason, I had her meet me there for a ride home. I was interviewing the Smothers Brothers, who were co-hosting their popu-lar TV show, and they were waiting to go on air with me. Leslie sat in the same green room with them, studying her law book. She was well aware of who they were but unstruck by their celebrity, nodding hello to them and then going on to study, without again acknowledging them or looking up. I went out to greet them during the break, kissed Les-lie, and then moved with them out of the green room into the adjoining studio. "That your girl friend?" Tommy Smothers asked me, nodding toward Leslie. "My wife," I replied. "Your wife?" he said as we left the green room and marched into the booth. "Does she ever watch televi-sion? She didn't seem to know who we were."

"Of course I knew who they were," Leslie told me later on when I asked her about the Smothers Brothers. "They seemed to be trying to get some acknowledgment from me, seemed to want me to recognize them. I honestly don't understand why that should be necessary to them." Years later Leslie would, for the first time, get excited about the prospect of meeting a guest, a conservative Hoover Institution scientist named Henry I. Miller who was widely published on biotechnology and whom she admired. When I introduced her to him and told him that she had never made such a request before he said he was "extremely flattered" and "not used to such celebrity treatment." Months after that meeting, another more famous Hoover scholar came on and said that Miller had told him, "If Krasny's wife doesn't come down there to see you you're nothing."

I enjoyed doing Eason's show; I liked meeting and interviewing show-biz types, favorites of Eason, who even then were old-timers like Rosemary Clooney, Victor Borge or Celeste Holm, but I also talked with a few of the writers he liked, including Calvin Trillin, George Plimpton and Tom Robbins. I got one call to fill in at KGO right before going into a graduate seminar I was teaching on the modern American novel, and I agreed to rush over as soon as the seminar ended and go on air as Eason's replacement. I interviewed John Davidson, another television personality—a kind of goofy, wholesome character who had hosted some popular TV shows. I went straight from discussing Flannery O'Connor and Catholic theology, grace and the metaphysics of evil in the classroom to jawboning on air with John Davidson.

I began to think it might be possible for me to land a weekend slot. Owens and others had told me that everything came down to the ultimate okay of the General Manager, who exercised tight control over all hiring.

I pretty much sized up The G.M. He was a Jewish guy from Detroit, an ex-salesman whom nearly everyone around the station seemed both to revile and fear, and it was understood that he enjoyed intimidating people. Station employees would actually walk around trying to determine what kind of mood The G.M. was in, and the place was rife with stories of his vindictive acts and bad-tempered pettiness. Yet there was something strangely likeable about him too, a weird kind of vulnerability that I realized I shared—a desire to be thought well of, though he was clearly a lot meaner and more ruthless than I could ever be. Every year he set aside twenty-four hours of air time to raise money to battle leukemia—the result, I had heard, of losing his brother to the disease. He enjoyed being seen as a big-hearted philanthropist and a *mensch* as well as a tough taskmaster. He had a reputation as a take-no-prisoners negotiator who never let go of the slightest slight. "He is," a local popular weatherman informed me, "the Antichrist."

I went to see him, and I suffered the humiliation of waiting more than three hours before he came out of his office and, with no apology, greeted me with a polite, "How are you, professor?" As I got to study him more, I became convinced that this first encounter, with its ridiculously long wait, was probably calculated. True, he was a busy guy. But, as I began to understand how he operated, I realized that ego and power were be-alls for him, that he got a thrill out of humiliating and dominating others. He shook his fist at me one night when I took calls from listeners asking for their thoughts about the station. He shook his fist, too, at Dean Edell and screamed "I made you" at him, audibly enough for many of us within range to hear. I heard him screaming one night at an on-air psychologist whose ratings had plummeted. He inspired strong emotion and great curiosity and was, you might assume, quite a personality. But there was something right at the center of his soul that seemed utterly empty, the sort of void that prompted a quip from famed San Francisco sportscaster Lon Simmons. Lon had gone off the air from a live Forty-Niners broadcast sooner than he was supposed to, and The G.M. became so enraged and verbally abusive that Lon told him to take the job and shove it. The G.M. told the press that he and Lon had a personality conflict. Lon's response was: "How do you have a personality conflict with someone who has no personality?" The weirdest psychological aspect, to me, was the fact that The G.M. showed up soon after at a station Halloween costume party wearing a Lon Simmons mask. Go figure.

His office was a testament to power. Full, panoramic view of The Bay, walls dotted with framed awards, citations and photos, including big pictures of him with his family, all of them on skis at Tahoe, Aspen and Vail and one of him with his arm around Brooke Shields. I wanted to be natural in the face of all these trappings of pontiff-like power, and gracious in spite of the more-than-three-hour wait. Not pushy. Nice. Respectful.

Despite his lack of an apology, he was cordial though noncommittal about what kind of future I might have at the station. After I explained that I might like a regular weekend gig, he was terse, words close to his vest, describing to me the fact that there were plenty of talented people in the wings who also wanted a weekend spot. One of them was Barbara Boxer, who had not yet stumbled upon the good fortune and timing of having the Burton machine push her into a congressional seat. "We're pleased to have you doing fill-in for us, but we make no promises and we make no guarantees." So that was it. I continued my weekly show in Marin and did fill-in, and that would be that. Or so I thought. Then, not long after my meeting with The G.M., I was called, to my surprise and informed that, yes, indeed, I would have a weekend gig.

.   .   .

I WAS DOING A SUNDAY NIGHT SHOW at KGO. Leslie had been hired by San Francisco's most powerful law firm, Pillsbury, Madison and Sutro. Both of us were now associated with big name operations.

KGO was a major commercial station, and it felt good to be associated with something so successful. But Bob Flanagan, a friend of mine who is a Stanford economist, asked me one evening at a dinner party, "What is it exactly you do on that radio station? Answer phone calls and read ads?" To my friends on the left, KGO linked me to a guy like Eason—an anathema to them because of his railings against protestors and his steady ridicule and disdain of leftist politics. " I used to be a liberal like you," Eason would sarcastically allow to me one day. Liberal had not yet become, as it soon would, a stinging pejorative. But it was beginning to be that, and by this point in my radio career I had been called a pinko, a reactionary, a Communist and a fascist, a nigger lover, a racist, a Zionist tool and a Palestinian puppet.

At the top of every hour an announcer's voice enthused, like a carnival barker, "HERE'S MICHAEL KRASNY." What was I, a scholar, doing reading ads aloud for everything from hemorrhoid cream to mouthwash? There were moments when I felt that I was simply a voice to fill time between ads; that the content of what I had to say or who I talked with was of minimal importance compared to the running of the ads. I heard myself on at least a few occasions referred to as a disc jockey and an announcer. Yet I had my own three-hour Sunday night show. I could make an impact on and educate the public, link my gown to town *and* get a pay check. Not a great deal more money at an hourly rate and after taxes than I had been making at KTIM, but with Leslie now commanding a corporate attorney's salary, our economic prospects seemed bright. At times, it even seemed too good to be true that I was getting paid for coming in to do what I enjoyed—which by this time wasn't only interviewing and educating but occasionally railing with my own reasoned brand of rhetorical invective. Venting strong feelings was clearly becoming more stock in trade for hosts, and I couldn't help but notice that Eason and Owens and the other evening host, Art Finley, were ratcheting up their rhetoric, sounding more firebrand. I had strong feelings about the Reagan Administration—what I saw as its wrongheadedness on foreign policy and lack of compassion for those in need—and about politicians who turned their backs on social welfare or behaved like bureaucrats or hypocrites, and as time went on, I felt more comfortable letting it rip. Still, I wanted to conduct a serious-minded, university-of-the-airwaves-type-program and invite on the smartest people I could to talk about a wide range of important subjects. Snide comments filtered back to me about my being not only too liberal but too much the pointy-headed intellectual, too intelligent for the station's listeners. I realized what I was doing was in part supposed to be entertaining. How to be serious and relevant without being boring and unsexy was the persistent challenge. Management wanted, above all, for listeners to stay with us through the ads.

In meetings of talk hosts, which they referred to as "alleged talent meetings," KGO management had a lousy word for what they claimed they wanted: infotainment. I realized, even after attending just a few of these meetings, that the principal talk hosts all copped attitudes of independence from management—in Eason's case, it was a kind of good ole boy playful combativeness, a quality he exhibited toward all kinds of authority on air that helped make him popular. The only regular host who was always pleasant and congenial at these meetings was Ray Taliaferro, who on air was so combative that a Kaiser doctor once told me that a man came into the emergency room in serious cardiac distress caused by listening to Ray.

One of the guys in management took me aside one evening and said, with what passed for intimacy, "You've got to watch that vocabulary of yours, Michael. You use too many big words that too many listeners don't know or understand. I worry about the truck driver in San Jose who hears you and feels stupid and wants to turn the radio off because he doesn't understand the big words you use."

At first, I did what I am often inclined to do. I apologized. But then I added, "Maybe he does understand me or will understand me in context. Maybe he'll want to learn. Don't you think it's important to keep the discourse level up?"

"I'm telling you, as someone who knows our listeners, you need to bring it down. Don't be afraid of insulting their intelligence. The great majority of them have very little to insult."

I believed he was wrong. Sure, there were yahoos and nitwits, but the audience was large and, I felt, full of informed, bright listeners eager to learn and to increase their word power. I did not want to insult or demean the intelligence of my audience. I felt if I maintained a fair and intelligent style and kept the discourse up, not only would I receive more intelligent callers, I would maintain and possibly increase my listener base. To my way of thinking, aside from New York, Boston and D.C., the San Francisco Bay Area was clearly one of the nation's centers for the highly informed, educated, intelligent and cultured. So didn't it stand to reason that listeners and potential listeners would want a brand of talk radio that operated on a higher level? On the other hand, the lesson again was clear—I had to watch my polysyllabic tendencies.

.   .   .

SAN FRANCISCO was one of the only cities in the nation that in 1984 went for Walter Mondale, Jimmy Carter's vice president, against Ronald Wilson Reagan. I railed against Reagan's downright miserliness toward those in need, against the U.S.-led invasion of Grenada, his administration's support of the Contra insurgents, the mining of Nicaraguan waters and his visit to Nazi graves at Bitburg. In San Francisco, I was often preaching to the choir. I went to lengths to put strong critics of the Reagan administration and its policies on air, including some pretty far-to-the-left types who helped fuel my reputation as a liberal (we were, by then, beginning to use the word progressive). I had on national Republican delegate Barbara Hoenniger—the first to talk of a so-called October surprise, an alleged but never proven deal to hold up release of the hostages in Iran to ensure the first Reagan presidential victory against Jimmy Carter. Barbara spoke faster than any woman I had ever interviewed, with the possible exception of Camille Paglia, and in the midst of our interview a caller who got through, and who I was too stunned to bleep, asked her if she wanted "to suck" his "big hard cock." I enjoyed bringing on political conspiracists like Danny Sheehan of the Christic Institute and *Realist* editor Paul Krassner and even the wildly idiosyncratic Mae Brussels, Dave Emory and attorney Mark Lane. I looked at a lot of this as simply good programming, the airing of divergent, nonmainstream, provocative and educational views. There was a tradition in nighttime radio of the far out and bizarre, and I was even open to occasional discussions of the paranormal and the weird. A woman came on who claimed she had been abducted by space aliens, and a psychiatrist with an Ivy League medical degree named Brian Weiss came on the show explaining why, after the death of his son, he'd become a believer in past lives. I put the local skeptics and debunkers on, so why not occasionally hear from the believers?

Russ Coughlin, the KGO television G.M. I had interviewed years before, was by this time doing a nighttime talk show. Whenever he saw me he asked, with good-natured sarcasm, if I had on my sixties hat or if I was going out to join the latest rent-a-mob of anti-American protestors. I didn't like being typecast as the in-house lefty, but I did feel I was a son of the sixties, attempting to promote social responsibility and raising political consciousness. I had a bully pulpit, and I was making a political and cultural impact. In the interest of fairness, however, I also put on conservative voices, even some right wingers and family-values bible thumpers like the Reverend Lou Sheldon, Roy Masters and Paul Cameron, who inveighed against abortion and homosexuals and got many of my more liberal listeners steaming mad. I argued with them, but I also let them spin their positions. If these kinds of men were the enemy, didn't listeners need to know how and what they thought?

When I was suddenly offered a regular nighttime slot, I had serious reservations. It was one thing to do a weekly show. But doing a show five nights a week, I knew, could be a grind. I still felt more a teacher and scholar than a broadcaster, communicator, pundit or personality. If I accepted KGO's offer, I would have less time for everything, including the writing time I still imagined I might covet between my twice-a-week teaching and once-a-week radio program. I felt I was at a crossroads. Should I stay in academe?

My four-course teaching load was becoming more onerous and intolerable, and I had been a full professor for years now with no place to move up to. Should I give up classroom teaching, which I loved, and become a full-time KGO talk show host? Could I do both? I sought advice, and the general consensus was that I should go for it and cut back on teaching. Digger pushed me to take the offer, and so did other friends. Some urged me to accept to give more airtime to left-of-center political views and more of a voice to the voiceless and oppressed. My friend Kent Gershengorn, a prominent cardiologist, told me that by doing both teaching and radio I could extend two distinct sides of my personality that would enhance each other and, more importantly, make me a better family provider. I had taught a course at S.F. State with a well-known Berkeley psychologist who managed to teach as well as maintain a full clinical practice. Why shouldn't I, too, bifurcate into separate career identities? KGO offered me a two-year contract. Why not try it for the two years and cut my teaching to half time?

During negotiation, The G.M. riveted his eyes on me with the most intense stare I have ever endured. I asked if I could have twenty-four hours to think the offer over. It wasn't a ploy. I felt my identity was being pulled two different ways. I also felt I was being lowballed with the per-annum figure The G.M. had thrown at me. Joy Brown, a woman psychologist KGO had let go, had been making nearly twice what they offered me. They had lured her from Boston after the success of Toni Grant, an L.A.-based psychologist who had racked up high ratings. Joy's ratings were mediocre. Psych talk, sports talk, money talk and all other specialized talk were proving to be not as durably attractive to a broad base of listeners as general news talk. Though psych talk would later have a major rebirth on radio with moral dominatrix Laura Schlessinger and on television with Dr. Phil, these were not good days for what had come more widely to be called shrink talk.

The following day I counteroffered a figure to a station executive that I felt was fair—not as high a number as I felt I might go. But it was above the lowball figure The G.M. tossed. The whole negotiating process made me uncomfortable and jittery. It seemed crass. I was trying to look out for my economic interests, but how was one supposed to know what constitutes a fair rate of pay in a strange business like this where money was made by the selling of air? The executive told me he had relayed my counteroffer to The G.M., who was waiting to get on a flight, and that The G.M. went wild with fury. I told Eric Solomon about this, and his response was: "You want to work for this guy?"

Ultimately, I did go to work for him because, with no small amount of nudging from the new program director, a slick but likeable attorney, my counteroffer was accepted. And so—despite my reputation for left-wing, intellectual discourse—I was suddenly a full-time, five-night-a-week radio talk show host.

.   .   .

I SOON CAME TO REALIZE that I could use the fact that I had a regular radio program to open doors and meet people. I still felt drawn to and fascinated by the movie world, so I made myself available to film festivals, as I did with Ann-Margret—with the added bonus that I now had a major nighttime radio show and could offer on-air promotion. I interviewed Australian director Peter Weir for the Mill Valley film festival and then actors Dennis Hopper and Natassia Kinski for the Napa Valley film festival. After interviewing Joe Esterhas and local filmmaker Phil Kaufman, I headed off to Southern California for *Mother Jones* magazine to meet with a number of Hollywood big shots—including Les Moonves, Dawn Steel, Brian Grazer, Barry Diller, Richard Donner, Matt Groening and Josh Brand—on the topic of film and television violence. It was something I was concerned about as a father. It was also something, I concluded, that everyone in Hollywood wanted to pass the buck on.

With my increasing audience, I was also being asked to host, keynote, or simply appear at all kinds of functions and events. Jewish organizations were especially after me for appearances and lectures, and I was saying yes more than I should have—often out of sentimental feeling for my mother or in-laws, who were all strong, devoted nonprofit and community organization supporters. If it was a good organization or a good cause, I found it hard to say no.

I became friendly with Bruce Labadie, who was in charge of summer music performances at the beautiful Paul Masson winery in Saratoga, near San Jose, and he invited me to come down to introduce performers. As time passed, I would go down with Leslie, Lauren and friends for evenings that included swimming and dinner with the headliners before I introduced them on-stage. I dined with and introduced Dave Brubeck, Woody Herman, Smokey Robinson and Ray Charles and provided an introduction for B. B. King, who kept calling me "Little Michael." There was also the black rock-and-roll legend who threatened not to do his show unless he was paid twice the amount he originally signed on for. Bruce Labadie was smart enough to give him a post-dated check and cancel it the next morning. It might also not be in the best of taste to add that the rock-and-roll legend, before I introduced him, was having fellatio performed on him by a buxom, bleached blonde, on her knees in the dressing room, while he chomped on an apple. "You're on, sir," the poor, embarrassed stage manager cried out, and the legend responded, "Wait til I finish this apple."

It was easy for me to get big-name and prominent guests on air because of KGO's large audience and the fact that 10:00 P.M. was a good air time for people making appearances in town. I scanned the papers and magazines looking for interesting, provocative or worthwhile guests, the greater in intellect and stature the better. I started having periodic phone conversations on air with people like Noam Chomsky and Ralph Nader. I had Stephen Jay Gould, the Harvard evolutionary biologist, on one night with Donald Johannsen, the paleontologist and discoverer of Lucy, and I also invited on Gould's nemesis Richard Dawkins, the author of *The Selfish Gene*, and Carl Sagan, the famed astronomer. I felt it was daring in a way to bring up the intellectual caliber on a commercial radio station and go after the higher denominator. Still, things happened to remind me that the listenership was, well, what it was. When Carl Sagan was on, a lot of the talk, predictably, turned to things like quarks, black holes, worm holes and time travel. At one point, he remarked to me that we had had no women callers. I looked at my screen and saw a woman's name and put her up, saying, "We now have Jane on. Our first woman caller. Welcome, Jane." Jane said she had just tuned in but wanted to know what it meant that her sun was in Libra and her moon in Virgo.

When I had Deepak Chopra on the air, Dean Edell told me that he'd seen a prepub copy of an article about to be released by *JAMA*. It charged Chopra—the Hindu auyervedic medicine man who would gain

great notoriety and popularity through his books and public television appearances—with being on a board that provided him kickbacks.
Chopra later would sue *JAMA*, claiming the article false, and he would
win, but he was blown away that I even knew about it and kept asking
me how I found out. In years to come, I would have some fairly intense
discussions on air with Chopra about wacky beliefs he had on longevity and health. He told one very funny story on air about a woman who
accused him, after a lecture that he'd given, of having raped her. "I've
never even seen you before in my life!" Chopra exclaimed. The woman:
"I'm not talking about this life."

Farmworker leader Cesar Chavez came on the air with me soon after
I began my regular 10:00 P.M. to 1:00 A.M. slot. I felt honored to have
him on and that there was something beatific about him—though years
later a Safeway executive, who grappled with him over the grape boycott, angrily dismissed him to me as "one frigging hard-headed SOB."
Whoopie Goldberg, then performing as Moms Mabley, came on the
night after Chavez and, though nervous and self-conscious, was funny,
doing a lot of different voices she had in her standup repertoire—a
black junkie, a surfer dude and a Valley Girl. I saw her metamorphose
from that early interview, when she appeared generally shy and self-
effacing, to a much stronger, more confident personality. By our third
interview, after she starred in Steven Spielberg's *The Color Purple*, she
came off like a diva.

More and more, I was talking on air to writers. I had Saul Bellow
on the night after I had interviewed him, on stage, at a University of
San Francisco event devoted to his work. It was challenging to get Bellow down to an accessible level, since he spoke on a lofty, cerebral plane
and could be halting and elliptical, even abstruse. But it was also embarrassing to be asking him questions and having to pause during the
show to read commercials.

Because of KGO's reach, promotion and publicity machines throughout the country vied to get their authors on the air. It was astonishing
to me to see how many books of little or no social significance came to
us over our transom. Reams of lumber-based paper telling how to get
rich or invest or how to buy a used car or find true love or cook cordon
bleu or have a lifetime of super sex. While Owens and Eason quickly

scanned photos on jackets of books written by women for pretty faces, I culled through the piles looking for books on serious topics. I could not lose my audience. I could not bore. I had to keep faith, ensure trust. I had to be engaged and up and aware of what listeners would welcome or reject. I had to stay focused, prep, prep, prep and perform.

My own writing was being supplanted by talk, shunted aside by obsessive preparation. I was busier than I had ever been, more of a recognized figure, and I felt that I was doing good work. But my growing success seemed sullied to me because it was gained from the spoken rather than the written word and from the often, I felt, meretricious and ad-plagued world of commercial radio.

There were overpublicized writers from back East for me to talk with—authors like Jay McEnerny and Tama Janowitz, or like Mary Gordon, whose fiction I could peg to a topic. But when someone was in town I especially admired, like the Canadian novelist and essayist Mordecai Richler, author of *The Apprenticeship of Duddy Kravitz* and *Joshua Then and Now*, I couldn't resist putting them on air and trying to make the audience respond. Richler, who came on at midnight, was liquored up and reticent, not the wonderfully clever word magician and humorist he was in fiction. He was mildly shocked to discover he was being interviewed by someone who had read his work and even published an article on him.

I was discovering the sometimes wide chasm that separates a writer in the text from the writer in the flesh—and that many fine writers, like Bellow and Richler, were not very good or effective public speakers. You would never imagine from conversing with them how clever and magical and funny they could be in their written prose. They didn't have to be good talkers because they had what they needed to perform in ink—whereas I appeared more and more to be talking out ideas with little or nothing to show in print. Perhaps I was the opposite of Bellow and Richler. A talker not a writer. But this was a possibility I resisted. Why couldn't I be both? Why not move forward in talk and simply put writing, for now, on hold?

I was invited to do an on-stage interview of Tobias Wolff, the author of the autobiographical work *This Boy's Life*, together with Richard Ford, author of the highly praised novel *The Sportswriter*. I much preferred

Wolff's work but had found him diffident earlier at dinner, whereas Ford
was voluble, full of southern boyish charm. "Tell me about you, Michael,"
he said, looking right into my eyes with his big blues. "I want to know
all about you." These two writers were both good friends of Raymond
Carver, and I was a Carver fan, especially moved by his marvelous 1983
story "Cathedral." Ford was an acolyte of E. L. Doctorow, another writer
I admired. I felt the three of us would have many things in common to
discuss in the interview, but I was concerned that Wolff would be too
reserved. I should have been concerned, instead, about Ford.

From my opening, rather innocuous question, he seemed prickly
and testy, a completely different creature than the man at dinner. I kept
up my professional interviewer persona, but I was confused and upset
by his tone. I quickly switched to Wolff, who was fluent and amicable,
much livelier than he appeared at dinner. When I turned back to Ford
with a question, he ignored me and spoke directly to Wolff. When I
posed another, follow-up question to Ford, he was nearly dismissive
and turned his attention again to Wolff. I then asked Wolff another
question, and he answered with what seemed to me a kindness meant
perhaps to offset Ford's rudeness. Ford continued to ignore me and talk
directly to Wolff or to answer me with a hauteur that was both icy and
palpable. Had I said something to offend him? Was he simply vicious
or, like Vidal, anti-Semitic? When the interview ended and I thanked
them both, the three of us left the stage. Once out of sight of the audience, Ford grabbed my hand, pumped it and told me, with a wide smile,
"Great job, Michael. I really enjoyed that. Thank you so very much." I
stared at him as if he had just landed from Neptune. It remains one of
the most bizarre performances of an interviewee I have ever experienced. Years later, Ford literally spat on a young black writer named
Colson Whitehead for writing a critical review of his work years before.
A southern white man spitting on a black man! Whitehead recommended
in print that anyone ever critical of Ford should wear a rain slicker in
his presence. I soon learned that Ford, despite having been adored by
Raymond Carver, had a reputation for being a mean critter. James Atlas
wrote that Ford received a manuscript from a young would-be writer
and hated it so much that he shot it full of bullets and sent it back. Herb
Gold reported that Ford, married for many years to a city planner and

without children, told a bunch of aspiring writers at a conference that if they really wanted to be writers, they had to choose not to have kids. "It didn't stop Tolstoy," Herb wisecracked. Of course, later, I learned that Raymond Carver felt that his children were his greatest barrier in being a writer. To this day, I have no clue how to explain what occurred with Ford. But, as with really bad students, you remember those interviews the best that are the most difficult or wretched. And they aren't necessarily the ones that others think they are. Many thought an interview I did with Nobel laureate V. S. Naipaul must have been excruciating for me because he sounded reticent and difficult, even unpleasant. But I knew where I was with Naipaul and never felt, as I had with Ford, a rife, motiveless malignity.

Another memorably antagonistic interview during this period was with LSD guru Timothy Leary. I was filling in for Ronn Owens on the morning show, and Leary seemed, from the start, to be distracted and flaky, talking in phrases that didn't quite make sense. I decided to be aggressive with him and asked about newspaper reports suggesting he might have finked on some of his left-wing cohorts to the FBI, reports that later proved to be true. Leary became agitated and called me "the Nazi Reagan of San Francisco." This annoyed me, and I fired back. "Do you feel any guilt or complicity over the deaths of acid droppers or kids still suffering from acid flashbacks because you urged them to turn on?" Leary went berserk and sputtered incoherently. But, unlike in the interview with Ford, I had brought it on.

When Ken Kesey came on, I got excited. This was the Merry Prankster, author of *One Flew over the Cuckoo's Nest.* I had taught the novel, seen the Dale Wasserman stage production of it and the film with Jack Nicholson. I had also read and thought highly of *Sometimes a Great Notion.* I had what felt like hundreds of questions to ask Kesey, but reminded myself that I was not conducting a literary interview. I was speaking to an author in front of a huge commercial radio audience and would need to tailor the interview accordingly. I remembered a talk Kesey had given years before at the local Unitarian church in San Francisco; two of the matters he had mentioned struck me as absurd and gave me a good way to open. He had talked about how passing by and not picking up a hitchhiker was bad karma, and he used that same phrase, bad karma, to talk about what men accrue who enjoy looking at naked female flesh in *Playboy*. I got right into it with him by recalling those two references, citing the dangers of not knowing who you might pick up if you should stop for any character with an outstretched thumb and mentioned that I enjoy the pleasures of looking at undraped women in *Playboy*. Why was that bad karma? And what about his karma, given what some viewed as the misogynistic portrayal of the horrific ball-busting Big Nurse in *Cuckoo's Nest?* And what did bad karma really mean to those of us removed from Eastern philosophy by being bred in the West? Kesey was thoughtful and playful in his response, and he handled my challenges with a sense of good-natured fun and aplomb, if not naiveté. Yes, there were bad people out there hitching, but we must try to expect the best in other people. We men were lustful creatures, but we must try to be better than that. He had no misogynistic intent in creating the character Big Nurse. Karma was complicated, yes, especially for those in our part of the earth. Kesey was easy to talk to. He veered off into anecdotes and a kind of nostalgic reverie of Merry Prankster stories, reminiscences of his times as a student at Stanford and as a worker in a mental health ward, experiences that gave birth to *Cuckoo's Nest*. Toward the end of the interview, Paul Krassner's name came up, and Kesey burst into an anecdote. " I tried calling Paul when I was last in town, but I kept getting his answering machine. So every time I'd call I'd say, in a deep, disguised Damon Runyon voice, THIS IS LOUIE, PAUL. THEY'RE AFTER US. I started to leave that message repeatedly, adding that they had knives and guns. Then I called and said they had Uzis and AK47s. Then that they had bazookas and missiles. And each call I'd start with that same funky, voice. THIS IS LOUIE, PAUL. THEY'RE AFTER US. So I finally see Paul and I laugh and ask him if he got my messages. He has no idea what I'm talking about because . . . it turns out . . . I had switched the last two digits of his phone number and had been phoning somebody else's answering machine. So Paul calls that number. A guy answers and Paul says to the guy, 'Hi. This is Paul. Did I get any messages?'" I laughed at the story, and it was a good story to end the hour with. I said goodbye to Kesey, and we broke to network news. When I came back from the break, I flogged the news topics I wanted to discuss with listeners for the next two hours, and I gave out the phone numbers.

The first caller was listed as anonymous. I went to the anonymous caller and heard Kesey, who was calling from a phone downstairs. "THIS IS LOUIE, MIKE. THEY'RE AFTER US."

When Allen Ginsberg came to town I noticed that Ronn Owens—who confessed to me that he never read any fiction, let alone poetry—had marked Ginsberg down as a guest. I told Ronn that I would like to interview him. Ronn, with his version of noblesse oblige said, "You got him." Ginsberg the poet I had met in the text of poems like *Kaddish* and *Howl.* I pictured him a ragged or naked man full of Blakean, visionary madness, humming Om as he sat in the lotus position. He appeared, instead, dressed in a smart three-piece suit. He rambled somewhat, but he also spoke with purpose and passion against the military-industrial complex and a litany of U.S. perfidies. He was impressively well-researched on the CIA and talked about Kerouac, Burroughs and Ferlinghetti. He needed little if any prodding from me to leap into a reading that necessitated bleeping the "f" word. Years later, after Ginsberg's death, I would have on Kesey, Krassner, Peter Coyote and Diane Middlebrook, who all spoke lovingly of Ginsberg despite his erotic attachments to young boys and approval of NAMBLA.

Grover Sales, a jazz critic and reviewer who had been on air with me since my KTIM days, wrote a cover story on me for a local, free paper in Marin, *The Pacific Sun,* all about my two lives as a teacher and broadcaster. In it he quoted Eason, whom Sales called "the dean of talk radio," saying: "Only Krasny could have brought off the kind of interview he did with Allen Ginsberg." That was the kind of respect I wanted—interviewing Ginsberg, being praised by the usually critical and churlish Eason. I was booking guests on a wide range of subjects, beyond the main staple of news stories and politics, including the radical environmentalism of Earth Firsters like Mike Rozelle, Dave Foreman and Judy Bari, holistic health innovators such as Norman Cousins, Bernie Siegel, Andy Weil and Dean Ornish, organic food advocates and spiritual transformation types like Ram Dass, Shakti Gawain and Jack Kornfeld. They were all part of the air I breathed in Marin County, and I began to realize fairly soon that, despite the program director's warning about not being "too Marin," there was an audience for all of that.

I studied up on whatever guest I had on and, if he or she had written a book, I read it. I constantly heard, with surprise, "You read my book!" The radical feminist and legal expert on sexual harassment Catherine McKinnon actually kissed me after our interview (an act I jokingly referred to on air as sexual harassment), because I'd read her book. It seemed a sad commentary that most talk hosts rarely take the time to read the work of people they interview.

People began asking me how I did it, how I read everything, and my boilerplate answer was that it was the wrong question. The real question was not how but why. But the simple, true answer was drive. I was driven to perform as I had been driven to write. "Larry King never reads books of guests he has on," I'd say. "I always do. That's why he's rich and famous." But preparation, thorough preparation, was a source of pride, a point of honor, a way of ensuring quality. I wanted to learn and to deliver learning. I wanted to be worthy of trust and confidence. I was a novelty—a literature professor and omnivorous, reading, public intellectual on commercial talk radio; hence I was getting ink.

My name started appearing in Herb Caen's column, which everyone in the Bay Area seemed habitually to read. He ran items when I referred to the poet Yevtushenko as "the Russian Rod McKuen" or asked how California's governor of Armenian descent, George Deukmejian, was going to deal with the so-called "young turks" in the California legislature. He also reported on the hour when I verbally battled a Livermore physicist on Reagan's Star Wars defense plan. When the interview ended, the guest said to me, "Let me present you with a gift." He handed me a sweatshirt that read: STAR WARS. NOT A WEAPON BUT A SHIELD. I read it aloud and spontaneously remarked: "Didn't we hear the same thing a while back from Dalkon?" Then there was the time Pat Conroy was booked and had to cancel due to a root canal, and I said I hoped the root canal wasn't like being on air with me. Caen especially liked that kind of self-effacing humor. I had a soft spot for him—though whenever I met him, he seemed aloof or just plain out of it, and he had a reputation among his fellow journalists at the daily paper as a bit of a prick and a *shnorrer* who ran gossip items that wounded. He came on my show to push a collection of his columns; many of them with some damn good prose descriptions of San Francisco, which he liked to call "Baghdad by the Bay." He drove up to the studio in a new Jaguar and wore, as was customary for him, Wilkes Bashford habiliments from the clothier of the same name. Caen's real name was Coen, but he was not a self-identifying Jew. He wrote about his "German mother," and when he died, they held a big ceremony for him inside the Episcopal Grace Cathedral. Most of Caen's cronies were gentile socialites, politicians and local celebrities whose names he loved to drop in his column. I wonder to this day if he was more admired because of his writing or because of the way he could ply gossip and clever quips. But admired he was. When he died, you would have thought, by all the eulogizing and memorializing, that he had been the pope of San Francisco.

. . .

ALEXA GILLIAN KRASNY was born, like her sister, at Kaiser Hospital in San Francisco on January 12th, 1986. Lauren, by this time a fourth grader, only a few months shy of nine, was extremely upset and angry over our having another child. When we informed her of the pregnancy and that we knew she was going to have a sister, she was furious. "You didn't consult me," she kept saying in anger.

I was a father of two daughters. Years later, following Bellow's death, I would sit on a panel with Gregory, his oldest son, and hear Gregory lament that his father had put art ahead of him. I wanted nothing to stand in the way of being a loving and attentive father, nothing to diminish it. But how would I manage to be the father I wanted to be and continue striving to meet high standards of excellence in two careers? Were the split identities of father, educator and broadcaster all compatible? And what of the still small hope that my literary voice might still emerge?

Teaching during the days and doing nightly radio were bleeding hours of sleep from me and taking me away from my family. With Alexa I simply could not put in the hours of child care I had with Lauren, and with Leslie working temporarily part-time as an attorney, we had to go the route of hiring a child care provider. But I was with my daughters as much as I could be and, soon after Alexa's birth, I took the family with me to Saratoga to the winery to meet Ella Fitzgerald, who held my infant daughter in her arms, rocked her and sang "Do You Know the Muffin Man." Lauren was in a private school—the tony, too affluent but allegedly academically superior Marin Country Day School, and that gnawed at me since I favored public schools and felt my old ambivalence about class and wealth. But, as my friend and English department chair Steve Arkin succinctly put it, "Schmuck! Don't you want to send your kid to the best school?" The irony was that we would discover over time that the public schools, where both our daughters eventually would wind up, were much more suitable.

I wanted to maintain on-air dignity and gravitas, civility and authenticity. Years of classroom teaching had taught me how to keep my equanimity with callers. A producer who worked with me—a mad Latino named Juan who passed himself off in bars around town as the station's program director—cheered me on when I went into a rare tongue-lashing mode. "Sometimes you have to take no prisoners," he instructed. But my on-air persona, like my classroom persona, was mostly the likeable and respectful educator. The mostly calm persona I had created was a far cry, mercifully, from the outbursts at Montgomery Ward's or the crazed episode with the baseball bat outside the Mill Valley theater. But I knew, too, that my calm and erudition were not compatible with the phenomenon beginning to take shape in talk radio, the emphasis on confrontation and controversy and the ratcheting up of emotion to boost ratings. The G.M. had marked me as being too intellectual—"an NPR type." With my steady criticism of Iran-Contra and the invective I directed against the Reagan administration, as well as my liberal views on racial and social justice and environmentalism, I was widely viewed, often with contempt, as a liberal. But being a liberal and trying to do what one local critic described as a classy, nonscreaming, polite, informed talk show wasn't hurting my ratings. Nor was the fact that I regularly had guests on who spoke about offbeat or intellectual and intellectually demanding topics, or who represented more invisible communities of color and poverty.

The key, I told myself, was ratings. I could do my brand of radio. I was in a popular time slot, without any talk competition except for Larry King and a few other syndicated shows and on a solidly popular, number-one-rated station. My ratings remained high. Moreover, I was building a following with the topics I tackled and the wide net I was spreading among anti-Reagan people, critics of U.S. foreign policy, advocates for the poor and underclass and Northern Californians who valued environmental issues. Even occasional shows sympathetic to an issue such as animal rights attracted many who supported that cause. I'd put on people like Harry Edwards, the black sociologist who led the famous raised-fist protest at the Mexico City Olympics, and Randy Shilts, the gay reporter and author of the first major book on AIDS, and I was seen as a friend to blacks and gays, which I felt I was. When I put on the local head of the anti-Arab discrimination committee, I was suddenly perceived as sympathetic to Arabs and hailed for a willingness to allow what was then a rarely heard point of view on to the biggest, most listened to and dominant of all local radio stations. I wanted KGO listeners to hear feminists and points of view never before heard on that station. I put on Andrea Dworkin and Susan Brownmiller. Naomi Wolfe—whose father Leonard, famous for his work on Frankenstein and Dracula, was a long-time colleague of mine at San Francisco State—came on and so did Gloria Allred. When Gloria Steinem came on my show, she caused a stir of excitement among the young women still around KGO that evening. I told Steinem, "You're from Toledo and I'm from Cleveland, so we're *lantzpersons.*" She liked that nonsexist permutation of *lantzman,* the Yiddish word used to describe Jews from the same European region. I asked for her autograph for my daughter, Lauren, and ironically grabbed the only piece of paper I could find in my briefcase, a copy of a poem I used in one of my classes, Sylvia Plath's pathological, Electra-driven "Daddy."

In a way, being a talk show host and building different loyal groups of listeners was not unlike being a politician and winning over interest groups—constituencies that would support you because they identified with you or saw themselves politically aligned with you. But I tried, too, not to be any kind of predictable ideologue. Yet despite the high ratings—and, to my delight, a fan club that cropped up in Vancouver—I heard rumblings about how a lot of my time slot's high numbers were "tonnage," a word used around the radio station's sales department for the fifty-five and older demographic, who were not as desirable to advertisers as younger listeners.

One night—after an extraordinary confrontation on my program between a member of the El Salvador leftist guerilla group, the FMLN, and a right-wing death squad militant who had become a diplomat—the

P.D., far too liquored up, told me, "I really like you, Michael. I like you a lot. I just hope I don't have to be the hit man from The G.M.'s death squad who has to rub you out if your ratings slide." It was a strange and, in many ways, unnerving moment, because it made me realize that no matter how much I may have been liked, no matter what kinds of guests or quality or class or level of discourse I brought to the airwaves of KGO, no matter how much public service I provided, I would live or die by ratings.

When the *Challenger* space shuttle blew up and seven crew members were killed, it was one of those moments in radio where emotions were at their most intense. Other events remain in my memories of those years—the tearing down of the Berlin wall, the nuclear explosion at Chernobyl, the blowing up of Pan Am 747 over Lockerbie, the protest in Tiananmen Square and the Exxon *Valdez* oil spill. I saw—up to and including 9-11 and the tsunami of 2006—the power that talk radio has to create community, disseminate information and analysis and allow for an outpouring of feeling. Although I still dreamt then of being a writer, a card from Kay Boyle, an internationally acclaimed author who had taught at San Francisco State, changed something inside me. As a professor of English, I hardly knew Kay, but I admired her work and knew the high esteem others had for her and her writing. She had been friends in Paris with Beckett, Pound, Hemingway and Joyce, and she had had a distinguished writing career. She was also a radical, a fierce opponent of Hayakawa during the San Francisco State student-led strike and a passionate supporter of radical causes and Amnesty International. Kay sent me a postcard saying what a joy it was to listen to me and how, when I came on air, it was for her "a purification of the airwaves." Of course the card made me feel good—but it also tapped into something else, a realization that I could go on publishing short stories in small literary journals and never be noticed or receive a fan letter from the likes of Kay Boyle. I had far more listeners than I could ever have readers. I had a base, my own radio program, and I could, I reasoned, use that as a springboard. Put simply, if I couldn't become respected as a writer—as it was increasingly becoming clear that I would not—then perhaps I could build on my success as a broadcaster and move on again to television or to a national radio audience.

A young journalism student came to my office at San Francisco State to interview me, and the first question she asked was, "What do you like most about your job as a broadcast journalist?" I talked to her about making an impact on people's lives, serving the public and offering knowledge and civic debate as an on-air educator. I hoped the play and interplay of ideas might change consciousness, lead to action and enrich lives. My words caught who I honestly had become. I knew I was able, an articulate and informed broadcaster, and a lot of people were still devoted to my brand of serious-minded and civil talk radio. Focus groups revealed that listeners trusted, liked and respected me—even though they often found me too intellectual or, worse, duller and less stirring than my more volatile colleagues. But the real question for me was whether I really was good enough to move forward and build on the capital I had.

I was continuing my one-man crusade to bring serious writers to the airwaves of big-time commercial radio. I had Salman Rushdie on to talk about his short book about a brief time he spent in Nicaragua, called *The Jaguar's Smile*. I had read *Midnight's Children*, and I tried talking broadly with Rushdie about his novel writing, but the on-air conversation moved to politics, including what was going on between India and Pakistan and U.S. policy toward the Sandinistas. It was similar with Mona Simpson, whose book *Anywhere but Here* prompted a conversation about stage mothers and Los Angeles rather than literary talk, and Ann Beattie, whose book on the painter Alex Katz led to a discussion about the convergence of literary and visual art. But in my world of commercial radio, I felt compelled to pursue serious literary and intellectual talk with some restraint. I liked my program being thought of as a classroom of the airwaves, but I did not fancy, and frankly feared, turning it into a classroom seminar. I knew instinctively that I risked losing too much audience if I became too literary or too academic.

I would have more interviews with Simpson, Beattie and Rushdie in years to follow—including an unannounced one with Rushdie, after the fatwa, when he came with heavy security. Eason called Rushdie a "Sandalnista" because *The Jaguar's Smile* was sympathetic to Nicaragua's Ortega regime. I related Eason's observation to Rushdie, and he reacted with amused good nature, though he obviously took seriously the plight of Nicaragua and the U.S. role in trying to head off what the Reaganauts and Bushites viewed as an encroaching, south-of-the-border red menace. Rushdie told me that Bellow's *Augie March*, with its brilliant and inventive use of the vernacular and its great, sprawling episodic adventures, was the incomparable great American novel of the twentieth century. *Augie March*. The model of the great American novel I intended to write.

A friend of mine named David Davis, a rabbi and Judaic Studies prof at the Catholic University of San Francisco, arranged for me to interview Bellow on-stage at U.S.F. I had lunch with Bellow afterward in the university cafeteria. It was strange hearing the great Nobel novelist ask me and my friend Irving Halperin for advice, as we ate, on whether he was too old to be considering marriage to a much younger grad student, a young woman he eventually would marry and father a child with when he was in his eighties. That night on KGO he sounded stiff and formal whereas, in front of the academic audience and face-to-face with me earlier that day, he had been much more at ease, full of aphoristic wisdom and levity, more himself. But I was still proud to have had him on, just as I was with Rushdie.

If I couldn't be a great writer, I would at least be an interviewer of great writers.

· · ·

I WAS BACK IN TELEVISION, too, as co-anchor of a simulcast weekly program called "Nightfocus." I was the sidekick to a sometimes quasi-logorrheic though likeable anchor named Pete Wilson. I had to battle Pete to shoehorn in a question or comment, but that was not a significant matter to me. I liked Wilson and was chummy with him, and he had gone to great lengths to demonstrate to me that he was not an empty-headed, airbrushed news anchor—a line reader, as I disparagingly called high-paid anchors. Pete was, in fact, a fan of mine, having gotten into the habit of listening to me on his drive home after his 11:00 P.M. newscast and, on occasion, calling in. He liked to tell me that people perceived him as a conservative when he really was a liberal—though a liberal who had served in Vietnam and had a style and delivery that could come off as swaggering. He seemed to want to prove to me that he was not as conservative as many liberal-minded San Franciscans thought him, and

I wanted to show him I was not as liberal as so many assumed I was. He expressed amazement when I objected to Robert Bork being shot down by the Senate as a Supreme Court nominee. I saw it as a partisan attack against a reactionary but well-qualified candidate—a politicizing of the judiciary nominating process that, with some prescience, I believed could all too easily lead to a slippery slope of political litmus testing and partisan battles over every judicial nominee.

As an opinionated talker, Pete welcomed having a nighttime television talk show, and since he was the station's main male anchor, he had the lion's share of opening each show and setting the framework for the program. When we got into content, he was dominant and I, unnaturally, was the quiet sidekick. Wilson was a television pro, and I was still a novice; that was clear when the director took me to dinner at company expense, insisted I order lobster, and fed me strong advice about ignoring the camera and allowing it to follow me. The important fact to me, though, was that I had a television show—that I was getting more exposure from it and possibly building greater career possibilities. Who knew where "Nightfocus" might lead? We were on right after ABCs "Nightline" and, since I worked for ABC, I might wind up subbing for Ted Koppel, the highly intelligent and incisive "Nightline" host. It seemed like a not-impossible dream. I was a professor with a radio and television show, even if I was second fiddle on TV.

Early on, Pete and I had on the white racist Tom Metzger—who came to the studio with his son, whom I called Baby Metzger after the son of the tyrannical Haitian despot "Papa Doc" Duvalier. Willie Brown, then a member of the California State Assembly, came on to debate Metzger, along with a couple of other people representing local minority groups. A brilliant African-American politician who later became Mayor of San Francisco, Willie informed me that he would always accept an invitation to battle rhetorically with a racist. I had my own strong feelings about Metzger, who reminded me, in his viperish hatred of all non-whites and Jews, of George Lincoln Rockwell, minus Rockwell's theatricality and intensity. It was a bit frightening to be going head-to-head with someone so fervent in his hatred of all minorities, including Jews. But it turned out that the interview was not head-to-head at all. Metzger refused to be in the same room with Willie and the other minorities so the producers set him up in a separate studio. Pete let Willie, a gifted debater, and the other two go at Metzger, while he and I mainly traffic-copped Metzger's answers back to Willie and the others. I was almost a silent partner, but managed to pipe in a couple of questions. When it was over, Baby Metzger and his friends, angry over what they called the unfairness of three against one, trashed the green room they were in and caused a good deal of petty damage; a few years later, he was in a notorious, violent TV dustup with Geraldo Rivera . There was a confab at the station about whether or not to sic ABC lawyers on Metzger and his White Aryan Resistance crew for trashing the guest room, but ultimately the local brass decided not to do so, lest the station and ABC wind up fighting a vicious enemy. Years later, attorney Morris Dees would legally battle it out and win huge, crippling settlements against Metzger and racist Christian Identity Movement leader Richard Butler.

Though I was getting used to television with this once-a-week nightly gig, I was more at ease in my old radio world. Television meant dressing up and putting on makeup, and even when Pete was on assignment or ill and I moved up to be main anchor, there was always another television personality with me. One of my co-anchors was Russ Coughlin, the former Channel 7 G.M., who had now moved back into on-air work doing TV editorials. I thought of the odd serendipity that now paired me with a man who was once in charge of the whole bloody television station and with whom I once played the role of young fledgling print journalist, while secretly coveting some kind of television gig. Now, years after those humiliating, unreturned phone calls to Jim Schock, I was on the cathode tube, although, for me, radio was the more natural medium—more a theater of the mind, more intimate and kinder to my vanity. I went into near shock when I first saw camera shots of my balding scalp.

I was on radio the night George H. W. Bush picked Indiana Senator J. Danforth Quayle as his vice-presidential running mate. My guest was Ken Adelman, a former ambassador who negotiated nuclear treaties for President Reagan, and he was trying to convince me that Quayle was smarter than people believed. Later Quayle would misspell potato and stumble verbally into a minefield of malaprops that would convince people he was, like the cowardly lion, in need of a brain. In fact, since Quayle and George H. W. Bush had been in the same fraternity, as was Bush's son George W., I thought the choice of Quayle as running mate was a surrogate-son choice, and I still believe that. To be fair, there might have been, in both Quayle and Bush Jr., a certain kind of intelligence that was not verbal. Years later Newt Gingrich would tell me that Bush Jr. was not verbally intelligent and would rather chop wood or fly a plane or engage in a video game than read a book. "He's not bright, not as you or I might be," Newt modestly assured me, "but he's really very bright." Which was pretty much what Ken Adelman was trying to convince me regarding Senator Quayle, arguing that Quayle understood the more sophisticated nuances of nuclear weaponry and was possessed of different, nonverbal but real intelligence. When we went to a commercial break I said to Ambassador Adelman, "I'm sorry, Ken, but I really do think your boy Quayle is a dim bulb." The ambassador quickly parried back, "Fuck you!" My immediate Pavlovian response back at him: "Fuck you!" Then we were suddenly on air again, and regular conversation ensued as if nothing had happened.

It was around this time that I met Larry King. He was dating Sylvia Chase, who had been a first-rate investigative reporter and was now working in the San Francisco market as a news anchor. She didn't seem especially suited for the role, but she had name recognition that Channel 4, then the local NBC affiliate, figured it could promote. King was king of talk radio at night for the mutual network and was already moving into his sinecure role as CNN TV host. I listened to him on the radio on my rides home and enjoyed hearing his brand of liberal politics, celebrity schmoozing and sports expertise. In fact, King helped keep me awake on drives home. There were a few scary times when, sleep famished, I would drive off the road or jolt awake a good distance from where I had remembered being—realizing that I had been driving asleep, even with the windows open and the radio blaring. On one occasion, the car actually careened off to the side of a road and turned over completely onto its side. I talked about it on air, and one caller, from Oregon, chastised me for driving sleepy—saying I, who had inveighed against drunk drivers, was no less dangerous. I had to agree.

When I met King, it was at a private home. Here was someone with whom I shared a craft. He was a talk colleague far more famous than I and diametrical in style, but I thought we might become chummy and exchange ideas about the work we both performed nightly. Yet it was clear that King, like the name he adopted, had a bit of an imperial sense of himself, at least in the setting we were in—a kind of remoteness that says you can approach me and ask questions and I will answer, but I will not deign to buddy up or respond in kind to your warmth. He even sat in a throne-like chair, with me beside him on a lower footstool. He was not unkind. He was just cool—even though we conversed for the better part of the evening, me playing interviewer to his celeb. King was much more likeable on air. His TV persona and gruff Brooklyn intonations accounted, I believe, for whatever appeal he may have. Talking to him made me realize that, though we were both Jews in the talk game, we were cut from very different cloth. King was by nature more simpatico with—and indeed would become pals with—Ronn Owens, as much as such schmoozer types can really be pals with each other. Both were New York born and bred, loved to cozy up to the rich and famous and had had heavy-duty gambling joneses. I, too, could be glib, but by nature I was bookish and scholarly, more of an educator. Years later, public radio's Ira Glass would tell me that there are book Jews and money Jews. A binary world. Maybe, I told myself, guys like King and Owens had more of what it took to be stars in the talk game. Maybe I was only fooling myself into thinking I could parlay my career into national syndication and television the way King had done; maybe my ambition in broadcasting, like my writing ambition, exceeded what I could achieve.

Still, I got a record-breaking volume of responses, most of them angry, after King helped to bring Ross Perot's presidential ambitions to prominence on his talk show. I went off on what a crackpot and fool I thought Perot was, presenting research I had done that raised serious questions about his character. So many people were looking for an alternative to Bush or Clinton that Perot had quickly garnered wide support, even in Northern California. People who claimed to have admired me wrote to tell me how disappointed they were in my criticism of this most unlikely of messiahs.

The dark side of commercial radio fame had to do with the enemies and crazies you set off in a talk pit that blares your voice, opinions and tastes into thousands of homes. But there was a high side, too, which I associated with King and Owens but occasionally had a chance to enjoy.

I did a live broadcast from Harrah's in Lake Tahoe with Harry Belafonte, who was the featured performer at the casino. Belafonte, who was billed as my co-host, was warm and charming, and there was something seductive about getting royal treatment during the show he put on before our live broadcast, including front row seats for me and my family. But the best part was being put up with my family in the penthouse at Harrah's, catered to by the chef and fawned over by by the hotel's head executive, Lou Phillips. Who doesn't like being treated special? Even a guy with prol roots and sixties' pretenses of enmity against the shallow and materialistic.

When we were on air, I felt overpowered by Belafonte's charm and magnetism and by his passion. As soon as we got on politics, he was fiercely ripping into Bush Senior and the policies of the Administration. Belafonte was the kind of natural talker I could be only when something really stirred my blood. He was a political firebrand, and judging by the calls he elicited, all the liberal haters of Bush and the GOP who regularly listened to my show adored him for it. I said to him—because it was so obviously the case—that he would make a terrific talk host because of his passion combined with the willingness to offend, if necessary, anyone who might disagree with him and his great, magnetic, powerful, inciting voice.

Tom Stoppard

"I'm a news addict. An absolute junkie," Tom Stoppard tells me as we wind into our second interview in two years. This time he is in San Francisco to talk about *Night and Day*, which is being resurrected by the American Conservatory Theatre. San Francisco theater goers love Stoppard. All his plays have been performed in San Francisco. He is lulled, he says, into a false sense of security when he comes to the City by the Bay. There's a warm, friendly swell of benign disposition towards him, and he doesn't think of San Francisco like any other city in the world.

Stoppard is telling me he reads as many newspapers as he can and gets a lot of what he melds into drama from them, and I tell him that I, too, am a news junkie and an omnivorous reader of newspapers, but wish

I had his creative gift. He muses about creativity being a gift from the gods, but also a psychological process. That's how it is for him, though it's not always intense. "Just sitting here with this microphone in my face I know this is so—a moment between not having the thought and having it when you aren't present." I tell him he sounds mystical. He laughs. "Yes. Rather east of Suez."

"I get up early in America," he says. From his teens he was fascinated by American culture. "I still read more American novelists than British." He speaks with a British restraint, a slow and measured thoughtfulness garnished by the slightest trace of a Czech accent. Others besides me have told him he bears a resemblance to Mick Jagger. He came to England at eight and loved being English, loved and absorbed all that was English—landscapes, architecture, school, language. He put it all on like a coat and felt comfortable in it. He had left Czechoslovakia at eighteen months and resented the idea that he should still be Czech, even though he spoke the language as a toddler. He was thirty-one when the Russian tanks moved into Prague, and he deplored it, but he deplored it as an Englishman. He felt he should have felt more, but it felt no different to him than if it had been Poland. Then, dissidents in Eastern Europe and Russia became a cause. He was making up for not shedding real tears when his own country of birth was invaded. "I was nervous when I began to find myself even beginning to be a public figure. I clammed up, and then I did become involved in speaking out on issues that affected me—Eastern Europe and Russian Jews. I just wanted to adopt a part of the globe as an area of my interest because I couldn't cope with all the issues and appeals that came at me."

There is modesty in Stoppard. He talks of having left college to do journalism, but says he felt that he was bluffing, that he ill deserved a byline since he was "a spotty young man without deep authority." He left boarding school knowing nothing about the world, but learned fast as a junior reporter; though he regretted not having four years at the university, he felt "delirious with pleasure" doing journalism. He is fascinated with trivial facts. "I'm not erudite," he says "in the way people credit me for." He describes himself as "very undisciplined." When I note that he seems modest, he says, "I don't like modest. I like things that engage me on an intellectual level, and I like to write about them in ways that entertain."

When a caller tells Stoppard she is the great-great-granddaughter of an obscure historical character from one of his plays, he tells her he is "speechless and delighted and amazed and shocked." When another caller phones in saying how honored he is to speak to Stoppard and adds, "I am also an entertainer. I play the guitar and sing," Stoppard immediately responds, "Two things I envy you for," and then goes on to ask the caller what kind of music he plays and performs.

Though Stoppard has written many film scripts, all are adaptations. "I think in terms of theater, not movies," he says. "Theater is a storytelling art form. All theater. You see a play in medium-wide shot. The whole stage and the bodies of the characters are there all the time. You never come in for a shot on the eyes or the mouth. The whole person comes on and speaks, and that's it. The whole equation is different. The audience is subconsciously aware of the physical limitations the play is working under." Storms and floods, he adds, "can't be done but can be rendered poetically," which Stoppard says he prefers.

Stoppard tells an amusing story of his work with Terry Gilliam on the film script for *Brazil*. He kept telling Gilliam that everything sounded too much like Orwell's *Nineteen Eighty-Four*. Gilliam told him not to worry. Two years after *Brazil* was released, Stoppard saw Gilliam, and Gilliam admitted he had never read *Nineteen Eighty-Four* before they worked on the film. He had read it for the first time just that week. He told Stoppard the parallels and similarities between the two works shocked him.

Why, I ask him, does he like *Arcadia* best of all of his theater oeuvre? The story, he says, fell into place in a way which was aesthetically and architecturally pleasing. "It has to do with structure," he adds. He is personally absent from his plays, though once he has pen in hand, the contents that are in his head pour out, sometimes explicitly, as in *The Real Thing*. Theater is a recreation, but there is a moral sensibility that must be laid down. "Every message has the right kind of bottle," he states, "but if you put the right message in the wrong bottle. . . ."

I ask Stoppard the proverbial interviewer question: "Which playwrights do you rank the greatest?" "In height or merit?" he parries back. Then he adds, "The question strikes me dumb," and I think he must mean it strikes him as a dumb question. But no, he means it makes him

mute, and he explains that some plays by the same playwright are wonderful and some are not. Beckett's more minimalist work doesn't engage
him, though *Godot* is clearly the twentieth century's masterpiece.

Stoppard says he loves Evelyn Waugh's *Scoop*. Stoppard even used
William Boot as a pseudonym. He adores parodies and fixated on them
when he was young. "Parody," he says, "is like writing to one side. *Ros-
encrantz and Guildenstern* is a first cousin to parody. I was too smart to
write my own Shakespeare verse."

Edward Albee

Edward Albee is talking to me about how he left
home at eighteen for Greenwich Village because he couldn't take it anymore—it being family, bigotry, reactionary views. He was afraid he
would turn out like what he couldn't take. The mother who adopted him
he calls something of a horror, though the older she got the more sympathy he felt for her and the more he admired her guts. The facts and
events of her life were grafted on to the lead woman character in *Three
Tall Women*.

Albee was thrown out of college. At thirty he was still an *enfant terrible*. He gave himself *Zoo Story* as a thirtieth birthday present. He had
shown Thornton Wilder his poetry, and Wilder had told Albee that maybe he should write plays, though Albee was certain Wilder hadn't seen
any playwriting potential in him. The avant-garde excited him. Brecht.
Beckett. Ionesco. Writing, he says, is something you have to do because
it's something that has to be done. Writers steal. He wrote *American
Dream* as an homage to Ionesco, but who was to say how much was theft?
American playwrights must choose between mediocrity and familiarity.
We want the familiar, the naturalistic. We expect or want theater to be no
different than our lives, Albee says, but most people live partial lives, and
we tell each other and ourselves lies. O'Neill told us in *The Iceman Cometh*
that we need pipe dreams to survive. Albee tells me that he said the opposite in *Who's Afraid of Virginia Woolf.* He says to get rid of pipe dreams.

Albee is calm and formal, a proper man. Affable and equitable. Pulling at his dentures throughout our interview. He tells me flatly that he
has no conflicts with his sexuality and is sexually "perfectly content." I
find it difficult to picture him as he was or might have been as a denizen

of Greenwich Village, when W. H. Auden may or may not have told him to write pornography. "Auden might have said that," Albee tells me. "I don't remember."

Albee talks about how television is determined to make us all children and how, even though we Americans clearly don't want arts education, we desperately need it. Mozart sonatas ought to be played in kindergarten rest periods and representational art flashed before children early on so that it can make its way into their unconscious. Arts education, he says, is a disgrace in this country. Without it we are making fools of ourselves.

He has found out what he thinks by writing plays. Unlike television or film, the theater is live and dangerous. No two people ever see the same play, and he assures me, he has never seen anyone asleep watching any of his plays—except critics.

Albee is looking for his biological parents, though he says it is extremely difficult to find out who they were or are. He is looking for them despite the fact that once he found out who he was, discovered his own identity, he no longer cared.

    Tony Kushner

No second acts in America, Scott Fitzgerald? How about Tony Kushner? We had anemic crowds at on-stage interviews we did in both Santa Rosa and at Chabot College in Hayward—then suddenly *Homebody Kabul* comes out after war in Afghanistan, and he's proclaimed prescient, and box office sales sizzle. On air we're talking so much about politics and his brand of socialism that he laughs and says he's worried we won't sell tickets.

Tony is very smart and incredibly sweet. Intensely opinionated but also admitting to me that he has always felt a little like a nerd. "It's too late to change," he adds.

Angels in America had its own second act when Mike Nichols decided to direct it for HBO with a cast that included Pacino and Streep. Even Middle America watched all that content about Jews and gays and AIDS. The play had much to teach when it first came out and won Tony a Pulitzer at a time when protease inhibitors had not yet been produced for the free market Tony rails against.

Tony came on air with me once after a debate about gay and lesbian marriage that included an evangelical who spoke in opposition. Tony said he was "awestruck" at my politeness and assured me there was no way to have a reasoned or rational conversation with a fundamentalist like the minister, who was from the traditional values coalition, because the man had such an immensity of bad faith, both Sartrean and religious. He was, Tony said, part of a great global evil of fundamentalism—theocratic, homophobic and bigoted. The minister's disguised hatred promoted violence. Tony claimed to see no difference between the Christian fundamentalists and the Islamic fundamentalists. A religious, Catholic occasional caller phoned in and in her meek yet forceful way told Tony he was out of line for calling the clergyman names and branding him violent. She added that gay marriage was a travesty and against natural law. Tony sounded firm but polite. "I don't know how to talk to you," he said. "I don't think I can, even though you sound nice." He then launched into a verbal sweep about "people like you" and called her prejudiced and conservative and she, like an indignant schoolmarm, told him that he was using stereotypical language to brand her. This is on-air drama.

Tony calls theater popular entertainment. Imagination in part is for empathy, for being able to travel places, including inside experiences of people with experiences unlike your own. I am tempted to ask if that includes those like the woman caller or various homophobes or fundamentalist religious types who believe biblical admonitions against sodomites. Instead I ask if he empathized with Roy Cohn or the Mormon character in *Angels in America*. Mormons, Tony says, are a people of the book, a people in exile and diaspora. He says he is like Roy Cohn—Jewish and gay and in love with America.

In our first interview, Tony told me that it was harder being gay than Jewish. That was before the anti-Semitism of the Hitlerian era had its second, post 9-11 act. He also said it was harder for him to come out in America as a socialist than it was to come out as a gay man. Now he says there are "interesting questions" connected to the socialist tradition, such as the possibility of a planned economy alongside democracy, with freedom maintained. Tony is giving me his political screed. Capitalism, he says, has created great things like bourgeois human rights. It has historically been a liberating force throughout the world. But it is wasteful and destructive of human life and has put too much emphasis on a loosely associated individualism. There is a five-hundred-year history of human community without anarchy or the handing over of human destiny to the extremely punishing free market. Even right-wing Nixon saw the need for wage and price controls.

To Tony, playwriting and acting are much harder than directing. Directors and playwrights have a kind of S&M dimension to their interaction because of power balances and imbalances. "It's all very Foucaultian," he says. He trained as a director and often feels he should have continued in that direction instead of playwriting. He closed the directorial door for good when he realized he'd been discussing wigs for hours on end. "I'm no drag queen," he adds with a laugh.

Wole Soyenka

Soyenka. Africa's first Nobel laureate in literature. A human rights and democracy activist. He comes into the studio wearing jeans and looking like he could be an academic colleague. He is as much a symbol of Nigeria and its potential as Mandela has been for South Africa. Both fought for liberation, both were placed in solitary confinement and both have dignity.

Soyenka and I start out talking about the bush. He goes there to hunt but finds great calm in the remoteness, the vegetation, the smells. It is an escape. A special communion unlike any other. In the twenty-two months he spent alone in prison, there were no books nor writing materials, no music, nothing to do but think his life through. Which he did. The one illumination he claims came through to him was his desire to be a gentler and more understanding husband. The marriage collapsed. But Soyenka doesn't write much about personal relations in his memoirs. The American public seems to believe in maximum exposure, no privacy. Temperamentally, that goes against his grain, though not if he is writing about his childhood. The age of innocence, he says, ended for him at age eleven. As an adult building relations for self and family you have no moral right to drag any of them into the public eye unless you collaborate.

Writing memoir disciplines Soyenka as opposed to his disciplining his characters, as he does in his dramas. With a novel or fiction, one is freer. He prefers the theater, especially street, guerilla and shotgun plays, which electrify him to direct. In drama you can visualize the figures on stage and move them mentally. He doesn't consider himself a novelist, even though he is. He praises novelists. "It's a very hard craft."

Soyenka is so Yourban that he went to Brazil on a crazy Indiana Jones type journey to capture a sacred artifact of Yourban heritage. His existence is wrapped up in the collective ontology of Yourban myth. Soyenka's Yourban sensibilities account for his own mythologies, and he sees Yourban myth as universal. Yourban sensibilities account, too, for his view of democracy. He has gone to great pains to dissect democracy. In Europe you have kings and queens and feudal structures, but they are democracies. In Yourban society, there is a monarchical system but it is "as democratic as you can imagine." The king is a spiritual figure but he is controlled, almost a captive. If he is told to commit ritual suicide, he does so. Soyenka muses that he tried to compel ritual suicide with Nigerian dictators, but it did not work. Abache was sui generis. Like Idi Amin. "I don't believe Abache was Nigerian." Soyenka quips. "He dropped from a planet."

Democracy in Nigeria, Soyenka believes, is in trouble. Oil wealth has bastardized and degraded it. The people want and deserve compensation and autonomy, resource wealth, but there is thuggery and bad leadership, power against freedom and truth, out-of-control power that must be stopped. They have passed the point of continuing to cast blame on colonialism. Soyenka says of all of Africa, "We must accept responsibilities for our successes and our failures." In most cases it has been a half century since independence. He levels blame at the Arab League for not condemning the atrocities, in Darfur, of the Janjaweed, who push a pan-Arab agenda.

African writers, Soyenka believes, are on an inward-looking search, probing contradictions. Without his own political activism, he fears he might collapse. It is what he has eaten for so long that it now eats him. "Something takes place that negates my raison d'etre or goes against my ideals, and there is self-seizure. I have no choice." I think about the time he took over a radio station to play a political tape he felt that Nigerians needed to hear. I ask him if he could give up art, and he says that fortunately there is no need to give it up. Even if he moves into senility, there will be creative urges. Most creative human beings would rather be doing something else. A creative template builds up inside of you and you want to actualize it.

Soyenka must be inspired to write. He is unlike those writers who sit down with espresso for a certain number of hours or turn out a certain number of pages. He writes when the material in his head has gestated and must give birth, even if caesarian.

Soyenka fought for rooting out the Boers and reclaiming the dignity of race, but he has had to watch his own race inflicting agonies. A lot had to do with the wrong leaders. But there is a lunacy and virus loose in Nigeria and across the globe in the name of Islam that politicians have exploited. When he grew up, there was a spirit of community among neighbors who were Christians, sharing the festivity of Ramadan as Muslims did with Christmas. There is great potential for Nigeria with the right kind of leadership. With its material and human resources Nigeria can be an example for the whole African continent. "Maybe not in my lifetime," says Soyenka. "But I believe it can happen."

South Africa as an example does not seem to be affecting the continent as it should. The horror in Rwanda, Darfur, the wars in Sierra Leone, the Ivory Coast, Liberia, the fires that raged in Congo. Rules need to be spelled out for a commonwealth of nations. Protocols. Soyenka has started a political party. He continues, unswerving and undaunted, to believe in democracy and ideal leadership. In social justice. In the transformative power of literary art.

Into the Hall of Fame and Off the Team

I CERTAINLY WASN'T FOLLOWING my old script, which
involved my becoming a respected novelist, but on balance life seemed good. I still loved classroom teaching. My desire to
make a mark as a writer was finally beginning to be eclipsed by the real
life I had made for myself. I was known more, even in the world of commercial radio, as one who talked with and interviewed writers rather
than a writer who talked about writing. It seemed natural to do what I
came to be doing in the public sphere. Questioning. Talking. Discussing.
Conversing. Analyzing. Quipping. Above all, whether with individuals
or panels, trying to pull out the best in myself and others.

I had academic colleagues who imagined, since I was with the leading radio station, that I must be making beaucoup bucks. I had long suspected that writers who had earned great respect often hunger for more
money or a wider readership and fame, and that ones who had money
or wider fame longed for greater respect. This was confirmed when I
split an hour between Anne Rice, author of *Interview with a Vampire* and
a number of tales of horror and eroticism, and Mavis Gallant, a much
admired literary figure and short story writer who wrote fiction for *The
New Yorker* and other quality publications. Gallant came into the studio
first. Having heard, before we even began to talk, that she would be
followed by Anne Rice, she launched into a diatribe about writers who
prostitute their writing, turning out vulgar potboilers for cult audiences.
Anne Rice, whose poet husband, Stan, had been a friend and colleague of
mine, came into the studio livid after Gallant left—dishing it out about
how coterie writers who couldn't compel a large audience were full of

whining and insult when the truth was that large audiences simply didn't cotton to them, usually for good reasons. Well, I would gladly take either of their mantles, best-seller popularity or high literary achievement, if only I could cut the mustard and create worthy work.

Leslie meanwhile had risen in less than a decade to become vice president and general counsel of Dole Packaged Foods. I was one of those men baffled by the notion that having a high-earning executive wife somehow diminished my masculinity. I felt proud of Leslie and more at ease about the present and our future because she could command a heftier income than I could. When she was in a law firm noted for representing Standard Oil, I kidded Sierra Club-minded acquaintances of ours that she did more to make the company comply with environmental standards than the environmental activists. But working for Dole presented a different set of questions. The company had long been associated with the use of cheap labor in Latin America and the Philippines, although Dole workers in those countries, ironically enough, had a better standard of living than many of their fellow countrymen and women. Many of Leslie's fellow executives, most of them likeable, amiable men, were conservative Republicans. I was that guy on the radio who was critically bashing Reagan and Bush, as well as inveighing against the corporatization of America and the overemphasis on profit over human value. Notwithstanding such on-air rhetoric, I still wanted to be viewed more as an unpredictable maverick than a yellow-dog liberal or even the unregenerate lefty that many believed me to be. In truth, I was becoming more conservative simply because I had more to conserve. I wanted a better life for my family more than I wanted to preserve ideological purity.

When the Weathermen were smashing storefront windows in an attempt to mobilize working-class youth against the Vietnam War, I was one of those who, though opposed to the war, empathized more with the storeowners and wondered if too many of the Weather Underground thugs were silver-spooned—not driven, as I was, by more conventional, upwardly mobile desires. Or maybe it was less that I was becoming more conservative than that America's political climate was changing, and I was blessed or cursed with the ability to see both sides. I never had doubt about my feelings of opposition to the Vietnam War, the need for racial justice and greater social equity or bringing important issues to public awareness. But I tended now, more than ever, to see both sides of many major issues, hardly a plus for the increasingly polarized world of talk radio.

The liberal in me argued that affirmative action was the best way to redress historic evils of slavery and white supremacy. Yet I talked about how attempts to implement it as policy were riddled with unfairness and how children of poor and working-class whites were more in need than offspring of the black bourgeoisie. I believed that the death penalty was barbaric and wrong in light of the obvious racism with which it was meted out—not to mention the simple, unassailable fact that someone could be executed, and indeed many had been, for crimes they had not committed. Yet when I commented to my listeners about the mayhem of some criminals, my visceral response was that a lethal needle in the arm was too easy a way for them to die. If they were clearly, incontrovertibly, guilty, why should their lives be spared? Doesn't a society have the right to make a murderer pay the ultimate price with the ultimate penalty? Particularly a democratic society with much of its citizenry in support of the death penalty—though a good deal of that support admittedly depended on who was polling and how they phrased the questions? I knew how perilous guns were lying around homes and that the proliferation of handguns was way out of control; colonial militia men used muskets, not Saturday night specials or Uzis. Yet I also commented on air that I understood the passion of NRA types who feared government authority would wrest away their firearms, who believed the Second Amendment was about their right to defend themselves, their loved ones and their property. I understood and vocally, forcefully defended a woman's right to choose, but I empathized with fathers who had helped conceive babies and wanted them—and, yes, empathized, too, with the anti-abortionists who felt horror at the sucking out of what they believed to be human life. I wanted Israel to survive in safety and peace, a phoenix nation built out of the ashes of the European Shoa, but I gave Palestinians opportunity to vent their cause on air, and I felt the pain of their plight. I still leaned left, and I was praised by the left for extending the commercial airwaves to people like Noam Chomsky, Alexander Cockburn, Christopher Hitchens, Jesse Jackson, Michael Parenti and others critical of U.S. foreign policy, neoimperialism and multinational corporatization. But I had begun to feel as if I could not legitimately call myself a lefty any more. I felt too privileged. I, who once went into prisons to help the incarcerated, now felt increasingly disposed toward being harshly punitive against violent criminals and pedophiles, despite wanting, against reason and logic, to cleave to the liberal notion that many somehow could be helped, rehabilitated, saved. I put on the air progressive voices for prison reform, but I found myself arguing for harsher punishment for violent offenders. Who was going to save the victims of the predators and the perpetrators who weren't locked up?

And despite the fact that I had fallen asleep at the wheel, I still railed against drunk drivers, especially repeat offenders, and advocated harsh punishment. Couldn't we deter drunk drivers from putting others at risk by meting out draconian sentences? I was sounding more conservative. I worked, after all, for a corporation, ABC, and I had been hired by a woman who owned a communications company to moonlight, as a facilitator, for a high-tech corporation in Menlo Park called Raychem—which, among other things, manufactured defense technology and weaponry for the government. I interviewed Raychem's CEO and president in a series of company-staged events. I liked the work. I liked learning about a corporate culture and its technology, and I liked the people I worked with, whatever their politics. I also liked the corporate check.

The truth was I was not exciting or controversial or outrageous like many now on the airwaves. I refused to shy away from taking positions, but I also fretted that emphasizing reason and seeing both sides would only be viewed as wishy-washy, compared to ultraopinionated, outspoken, bombastic and pompous talk hosts who were gaining audience.

How could I go on being civil and courteous when the gold standard increasingly appeared to be contention, elevation of adrenalin and demagoguery? Like many serious students of literary art, I saw grays. I liked listening to what others had to say, welcomed exchanges of ideas with callers and discussion of all sides, a free, bustling and varied marketplace of ideas. Wasn't that what the whole defense of George Lincoln Rockwell's right-to-speak was all about back when I was an undergraduate? Or was all that too passé and ACLU? I was admired for possessing balance and fairness but well knew, as time slipped on, that the medium I worked in was veering toward galvanizing hosts who could incite, fire up and entertain, toward more heat and excitement rather than thoughtful, critical analysis and debate. I had my fans and admirers. I knew, though, that I was unlikely to vault up to a higher level of success.

Radio wasn't the only medium that was changing. Television was, too. The Dick Cavett or Bill Buckley intellectual style of talk that many associated with my approach was becoming passé—as, soon enough, would the woman-friendly, warm and fuzzy, Irish Catholic, liberal and sometimes public-service-oriented Phil Donahue. Geraldo and Oprah were leaving Donahue in the ratings dust, and they soon would be followed by a spate of tabloiders trying to out-tabloid each other in a trajectory that would lead to Rikki Lake, one-time San Francisco TV host Maury Povich, Jerry Springer and Fox TV's Bill O'Reilly. Except for Ted Koppel, all nighttime television hosts were stand-ups, and Koppel's days were numbered. In radio, I heard more and more frequently the names Rush Limbaugh and Howard Stern. I made it my business to listen to both. Limbaugh was humorous, glib and controversial but, I thought, not the raving fascist people on the left made him out to be. He was pompous and biased, frequently wrong and a conspicuous Republican shill. But he was also appealing, entertaining, and a welcome voice to many from a different America than the one I lived in and broadcast from. His brand of talk radio would soon become the national gold standard. Saturday Night Live's Al Franken would launch a best seller and a radio career years later by ridiculing Limbaugh and going after his mendacity. Another Air America voice, Ed Schultz, would sound a lot like a bad version of Limbaugh on the left. The left would also hail Bill Moyers in TV and try, without success, to make popular talk hosts out of Jerry Brown and Jim Hightower. Howard Stern struck me as astonishingly puerile and cruel, with too much over-the-top sexism, too many farts and too much joking about mental retardation; but he could also be funny, very funny. His bad-boy appeal , his cutting brand of humor, his obsession with sex , his infantilism and willingness to flagellate anyone—including himself—was something I understood. However, if it took right-wing, blustering politics or jejune sophomoric locker room humor to be a national hit, I simply did not have the right stuff, and I could never make the Faustian bargain if I did.

In 1989 I anchored, solo, a "Nightfocus" segment on the *Exxon* Valdez oil spill and nursed a faint and preposterous hope that someone from ABC might notice and invite me to fill in for Ted Koppel, just as I secretly hoped that someone like Ed McLaughlin, who helped launch Limbaugh, might take to my brand of high-quality radio and do for me what he did for Rush. I would welcome a larger, national arena, the opportunity of reaching a wider audience beyond the Bay Area. Wasn't that often the ambitious trajectory of public servants? The mayor who feels he can do more as governor, the local assemblyman who wants to go to Washington and serve a greater constituency on Capitol Hill?

Television that year had a number of big, riveting international stories with strong and lasting images, like those from Tiananmen Square, the Panama invasion and the fall of Romania's Ceausescu. International stories were of less interest to the public compared, for example, to a local program we did on "Nightfocus"—one that got nominated for an Emmy—on a man named Ramon Salcido, who murdered his own children. I relished geopolitics and international issues, but the public appetite for those stories, excepting the really big ones, was on the wane and would continue that way up to 9-11. More and more, I heard the cliché about news coverage being local and the maxim "if it bleeds it leads." More and more there was in both television and radio the drive to excite, to sensationalize, to pull in the biggest numbers with the biggest net stitched of controversy, bluster and unwavering certainty.

.   .   .

THE P.D. AT KGO, a former news director named Bruce, was a likeable guy who started preaching the gospel to us of sensationalizing. He spoke nearly reverentially of the work of Alan Berg. I ignored Bruce's frequent importunings at meetings about how our radio programs were like parties, how we needed to get as many people to our parties as we possibly could, by whatever means, and get them to stay as long as possible. When he died of a painful prostate cancer, his position was filled by a young news director who had the same kind of dulled-gray-matter, frat boy quality I associated with Dan Quayle and would later see, to a lesser extent, in George W. Bush. He believed in bizarre stunts and any outrageous action that might bring ink from the press. He delivered his first newscast to the opening sounds of ringing gunshots.

There is no tenure in broadcasting. The litmus test for performance, besides ratings, is the volume of listener response. The other regular hosts got a lot more. They stirred things up more and elicited more emotion. I continued, anomalously, to opt more for civil and intelligent discourse—though I did enjoy editorializing when I could fuse it with real emotion, on occasion getting strong responses. But I had little appetite for being contentious for its own sake or stirring things for the sake of ratings. Maybe if I could simulate or fake passion more or not see so many grays—but, I thought, I am who I am.

When a young woman known for her love of abrasive radio and her peremptoriness with underlings was hired as executive producer, I began to feel uncertain about my status—even though this young woman, who resembled Heidi Fleiss, invited me to lunch and told me how great it was that I interviewed writers. I had just had on Jean Auel, author of *The Clan of the Cave Bear*—in my mind a more commercial and less literary writer—and the new young woman executive praised the interview and asked me if I would read her fiancé's novel. I read it and made notes and suggestions, though I remained silent about how vapid I thought it really was. Then Craig Spear, one of the KGO producers and a friend, informed me that she had said to him: "What's with Krasny and all these writers? Our listeners don't give a shit about that stuff. It belongs on NPR, not on our air." The G.M., too, continued to tell people that I sounded "too NPR," though he also seemed to have taken a liking to me, even calling me "boychick"—an affectionate Yiddish diminutive that a few of my closer Jewish male friends also called me. "He almost likes you," Ronn Owens said of The G.M., whom years later would become his mortal, feuding enemy. "And with him, that is as good as it gets."

I was invited to an elegant party that The G.M. threw to celebrate his birthday. It was at the Mark Hopkins, a swanky San Francisco hotel, and attended only by his close associates and the five regular talk hosts. I bought him a bunch of fiction, including some Bellow, and included a warm note. Soon after, I was honored with a commendable achievement award from Media Alliance, a lefty journalist group, and then by the San Francisco office of the Hebrew University, which presented me with the S.Y. Agnon medal for intellectual distinction. Such prestigious awards, I felt, could only solidify my position. The G.M. sent a note of congratulations to me for the Media Alliance award, and he attended the dinner that the Hebrew University threw in my honor. I assured myself that I was on his A Team.

·   ·   ·

I HAD JUST BROADCAST right outside the grounds of San Quentin, while California and the world awaited the execution of Robert Alton Harris. I was jacked up and full of adrenalin because there was fear raging inside me, the fear I always have had of my own aggression. I wanted Harris to die. Harris was beaten nearly to death as a boy, far more mercilessly than I ever was by the sixth-grade British teacher who periodically erupted and took me literally by my ear into the boy's room and punched and kicked me and once shoved my head into a toilet. I wanted the appeals to fail and the wailing of protestors opposed to his dying to be choked and stilled by his death. I had let the public know in strong, deeply personal ways how much I wanted Harris to die—the man who snuffed life from two teen boys, two brothers, two children, and told them to die like men, then murdered them and finished off one of the boy's hamburgers. I felt as though I could kill the motherfucker myself, and I unsheathed all that aggression and put it into strong language. Yet I felt anything but demagogic. My tone and passion and clarity all felt right. The new P.D., for whom I had no respect—because he was so dull and shallow that those adjectives were much too flaccid—told me after the broadcast how magnificent I was, what a fantastic performance I delivered, and yet I didn't feel good about it. He had taken me to dinner a few weeks before and offered advice on how I needed to jack things up and give the public more sensation. I had just, the night before, interviewed Harvard philosopher Robert Nozick, and here was this philistine frat boy telling me, with all the sham friendliness of a car salesman, that I needed to come out of the chute at 10 P.M. with more hard-hitting stuff, like "A Current Affair."

Well, I delivered at San Quentin, and it was what I felt—or at least it felt like what I felt—but it was fueled, too, by inchoate fear that I was doing what I knew I needed to do, given the new commercial broadcast standard where everything suddenly had to be hot hot hot . . . I knew I was also going against the grain of the left, sounding like one of them—those Americans whom so many educated Europeans had contempt for—and I wondered if I, too, were made of the same stuff. Did a good man hector for capital punishment?

I was on the dark side of forty, and still, I realized, I did not have a true sense of who I was. Was I a novelist? If I were a novelist, I would be processing ideas and thoughts, impressions and descriptions, birthing characters, plotting. I would not be accepting one public appearance invitation after another or doing stand-up evenings of Jewish humor or cranking out book reviews or running to see new films or taking on corporate jobs, joining with old friends or even giving precious time to expanding my social circles. The work would take over, and all of this other feel-good or money-making stuff, all of this do-good-for-others, community and being-the-public-person stuff and maybe even family too, would be shunted aside so I could focus on writing. If I were the novelist I had long hoped myself to be, I would not be interviewing writers. I would be the interviewee.

· · ·

I WAS INDUCTED into the Heights High Hall of Fame. Since I was a teacher, they asked me, following the ceremony, if I would like to teach an English class on Hamlet. I agreed. The school was now 60, maybe 70 percent black, with metal detectors at the entrances. I was filled with longing and strange waves of nostalgia as I delivered my speech with the cadences of the broadcaster and teacher I had become, with the intonation and power that I knew would bring applause. Then I was in the classroom doing what I was born to do—teaching, and entertaining too, playing to the largely black student class by explicating the Oedipus complex, throwing in how the MF word might connect us to Hamlet's possible feelings for his mother, Gertrude. I was talking hip, dispensing knowledge, tossing in pop-culture references and tickling them with rap jargon. Keeping it up and keeping it steady, real. This was my métier—exchanging ideas, inspiring thought, making thought come alive. All those writers who wrote so well and talked so poorly!

Some I nearly had to pull teeth with—Janet Malcolm of *The New Yorker*, one of the nation's best and most formidable essayists, who spoke on air to me with quivering trepidation and near inarticulateness, even as I tried steadfastly and with gentle assurance to make her feel at ease, to pull her brain power out through her tangled tongue. Joan Didion was another quivering talker of rare mettle and perspicacity on the printed page. Or David Byrne, impressively creative with his music and his lyrics, yet on air with me a dud of monosyllabic grunting. I had the verbal gift of fluency. Why not relish that? Cherish it!

I was at the top of my game with much to be thankful for. And yet . . . "Nightfocus" had been dropped—with the usual euphemistic, publicized PR phrases that it was put on hiatus—so once more I was no longer on TV. I was beating Larry King, Tom Snyder and a recycled Rush Limbaugh in the nighttime radio ratings, but it was not all about me. As my colleague Lee Rodgers put it, radios in the Bay Area were soldered to KGO, and listeners, at night especially, preferred a locally based talk program, the reverse of the television trend that was now canceling local morning programs for ones that were in syndication. I still coveted a national show with no likelihood of that coming to pass. And if I had a shot, I told myself, what kind of a sick whore would I have to become? Dean Edell got his shot at a national TV show, and a producer clamored in Edell's ear for him to get real tears from an audience member for the camera. Sensation and quick emotion, hot hot hot, the new yellow brick road to high ratings.

I was at the top of my game on air, but felt unappreciated. The nitwit P.D. loved me at San Quentin, but what about that talk he gave me in the Union Street Italian restaurant about needing to be more sensational, to clobber and slug out more controversy? He left a copy of Madonna's *Sex Book* in my mailbox, with a note that it would be great programming for acquiring young demographics. His underling—the young woman who pretended to think it was great that I had on authors, and complained about it behind my back—called me at home about a show I was doing on golf with some Monterey golf pros, advising me that no one young really cared about golf. "It's an old man's game," she said. I told her I personally had no interest in the game but wanted to keep my program eclectic and unpredictable, full of variety, and I wanted, too, to do different, offbeat hours—to keep learning, with my audience, about myriad matters, including areas I knew or cared little about, like golf. I didn't tell her that I also wanted to test myself to see if I could discuss a subject I had little or no interest in—but I did tell her that there were fascinating class issues about golf players, and that she was wrong that golf was an old man's game. "It's probably more a Republican's game," I joked. Young was what these new executives craved, parroting the avarice of The G.M. for the all-important young demos. The G.M. wanted the double-digit ratings numbers of yesteryear when KGO, still to this day on top of ratings in the market, trounced, crushed and eviscerated all competition, with fifteens and twenties of overall market share. Now it was dominant still, but registering only in the sevens, eights and nines. And too much of those single-digit winning numbers, they felt, was tonnage. They wanted the young demo digits to spike and zoom.

I remembered, months before, seeing the P.D. walking out of The G.M.'s office—looking as if he had just been in a boxing ring for a few rounds as a sparring partner for Jake LaMotta, because the younger demographic numbers had dipped. "Rush is killing us in the drive-time morning hours," he explained to me. "He's fucking killing us." The G.M. had turned his anger on him, and the P.D. was reeling from the temper assault. The female executive would-be golf-talk silencer, and the zombie news director—whom the news guys called Mengele—were both, I knew, fearful of The G.M.'s outbursts and pirouetted to his vampiric demands for huge numbers of young-blooded listeners so he could sell ads at higher rates. I felt above it all. It was too venal, and as long as I did my job and put out quality programs that attracted and kept a large audience, the hell with their number crunching and bean counting.

.   .   .

RIPENESS MAY BE ALL, according to Shakespeare, but choices, in my experience, were really all. I chose to play hardball, but first I chose softball. Let me explain. San Francisco city employees challenged KGO to a softball game. I had long thought of myself as a pretty fair softball player. I regularly organized games each summer for years, inviting colleagues, students, friends and acquaintances. All very politically correct, with both genders on the field, followed by a picnic. I would pitch. I often thought of myself on air as a pitcher—serving up one question after another and trying to experiment with different spins and varying speeds. Larry King seemed the ultimate softball pitcher, almost like one of those machines used in batting practice, usually for hardball, that keeps loading the ball up and sending it across the plate. I thought of myself, too, as a decent hitter. I liked softball so much, in fact, that I got a team together, a bunch of fellow English professors. We joined a city league and called ourselves, from Othello, the Two-Backed-Beasts, playing against and usually getting defeated by teams like the San Francisco Sixty-Niners, made up of Mission District blue-collar Hispanics. I hit for an average of above 300, which I computed after every game, so when the call went out for KGO to play softball against Mayor Art Agnos and city employees, I chose to play. It was hardly a momentous decision. I enjoyed the prospect of beating a team led by Agnos. He would later become someone I would like, but at that time I beat him up on air because I found him arrogant, and I felt it served me to show that I could flail liberals. None of the other talk hosts signed up to play.

On Saturday, game day, I felt lousy, run down and fluish. I told my brother Vic, who came by to watch the game, that I probably shouldn't be playing, but there I was swinging an assortment of bats to see which one I liked. An umpire, hired by the mayor's office, explained the rules and told me, the pitcher, that I had to put an arc on the ball. I never had to pitch with an arc. I protested, to no avail. I walked the first three batters and quickly went to the showers. Newsman Ed Baxter took over on the mound, and I conceded to him and the others that pitching with an arc was not for me. I went into the outfield and told myself I would show my mettle at the plate. But when I got up to bat, the high-arc pitching confused me, and I felt weakened and ailing. I wanted to hit for distance but wound up fanning on three pitches while The G.M. shouted strange catcalls at me about being "a guy from Cleveland." Weird, I thought. We were on the same team. Why was he razzing me? When I got up to bat later, for a second time, I swung twice and missed the ball, then barely connected for an easy grounder right to Agnos, who was playing first and tagged me out as I came toward him, smiling and gloating, "Boy did I enjoy that!" By contrast, The G.M. hit a line-drive single his first at bat and was cheered by his minions as if he had delivered a game-winning blow. His second at bat was another infield single that he managed to beat out hustling. I saw him as the inning ended and went over and complimented him on his hits, adding something about how I got confused by the arc and didn't feel too well. "Believe it or not," I hastened to add, "I was a pretty fair softball player in my day. I even played on a city league team." An enormous grin burst forth on his face and he said, "And what kind of team was that? Paraplegics?"

I playfully mock-punched him on the arm, while that grin at his own cleverness stayed on his face. I knew I had humiliated myself and lost macho points—just as I did when I complained to him and Ronn Owens of vertigo on a Bay cruise, only to have them both pipe up that they weren't dizzy. Yet I knew he had a kind of held-at-bay affection for me, and there was, after all, the Jewish tribal connection. So when it came time for me to re-up a contract, I chose to play hardball.

Everyone had their battles with The G.M. or his P.D. proxy over money. He had let all of us know that he wasn't going to let things get out of hand, as in professional baseball, where players dictated ever more astronomical salary terms. In fact, when Lee Rodgers asked for a raise he felt fair to the market and the share of ratings he was posting, he played hardball and wound up walking. His leaving was a big loss to the lineup, and it took a while before the P.D. could smooth things over enough to get him to return on terms acceptable to all parties. Lee counseled me to ask for a considerable raise before I signed a new contract, assuring me I had a loyal following and was a proven, hard-working performer who deserved a healthy bump in pay, all of which made sense to me and sounded fair-minded. So did Lee's notion that I would have to be willing to play hardball, to put my job on the line—though, the way he figured it, they wouldn't want to go through with me what they had just gone through with him. Moreover, they needed me and had no one in the wings except a loudmouth, leftist, Israel-hating ex-priest named Bernie Ward. "They've got hundreds of demo tapes from all over the country," Lee assured me. "I've heard the supposed best of them. Believe me, there is no one even close to being as high-quality as you are, and you're a proven and popular performer in this market."

Bernie Ward, who did a kind of weekly crossfire duel with Lee, had coveted my slot for years, and I knew he had lobbied and pestered nearly everyone in management, especially the Dan Quayle-like moron P.D., that he should be the one sitting where I was because, Ward felt, he was much more controversial. In my mind he wasn't wrong about that, since he ranted a lot more than I ever did or could. But the former P.D., the one who had told me he didn't want to be my assassin and then left for a more powerful position in Seattle, also told me that he believed Bernie, with his sandpaper voice, would be a miserable choice for a regular slot. I knew, too, despite the fact that Bernie more easily stirred controversy, that he was not as liked as I was or seen as being in the same league. Whenever he saw me he greeted me effusively, both on and off the air, bellowing, "it's the erudite one." But he wanted to replace me. On one occasion, the station announced that he was filling in for Lee and talking on the air to a naked woman, who turned out to be porn star Nina Hartley. Was this where the work we were doing was headed? Not that I was a prig about porn stars, having interviewed both Marilyn Chambers and Annette Haven, though without the kind of prurience I saw in Bernie's eyes and not with the guest au naturel. Lee, who liked Bernie, and Ronn, who detested Bernie, and others in the know thought there was no chance of Ward ever getting my slot.

I asked for a raise—not as large as the one that sent Lee packing a few years earlier or that he, as a former P.D., assured me I was entitled to, but enough to prove that I was worth dipping into what they cared most about, their pocketbook. THEY were The G.M. and his crew of managers, but THEY also meant something more amorphous, something that seeped into the ego and clamored for validation. How much were THEY willing to pay ME, and how much did THEY truly value and want ME? Ronn Owens was making twice as much. Was Ronn really worth twice simply because he was on in drive time, when the ads ran for a lot more? I'd been with the station for over a decade. Surely they appreciated my work. Surely they would pay what I was asking, and if they wouldn't meet what I felt was a fair figure, I thought—well, then, we would negotiate. I hated the whole game, but I knew from veteran and more savvy-at-the-game guys like Rodgers and Eason and Owens that you had to begin high and ballsy.

It wasn't, truly, that money was a priority to me. I liked what I did on radio and only thought of money as a way of providing more and better for my wife and kids. Were I to win the lottery, there would be little I would actually want for myself. I liked travel and good restaurants, sure, but I was my father's son, a man of modest taste who still eschewed materialism. I honestly felt—knew—I could as easily live in a garret as in a mansion. But my kids were in private schools, we had a regular housekeeper and steep expenses. "Nightfocus" was on hiatus, and Leslie was quite possibly leaving her job with Dole because the company was moving to Southern California. I added all that in to the mix of what I fancied would be my pitch—give me more money and entice us to stay in the Bay Area because my wife was wanted elsewhere. Why shouldn't I get more money, I told myself. I deserved it!

The fates converged. Weeks after the San Quentin execution broadcast I had on Doris Lessing, one of the world's great women novelists and the author of a book on Zimbabwe. Somalia was beginning to erupt, so it was good programming. I also had on, two days later, Jessica Mitford, the journalistic doyenne who had written *The American Way of Death*, an extraordinary, loftily praised book about the mortuary business. The P.D. cornered me in the hall. "Kraz," he began. "You gotta stop putting old broads on. You think they're gonna bring us young demos?" Soon after that encounter, for the first time, I had a lousy "ratings book." I expected it would rebound in the next book, which it did. But I had already set actions in motion and had let the P.D. know that I wanted more money. I had no idea how one bad ratings book was destined to play out, though Lee Rodgers and a number of others assured me that a single bad book following years of strong ones meant squat. But I also remembered how The G.M. had become furious at my demand for more money before I first signed on—and here I was, insisting on more than the 2.5 percent cost-of-living raise I assumed The G.M. had in mind for me.

The P.D. had to win his bones and not allow other hosts to think they could crank more dough out of the company, and who knew what orders he was getting from above. He told me, in our first formal contract talk, that he didn't want to sign me up again and that he had someone in mind to replace me. I assumed it had to be Bernie Ward, but he let on to me that it wasn't. Some hardball player! Even though I thought he may have been bluffing, I felt crushed that he could actually, really talk about letting me go. I told myself that it probably was a ruse, that of course they wanted me and were simply trying to get my money demand down, especially with the leverage they had from the last bad ratings book. So I ate crow. I told the P.D. the truth, that money had never really been my objective. That the job was what mattered and that I would sign up again if only they would tell me what they believed was a fair dollar figure. I reminded him, too, of how much praise he had heaped on my performance at San Quentin.

"Let me walk around the park on this and get back to you," he said with weighty-sounding seriousness, like a kid impressing himself by playing the role of an executive. As I left and as we shook hands, I noticed something I had not noticed before. Off to the side in his office, there was a large plaque that a listener had made for me in my early days of doing radio at the station—when I would go off the air saying, "This is Michael Krasny signing off." The plaque had those words nicely engraved, with a beautiful waterfall scene. I had lost track of it. Why, I wondered, was it nestled here in the corner of the P.D.'s office now? Was he signing me off? After all these years of diligent, hard work on the air and innumerable public appearances, was there really someone else waiting in the wings?

I called The G.M. at his home that night. I felt I needed to make him understand that I had good motives and was not just trying to hold him up for more money. I felt that I could reason with him. From the outset, I felt that my whole negotiating stance was foolish, wrong for me, the kind of role that I was ill suited for. Where money was concerned, I liked Kafka's aphorism that he who seeks shall not find but he who does not seek shall be found. I explained that all I had really wanted was to negotiate. I heard what sounded like a sneering snort as he repeated the word, "negotiate," and then I heard him add an elliptical snatch of words about me hating to read commercials and not having enough respect for the sponsors. He then muttered, "Usually I like to let guys go, to kick them when they're down when their egos get too big. But this is one I don't enjoy." Was my ego getting too big? Hell, egos swell enormously behind microphones, but really, mainly, I only wanted to find out what I was worth to them and to get fair compensation for hard, quality work. I was also—like trying to pitch and hit softballs with arcs—out of my league.

Although The G.M. said he would consider my situation, I was beginning to realize that they really did want to get rid of me. Apparently I was not worth a decent raise. I refused to beg or demean myself, but I made it clear once more that I wanted the job. He knew I was no ego-bloated hotshot inflating my own worth. But why had I broken my own principle of not making money the issue?

That night, I dreamed there was a wedding and all of them were there—the G.M., the P.D, the anti-golf female executive and the newsroom's Mengele. I woke up remembering that Toni Morrison, in a novel called *Sula*, included the dream of a wedding, which turned out to be a harbinger of loss, the presentiment of an ill wind of change. Later that morning, the P.D. told me in his office that he had thought a lot about it and had decided not to renew my contract, effective immediately.

I took the news, as the cliché would have it, like a man . . . but it came as a steel blow. I managed to ask that I at least be able to say goodbye to my listeners with a final broadcast. He reluctantly agreed.

I was stunned. I was being booted out, and I felt dazed by it, shamed. I was in the dark. Was it the demand for more dough? The one bad ratings book? My not reading commercials with enough enthusiasm? My performance at the softball game? My still-unnamed potential successor? The fact that they always had me pegged as too cerebral? Too intellectual? Not entertaining enough? Having Lessing and Mitford on in the same week? I asked the P.D. why. All he said was, "We want to go in a different direction." He said the same thing to a columnist weeks later, who wrote, in response, "Down?"

After being told I was fired, I needed to walk. I left the ABC building and headed straight up Broadway, only to step into a pothole and injure myself so badly that I had to hail a cab to take me to Kaiser Hospital. I wound up hobbling in that night on crutches for my last show, a pretty pathetic figure.

I was wounded, sad and full of self-pity, but I wanted to do my last show with dignity and professionalism. I also wanted to let my listeners know that this would be my last show. I found out later that The G.M. wanted me cut loose before I could get on air that night lest I possibly badmouth him or anybody else in management, something others had done following firings in the past. But I honestly never had any intention of doing that. The G.M.'s thinking, I suppose, was that I would just disappear, and that whatever fans I had would not be as exercised or upset as they might be if I went into a swan song or a denunciation. The press would mostly be told that I was leaving due to creative differences and that, so to speak, would be that. To his credit, the P.D. stood up to The G.M. and insisted that I be allowed to do a farewell final show as he had agreed, even though, I subsequently discovered, he had put on alert the regular news anchor, a crony of his who liked to brag about the seventeen-year-old-girl he was planking. If I started laying into anyone in management, I found out later, the newsman had been instructed to shoo me physically out of the studio and take over the microphone. That would have been quite the audio spectacle—but I said goodbye the way I wanted to say goodbye, with emotion in my voice but with self-control, followed by a quick turn to the news and issues of the day. I stated that I did not want to discuss the reasons why I was leaving, but preferred to go out doing a regular, normal program. The flood of calls of outrage and outcry followed instantly, and I put a few of them on after they were screened, including a foreign-born taxi driver who sobbed uncontrollably. After that I put a clamp on, asking the screener and my listeners for no more such calls—saying that I did, truly, want only to discuss issues until this show, my last show, was over; to go out talking and listening, as I had done now for years. I was also fighting an inner battle, feeling sorry for myself and wanting to hear the outpourings of love, fealty, loyalty and commiseration. I had been their companion, their voice in the night, their source of information and their opinion shaper, their font of nightly serious reflection, intermittent lightheartedness and fun, a fixture and a friend to many for eight years and thousands of hours.

The best thing for me personally about being let go was being able to do that last show with the kind of self-restraint and dignity I admired and to realize, in the weeks and months that followed, that my work mattered and how important I had become to many—something that I never truly realized until that last hour. The expressions of regret, the anger, the consolations I received after that final show moved me tremendously. I learned from droves of listeners what I was probably seeking to have management affirm by giving me a raise—that my work was valued. Now my voice, which had been a steady, trusted companion for some and doubtless a nuisance to others, the voice of a flaming liberal to some and a soothing counterpoint to contentiousness to others, a voice of intelligence and reason to some and pomposity and sententiousness to others—that voice in the night would be silenced. "You've made your mark, and people will miss you," the sportswriter Lowell Cohn told me, and those were words I clung to. But the truth was, no matter how much people told me, in the days and weeks and months that followed, that I was too good for KGO, I felt I was being let go because I was somehow not good enough.

The replacement they hired for me was a guy whom Bruce, the P.D. who died of cancer, had become acquainted with when he worked in Denver—a guy with a nice, pleasant-sounding voice known for "wild and zany stunts" (always the two conjoined adjectives) that had received Denver newspaper coverage. I listened to him as much as I could bear, usually in moments alone at night in the car, and—without a shred of enmity toward him personally—I concluded, as many listeners and the other hosts did, that he was a vapid lightweight who made me look all that much better, and whom I even began to feel sorry for since he was so out of his league, so obviously a poor and intemperate choice, a would-be but not funny clown in a lineup of men who provided a staple of serious newstalk. He set off an avalanche of complaints, especially after using the word Chinamen and asking listeners to weigh in on whether or not they would set fire to the homeless for cash, and he was gone in a few months. Then Bernie Ward got the job. Later the P.D., epitomizing both the Dilbert and Peter principles, moved up into the highest executive ranks in ABC.

I felt as if I had been murdered. That sounds terribly hyperbolic, but nevertheless expressed my state of mind—and that was how a *San Francisco Chronicle* columnist said it sounded when I bid my farewell and got those on-air calls. I felt The G.M. probably ordered the hit. I had the feeling that everything was out of kilter, and I was suddenly looking at a world in which nothing essentially had changed and life went on just as before, but somehow everything had changed, and I was not in it in the same way anymore. It was almost as though I had been removed and put into some sort of limbo—despite the fact that the local papers played up my departure, in some instances, as if it meant the death of quality radio, a defining moment. Liberals and lefties mourned my loss, little realizing that it had been more about money and young demos than politics. In many ways, Bernie Ward was far more to the left than I and even began modestly to call himself the lion of the left. He would later get into a major flap with the Jewish community by making some stupid, rank remark about Jews not being as advanced as Christians in ways of forgiveness. With his anti-Israel fervor, I heard constantly, especially from Jews, how much they wished he hadn't replaced me—even though he was not the choice to replace me. Truth be told, Bernie was far superior to the man they chose.

There would be a hue and cry long after, once conservatives became dominant as talk radio hosts, about the inability of liberals, progressives or lefties to take hold in talk radio. My name was tossed out locally and throughout pockets of the West as a prime example of the purging of the left from the commercial airwaves. Laments also flooded into print when I left KGO about the sad dumbing down of talk radio, about how Rush Limbaugh and Howard Stern wannabees and shock jocks and prurient morning zoos were ruining radio and hijacking it from serious discourse. I believed a lot of that to be true, too, but I also believed that none of it quite applied to me. Talk radio would increasingly become a right-wing phenomenon and play hard on controversy and sexuality. Even an old-fashioned quasi-liberal like Tom Lykis, who once fanned the flames of serious discussion over political issues, would see the light in the heat and reinvent himself as the nationally syndicated Professor Lykis, an obese, salacious and misogynistic adviser to the all-important young-demo males on how to get more tail for less money and how to keep women under their thumbs. Right-wing characters like Oliver North and G. Gordon Liddy would move into national talk show quarters, and a favorite local San Francisco-based station, KSFO, would become, after being purchased by ABC, a totally conservative hot talk station, "sieg heil on your dial," as one local wag called it.

Despite all the sympathy and generous, consoling "you were too good for them" sentiment, I felt Herb Caen's item, simply announcing to the world that I was "bounced," reflected what people were thinking—which is to say, even though I was repeatedly reassured otherwise, that I had failed, been cast off. I wondered why I felt little anger. That would come later, when The G.M., would say, in a public forum when asked why I was let go, "He just wasn't well enough prepared." Jesus! If there was one thing you could put on my tombstone, it was that I was always prepared. Overprepared. But for the time being, I felt mostly numb and sad, like a failure. Digger and other friends told me they felt mad enough to kill for me while I, who had always grappled with feelings of rage, bore myself with dignity on that last broadcast and remained, despite feelings of depression, surprisingly rancorless. Well, I had chosen to play hardball, and now, for the first time in over a decade, I faced a life outside of radio. It could be worse. At least I had a professorship and could go home again full time, back to my first love of teaching literature. Or perhaps I could find another venue for myself in radio or television, though I had no idea where that would be. I had found my voice, and now it was rendered mute. I wouldn't go begging again like a mendicant, as I had years before with Jim Shock. I was suddenly, literally overnight, an ex-public figure with no microphone for my broadcaster's voice and no literary voice to fall back on, mute and flooded with feelings of waning respect, failure and ruefulness. Funny how my career dreams of doing both television and radio and eventually hosting a national show had evaporated, and I had only the classroom to return to with no likely media work in sight. Where could I possibly fit in this changing, young-demo-hungry, right-turning, Geraldoized market? I suddenly felt like a dinosaur, an old-schooler—jobless, rudderless, and wondering what I might be willing to settle for.

Well, here was the opportunity for another choice. I could see at last if I really could coax out a novel. Though it sounded too harsh, maybe I had even been a kind of faux broadcaster all along, using it to sublimate the need to write and the higher calling of the novelist. Like teaching, broadcasting had felt like a calling, a métier—but then so had writing. Could I go back to my original blueprint for a life filled with only teaching and writing, give writing the wall-to-wall, full-court press, my last push for my first real writer's hurrah? I was cast out of broadcasting at an age at which novelists weren't born, rarely emerged and were highly unlikely to deliver. Yet somehow I would come back from this blow, rebound, pick myself back up and perhaps even, at last, find my calling.

Except it didn't happen that way. I continued to feel like a man who had lost his post and had to face failure. It was Ronn Owens who helped start me off at KGO, and it was Ronn who gave me what may have been the best advice. The week everything fell apart he had been out of town, on vacation, and he called me when he returned. You could always count on Ronn to avoid real sadness, emotion or lamentation. That sort of seriousness was more the province of a colleague like Lee Rodgers, often labeled a right winger, who seemed troubled and saddened by the way my career had apparently reached its denouement and assured me, "There are a lot of people who are pretty upset and angry about what happened to you. You are a very well-liked man." Ronn, on the other hand, tried humor, exclaiming "I leave town for just one week and look what happens! Listen," he offered, "the best thing for you to do is to find another talk show. In no time people won't remember who you are, and you'll be like one of those disappeareds in Argentina. Get something while you're still fresh in the public eye." It was good advice. And who was I fooling? I wanted to continue doing a talk show, to continue having a public platform. It was truth time. I was a talker and not a writer. There. I'd said the unsayable. But a platform? Where? How? I was not leaving the Bay Area.

Leslie and I went off with our daughters for a week vacation that we had planned months earlier, to Club Med Ixtapa. It felt good to be away in a place where no one knew I had been bounced, where we could fill our days with mindless relaxation and recreation and the indolent hedonism of eating and drinking and lying around in the sun. Still, I had to stave off the depression that was constantly dragging me down.

I thought about writing a piece on my experiences in commercial radio, coupling it with strong rhetoric about its decline, but it was still too fresh. I prayed that the idea for a novel would come and fiercely take hold of me, unleashing a relentless outpouring of language and storytelling. Augie March trained eagles in Mexico, and I was lying poolside at Club Med. I needed an idea, a concept, a plot, an image, anything that would take hold and send me into the throes of creation. Perhaps a dream might magically arrive, as it had for Robert Louis Stevenson, carrying him to the idea that gave birth to Dr. Jekyll and Mr. Hyde. Just give me the grist for a hit, or a novel of literary quality, and I would find my way out of the doldrums and back into the light.

But this, I admitted, was just more pipe dreaming. Magical thinking. No ideas came. My voice belonged behind a microphone. That was where I had found myself and where I was supposed to be. While I was in Mexico, a friend called my voicemail at home to tell me there was a job opening for a morning talk host in public radio with KQED, the local National Public Radio affiliate. Wouldn't that be a good fit for me? Shouldn't I consider it?

I was not keen on public radio. What little I knew about it from occasional samplings was that it sounded too stiff and formal. Plus, commercial broadcasting was where most of the action seemed to be— despite the fact that I had been told for years, especially by fellow academics, that the only radio they listened to was National Public Radio. The money they were offering was considerably less than what I had been making at KGO. But if I had really wanted money, I would have followed a different path from the beginning. What I knew of public radio, however, also made it seem like a real university of the airwaves, just the sort of phenomenon I had been trying habitually to create (golf hour, psychic and porn stars notwithstanding) in commercial radio. I was most resistant to the idea of public radio, however, because of the simple fact that The G.M. had for years labeled me an NPR type, and I did not want to become what he thought I was. I would have to try out for the position along with at least five or six others, a few whom I recognized as quality and seasoned broadcasters. I didn't know if I could take going down to defeat against any of them, and I knew enough about public radio's reputation for political correctness and affirmative action to realize that I would have a disadvantage competing in a lineup of tryouts that included women—especially a smart, celebrated feminist, a Filipino-American and a lesbian.

The job, I learned, was for a two-hour morning show called "Forum," and the host had been pushed out in a nasty power struggle. That, too, didn't sound auspicious. Nor, as I learned more, did the fact that the show was essentially all about public policy, particularly local public policy— definitely neither a strong interest of mine nor my strong suit. The host's role was more of even-handed moderator than editorializing shit disturber, and the content was serious rather than geared toward so-called infotainment. The show had only one short break each hour, rather than the three hours I was used to, with breaks every few minutes for commercials. A lot seemed wrong about it—but I felt I needed to take a shot.

Louise Erdrich

The first time I interviewed Louise Erdrich, I was on commercial radio, and she was with her husband, Michael Dorris. They were a glamorous couple. Not only their youth and good looks and Native bloodlines and writerly status. They were like a pair of teens in love, and they were, both of them, incredibly nice. All the darker stuff had not yet begun to smash into their lives.

Erdrich and I are fond of each other, pleased to be together again years later for yet another interview. She is ineffably sweet and exudes a fine kindness. On this particular morning she is upbeat, enthusiastic, girlish. I describe the nonlinearity of her newest novel, *The Painted Drum*. She laughs her spirited, hearty laugh. "Nonlinearity. That's me!"

Soon we are talking about relationships. Erdrich speaks of the necessity of risking one's heart as a purpose on earth. She is, she says, overwhelmed by the chaos of family life, but loves it. She sneaks off to her room for necessary writing solitude, but continues seeking new kinds of chaos. A new puppy. The dental office she and one of her daughters decided to turn into a bookstore.

I talk with her a bit about *Love Medicine* before broaching the subject of Michael, her late ex-husband. I allude to June Kapshaw winding up as a car her sons take home at the end of *Love Medicine* and ask her whether she knows that, according to Faulkner's biographer Joseph Blotner, the only television show the great Mississippi author ever watched was a short-lived one called "My Mother the Car." I get another laugh. She tells me the only television show she ever watches is "The Bounty Hunter."

I bring up Michael. It is easy to do because I heard her tell an NPR reporter that she didn't miss him, that she knew it was terrible for her to say, but it was what she honestly felt. She misses him, she says to me, but in other ways. In family for instance. But not in collaboration. There's a big box from those days that she hasn't opened. She doesn't know if she ever will.

Her grandfather felt comfortable with both Indian and Catholic traditions. They don't work together in Louise's mind, but came naturally together for her in her work because of him. "A lot of Catholicism has been taken into Native practice," she says. "The Vatican wouldn't approve. You don't change human values in Native or Ojibwa culture. You exist and be in the world as it is. Catholicism is the opposite. Searching out gay seminarians."

She and her sister teach writing at Turtle Mountain. Another sister is a pediatrician on the reservation. Trying to force assimilation onto Native Americans isn't working. It never has. I talk about all those who take up and copy Native ways. "I'm a quarter, and this belonging to the continent draws me in," she says. "People want to belong to Native cultures," I say, "Especially if it can help them gain entrance as a minority or buy in to a casino." Louise laughs.

We talk about writing. For her, character and place drive form, plot and everything. "Story comes out of character for me. Writing a story is entering an altered state. I rejoice. The story keeps going. The wonderful perk is getting the story. People come made up already. It's just like I'm hacking away the brush. It seems I'm open during hours I write and someone enters."

Louise has boxes of rejection slips. Unlike the big box that she has never opened, these are boxes she says she looks into all the time.

Cynthia Ozick

I met Cynthia Ozick once at a synagogue, years before I first interviewed her. I was with a Jewish historian named Fred Rosenbaum, who gushed to her that she was the best living Jewish woman writer. She sternly told him he ought not to make such gender-specific comments.

It is a far softer Ozick I meet in my studio for the first time. I may have softened her by mentioning my late friend Irv Halperin before we go live. Irv was a Holocaust scholar who helped her find her way after she literally got lost in the wrong building at a Jewish writer symposium at Berkeley. She was as grateful to him as if he had been her knight. The two corresponded for years.

We are on air talking about literature and the division she establishes with me about being a writer and being a citizen. Citizens, she says, are worldly, down-to-earth; they fulfill commitments. Writers are wild, free, demonic, irresponsible. She says she would rather be a writer, and I ask if one can't be both. Of course, she says, but it is a difficult double life because one is in the present and the other is not. Essays and novels, too, are divided. Sometimes essays can be a branch of fiction, but usually they use more intellect, and you know the subject and have great freedom, whereas when you begin a novel you are in inchoate territory. Fiction comes from images, and Ozick, a drugstore owner's daughter, tells me essays are prescriptions. Fiction for Ozick has no source in autobiography. "I just want to make things up and be free of any connection to self in writing fiction. That's the bliss." Was there bliss, I wonder without asking, in entering the vivid world she created without living in—the surreal horror of the Shoa in her great short story "The Shawl"? She would tell me in a later interview that writing that story was the only time she felt directed and that she hoped it would not ever happen to her again.

The demonic and evil soon emerge in our conversation, and Ozick says evil is what humans do. It is what we are capable of. Writers see evil more deeply than society—American society with its enlightenment values, its optimism, its myths of the frontier and, though shrinking, its opportunity. Twain used the phrase "evil joy" and that, she says, is something hard for Americans to acknowledge, though all of us saw it in New York on 9-11. Kafka knew what it was to give in to demonic irrationality. That was what murdered his three sisters and would have killed him if he hadn't died before the Nazis started their killing. Kafka's work is metaphysical, she says, but hers is not. She was never smart enough to be a metaphysical writer. I gently chide her and tell her she is one of our brainiest writers. "I flunked elementary algebra," she quips. Soon we are discussing Job. Ozick denounces the theologians who are apologists for God, who tell us God is just and that we cannot understand divine will on earth. "The world is unkind," she declaims. "There are fascists. There is sickness and evil joy, and people who want to crush others, and God is the one who crushes in Job. The frame of the story is false consolation. What happened to the first group of children that were wiped out? Has he lost his compassion or forgotten them? It's like the producers of the first Anne Frank play in the fifties. They offered us uplift, not history."

Ozick says she has recovered from New Criticism, the once nearly sacred textual approach to literary interpretation that negated the personal or biographic role of the artist. In order to get into Lionel Trilling's seminar at Columbia, she made a false conversion from it and agreed with him that full emphasis on the text left out psychology, sociology and history. But now she is a real convert and sees how character can influence content and shape a writer. A writer can lack compassion and be cold to his or her family and still create a masterpiece. She would not have wanted to have been either a lover or a friend to Henry James because she'd have been shunted away from him, but the selfishness of art gels as a compact with the selfishness of the worshipful reader. Conrad's son wrote about supposedly sitting in James's lap while James fondled and squeezed him tight until his mother rescued him. "I never thought of Henry James as a pedophile. But there it is. Does it matter? No. His work is extraordinary, certainly worth a few squeezes of Joseph Conrad's little boy." When a caller berates her as appalling and insensitive and ill-informed to suggest that molesting a small boy could justify anything artistic, she says she was joking and doesn't believe James ever molested a fly. "I admire art extensively," she declares, "but never at the expense of a human being. Anyone aware of Mozart being played at the gates of Auschwitz should realize what I mean."

The camps are never far from Ozick's thoughts. In a later interview, she will tell me how happy she was in high school until everything shattered for her when she acquired knowledge of the Shoa and was plagued with guilt. Good people, people of value and integrity, have invited her to Germany, which she characterizes as a great democracy because of the Marshall Plan and the war defeat that crushed its evil joy. She does not want to go. Nor to Poland, nor to any part of Eastern Europe. It is a personal expression for her of memory. With rising European anti-Semitism, she would not even want now to go to Paris.

A caller mutters the words post-colonialism and imperialism, and Ozick is on fire. "They are lies if you are applying them to Israel! They are from-the-left clichés, dogma, ideology, a template where there is no applicability. Britain didn't fulfill its mandate. It regarded areas of the Middle East as empire and treated the people there as colonial subjects. Who created these countries? Some British bureaucrat!" And what, I ask, of those who apply "demonic" or "fascist" to describe modern militaristic Israel? Ozick is fierce. "I say balderdash—which is polite for what I feel." She talks of murders of Jews in what is now Israel throughout the twenties and thirties and forties. Of the offering of a state to Arabs that they refused. Of the 1956 incursions into Israel of fedayeen killers. Of the wars in 1967 and 1973, attacks on Jews by Arabs. Of homicide bombers. I had been talking in the previous hour to Tony Kushner, who expressed the view that he would bring as scriptwriter to Spielberg's *Munich* that both sides in the Middle East are culpable for the vicious cycle of violence. Could Ozick have heard him while she was sitting in the green room? For her there is no conflict, no two sides. Just Israel and those who want no Jewish state. She tells of a cousin of hers, a musically talented fourteen-year-old, shot dead in the road by Arafat's people. Israel is the object of evil joy since and before its inception. "The leadership of the Arab mindset has no room for anyone other than Muslims in the Middle East. They recognize no one else's history and want no land for Christians or Jews. The Arabs don't want a Jewish state in the Middle East."

A caller phones in and identifies himself as an American Jew and co-coordinator of Jewish Voice for Peace. He has just returned from Bethlehem, where he was a human shield for Palestinians. I hear Ozick groan. The caller says he resents Ozick. Her facts are outrageous. She is a racist. He will not be lectured to and he will not let her speak for him.

"Thank God," says Ozick. "You're a very small minority. Like Johnny Lindh Walker."

"That's inflammatory," shouts the caller.

"You called me a racist and that is inflammatory, sir. You want to protect Arafat and that is enough said."

"No I don't!"

I intervene. I see this will take us nowhere, so I go to another caller who is also enraged and brings up the United Nations resolutions, asking Ozick how she can possibly justify that people who went through what the Jews went through are destroying a way of life of another people. The caller yells, "Israel has the biggest army."

"Thank God," says Ozick "because if the Palestinians did there would not be a living Jew." She hears the caller say genocide, and she shouts "shame" at him—believing he is talking about Jewish genocide against

Arabs, when he is actually asking, once again, how she can justify the actions against the Palestinians by a people who themselves suffered a genocide. When the caller speaks up and tells her what he really said, she apologizes for misunderstanding him but adds, after I bring up the massacres in Sabra and Chatilla, "Sharon did not expect the Christian phalangists to be murderers. He was not racist or genocidal. He never dreamed or imagined they'd be slaughtered."

We are at the end of the hour. I know that Ozick has become quite worked up, and so I apologize to her for such a physically exhausting hour. After the microphones are off, she asks me if I think she has anything to fear in the way of safety for a scheduled on-stage appearance later that evening. Irv Halperin played Galahad to her at Berkeley, and I try to do the same now, reassuring her that the crowd will probably be mostly literary and not likely to have anti-Zionist zealots seeking to harm her. "Would you do me a big favor?" she asks. "Of course," I say. "Would you hug me?" "Of course," I say . . . and I do.

When we meet the next time, it is to talk about her novel *Heir to the Glimmering World*. I have not broached the Israeli-Palestinian question. Our conversation has been about how she had to miss a book tour due to flu and how she's relaunching herself, with a new agent and new publisher, into the book-peddling process. We talk of the novel and, again, of essays versus fiction. I ask which she trusts more, and she says fiction. Essays are too linked to autocratic authority, belief or credo, arrogance of the intellect that another essay can completely contradict. Fiction is more trustworthy because the belief it induces is make-believe. If she has any credo, it is that ideas are emotions and emotions are ideas. She calls herself a dyed-in-the-wool rationalist, unsympathetic with mysticism and the idea that the creator is in creation. Then a caller brings up Israel and the Palestinians, and she, saying she anticipated such a call, brings out a piece of paper, a statement written the night before on a hotel pad. She says it makes her tremble to be asked a political question because it demands a different voice than the one she speaks comfortably in about literature. That night, on stage with me at the Herbst theatre, she will also mention her distrust of the interview process, of words exchanged in the moment. But now her feelings are inscribed. She reads that she stands with George Eliot, Einstein, Churchill and Gershon Scholem. Zionism is a beautiful ideal, as beautiful as any other redemptive revolution in the history of humankind. It can be classed with the repudiation of slavery, the invention of anesthetics for surgery, the social equality of women or countless other human decencies. She concludes:" I hope this will take care of all of Berkeley."

That night we talk on stage mainly about her novel. As we walk off she asks, in a nearly plaintive voice, "You don't agree with me about the Middle East, do you?" I simply tell her I see things as more complicated and understand the Palestinian hunger for land they see as their own. As we walk together toward her waiting fans, she nudges me aside into an alcove. "I'm so enamored of you," she says. "Would you please hug me?" I do.

Isabel Allende

Isabel Allende once said to me on air, during the Clinton impeachment, that the world had never witnessed a more expensive blow job. She also talked openly another time about having a dream of biting into a tortilla wrapped around Antonio Banderas. She is still the heretical, fallen-away Catholic girl who delights in bawdy talk and sensuality and what I oxymoronically like to call, in her case, female virility. The only sins of the seven that really interest or entice her, she once told me, are gluttony and lust. When she came to the United States, the immigration officer insisted that she was not white as she had written on the forms. He, a Latino, insisted she was an other. So she showed him her breasts and asked him if they didn't look white to him

Allende is making one of her periodic guest appearances on my radio program. My brother, Victor, is in the studio because he has wanted for quite some time to meet her. She is herself not unlike a house full of spirits—full of warmth and charm and hearty laughter and love of good conversation. She relishes male attention and sometimes acts like a schoolgirl around her husband, Willy, a California lawyer whom she adores. Her father left her when she was a child, and she grew up knowing she was much smarter than her brothers. She resented that they had so much more opportunity. She left her husband and the church and she left Chile after the coup against her uncle—whom a surprising number of people still think was her father and whom the TV talk show host Tom Snyder once confused with Pinochet. She felt, since childhood, like a misfit and then grew up to love feeling like a dissident, finding other women and a magazine and change as ways to channel her anger, discovering both feminism and journalism the best outlets for the immense anger she felt. Had she not found ways to channel her anger, she assures me, she would be "a total bitch." Had she stayed in Chile she is certain she would have been arrested for hiding people or trying to smuggle out information or trying to get people into embassies. She spent thirteen years in Venezuela, then met Willy and settled in Northern California. She has sold tens of millions of books, including *Paula*, the heart-wrenching portrait of her daughter who died, the book for which she wanted no money. Fans swarm to see her in Europe and South America. She is a grandmother who occasionally will slap her grandchildren and whose own grandmother was supposed to have moved a bowl of sugar by telekinesis. She hates nationalism and swears that a good prayer, the Lord's prayer, can always catch a taxicab.

Memory, Allende tells me, is like smoke. Imagination and memory are the same process, and language is like blood. Separation made her a writer. Once she left Chile she always had an accent. She wouldn't be a writer of fiction today without having left everything behind.

Jane Smiley

The first time I saw Jane Smiley she was at a party in San Francisco, making out like a teenager with a new boyfriend she brought with her from where she now lives in the Carmel Valley. Tall, lanky and equine and a head taller than the boyfriend, she is a horse race aficionado, but she is also a trained medieval scholar and the author of a book on Dickens. When we did an evening of conversation together onstage, she started right in before I could ask my first question, calling attention to her recently dyed blonde hair. Then she talked about being at the Santa Anita racetrack and going through the wrong gate and asking an attendant for directions. Though the way to the correct gate was easy, his explanation and gestures were so detailed that she thought, "He sees me as a blonde." She says it has been a revelation. She thought about writing a book like the 60's *Black Like Me* called *Blonde Like Me*. I ask her if blondes have more fun, and she says, "They get things explained to them a lot more."

A lot of what Smiley seems to be about is fun. I think of her public display of affection at the party and the absence of any self-consciousness in it. There is a side to her that belongs in Cyndi Lauper's " Girls Just Want to Have Fun" video. She tells of being asleep on a plane to New York from San Francisco. She wakes up to see that the woman next to her is laughing and reading *Moo*, and she thinks this is the best thing that has ever happened. What fun! The woman keeps on laughing, then puts the book down. Jane says to her, "You know I wrote that book." The woman looks at her and then at her picture on the cover and says, "Yes. You did." How wonderful to wake up to a person laughing at things you thought were funny.

Smiley loved writing *Moo* so much she didn't care how much readers would enjoy it. The joy of writing comic fiction is you are your own best audience for your own jokes. David Lodge was "a big influence and a great inspiration" in the writing of *Moo*. She loved getting a complimentary letter from him about it. Like *Moo*, her book on horse racing, *Horse Heaven*, is a group of interlocking stories. She describes it as magical realism and says she adored writing it, was sorry to see it go until she saw her tax bill.

It was fun, too, to win the Pulitzer. Her phone wouldn't stop—a reporter from Reuters calls and she hangs up and then it's a local station and she hangs up and then it's *The New York Times*. "It was chaotic in that way, but really fun. Though I realized if it weren't a journalism award you wouldn't get nearly as much press as you do. But no downside certainly."

Smiley loves living in Northern California and says she hopes she won't be exiled to somewhere else for something like lack of funds. While she was in Tuscany she was wondering why she wasn't back in Carmel with her horses.

It was Smiley's mother who made her a storyteller. If her mother, who was a journalist, wasn't going to be a novelist, then she would make her daughter one. Jane, a compliant child, says she took the path of least resistance. She wrote a novel as a senior in high school all about friends who were living passionate, Dostoyevskean lives. "I enjoyed it a lot. About page sixty it clicked. Before that I was trying to figure what to say, and after that I knew what to say. I went from idling to dynamic."

She had read a lot of Icelandic sagas, and quite a few of the medieval stories were strange and fascinating to her. She was studying them, getting her Ph.D, and then she went to Iceland, and it really gelled for her while reading contemporary accounts in *Icelandic Annals*. *Greenlanders* resulted from four or five sentences about a ship of Norwegian and Icelandic sailors stranded in Greenland and a Greenland man burned at the stake aboard the ship for adultery. It seemed amazingly dramatic to her. With *A Thousand Acres*, *King Lear* came first and Kurosawa and farming second. It grew out of her interpretation of *King Lear*. The book was laborious to write, and she could never write it again and even repudiated it with an article in *The Washington Post* that had another interpretation of *King Lear*. "I'd never go through that door again." The farm crisis at the end of the seventies was the historical moment for *A Thousand Acres*. It was not an uncommon event, but it was a big financial crisis and many suffered. It was the occasion for a different way for her of looking at Lear. Kurosawa made Lear's daughters sons, but he also wisely made them the result of their father. It's as if history begins when Lear decides to divide the kingdom—but that's also psychological reality for a certain type of narcissist, who experiences every new feeling as if nothing else had gone before. With such emotional tumult the past means nothing. The film of the novel meant nothing to Smiley. She wasn't at all involved in it and had no feelings about seeing it made into a movie. "I liked it but I don't have a copy of the video. I liked Steve Martin's *Pennies from Heaven*, where he dances, much more."

For Smiley novels and reading are the ultimate freedom. You can read a novel or stop reading it, burn it, give it away. The writer has no power to coerce you or get you to do anything. Reading, especially art, is an act of freedom, as we see in oppressive regimes and even in our own culture, where there seem to be no subversive acts. Every reader is a creator of the book and can recreate it in discussion with others. Like Proust, Smiley sees all novels as gossip. She says this not as denigration of literature or elevation of gossip but simple truth. Her family were "tremendous gossips—the men all rednecks, the women all liberals," which meant a lot of strife, though they all get along. Gossip is trying to come to terms with something unusual, assimilating views into a moral fabric. When two people are gossiping, it means they are telling a story and interpreting it. "I don't see that as pejorative. It's a form of assimilating specific behavior to general rules. How we think about what someone does, a way of understanding. I think it's good, not bad."

The works artists make do vanish. By the time they are read or seen or heard, the artist is onto something else, and there are only vague memories of the work. Your work is almost a history of mistakes in your life and thought before you got to where you are now. I cannot resist. "To being blonde?" "Yes," Smiley says. "To being blonde."

We wrap the interview. The final words are hers. "It was lots of fun."

Professor Michael Krasny greeting his literary idol Saul Bellow (left) twenty years after their first meeting in Chicago at a reception for Bellow held at the University of San Francisco.

With Joyce Carol Oates after an interview in the KQED radio studio.

With E.L. Doctorow before an on-stage conversation
together at San Francisco's Herbst Theater.

With Kurt Vonnegut after an on-stage interview at
the Marin Jewish Community Center.

With David Mamet before an on-stage conversation at San Francisco's
Herbst Theater to benefit the Magic Theater of San Francisco.

With Joan Didion at KQED radio after an on-air interview.

With former U.S. President Jimmy Carter after an on-air interview at KQED radio.

With former California Assemblyman and San Francisco
Mayor Willy Brown at KQED radio.

With Grace Paley after an interview on the air at KQED radio.

With Margaret Atwood before an on-stage interview
at San Francisco's Herbst Theater.

With Cynthia Ozick before our first KQED radio interview.

With South Africa's Archbishop Desmond Tutu after an interview on KQED radio.

An on-stage conversation with James Watson and E.O. Wilson at the
Gordon Mohr estate to benefit Conservation International.

With Isabel Allende at KQED Radio after an on-air interview.

With Salman Rushdie before an interview on air at KQED radio..

With Francis Ford Coppola after an interview on air at KQED radio.

8   A Smiling Public Man

I WAS A PUBLIC RADIO HOST. William Jefferson Clinton was President of the United States, a seeming liberal Democrat with a strong sense of pragmatism. A man with warmth, charm and fine communication skills who seemed especially comfortable and at ease with black folks and Hollywood glamour. A former Vietnam war protester who appeared to be driven to get people to like him. A president who seemed to me in many ways a lot like me, close to my age and also a policy wonk. Which was what I had become in my new berth as host of the daily "Forum" show. I had expanded the steady diet of "Forum's" public policy programming to include programs on national and international news, as well as the arts and culture and, especially, literature, and I had begun corralling every leading writer appearing in the Bay Area or on tour peddling his or her newest book.

I had established a sizeable following and, within two years, I had managed to more than double listeners and gain a new kind of gravitas. I could now do what I had done for over a decade at ABC with greater depth and no concern about capturing young demos or seeming too literary or intellectual. The listeners were the strength of the program. Keep the discourse and intellectual level high, and they will come: I believed that all along, even in my days in commercial radio, and that belief was proving abundantly true.

"We journalists get the audience we deserve," the left-leaning, syndicated, Texas-based columnist Molly Ivins said to me on air, then added sweetly, "Yours, Michael, is the best." I now heard more compliments about the callers, my preparation and the intelligence, range and quality of the program than I ever heard as a commercial broadcaster. Everyone seemed to feel that it was the right niche for me.

My program was for many becoming the program to listen to, the Bay Area flagship public radio program, a program where policy wonks and public officials and activists and people in positions of power and responsibility appeared and called in. As the fan base and the quality reputation of what is now called "Forum with Michael Krasny" grew, it began to seem as if a great many of those in Northern California who cared about issues and ideas were listening in.

I sounded in command on the air because I was. As a boy, I had watched Jack Paar, Johnny Carson, Merv Griffin and Mike Douglas. I learned from them, without realizing, about on-air technique, voice and style, although I grew into a young man who wanted the voice, style and technique of master storytellers. I'm not certain how much came from osmosis, being a bored kid watching TV talk shows. A lot came naturally. My role was like that of a symphony conductor or an airline pilot. I was doing more panels as well as having individual guests on, striving for balance against all the lefties in my Rolodex by ensuring that conservative and Republican voices got on too. Despite complaints that regularly came in about leftist bias, and a story that appeared in the local *Guardian* that labeled me "the last liberal talk show host," I regularly pulled in guests from the local Stanford-run, conservative Hoover Institution and did one-on-one conversations with conservative luminaries, in addition to the retinue of left and lib voices. Bill Buckley, William Safire, Dinesh D'Souza, George Gilder, Shelby Steele, Linda Chavez, Christina Hoff-Somers, Francis Fukiyama, Pat Buchanan and Richard Perle all appeared on "Forum."

I missed the editorializing and sounding off on whatever news grabbed my attention, the staple of commercial radio, but I believed I was creating an even stronger image of fairness, balance and high-toned quality, programming a steady stream of authors and public policy makers. The smarter, the better. I was once again reinventing myself. Now more subdued, I conducted programs befitting public radio. Favored guests become Rorschachs of a host's identity. Ted Koppel and Henry Kissinger. Don Imus and Michael Beschloss, Tim Russert, John McCain and Kinky Friedman. Howard Stern and Ozzy Osbourne,

William Shatner and Pam Anderson. Sean Hannity and Newt Gingrich, Oliver North and Dick Morris. Michael Kraṣny and writers, thinkers and intellectuals. Soon I would surprise everyone, including myself, by becoming the local ratings leader in the all-important 25-to-40 age demos, eclipsing my former commercial employer.

I still wanted to keep the flow of talk brisk, lively, animated and intellectually compelling, and I still needed to guard, even somewhat on public radio, against shows that sounded too esoteric or scholarly. I still made my work habits a badge of honor. Still teaching, lecturing, publishing, shoehorning in private-sector jobs and public appearances. Still meeting with students religiously and still grading, since fobbing off to a grader seemed sacrilegious. My boilerplate line was that if I was teaching them I should be grading them—though that in time would change and I, too, would succumb to taking on my best graduate students as teaching assistants. Reading theses, writing letters of recommendation, being a good committee man and still reading work by authors I had on as guests—distinguishing myself from other talk hosts who could not be bothered, who would wing it or go to preprepared publicist or producers' questions.

"You are the busiest man I know," I heard from friends and acquaintances. Whether in class or on the air or at a public or corporate event, I was always up and prepared, prepared and up. Like Bill Clinton, I liked eyes on me. There was a sliver of power in what I did. I helped to shape opinions. Influenced thought. Stimulated. I decided who I wanted to interview among the hungry-for-air-time pundits, book floggers and opinion shapers. For a man of wide curiosities who liked pleasing people, it was hard to choose.

This was public radio. Dan Schorr, after leaving CBS, would liken working here to entering the promised land. It felt strange in many ways. No glamour here. No sales offices. No specialized personnel dissecting Arbitron ratings. Journalism was what was supposed to matter. The G.M. and P.D. were both women. Women, homosexuals and people of color were everywhere here, whereas, at KGO, though there were a few women and people of color around, it was mainly a culture of men. White men. Heterosexuals. Public radio, here, seemed more to me like the public university, a retreat from the hardscrabble, much more competitive, show-biz world of mainly hetero men.

My producers, Robin and Candace, both wore nose rings. Both viewed journalism with great seriousness. Robin was also a bit distrustful of me at first, since my broadcast history was in commercial radio—that place, she kept reminding me, that was dramatically unlike here. She would have preferred they'd hired a woman host, but she loved the fact that, from the outset, I insisted on extending the program into the arts and humanities. In time we would become very close. Candace, who is African-American, seemed too hung up on race. Unimpressed by my pedigree as a scholar and teacher of black literature. I shouldn't have referred to Somalia warlords as warlords. I shouldn't have referred to South African violence in the townships as black on black violence.

There, management fought bitterly with the unions, and The G.M. talked about "hurting" and "punishing" them, while his young Quayle-like P.D. called the shop stewards and union leaders "union fucks" and was avidly at war with them. Here, the union seemed most often to be placated by management out of some stirring sense of a need to honor labor.

No intimidating, often scowling, megalomaniac G.M. in an office with a full Bay view and a wall full of plaques all honoring him. KQED's G.M. was a kind and calm, soft-spoken NPR public radio veteran, a woman who early on joined the NPR gynarchy of Linda Wertheimer, Cokie Roberts, Susan Stamberg and Nina Totenberg and who won her spurs sitting through countless budget planning and marketing meetings. In her office there were old, youthful photos of Bob Edwards and Cokie along with NPR banners and journalism and reporting plaques and awards. Journalism and prestigious honors mattered here. So, fortunately for me, did many of my stronger suits—bookishness and the desire for deep, fair political analysis, including on international relations. My work here was respected by management. The woman CEO, a master at fundraising and stroking donors and underwriters, brought the fat-wallet gift givers and visiting community dignitaries to my modest work space—introducing me with adjectives like "erudite" and "dashing," quite a shift from the KGO G.M., who was notoriously miserly with praise. My smart executive producer, a Cuban-born former newspaper reporter who was universally well-liked and a respected journalist, was also, from the get-go, supportive and honoring of my work, praising me without being fawning. He was able, too, to give well-reasoned, useful, sensible advice, constructive criticism that I found dependable and sound. Numbers and young demographics mattered there, not here. Depth and seriousness of purpose and quality all mattered here; infotainment there.

Commercial radio had been home for over a decade, and I had managed to fit in and get along. Yet I always felt strangely alien there, as if I had been an imposter selling my soul to the devil of crassness, superficiality and its real raison d'etre—selling air. Here we had underwriting instead of ads, a strange way of softening up and subterfuging commercials. Even though the underwriter's messages were more tasteful and subdued, listeners still complained about how they interfered with the purity of presenting news without influence or contamination from private interests. There, my bookishness and intellect were respected by many but devalued, not coin of the realm, while here they were valued, period. Yet here, too, was the endless begging of pledge drives, and people were more serious. Here we did live broadcasts from the mayor's chambers in city hall or from the Oakland Museum of California or on the campus of San Jose State, while there I went to Harrah's at Lake Tahoe to join Harry Belafonte or did a live show on the singles scene from a popular San Francisco watering hole. Here there was little if any smarm, excitement or show biz.

Jim Lehrer had made "dare to be dull" his anthem. Was that to be mine now? No! There was no necessity for me to have serious talk turn dull, and there were too many times when commercial radio, too, felt dull, those hours well into the night when nothing seemed capable of lighting up the phone bank. I decided, early on as a public radio broadcaster, that I would serve public enlightenment through news, public policy, arts and culture in ways that would not make them sound boring. I would mix my programming up so listeners would not know what or whom to expect, though they could always expect depth and quality. I would keep heads spinning by the sheer range of programming content!

Here, guests came under more careful scrutiny in terms of the mission of public service. In commercial radio bookings, there were no such standards—only getting and keeping numbers. In reality, almost any serious newsworthy subject could be labeled public service, but here, in public radio, they really believed in programming serving the public. We veered away from mainstream news, which was why we did only one show inspired by the crazed O. J. coverage, and it was on domestic violence.

When I was at KGO, my parents bragged to their friends because I had on Alex Trebek, who at that time was hawking a "Jeopardy" board game. Mom and Dad never missed "Jeopardy," and my dad loved going up to Trebek in Cleveland, a week before he was scheduled to be on my show in San Francisco, and surprising him with the date he was going to be on live radio with ABC in San Francisco, then coming clean and revealing how he knew. I truly entered another culture at public radio. More listeners loved and appreciated Shakespeare, the ballet, Bach, Mozart and Beethoven, bird watching and the fine details of what so easily and often could be the yawn-inducing world of public policy issues. There, the listeners and managers craved red meat. Here, they wanted intelligence and what I wanted to give them—authors, artists, scientists, world leaders, men and women of distinction, serious and high-minded debate. There, they loved discord, laughs and showmanship, controversy and the bizarre. There, they felt superior to pointy-headed public radio. Here, we felt superior to low-life commercial radio. Jim Eason once posed a question to the P.D. at KGO. If putting non-stop flatulence on the air were to bring in high ratings, would he, the P.D., agree to have hours of farting as preferred programming? Absurd hypothetical, I grant you, despite the fact that Howard Stern actually did just that on Sirius radio years later. The P.D. took the question seriously. His answer was, "You bet. Our listeners would hear nothing but farts all day long, if that brought in the numbers." Talking had begun to gain a new importance to me in public radio because of its high-mindedness and ideals.

In my first two years as host of "Forum," I had on a slew of writers of national and international stature and prominence. I was reading so much that it was no wonder I had no time to write. E. L. Doctorow, A. S. Byatt and her sister Margaret Drabble, Barbara Kingsolver, Nicholson Baker, Tobias Wolff, Maxine Hong Kingston, Louise Erdrich, Norman Mailer, Joyce Carol Oates, Margaret Atwood, Carlos Fuentes, Carol Shields, T. C. Boyle, Bobbie Ann Mason, Diane Johnson, Ian McEwan, David Foster Wallace, Wole Soyenka, Dorothy Allison, Jane Smiley, Roddy Doyle, Ethan Canin, Isabel Allende, Grace Paley, Ursula LeGuin, P. D. James, Edna O'Brien, Paul Theroux, Frank McCourt, Alice Walker,

Russell Banks, Evan Connell, Mary Gaitskill, Ernest Gaines, Edmund White. Quite a list! I was becoming the writer's interviewer. But I wanted to cover all subjects, not just literature—wanted to be wide-ranging, eclectic, a movable and ever sumptuous intellectual feast.

I was invited to a dinner with Amy Tan and Isabel Allende by Elaine Petrocelli, another friend to writers who runs Book Passage, an independent bookstore in Marin County that regularly features authors who are on tour. Elaine had put this dinner together to honor Louise Erdrich, and there I was having dinner with three solid-performing and much admired women writers. Louise, whose work, *Love Medicine*, I had taught, seemed upset and preoccupied, compared to her appearance on air with me earlier that morning, and so I privately took her aside and asked her if something was bothering her—little knowing or suspecting that her turmoil was connected to despair over the still-not-visible-to-the-public boil about to burst, her marriage to Michael Dorris. They were headed for a crash that would bring charges of child molestation against Dorris and culminate in his suicide. Louise could not fathom how I sensed her pain beneath what she believed was her unflappable exterior. Amy, too, I would later learn, was suffering—with loved ones having died all around her and some nut case posting notices on the Internet that said AMY TAN MUST DIE,—as was Isabel, whose daughter, Paula, was dying slowly from a long-suffering, horrid disease. But for me this evening was one of literary chitchat and repartee with three celebrated women writers whose real lives had not yet opened up to me. Unlike Pat Conroy.

I interviewed Conroy right before an evening party at the mansion of Gordon and Ann Getty. It was part of a weekend built around the National Kidney Foundation's annual literary luncheon, featuring six different writers and attended by well over a thousand people. I emceed the event. On our way to the Getty's, Pat began to unwind to me about his travails—family members still angry at him over his books, the daughter he had iconized in fiction not speaking to him, alcohol tribulations and a difficult divorce—all of which stayed in my mind when I watched the next day as minions attending the luncheon gushed and fawned over him. Talented Pat had literary fame, show-biz links and tales he had acquired from having had novels like *The Great Santini* and

The Prince of Tides turned into films. But I asked myself if I, roughly the same age, would be willing to endure such psychological baggage and pain for literary success.

Hunter S. Thompson came on air with me, fifteen minutes late and somewhat inebriated, holding a champagne glass in one hand and a bottle in the other, with a face all cut up from—according to him—swimming out to some rocks the night before from the Seal Rock Inn to try to meet up with a number of sea lions. I was annoyed by his lateness. I, like many sixties kids, had been drawn to his writing, though put off by his excessive substance abuse, regardless of how much he might have been confabulating. He would wind up committing suicide, driven by physical pain. I knew authors led lonely, isolated lives, yet too many also seemed to have Job-like personal suffering. Neurotic angst and visionary lunacy could provide literary octane. But suffering or dissolute excess notwithstanding, there were still undeniable perks to literary fame. Thompson, hardly an Adonis, had a lovely, well-coiffed fiancée with him, an attractive woman whom I initially mistook for his publicist; she joined us in the studio after the interview ended. Could I allow myself to be as unhappy as Pat Conroy, as boozed and drugged up as Hunter Thompson or as racked by life's traumas as Amy, Isabel or Louise if Mephistopheles told me that that was the price to pay for literary success? It didn't matter. If I was destined to be an artist, it was abundantly clear by now that it was an artistry of the spoken and not the written word.

I was a kind of recognized literary figure in my own right—a literary figure without an oeuvre. I was being called upon more and more frequently to interview writers on stage and in print and to emcee literary festivals and events. Keynote speaker at the Bay Area Book Reviewer's Awards and emcee of the Western State Literary Awards. Interviewing stars from my own firmament of literary criticism—such as Yale's Harold Bloom or the new historicism critic and Berkeley and Harvard English professor Stephen Greenblatt. These were high-powered scholars I would likely never have met up with in my academic life. Harvard's famed Henry Louis Gates would become a regular guest. Early on in my career in public radio, I played gentle provocateur. Bloom and Greenblatt, once bound by a teacher/student relationship, took Oedipal snipes at each other with my on-air nudging. I coaxed famed black political conservative Shelby Steele and his identical twin, Claude—a Stanford prof who, unlike Shelby, supported affirmative action—into taking shots at one another on air. Threats of a lawsuit erupted. I nudged Camille Paglia to take shots at the austere Susan Sontag; when Sontag came on, she responded to Paglia's invective against her, saying: "Isn't she that woman who wants to be in a rock and roll band?" I nudged David Rieff, Sontag's son, to express his contempt for red-diaper-baby-turned-arch-conservative David Horowitz, which later culminated in a public episode featuring Rieff spitting on Horowitz. And, of course, I nudged Horowitz to vent his reactions to Rieff.

An international Jewish writer's festival came to San Francisco, and I was enlisted to do on-stage interviewing. Without asking for it, I got top billing and equal pay with marquee names like Grace Paley, Cynthia Ozick, Elie Weisel, Aharon Appelfeld and Mordecai Richler, even though I was the talker and not the writer. Thanks to Ethan Canin's string-pulling I went off to Sun Valley, Idaho, to lecture and lead discussions with celebrated literary figures like William Styron, Mona Simpson, Lorrie Moore, Anne Lamott, the poet W. S. Merwin, and the king of the blockbusters, Stephen King. I was listed in the brochure as one of the writers. NO! A MISNOMER. A MISTAKE. AN ERROR. I was the interviewer, the talker, the facilitator, the master of ceremonies, not the master of prose or narrative or storytelling or even of comedy, like Dave Barry, who was also there at Sun Valley. My gift came from my mouth and not my pen.

.   .   .

THERE WAS NO DENYING that I was getting recognized in ways that eclipsed my fame in commercial radio. I was chosen as one of the commencement speakers at Berkeley, as well as the commencment speaker at Sonoma State and Napa Valley College and at my daughter Lauren's high school. There a then-aspiring right-wing talk host—a New York Jew who hid his Jewishness and venomously detested all liberal or left-leaning Jews—heckled my garden-variety inspirational speech. His daughter was in the same graduating class. I characterized his heckling to a local newspaper reporter as "oratoric penis envy." But I would, later on, feel involuntary twinges of envy for this despicable man, a toxic, incendiary gasbag with a growing, undeniable appeal—who would go on to build a major national career out of a frappe of jumbled extremist views and the sort of kook and shock-jock excess that I had come to speak publicly about as giving talk radio a bad name. To him, I was surely liberal poison. All of what I regarded as my best instincts—putting out humanistic and thoughtful discourse—must have seemed like nauseating, pontificating pap to him. He characterized my commencement speech, with rhetoric designed to stir feelings of community and racial inclusion, as "garbage," and referred to me on air as "Michael Crapny." A year later, when his son was running for a public office, he tried to show a touch of good form by extending thanks through his son, whom I had put on the air and treated with the same courtesy I would extend to any public office seeker. Years after that, when this broadcaster became one of the nation's most notorious and listened-to talk hosts and got booted off television for ugly, homophobic remarks, a reporter with the *Los Angeles Times* told me the heckling host claimed to have no idea who I was and could not recall heckling me. But his brand of egomaniacal invective, pathology dressed up as conservatism, and drive to push the limits of the outrageous with humor and hate was the new currency of talk radio, the breeding ground for Ann Coulter and a host of others who traded on bile.

I was still feeling like the yokel who couldn't get national. When people hammered me, which they did, as not being as good as Ray Suarez or Terry Gross, it was generally, I told myself, because they preferred a softer, more languid, less aggressive style and a more subdued ego, not the showmanship and exhibitionism that would sometimes creep into my work or the political views I'd occasionally inject—though as time passed, those vestiges of my commercial radio style would dissipate. I loved disseminating knowledge, an educator's weakness, but I also loved getting knowledge, the splash and burn and flight of ideas and analysis, the feeding of minds.

I also got called on more in the private sector to lead discussions with CEOs and executives, captains of industry. I was a brand name, a go-to guy for emcee or facilitating work, particularly in the high-tech world, and as the economy boomed I earned more paychecks from corporate giants with company names that many of my more radicalized guests or callers might have abhorred. I liked the work and the pay, though I sometimes felt a bit like a high-priced hooker.

When I did a big job for Visa International in Maui on "The Future of Money," with the CEO and a number of high profile panelists, I complained to Ethan Canin that I was shilling for a credit card company and wondered where my old sixties values had gone. "Schmuck," he rebuked. "You're staying at a beautiful resort in Maui with your wife and getting great pay for it. If that's selling out, show me where I can sign up."

. . .

MY MOTHER WAS DYING, and so I headed east to see her as she lay in all but lifeless immobility in her room at Cleveland's Jewish Home. My feelings about her were so mixed and intense, and the tenderness and helplessness of seeing her in suspended animation so piercing that, as Yeats said of his heroic young aviator, it took my heart for speech. Was my mother heroic? No. Frightened and helpless and wanting, her entire life, to please and win over all her neighbors, friends and relatives. To nearly everyone outside our home, she was the sweetest and kindest of ladies, but she was also the mother who screamed at her children and worried, sometimes in near desperation, that we would not please or placate the outside world, which my sister and I accused her of putting ahead of us. Yet she loved us deeply. Me, the baby, she maybe loved more, or at least cosseted more; my outgoing personality pleased her and reminded her of extroverts in her own family. Still, it was my dad's side she always seemed in need of pleasing and made us feel that we needed to please—to such a degree that we began increasingly to find fault with them and resented their lack of attention and responsiveness. I wanted to talk to her, to tell her how much over a lifetime I had loved her despite her imperfections and weaknesses. I was like that foolish Flannery O'Connor son who cried out for his mother—"Darling, sweetheart"—as he tried to bring her back, revive her from the darkness that had descended on her from a stroke. I could not revive her. But memory I could revive. Her sitting me—a child not yet old enough for nursery school—on her lap, telling me she would always love me and I would always be her darling, her little boy. How could such plainspoken, clichéd maternal words still move me so, a man years older than she was then? She had dropped out of high school in her junior year to work in a department store. She had told me repeatedly how proud she was that I went so far beyond her in education. In her senility she would tell me that I was an accident. It made all of us laugh, and my dad assured me that it wasn't true. They had planned and actually wanted four children, he said. But, then, who knew, really, what she wanted? She seemed to desire little more than the paltry things we had and a better life for her children, yet she often seemed unhappy, even angry. Perhaps she resented the role life had consigned to her, what Kate Chopin called the mother wife identity. I used to kid her that all she really must have studied in high school was home economics, but she might have wished for more in her life than gabbing on the phone, cleaning the house, working for Zionist organizations and preparing dinner each night for a tired and overworked husband. Sometimes she would be so angry at my brother and me for roughhousing or not complying with her wishes that she would unload on my dad as soon as he came in, and he would take us into their bedroom, make us lay across the bed and strap us with his belt. But, in simplest terms, the three of us knew both our parents loved us, and we knew, above all, that they were good.

My father would have kept caring for my mother if a social worker and the three of us children hadn't insisted that he, getting more frail and weak with age, stop dressing and undressing and feeding her, stop lifting her into and out of the bath and onto and off the toilet. "Please, Dad, let her go where people are trained to care for her," I had pleaded with him. "Medicare will cover most of the expenses, " I assured him, and finally he relented. He went to her every day and sat by her bedside until closing and continued his same routine, even as she lost speech and became a dying body breathing, bereft of movement or speech. As I confronted the reality of my own mother being closer to death, so much inside me kept echoing that life really was too short and really ends. Death always had dominion.

. . .

I'D BUILT A LOYAL FOLLOWING and fan base of smart listeners. I had been hearing for years how I deserved a national show, how it was absurd that a quality show like mine wasn't national. Thanks to Amazon.com and new technology, we, as well as publishers, had determined by this time that "Forum" sold more books than any other locally produced talk program in the country, public or commercial. We had more listeners than any local public radio program in the nation. So following my visit to Cleveland, I tried out for the job as host of "Talk of the Nation," the nationally syndicated NPR show that originated out of D.C. My show, "Forum," was often compared to and at times confused with "Talk of the Nation." I felt I had a superior group of producers working with me in Robin Gianattassio-Malle, David Minkow and Holly Kernan, and I thought we did a superior show despite being local. A number of broadcasters had been asked to try out for the job hosting "Talk of the Nation." I was not. I had never really been on their radar screen. My limited experience with the national NPR people in Washington had been in on-air interviews in San Francisco with people like Dan Schorr, Robert Siegel, Cokie Roberts, Ray Suarez, Terry Gross and CEO Kevin Close.

I had called an NPR executive named Pete Michels, who had no idea who I was, and I had made a pitch to him to include me in the field of those trying out for the job. Ray Suarez had resigned as host to become an anchor with "The News Hour." I had called Ray as well as the main anchor of "The News Hour," Jim Lehrer, and I had called others I knew, including Bill Moyers. If I was going to toss my hat into the ring for this national post, then I'd use every contact.

Going national seemed the logical next step. I felt like a state assemblyman eyeing a congressional seat. Maybe I couldn't be a great novelist or succeed in commercial radio, but I was surely succeeding in locally produced public radio in San Francisco, and I knew or at least believed that I had the right stuff to go national as host of "Talk of the Nation."

Did I really want to move to Washington, D.C.? To trade the good life I'd made for myself in Northern California for a wider, national pasture? Truthfully, if they had wanted me, I probably would have gone on to host, but they didn't. Six of us from around the country each did a week of auditioning on TOTN. I felt that I performed at the top of my game. No stunts. No fast talking. No show-off splurges of erudition. No trying to be cute. Just top-notch, serious, professional, highly intelligent radio. In the Bay Area there was effusive praise. I heard choruses (perhaps not objective) about how much better I had performed than the competition, and people pleaded with me not to leave them for the big time.

Some big time! TOTN is nationwide, the biggest public radio call-in show in the country, with a succession of fine hosts including John Hockenberry and Ray Suarez. But it was small potatoes compared to Limbaugh, Stern, Imus, Dr. Laura, Tom Lykis, Bill O'Reilly or Sean Hannity, and it was under the full control of the NPR news department. The studio looked similar to ours in San Francisco, except that it had more space and many more lines on the telephone switchboard. In addition to a producer in a separate booth who screened calls, there was a director who cued me and the engineers.

During the first day of my audition, I did an hour on irradiation of meat, and I suddenly heard a woman's voice in my headphones, badgering me to ask certain questions. When I asked the head producer, after the hour was over, what that had been about, she told me that the woman was a news reporter who was monitoring my content in the booth. Still, I worked well and easily with the TOTN producers, a hard-toiling, dedicated, diverse lot who got little glory—a friendly, industrious bunch who reminded me of my more serious grad students. I came in hours before air time each day in the D.C. uniform of jacket and tie, and I believed I had won their respect and good will. I liked these people and enjoyed working with them.

I was prepared and on and up. Al Gore had selected Joe Lieberman as his running mate, so we covered that major news story, the first nomination of a Jew for Veep. I mixed up news stories, as I usually did, with topics of interest including hours on jargon, the Q factor or likability in politics and distinctions that separate highbrow, middlebrow and lowbrow. I liked receiving calls from all over the nation and army bases in Europe. But I just didn't know if I was a fit for NPR, for the kind of sound that I had come to associate with many of the broadcasters there. Plus, there was no big thrill in it. And NPR may have been big-time for public broadcasting, but the studios were right in the heart of metropolitan D.C., with no glamour inside or out—a building with the kind of utilitarian plainness, workers and dull sobriety I associated with factories. I met up with a former ABC television anchor friend, Lisa Stark, with whom I had co-anchored a couple of "Nightfocus" shows; she was still working for the ABC network on radio and came to NPR to have lunch with me in the cafeteria. As I looked around at those seated near us, I thought to myself that I could be in the cafeteria of a Ford plant in Detroit or a data processing factory in Silicon Valley.

Except for the fact that this was the big-time of public radio, and that the job of TOTN host had national stature and a national audience, there really was nothing about NPR in D.C. that excited me. I also remembered stories told by another TV anchor acquaintance of mine, Marcia Brandywine—who had left commercial TV news to do a brief stint at NPR as co-anchor of "All Things Considered." Marcia complained about how chilly everyone was. But I kept reminding myself that this was the summit of public broadcasting. If I made the final cut and was offered the post, I would take it.

Still, I believed early on an offer was unlikely, perhaps even implausible, because Juan Williams was one of those trying out. A Pulitzer Prize-winning black journalist and creator of the civil rights odyssey "Eyes on the Prize," Williams had published a column for years in *The Washington Post* and was a veteran reporter for that paper. He was a big name, a beltway insider and a buddy of NPR's CEO Kevin Close. Plus, he had national exposure as one of those weekend political pundits on a Fox network news show.

Others in the competition—Korva Coleman, a black newswoman, Mike Schuster, an international reporter, and Melinda Penkava, who had done fill-in on TOTN—were all broadcasters and well suited for the job, given the talk show skill set it required. I liked Juan. I'd had him on air with me and got some good stuff from him for a print piece I did for *Mother Jones*. He was affable and smart and wrote a fine biography of Supreme Court justice Thurgood Marshall. He was a man worthy of respect, although he had no experience as a regular talk show host. NPR felt they could "get more from Juan," an executive informed me soon after the decision was announced. They were clearly thinking more about the cross-promotion from Juan's Fox network job even though, with its emphasis on sharp opinions, many thought it clashed with the reasoned, balanced style of TOTN.

Within a year and a half, and after the loss of TOTN listeners in New York City, Juan was gone—moved to give commentary and replaced by the more veteran talk host Neil Conan. Deep down I was relieved. I would have loved having the NPR national talk show, but I really didn't want to go to Washington or work in the claustrophobic, newsroom-dominated TOTN.

. . .

ONE CAN ALWAYS BELIEVE in new beginnings. New starts. They are quintessentially, archetypically American. I got pushed out of commercial radio and wound up in public radio. I was rejected by NPR, but soon after I was back on commercial television, ironically enough, at the cable outlet for KRON—the NBC affiliate where I once pestered Jim Shock for a return phone call. Now the station, Bay TV, wanted me as a host, and I accepted. So I was doing my morning radio show, teaching two classes and doing an hour TV show four nights a week, not to mention corporate gigs and pro bono, good-cause-appearances and stints as a lecturer and emcee. This, I told myself, was how people burn themselves out.

. . .

AFTER MY AUDITION, I went back to Cleveland to see my mother once again at the home for the aged. My brother and sister and I had made the decision at that point to put her on a feeding tube, even though others advised us to let nature take its course. My siblings and father deferred to me, the baby, in this decision. Lord knows I did not want that. I consulted with friends, physicians, bioethicists, and their consensus was that we shouldn't let my mother suffer with a tube. Letting her die seemed the right thing to do. But this was my mother! She did not appear to be suffering; though mute and immobile, she appeared to show signs of recognizing us. Still, I wondered if these moments of responsiveness were really figments of my imagination—even though, when my father whispered to her that it was their sixty-fourth wedding anniversary, we all heard, after weeks without an audible word from her, "Yes."

She died a few weeks later. I struggled to summon memories of her, not as she had most recently been, dying in a vegetative state, but when she was vibrant and waltzed around the kitchen singing or sat smoking a cigarette, talking to her sister Esther, my dad's sister Gea or one of her old friends from high school. I pictured her playing mahjong with her regular foursome and got involuntary flashes, too, of her yelling at me and shaking her finger in anger or sneaking up on me to plant a kiss on my cheek.

She died on a day I was to interview Isaac Stern, but before her death, I did an interview at San Francisco's Herbst Theater with Joyce Carol Oates, who teared up as she spoke to me, before we went on stage, of how elderly and feeble her parents had both become, how she strained and battled to remember them, not as they were then, but as they had been when they were younger. Like Proust seeing his mother dying, unable to link her frail and desiccated flesh with the beautiful and youthful mother of his memory. If Proust and Oates strained to pull their mothers out from the craw of memory, what about those of us less equipped, with or without the artist's touch? I would have liked to make my mother live again through the strength of memory, to wrench memory into words so that I could, miraculously, give birth, in prose, to my own mother.

The next morning I interviewed Oates on the air, and I brought up, toward the end of the interview, the name of her Bay Area-based editor and friend, who had worked with Lillian Hellman and a number of other major literary figures. He had died, and I knew many Bay Area literary people remembered him fondly, even lovingly. At the mention of his name, she went mute and sobbed, her hand against her mouth. I tried comforting her by holding her, and then I filled the dreaded dead air with my voice as we went to the network news that came at the top of every hour.

After my mother's funeral, Phil Kaufman, the film director, called me. His mother had just died, too, and he was remembering to me the gardens she used to plant and the sweet taste of her tomatoes. His Catholic cousin had tried comforting him, telling him she believed his father was in heaven, waiting to take his wife in and spend eternity together. "It's metaphor," Phil said. "You can understand why it's comforting to believe. I miss my mother terribly. It's painful. She was a wonderful, strong, giving woman of real character, and she had her senses and her wits about her right to the end. "

Sorry if it sounds like parody of Clinton, but I felt his pain. Felt, too, how hard it is for any one of us to find language to paint what loss means, let alone to paint the ones we love in eulogy. I offered Phil the usual consoling words, not unlike those offered me, my siblings and our father by those at the funeral who knew and liked, even loved, my mother. And then I recalled my interview with the film actor Billy Dee Williams, who was in San Francisco to be honored by the black film festival.

Once known as the black Clark Gable, he looked a lot older and weathered when I interviewed him than when he beamed those matinee idol good looks of his youth, and his reticence on air quickly took the bloom off his initial star status. He was, in fact, soon apologizing for what a caller aptly described as an on-air reserve that made him sound as if he didn't want to be there. "I just lost my mother," he confided. He recalled how his mother had loved yellow roses and went on to tell a story of sitting with his manager in a restaurant and seeing a doe, then suddenly noticing a large, single yellow rose. He felt it was a sign that his mother was okay. He then spilled out a hagiographic story from his boyhood: his mother had only one dime for transportation home, but she gave it to a poor man and walked home by herself. "That was mommy," he said. I thought of the kindness of my own mother and responded, "You are obviously your mother's son." Billy Dee was suddenly too choked up to speak. He managed, in tears, with his voice cracking, to say, "You got to try to be kind. I believe in kindness."

I believed in kindness too. The kindness of strangers as well as of intimates and talk hosts and listeners. But the message left for me on the listener response voicemail following that touching, empathic moment with Billy Dee was: "MOTHERFUCKER. YOU MADE BILLY DEE CRY."

 Kazuo Ishiguro
"Call me Ish," the famed author of *The Remains of the Day* tells me as we shake hands. I find it odd to hear the shortening of both Melville's famous whaler's opening sentence and his last name when I am talking to an obviously Japanese man with a well-attended British accent. I tell him I know he is also known as Ishy, but that Ishy would be way too strange on my tongue. So Ish it will be.

The hour before I had spent on air with the French ambassador. I introduce them, and the ambassador looks blankly when I tell him Ish is a 1998 recipient of the French Chevalier literary award. Perhaps it is odd to the diplomat, not recognizing Ish by name, that a Japanese man has received one of France's highest literary honors.

Ish was five when his family moved to England from Nagasaki. His father was a scientist, and the family plan for year after succeeding year was to move back to Japan within a year or two. Outside of the home were conservative English values. Inside, the opposite. It allowed for a certain distance in Ish from British culture, mores and ethics.

The Ishiguros settled in a near-rural setting only fifteen years after the war, among people who had little experience with Japanese but "were incredibly kind." Ish says: "It helped that colleagues of my father's were there, but there were no preconceptions. There is that side to the British that's very tolerant, and I think it is still there in that culture."

Though Ish is quite famous, he is wont to point out that his generation of literary fiction writers was really the first in Britain "to be sucked into celebrity culture." They were learning on the job about being celebs. Their senior literary figures—Kingsley Amis, Iris Murdoch and even William Golding—had no limelight like those of his generation who, if they were interested in the arts, initially gravitated toward theater, television or, like him, rock music. When he was a teenager in the eighties, Ish wanted to be a songwriter. He learned a lot about writing fiction from listening to and writing songs. It was terrible for him to admit, but he didn't read much then. His influences were people like Bob Dylan, Neil Young, Joni Mitchell, Leonard Cohen and Jackson Browne. To think of being a literary superstar would have been laughable. When he began his writing career, serious novelists were shabby people who lived in shabby places and didn't eat in fancy restaurants. They just got on with the work and had other vocations like teaching or being a civil servant. That's how Ish always imagined it would be for him. But he had a serious literary identity with two novels under his belt before *The Remains of the Day* brought fortune, a film, fame and a Booker.

Ish always starts with abstract emotions and questions before turning to characters and relationships. Settings are a problem. He has the story before he goes location hunting. At fifty it all comes harder to him than it did when he was younger and more instinctive and he could hold material, including massive details, in his mind. He has to work much more incrementally now. It's clear that age is on his mind. He talks about how writing is like a football career—gridiron or soccer. Few novelists do their best work after forty-five unless they start late in life or are imprisoned in midlife like Dostoyevsky. Both *Pride and Prejudice* and *Wuthering Heights* were written by twenty-two year olds. Both Brontes were dead by the end of their thirties. *War and Peace* was written by a thirty-seven year old. So was *Ulysses*. Kafka and Chekhov were dead around forty. No one reads any of the work Faulkner produced after forty. I tell him wryly that all this bodes bleakly for me as a novelist and he says, "No. The encouraging thing for you, Michael, is you haven't started yet. The problem is complacency. Suddenly you are fifty and you are asking yourself 'So what do you feel now?'" Awards for young or promising writers can create a problem. Lifetime achievement awards for novelists are usually for work produced earlier on. "Where do we peak?" Ish asks. He mentions Dylan, Miles Davis, Picasso—all lived three or four different stages as artists. "How do you have the courage to let go of what you did successfully?" Still, he talks about how there is a perverse side to his character. He moved into a different realm after *The Remains of the Day*, with the surreal dream language and narrative option he took in producing *The Unconsoled*. "I'm glad I did that. I could move on as a writer. I couldn't have done that if I hadn't had the time when I was left alone to get on with it, before the publicity and celebrity culture swept me along. I can compartmentalize. When I'm at home writing, I'm the same guy I was back in 1982. I'm aspiring to be one of those shabby, nonglamorous senior authors of that time."

Ish is thankful he was able to form a clear literary identity. It must be very tough for young writers today being asked to get on a best-seller list around the world and satisfy the most stringent literary criticism. "That's a very tall order and makes it hard when you're alone in your study to know your priorities. Do you have a smash hit or break new ground in literature and express yourself uncompromisingly? It's a balancing act that's very hard for an early career."

He says he can be very serious, then turn himself into a kind of salesman for the book tour and promotion " I try to be a good salesman. It's a second job. But it's difficult for new writers. They don't understand it's two separate hats." The positive side is you get readers and a real sense of your audience. Money is some of it, but with his film work (*The White Countess* most recently), he and his family could live well if he never published another book. Being a salesman stops you from becoming self-indulgent and, to some extent, from becoming stagnating and provincial. The danger is that you become self-conscious about why you write and how you write. "Perceptive people tease out unconscious motifs in your life. That has a profound effect."

Ish never worries about the gender divide or writing from a child's point of view. "I've had to think through central characters, usually narrators, who are so different on the surface from me and often unreliable. An English butler forty years older in a different time and place, of a different generation. Such large leaps make a female minor." A child's point of view is "alarmingly easy" he says. He regresses very rapidly. "Most of us put on a veneer of civility and disguise our urges, impulses and angers but are maybe not that different from how we were in our childhood or adolescence. All I need to do is let go. I don't look at or study children. I try to think and behave like a child. That comes easy to me. I worry about that."

Worrying about aging and worrying about being like a child. No wonder Ish wrestles so much with memory and mortality. In talking about his newest novel, *Never Let Me Go*, on doomed human clones, he notes that their life spans are more limited than ours. Then he adds: "We'll all lose control of parts of ourselves and fade away if we live long enough. We push all that to the back of our minds. Which is as it should be. We would get little done if we thought about how it all ends in dust."

 *Francis Ford Coppola*

Francis Ford Coppola is in the studio. He talked with me by phone on air after the release of the director's cut of *Apocalypse Now* and then again to promote a project he helped create to aid the homeless in San Francisco's North Beach. But this time, with release on DVD of *One from the Heart* and claims by his PR people that he wants me to interview him, I insist on meeting him—despite efforts by his PR reps to make it another hour by phone. I even enlist Eleanor, his wife, who talked with me on air a few weeks before about the installation she and a number of other artists created in Oakland to memorialize children dead or lost. The Coppolas' son, Gio, was killed in a boating accident. I tell Eleanor, "beat him up if necessary, but get him to come to the studio." It is important to me to get him in the flesh.

So here he is. In my lair. Fleshy to be sure, with a button by his navel unbuttoned and his stomach peeking out and a sweetness about him that is palpable. His daughter, Sophia, is more in the limelight now with *Lost in Translation*, and he is talking to me with pride about her directing, while I remember the dreadful acting she did in *Godfather III*. But Coppola identifies with failure as well as success and versatility. Films have been his gateway to success, but there have been the failures, too, including the re-release now of *One from the Heart*, a musical that critics loved hating. Doing musicals is part of being versatile—like his old man who, he tells me, arranged and composed music and loved covering the widest of terrains from Beethoven to Gershwin and went off to his workplace at Radio City Music Hall, where Francis the boy sat in the orchestra next to the clarinets. The boy had polio at nine, but by ten he was out shooting film with an 8-millimeter—the boy whose father's father gave movies their voice with the Vitaphone and whose mother's father imported films. Coppola was crazy about his actress mother and musician father. I'm bringing back that boy for a few nanoseconds through the man who is talking to me on the other side of the microphone. He brightens, recalling when he was a teenage drama counselor at summer camp and worked with six-, seven- and eight-year-old boys and girls and loved it—loved the feeling of working in community and loved the end of the summer when the plays went on. Once again I'm doing what I often do. I'm trying to picture the boy in the man. And I'm thinking of how much I loved being a camp counselor, and then I'm hearing Coppola on how he loved inspiring kids and still loves inspiring young filmmakers, and I'm thinking how I've loved inspiring students and would-be writers. There's a teacher in him as sure as there is in me. The identifying continues as he describes how he came to be associated with darker and more masculine forces in making films like *The Godfather* and *Apocalypse Now*, and then, following *Apocalypse Now*, how he needed respite with a musical, as he had done earlier when he directed *Finian's Rainbow*. The more masculine, darker-subject films, with all the violence in them, brought success, he says, due to cultural addictions. I ask him if he is more artist than craftsman or more craftsman than artist, and he tells me he is an artist and adds, "I'm all emotion." The craftsman in him seeks ways to get the emotion out.

Another interview is over. I am again thinking about Francis the boy struggling, as I had throughout my boyhood, with emotion, wanting to prove versatility, wrestling with masculine and feminine sides. And in Coppola, above all, like me, there is love of family—an ingredient which, when added to *The Godfather*, gave it greatness and gave him his non-refundable ticket to grand success.

Philip Roth

Roth was a boyhood idol. I had met him once, backstage at a City Arts and Lectures event. He had read from *Patrimony*, his poignant memoir about his father, read it with a bad cold, frequently dabbing gently at his reddened nose. After the reading concluded, I vaulted onto the stage and went behind the curtains, startling the impresario. I had to meet Roth.

I remember him as pleasant then. Chatty. We got to talking about an early, and by then obscure story of his, from *Goodbye, Columbus*, called "You Can't Tell a Man by the Song That He Sings"—a tale of a high-school teacher pushed out of his position because of Communist sympathies. I could tell Roth still felt fatherly about the story. Talking with him felt like talking to a chum. A radiant Claire Bloom, then his wife, came backstage and embraced him, full of raves over his reading performance, which had struck me at the time as ordinary, perhaps even lackluster, due perhaps to his cold—an all-too-easy way to pick up a check.

When I finally interview Roth, it is soon after he publishes *The Plot Against America*, a counterhistory of a Charles Lindbergh presidency, reminiscent of the dystopian 1930's novel of fascism in America, *It Can't Happen Here*, by Sinclair Lewis—a book Roth claims never to have read, by an author he calls "unreadable."

Roth speaks with thoughtfulness; deliberate, though fluid, he takes questions in and often breathes out a considered-sounding umm before answering. To my ear, he sounds oddly sweet and kind, charming too, if just a tad effete. Which is at odds with the masculine, virile image I have always had of him. I talk with him about his new novel and the similar, central role given history in Faulkner's *Absalom, Absalom*, and he responds by saying that the density in Faulkner's novel puts it in another category from Roth's own work, adding, "as does its greatness."

Roth is a septuagenarian. An intellectual. A writer's writer and child-
less man who spends most of his days isolated and alone with his and
others' words. Despite nearly a lifetime devoted to capturing what is
real, there is something soft, dreamy and poetic about him to go with his
tough-mindedness. He had to have been tough, I figure, to have with-
stood the scorn heaped on him from some bitterly critical fellow Jews
over the Jews he sought to capture in his early writing—scorn from the
towering literary critic, Irving Howe, who accused Roth of Jewish self-
hatred and minimized his talent. Though along with the scorn came
success, wealth, adulation, and from it, too, more writing. Who among
American writers has produced more work or won more coveted awards,
excepting a Nobel, than Roth?

I am suddenly remembering a story, told to me years before by a psychoanalyst acquaintance of mine who knew Roth and Claire Bloom—a
credible source who lived near them in New England when they were
man and wife, and who, with her famous playwright husband, got to
know them. She told me, without rancor, that both were constant in their
hammering and derisive joking about Jews. True? I don't know. I remember Nixon's Jewish lawyer, Leonard Garment, defending Nixon's private
anti-Semitic remarks to me by telling me it was common for most people
of any psychological complexity to disparage minority groups in private,
even their own.

The Plot Against America features Roth's own family. People assumed
his early work was about his family, and it didn't matter if he said otherwise. He has always written about Jews. All that early castigating he
got for his negative portrayals of Jews is ironic in light of his response
to a question I ask about two of the characters in his new novel, Rabbi
Bengelsdorf and Aunt Evelyn. Both toady up to the Lindbergh administration, champion its policies of international isolationism and volun-
tary Jewish assimilation. Are these not Jews trying to be on the inside, I
ask—thinking of Nixon's sycophantic rabbi supporter, Baruch Korf. Roth
mildly chastises me. "Don't generalize too much. I don't know about
Jews. I know about Aunt Evelyn and Rabbi Bengelsdorf."

Roth's politics are up front. He laments the reelection of George W.
Bush. He has written a piece in *The New York Times* in which he says
President Bush is "unfit to run a hardware store, let alone a country like

ours." When I mention that statement to him on air, he informs me that he received an angry letter about it from the Hardware Store Owners of America. He adds: " I meant you no harm, fellows."

Roth also mentions a four-page letter he recently received from someone who went to his high school, a man he had not known, who was a few years younger. Roth becomes highly animated talking about reminiscences, in this letter, of the "Jewish neighborhood" he and the letter writer grew up in." Ghetto," he notes, "is too pejorative." It was, he assures me, like a small town, cozy, with a strong neighborhood feeling. The people in his neighborhood were the people he wanted to populate his novel with. Real Jews. Jews he knew. Except for brief forays into fantasy, like his novel about a man becoming a breast, or the one featuring a baseball league full of midgets and Nixon and Billy Graham in hell, Roth has wanted to be true to his ethos of representing what was or what is. No polemics. No didactic intent. When I tell him I found utterly believable a Kristallnacht scene on U.S. soil in *The Plot Against America*, he lets out a strong, contented, audible laugh, and says, "Good. That was what I was hoping for."

He wants, in most of his work, to represent reality, even though confabulation and imagination are the transports for getting there. No violence ever occurred in his own home, but it occurs in *The Plot Against America* because of the exigencies of the time, the history the family lives under. If that history had been real, Roth assures me, such violence could have or might have resulted. A leading French intellectual friend of his, a survivor, told him he got that reality exactly right. Which is what he wants. He never personally encountered the lash of anti-Semitism. But he knew as a boy that it was out there, an irrational disease that wanted to exclude him and do him harm. In this novel, he wanted to show things as they were through what could have been.

"Blessedly," Roth says, nothing like his counterhistory ever occurred. Then he adds, almost solemn but unquestionably up, "It's quite wonderful."

I bring up *The Plot Against America* when I interview Roth for a second time, soon after the publication of *Everyman*, after he says, "Let's play ball" and our microphones get turned on. I tell him how an Indian immigrant in my sister's book club in Cleveland said she hadn't known Lindbergh was a U.S. president. Roth: "A lot of people didn't know that.

Me included." Then I tell him about Adrienne Barbeau, a pop culture television icon of the seventies, who has just published a memoir in which she confesses to losing her virginity to a young man who told her he was the novelist Philip Roth. Roth: "I hope he had a good time."

Roth explains his new novel as grim but affirmative of life's sweetness, heightened consciousness, bliss and love. He is unfailingly polite, excusing himself for inadvertently interrupting me at one point and, later on in the interview, apologizing for a moment of cross talk. When I bring up the source of his book's title, a fifteenth-century morality play, he quips about having had to read it in college "before education was abolished in English departments."

He talks about process. There is much in the new novel about the jewelry business, the ad business, medicine and grave digging. He writes, he says, about what he knows and then finds out what he doesn't know and talks to people who do.

I ask about a scene in the novel in which the main character gives his phone number to a fetching young woman who seems to be flirting with him. Why didn't the man ask for her phone number? Roth laughs. "You want to get down to technique, Michael?" He explains. His character is in terror of being laughed at. He is yielding to terrible longing and knows he can be humiliated. He is trying to avoid being humiliated and doing what is bound to cause him humiliation. Roth speaks of his character as though the man was flesh and blood. His character, in this scene, is the same age as Roth, in this novel all about the ravages of old age. I recall to Roth a central line from the novel: "Old age isn't a battle. Old age is a massacre."

Old age, Roth says, is, with few exceptions, about the emptiness that comes after the man or woman has been made, the returns are in, the precincts all heard from. Men and women who worked all of their lives or raised a family now lose their faculties and facilities and get hit with loneliness, diminishment, yearnings that can't be satisfied. "The golden years" is a bogus slogan. Just walk into a doctor's waiting room or a hospital full of gurneys or a cemetery while a funeral is going on. Though people seem to go from middle age to death in our era and think of themselves as not inhabiting old age, the so-called golden years are tough years—requiring stamina, endurance, courage and stoicism. Illness, sickness, suffering and the approach of death can deform people, and you're left with the consequences of your "inescapable mistakes."

Roth talks about his forty-five year high school reunion, the prototype for the reunion in *American Pastoral*, an event which he obviously enjoyed. But, he cautions, you knew what happened, who had become what and what friends and acquaintances had made of themselves. He was called on to speak at the reunion and observed from the booklet of biographies that there were still more classmates of his in Florida than there were in the grave. He said then that he hoped for the same five years hence, but that was ten years ago. "Maybe," he says, "it's even up by now."

His entire literary life, his readers and critics have looked for ways to read him autobiographically. Knowing how much he has personally suffered from physical and medical travails, I ask him the risky question of whether there is a connection between his character's hating his older brother for being healthy and his own feelings toward his older artist brother, Sandy. Roth says he doesn't remember using the word hate. It's envy. But I have the text in front of me and read to him that he did use hate, which he then quickly acknowledges. He says he has knowledge from his own life of a family with two sons in it, and there are brothers in many of his books, likely not accidental. Knowledge from life one derives for fiction, particulars are taken from this and from that and made up. The writer uses imagination, invention, the gift of intuition.

Roth's everyman character is a good boy who strays outside the conventions and, as much as he defies conventions, gets burned. Portnoy was both a good boy and a bad boy, and Mickey Sabbath of *Sabbath's Theater* was a bad boy. Characters can be ordinary too. Tolstoy was too harsh in calling ordinary terrible. Roth's protagonist in *American Pastoral* was ordinary but destroyed by an "American berserk" daughter. The daughter in *Everyman* is loving and wonderful. Roth is, really, a brilliant dialectician of life and counterlife. I am surprised at myself for my slight burst of fawning as I conclude the interview.

Colson Whitehead

Before meeting MacArthur genius award recipient and much praised, Harvard-educated, Gen-X black novelist Colson Whitehead, I was expecting a different young man than the T-shirt-wearing quasi-"nerd,"—as he described himself—with the nervous laugh and slight stutter who greeted me pleasantly. We start right in talking about names. His is Arch Colson Chipp Whitehead. The name Whitehead is Seminole and literal. "We're not so whiteheaded anymore," he quips, and says wryly that he saw a bar on the New York's Upper West Side called Chipp's and wondered if he might have been conceived there. That's how his imagination roams. The fantastic and absurd seem normal to him. Beckett's blasted plain and Borges' worlds seem normal to him. Pynchon and Ishmael Reed are real, not surreal. "It's the way I see the world. Walking down the street is postmodern."

Raised in Manhattan, Whitehead now lives in Brooklyn with his wife and daughter. It's cheap there, and he has met other writers like Jonathan Lethem and Myla Goldberg. They play poker, trade manuscripts, pal around. He is a binge-and-purge writer—for eight months he will work hard, then do almost no writing for the next eight. He is in effect always writing, but he writes in big chunks and never-understood drafts. He is always skipping around depending on what he feels like working on. It all comes down to getting it down, getting it truthful and getting it right.

He started writing for *The Village Voice*. He was an assistant in the book section, and they gave him a shot, and soon he was doing book and music reviews and writing a lot about television, what he describes as "a snarky TV column." He still watches TV. It's a good way to unwind at the end of the day.

His first novel, *The Intuitionist*, was all over the place. No one liked it. He was binging afterward on detective fiction like Walter Mosley's and Elmore Leonard's, so he decided to go linear and build a plot with stock mystery characters. *The Intuitionist* started out as more of a parody of mysteries. He invented the subculture of elevator inspectors and did the same with corporate namers in his third novel, *Apex Hides the Hurt*. He had too much time on his hands and wondered how such strange jobs played out. It was different with *John Henry Days*, which he researched because of all the permutations and different local identities associated with the mythic figure of John Henry. In that novel, he could inhabit different people at different times.

He got homesick for New York living in San Francisco, but now he feels nostalgic about San Francisco. He and his wife saw the second tower fall, and it put both of them into shock for a while. Tragedy and beauty, he feels, coexist on any street corner in any city—but in writing essays about New York, he was really writing about the changing idea of home.

I ask him about Richard Ford's spitting on him. He says it was one of the most bizarre things that has ever happened to him. He says, "It's beyond my ken." He thought Ford's collection of short stories was "terrible" and said so in print. "We all get bad reviews. But this is years later, and Ford pokes me on the shoulder and says, in this Clint Eastwood voice, that he's been waiting a long time for this. I spat on his book. he says. So he spits out drunken-breath red-wine saliva all over me. Maybe he was channeling voices telling him I was too uppity. You would think after a certain amount of success. . . . "

A listener, confusing Richard Ford with Richard Powers, wants to know if Whitehead has problems with Ford doing black characters. Whitehead corrects the caller and says he has no problem with white writers creating black characters, so long as they do it well. He is too young to remember the brouhaha over William Styron's *The Confessions of Nat Turner*, but he knows about "the radiation" it caused and says the argument over white Styron trying to become black Nat Turner made him not want to read the book. Critics have complained about his work. But no one has yet to complain about him doing white characters.

Yes, he has received much praise. But a bad review can stay with you for a couple of days. Praise doesn't swell your head, since writing beats such feelings out of you and keeps you humble. "It's just you and the computer and the blank page. The critic isn't in the room with you."

9   Attacks from the Air

G EORGE W. BUSH was the nation's chief executive. It was neither a clean nor convincing nor fair win, but there he was, this genial Texas silver spooner with charm and inner drives barely visible beneath a frat boy's reformed boozer exterior. Carlos Fuentes related to me on air a dinner he had had with Gabriel Garcia Marquez and President Clinton, at which the former president spoke with impressive knowledge of Faulkner's work, revelatory of a southern boy with an even greater intellect than the formidable one that showed, and which he concealed lest he inherit the Adlai Stevenson curse of being branded too intellectual. His successor, W., had no such concealed intellect. Though his former librarian wife promoted books and reading, he was the anti-intellect. He was also leagues behind Clinton in guile or dissembling, and yet Bush had managed to beat out Ann Richards in Texas for the governorship and then to defeat John McCain for the Republican nomination, and he had now grasped a questionable victory from Albert Gore that liberals and Democrats saw as the result of deceit and corruption—a brother at the helm of the Florida government, a father with CIA know-how and a politicized and stacked, partisan Supreme Court.

For those of us who worked in media, the election had been a thrilling ride, rife with dramatic events as they occurred, great fodder for analysis and talk. I was right in my element with it all, both on radio and on television, providing dissections and orchestrating voices of analysts of all stripes and hues, experts and journalists, correspondents and callers. Here in the Bay Area, where Democrats dominated, there were few

Republicans to draw from for television, though guests could be brought in from anywhere via phone on both radio and television and, since my television show was part of NBC, I had network resources at my command. But when the Young family bought KRON I knew instinctively, given their reputation for cutting and slicing, that my days would be numbered as a television host. When I got my pink slip, it was anticlimactic. I felt none of the anger I felt at KGO and was relieved to have my evenings at home again. I didn't want to get caught in the trap of worrying about fair compensation from my radio job to make up for the income loss from commercial television because I knew, for the quality of the work I did in radio, there was no fairness. I was, after all, working for a nonprofit.

My role on both radio and television, in the increasingly partisan-filled media world, was now more than ever that of the reasoned, fair, professorial arbiter of ideas. A dinosaur perhaps. Unlike the contentious hosts who filled the airwaves, I stayed in control, even when incidents erupted like one that occurred on air with Betty Friedan. The icon of early feminism and author of *The Feminine Mystique*, Friedan had been on air with me before. But with her autobiography, *A Life So Far*, she had been roughed up by reviewers and the press, who went to her ex-husband for his response to allegations she made in the book that he had beaten her when they were married. She even wrote of going to a NOW meeting with a black eye that he had given her. All of this her ex denied, and he was making rumbles about suing her. When I brought it up on air, she seemed guarded at first, but then quickly said, of her husband's alleged violence against her, "I gave as well as I got." She also wrote about feuds she had had with Bella Abzug and Gloria Steinem, and I knew Friedan had public differences and disagreements with Susan Faludi. So I asked about her feuds with other feminists. A caller scolded me for trying to make it seem that there was divisiveness among leading feminists. Well, apparently there was! But Friedan blurted out, "I agree with this caller. I'm sick of you god-damned media people." I took instant offense, and firmly told her so—whereupon she ripped off her headphones, got up from her seat, and shouted at me, "This interview is over!" She then threw the headphones down and started to leave. I spoke to her as if I were speaking to an upset child, with firmness and in a calm tone. "Sit down, please. This is not the enemy camp. You are among friends here, and you and I have talked together before without asperity. Please. Calm down and let us finish this interview." It served to mollify her because she did sit back down and put on her headphones, and we concluded the interview.

Every talk host has war stories like that. We all encounter the irrational, the unpredictable, even the deranged. That, excepting the deranged, was part of what added to the excitement, especially when doing it live, without a net. I had my incidents with Gore Vidal, Richard Ford, Timothy Leary, Lynne Cheney and a number of others like poet, playwright and black-nationalist-turned-Marxist LeRoi Jones/Amiri Baraka. I asked him if it was true that he had once, in his excessive black militant phase, told a young white woman—who asked him how she could help bridge the racial divide—that she should die a slow and horribly painful death. He admitted to "owning" the remark but he accused me of being in the CIA. Of course I was the one provoking the incident, but I was also doing what good journalists are supposed to do, asking tough questions. The important fact for me is that I remained professional on the air and never lost control of my anger.

On the other hand, off air, there was Will. He signed up with me for an independent study and was full of flattery. Norman Mailer, he assured me, had agreed to write the introduction to his novel, an obviously autobiographic story about a foundling born without lips who was tossed by his birth mother into a garbage can. I read the novel as part of Will's independent study. I politely gave him advice on possible changes and listened to him rail about how he and all disabled writers were unconscionably being ignored by publishers. Why were there no special shelves in bookstore fiction selections for books by the disabled? What an egregious injustice that these books were not published and promoted. I soon began to realize that Will's rants about neglect of the disabled were really about his desire to see his own work in print. His writing had some life in it, and there were moving moments. But the book was messy and highly unmarketable—even though I guessed that Will hoped to get it published with his militancy about the disabled and what he assured me was his connection to Mailer.

I made the mistake of telling him that Mailer was booked on my show. He pushed and wheedled me to put in a word and remind Mailer about the promise he had supposedly made to Will to write the introduction to his novel. He accompanied his pleas with intense railing about how Jack Abbott was dog shit. Abbott was the convict who wound up killing a young Manhattan waiter soon after he was released from jail, after Mailer did a lot of the pleading for him to be released. Mailer also helped Abbott get his book published. If he helped Abbott, Will insisted, why couldn't Mailer keep his promise and help him? I told him that if time allowed and if it was appropriate, I would bring his name up with Mailer. I meant to be kind. In the meantime, though, I began to hear disturbing tales. Will was dumped on the university. He had stalked a woman professor and charged a gay prof with sexual harassment. Will had done time. He was a nut case. From my own experiences I found him incredibly pushy. Try as I might to fend off his rantings, they would simply erupt. When he finally took his leave from me, he would invariably try to hug me. I managed to stave this off, but it was becoming increasingly annoying, as were his maudlin profusions of gratitude. He would leave long voicemail messages, swearing like crazy every time the beeping went off indicating his time was used up.

Mailer's assistant called one of my producers. Had I given Will permission for some private time with Norman immediately following our interview? The SOB had written to Mailer saying I had approved such a meeting. I called Mailer's assistant back. She told me that Will had been bugging them for years. Mailer had made no promise to write an introduction. He had, in fact, tried to discourage Will. She understood how Will had tried to use me. "I'm going to pin his ears back," she said. The truth is I was furious.

Will came into my office, full of his usual friendliness and flattery, and I exploded. I let loose a torrent of anger and fury the likes of which I have never unleashed in a professional setting. So much, in fact, that the writer Michelle Carter, whose office was down the hall, told me the next day that she had heard me screaming and could not believe the decibel level until she looked out from her office and realized it was Will and then immediately understood. My blood boiled at the way he had tried to use and abuse my generosity. Ironically, he told me with awe how much he admired the passion of my tirade. Fuck Mailer. Who the hell was he? Will just wanted to be my friend. He went to hug me, and I pushed him away. " I'm sorry I lost my temper, but you did something without my permission, and you stepped over the line. This relationship, if that's what you want to call it, is over. Finito." Later on I regretted my fury. He was, after all, though a bad case, a fellow wannabe writer.

Ironically, Mailer wound up phoning Will, briefly talking with him and providing a plum Will described to me as the "most wonderful thing that ever happened to me in my life." When Mailer came into the studio, gray and hobbling with a cane because of a bad knee, he spoke to me, before we went on air, about "our friend." "Pathetic" and "sad" were his operative words, but I let him know how furious I had been at Will's attempt to use me to get to him.

Since Mailer had put out a literary retrospective of all his work going back to *The Naked and the Dead*, we talked a lot about his work, then about his idol, Muhammad Ali. Mailer is easy to talk to. This was our fourth interview; we enjoyed each other and were comfortable, even affectionate with each other. Some of my feminist women friends still found him worthy of their wrath for some of the things that he had said—though he told me years before that someone who loved women as much as he did could hardly be called a misogynist. And, as Germaine Greer noticed when she battled with him over sexual politics, there was something sweet and loveable in Mailer that won you over, if you were open to that side of him. He was a nice, avuncular Jewish man, and at seventy-five he realized, he conceded to me on air, just how much a part of him his Jewishness was. He talked about how writers and writing in America had become a woman's empire. He was speaking, I thought, more about book purchasers and the Oprah phenomenon than about the often lamented feminization of American culture. I mentioned to him an article by Francine Prose that had appeared in *Harper's*. She quoted a passage from *Advertisements for Myself*, in which Norman said women can't be writers because they lack balls. This sparked a strong, visible response. The color rose up in his face, and he was suddenly punching back. "That was a stupid thing to say. I'm sorry I said it. But some people take something you said like that and keep poking at it as if it's a bruise. How would you like to be married to someone like that? Someone who just keeps poking over and over again at a bruise?" Years later Francine Prose told me she'd heard Mailer's remarks, and went on to inform me that her husband had now and then taken to shouting at her, "How do I like being married to someone who keeps poking as if it's a bruise?" I couldn't help thinking that maybe Mailer believed he was married to someone like that, the wife who got him into Bellevue, whom he stabbed in a violent tantrum, an incident many women still would not forgive.

Mailer and I spoke about the writer as celebrity and public figure. He noted how the sort of celebrity status he possessed put him on a level with people like Madonna, where he could approach her on a kind of equal footing. He talked about how novelists are godlike—creating and controlling characters, putting them into situations, placing words in their mouths and then facing the difficulty of going back to the real world, having to deal with real people. That disparity between the omnipotence and aloneness of the novelist and the real world with its lack of control was partly why I found it difficult to invent myself as a writer. I sometimes thought of Kafka, who said he preferred being without human contact. I liked the stimulation I got from others. I never wanted to be the writer who sat apart from the world godlike and, in Joyce's words, pared his fingernails.

I spoke with another great war storyteller and American fiction writer, Robert Stone, about the decline of the novelist—the precipitous fall that Styron lamented as the novelist's loss of grace, high status and wide popularity. Stone, the son of a schizophrenic mother, talked with me of battling bouts of depression and an inability to write, then passing through and entering back into the flow of language, plot, character and narrative. Wizened and all gray, a one-time Merry Prankster with Ken Kesey—whom he described as an artist turned public shaman—Stone had an imagination that sank into the tangled inner lives of outcasts, exiles and misfits, a writer whose work was filled with dark edges and paranoia but who came across in the flesh as the most genial of men, kind and collegial, nearly docile, an autodidact who never finished high school but taught at both Harvard and Yale. This was a writer who quoted Kafka's line to me about there being "a vast amount of hope but not for us."

Stone, a pal of Paul Newman, also had that special status of belonging to the famous writer's club. Perhaps, though, Mailer was right, that the writer's club was now more a woman's club in an America of shattering glass ceilings and new woman networks. Two old-boy literary warriors like Mailer and Stone. Their status as novelists declining with new gender power, age and generational shifts, declining readership and the overall fall of the novelist's once Olympian clout.

. . .

AFTER AL QAEDA ATTACKED US from the skies on September 11th, even Howard Stern got dead serious. So did the nighttime talk shows, as America debated whether or not irony had died. Patriotism that had been dormant in my heart—even when I was angriest at my nation's government and scowled at what I called flag wavers—emerged in me as never before. My immediate response, aside from the horror and pity, was love of country and smoldering anger at the perpetrators and their misogynist, fanatic Taliban hosts. Since the Taliban gave sanctuary to bin Laden and Al Qaeda, it seemed elementary to me that we had to take action against them. I made my views clear on the air, and I was not at all surprised when pacific folk of the Bay Area let me know their displeasure. There were even website postings expressing incredulity at my "turning hawk." Most listeners, however, appreciated the serious coverage and open community forum that we provided at so crucial a time, and I was amazed at all the personal thanks I received simply for doing what I had been doing for years—putting on an in-depth, calm, reasoned and civil discussion. Like many Americans, I felt the true heroes in the wake of 9-11 were the firefighters, rescue workers and everyday people who displayed courage and endurance; like many Americans, I was deeply disturbed and to a degree, personally changed. I had done so many shows and news stories on horror and carnage— Rwanda, Bosnia, Pol Pot's Cambodia, and so much more—and had felt many times the sick helplessness one feels in the wake of mass murder. But 9-11, though it was on the other coast, literally struck home. I tried imagining the horror, the terror those on board the planes must have felt as they watched the hijackers slitting throats and taking over flights to commandeer them into the whirlwind. I tried feeling what those trapped in the towers or inside the Pentagon must have felt as planes turned into missiles furiously sped at them, then hit and exploded into mammoth conflagrations, incinerating thousands who were living lives they believed had futures—thousands who were instantly snuffed or, worse, left with a choice of leaping from flames into death's jaws or being consumed by fire. My mind could not make real the suffering of the loved ones who found themselves grieving over corpses that had turned to ash. The true artistic imagination, perhaps, could comprehend a picture of the horror and suffering, match images to empathy and stretch empathy into palpable consciousness. Not having that kind of imagination might be a blessing.

I used to warn my students, when I discussed deeply tragic literature, not to internalize the pain. Lear holding a dead Cordelia in his arms. Feel that kind of thing too deeply, and you risk having it overwhelm you. Look at the Shoa flames too long, Elie Weisel used to warn, and they can burn you. But, as every good talk host and serious instructor of literature must know, talking about it, putting thoughts and emotions into words, can also provide release and psychic sanctuary. Though I had spent nearly a lifetime believing that the written word was superior, I knew that talk could be, if not the cure Freud believed, at least an anodyne.

When the airplanes hit the trade center and the Pentagon, followed by news of the heroically diverted plane that went down in Pennsylvania, the United States had been experiencing an ongoing plummeting of interest in international issues. We had become a largely celebrity culture. Following the tragedies of 9-11, however, our "Forum" listener numbers spiked enormously and people were hungrier than ever before for international analysis. Despite my own hawkish feelings, I wanted to hear from the peacekeepers. I wanted to hear what arguments they had to counter my strong belief that the Taliban had to be taken out, that there was no other recourse for us in the wake of such mass murder, even if we didn't capture bin Laden and his cadre of villains. NPR asked me to do a week of national broadcasting, and they got skittish when I said I wanted to hear one hour solely from peace advocates. I think the NPR brass were afraid that, with over 80 percent polling in support of the Afghanistan war, there would be hell to pay from the mainly GOP legislators on the hill who were threatening to slash public radio's funding. This, of course, was before Ray Kroc's widow died and willed NPR millions from cheap beef and greasy fries. NPR had been toadying up to the Republicans by trying to be more balanced, airing more conservative voices, and its producers loved that we had booked some big name Republicans for the national broadcast. But, when it came to me doing a show featuring an hour of doves and peaceniks, they tried pressuring us into putting on a countervailing Bush administration naval officer. My executive producer, Raul Ramirez, and I pushed to hear the hour of peace voices only, and NPR ultimately relented.

I wanted, too, to present balanced voices, in local and national programming, from Arab and Muslim communities, and I drew on the many with whom I had built mutual respect. As much as I felt we must fight and depose the Taliban, I was concerned about the specter of discrimination or vigilante bigotry against Arabs and Muslims. So, in both local and national programming, we gave voice to the more reasoned and peaceful activists of Islam, even as I realized there was a new mutant, nationalistic strain of the religion which was lethal and spreading. Karen Armstrong, the British religion scholar and former nun, had been on air with me not long before September 11th to talk about varieties of fundamentalism and about how Christian, Jewish and Muslim fundamentalists all feared progress, advancement and secularization. But this was an enormity the world hadn't seen before—a love of martyrdom that had been right beneath our Western eyes, festering in Saudi Arabian and Yemeni soil and moving into a mobilization phase in Afghanistan, now full of growing militant factions with operations and operatives and sympathizers nearly everywhere. I listened as the usual array of Bay Area lefties called in to talk about how America had this coming, how we were hated with good reason for our many sins. Bombing Iraqi children. Keeping troops left over from the immoral Persian Gulf War on the holy site lands in Mecca and Medina. Support for Israel. Yet martyrdom and mass murder weren't in the hearts of Mexicans, Vietnamese, Nicaraguans or Chinese, or the Chileans whose government was overthrown by a U.S.-led coup on another September 11th. Hadn't these people and others in Africa been affected to a greater degree by America's foreign policies or by the European colonials than those in the Arab world—especially the rich son of a fabulously wealthy Yemen-born Saudi construction engineer?

I had long contended that Israelis and Palestinians were cousins set against each other by the horrors of the German-initiated Shoa and European colonialism; the historic acts by Europeans had resulted in what seemed like eternal war between perhaps the smartest and most resourceful tribes of the Middle East. But this was before the rash of suicide bombings. Many of the Palestinians, it turned out, loved martyrdom as much as did the Wahhabi followers of bin Laden. How did a people who shouted "L'Chaim," to life, and so often worshipped and adored their young, relate to a people who also claimed to love their young but wanted them to die for the glories of martyrdom? This was kamikaze stuff. And I wondered if it wasn't also, as Bernard Lewis and others were proclaiming, a clash of civilizations, of Westerners who wanted life to move forward and Muslim fanatics who wanted to go backward or die.

I got support on air for my hawkish views on Afghanistan from other old lefties who came on as guests—Todd Gitlin, Christopher Hitchens and Sebastian Junger. They all saw the necessity of the U.S. war in Afghanistan even if, like me, they deplored innocent casualties that resulted from aerial bombings. Junger had been in Kabul when it was liberated, and he said Americans needed to know about the rejoicing and elation among Afghans, how they were shouting "America, America" like hosannas. It is just what many Bushites and Neocons expected and foolishly hoped would occur in Iraq.

I hit a nerve with some in my listening audience by putting on former SDS Weatherman Bill Ayres. He had been scheduled a month before to be on soon after 9-11 to discuss his memoir, which included a chapter about how he and his band of radical sixties bombers tried to blow up the Pentagon. Emotions were still raw, and I knew many listeners would be upset simply hearing Ayres. Many indeed were; he spouted angry anti-American rhetoric even as he condemned the Al Queda attacks and "the fascism of the Taliban and Muslim fanatics." I felt justified in putting him on air, despite the timing, because I wanted listeners to hear how a one-time homegrown terrorist thinks. I also asked him off air if his Weatherwoman wife, Bernadine Dohrn, had really praised the Manson clan for butchering the poor LaBiancas, whom she allegedly called "bourgeois pigs." He denied she had ever said it, or anything like it, but somehow I didn't believe him. At one point in the interview, I told him that I, too, had been against the Vietnam War but never saw the necessity for building bombs and that, as a working-class kid, I resented that he and his semi-affluent Weather Underground thugs presumed to speak for working-class youth. He said, with a touch of whimsy, "You probably would have turned me in," and I responded, "Maybe so." Ayres was still an ideologue. Still a fanatic. And it was ideologues and fanatics like him who had turned me off years before when, as a Vietnam War protestor, I felt soiled by their arrogance and rigidity. Ayres and his wife, and the other would-be soldiers of the left, hijacked the protest movement against the Vietnam War transforming peaceful mobilizations into glass-shattering, bomb-making chaos. Now religious Muslim ideological fanatics, who bowed toward Mecca, were trying to kill us, longing to do greater harm to Western civilization than even what the Nazis did to European Jewry. They and Ayres seemed to be brothers under the skin. Yet I kept my cool with Ayres.

This was a new kind of war against a new kind of enemy that had no borders, that hid in cells and wanted those of other faiths and even their less fanatical fellow Muslims to die, to be blown into pieces—like the blown-up bodies that the frustrated versifier bin Laden glorified in his bad poetry about the bombing of the U.S.S. Cole. Before anthrax and rampant talk of biowarfare , dirty bombs and nuclear peril, I announced to my listeners that I believed this threat from the dark side of Islam was the most serious, perilous and invidious the world had faced since the Austrian house painter spread his evil virus. And evil, I added, was not too strong a word to use, even as President Bush had used it, in the face of the murder of thousands by airplanes taken over by men with box cutters, the worst stereotype of Arabs—stealthy, sneaky slicers of throats.

So many of my listeners were old lefties that I found myself in the uncomfortable position of sounding to some of them like a Bush administration camp follower, simply because I made no secret of my view that the war in Afghanistan was necessary and just. The peace show we did convinced me of that to an even greater degree. None of the antiwar activists—who advocated inaction, food and love bombings or international police action to capture Al Qaeda leadership—made any real sense in the wake of the horror that had been thrust on Americans. I wanted to continue to be a steady, soothing, fair-minded voice that listeners could trust for rectitude, sanity and depth, but I was fully aware that my own biases and feelings were leaking. Still, the old phrase came back to me: "In an uncertain world, a steady voice." Never, since my final broadcast on KGO, had I realized more the importance of the role I played.

If there was great empathy here on the left coast for what occurred back East on 9-11, there was also a sense of being removed and apart from it all. It wasn't until I went back to New York in December 2001 to emcee a corporate event that I realized fully, not just intellectually, how terrible this had been for those close to the action, how the World Trade Center, at ground zero, had become a kind of holy shrine site and how firemen and rescue workers were now indeed, at least temporarily, iconic. The event—an executive symposium put on by the high-tech Silicon Valley company BEA systems in conjunction with *The Harvard Business Review*—was all about the staying power of leadership. The producers planned a grand finale for the symposium, featuring a New York City fire department brigade of men in uniform coming out on stage with Fire Commissioner Tom Von Essen in a stirring display of real staying power.

The BEA symposium was an impressive event, featuring a number of high-powered speakers such as Richard Ketchum, the president of NASDAQ; Jim Collins, the author of *Built to Last*; Jim Lee, vice chair of Morgan Chase; and Suzy Wetlaufer, then still the editor of *The Harvard Business Review*, since the story had not yet broken of her affair with General Electric CEO Jack Welch. But the big marquee name was NBC anchor Tom Brokaw, and the two of us talked while we sat in chairs getting our makeup applied. Brokaw had a daughter and son-in-law living in San Francisco and—once past the talk about their lives, San Francisco politics and what he loved about the Bay Area—we got to talking about how New Yorkers were living every day with the horror of 9-11, literally still breathing the foul air. In the shadow of 9-11, I felt I was simply having a serious conversation with another Midwest-born media guy who now, as a New Yorker, carried aftershocks and talked about his main aide-de-camp receiving anthrax in the mail. Fame ruled America before 9-11. Now we were all of us—the famous and the non-famous, the East Coasters and the West—in something together that was different than anything we had known or imagined.

.   .   .

SEPTEMBER 11TH helped to put my priorities back where they needed to be. I had a small American flag in my lapel that I felt fine wearing, and I continued to wear it with no sense of being a sold-out former lefty. I felt more committed than ever to my family and its future, to the need to do and be good in my role as a servant to the public and to a higher discourse. Corporate jobs were financially rewarding, but they took me from home more often than I wanted. Both my girls, fortunately, had become lovely, bright, kind, poised and graceful. As my parents wanted a better life for their children, I wanted a better one for mine. Al Qaeda and Islamic fanaticism against the West was a threat to my and every Americans' posterity. I wanted for my daughters what my parents wanted for me and my brother and sister—a legacy of love and virtue and a secure future.

My feelings as a father were intensified, too, by the knowledge that my girls were growing up. A good book needs to be written about how fathers feel as they lose the childhood of their daughters with time. It is a loss many parents feel but, for fathers with daughters, it carries its own peculiar poignancy. The sweet and utterly dependent little girl grows up, and we remember her girlhood only as best we can with videotapes or photographs. Even Alexa, then emerging from the throes of a rocky adolescence, shrewdly commented on it one day as the two of us sat in a pizzeria; there, sitting next to us, was a thirty-something father and his small daughter. He held her and played with her, acting silly and affectionate, all in ways that reminded me of how I was with both my daughters, and Alexa suddenly said to me: "Sometimes I wish I was still like that. That we were still like that."

Amy Tan

Amy Tan loves Nabokov. It distresses her that she lived in the same town in Switzerland that he lived in and that she never got to meet him. The language in *Lolita* is what keeps her coming back to him time and again, even though reading *Lolita* makes her feel inadequate. She remains enamored of and will stay enamored of the language in *Lolita*, she says, for the rest of her life.

She may have to suffer for the rest of her life with Lyme disease. It took years to discover what was afflicting her—the cause of hallucinations, neuropathy and a witch's brew of symptoms. But she can afford the best medical care. She tells me an amusing anecdote about a kid who asked at a reading if she was loaded. She was confused. Did he mean boozed up? Burdened? No, the kid's mother told her. "He wants to know if you're rich!" Tan was sure the mother would apologize for the boy's faux pas but instead the mother asked, "Well, are you?"

I know she is. Many books sold and a film of *The Joy Luck Club*, as well as one in the works of *The Kitchen God's Wife*. Luxury apartments in both San Francisco and New York. Fortune and fame. But this is still the little Chinese girl whose minister father and brother were both taken from her by brain cancer, who listened raptly and fearfully to the old-world bugaboos and imprecations of her mother, Daisy, who told her that if she kissed a boy she would get pregnant and wind up trying to flush a stillborn down the toilet. She wishes she had met Nabokov, but since she believes in spooks and the supernatural, she wishes more that she could have a long conversation with her dead mother, talk to the spirit of pre-Alzheimer's Daisy, who also had a brain tumor. She can't put into fiction that all three, father and mother and brother, had brain tumors. That would be too implausible. Fiction is emotional memory. It's also the stories her mother told her. But she couldn't write in *The Kitchen God's Wife* how truly evil the husband of her mother was back in China, the husband Daisy cuckolded with Tan's minister father, an adultery that put Daisy in a Shanghai jail. As much of a villain as that bad man was, Tan had to tone his badness down in *The Kitchen God's Wife* because no one would have believed how bad he really was from the picture Daisy painted. Daisy, Tan tells me, will always be there for her—like *Lolita* and her struggle with Lyme disease, but as the stubborn defender of hope.

Fame and fortune have fulfilled many of her young girl's fantasies. She's made it. Through storytelling written in English prose, despite scoring in the 400s on the English SATs. You create yourself as an American, Tan tells me, and you become who you want to be. She was drawn as a *Playboy* magazine cartoon with substantial cleavage, then saw her first novel turned into Cliff's Notes, and she also became a lead singer in a rock and roll band, the Rock Bottom Remainders. But fame and fortune have their dark sides. Sweet, innocuous Tan has been threatened and menaced by Internet postings. She tells me a short parable about the downside of fame, about when she was recognized in a doctor's waiting room. "It's the famous author Amy Tan," someone exults, and then Amy, there for a sigmoidoscopy, is asked by the receptionist if she had had her enema. On another occasion she entered a lady's restroom, and someone began talking to her through the partition. And even when you're as famous as she is, there are those who continue to misidentify her—like the caller who rambles on about her home burning down in the Oakland Hills, when the writer whose home burned down is Maxine Hong Kingston. Writing as a ticket to fame and fortune is no walk in the park, even with the gifts she has. She recalls Daisy looking at her writer daughter as she worked through long, intemperate blocks of time, staring at her and then suddenly saying to her, "Poor Amy. You squeeze all your brains out to write."

Tan wanted to be an artist as a child. She describes herself as a failed painter. Art was part of the draw for her to go to Burma, the setting for her new novel. She was in turmoil and moral uncertainty about going. The Nobel peace symbol of Burmese resistance, Aung San Suu Kyi, had urged tourists not to go, not to spend their money in a corrupt and inhumane military state. Tan thrashed for an answer. How do you morally decide when you don't know the outcome or whether your intentions will be realized? What of the arguments for constructive engagement, better understanding or spending money that will help the impoverished? Going to a country that bans writers was subversive, so she went. Then she bounded onto the road to political didacticism. Her fiction, she says, at least this fiction, is now her subterfuge. She wants readers to know about Burma, the Myanmar military regime—the rape and torture and killing, the human rights violations. "It was my absolute intention to make people aware of the Karen in Burma, but I had to wrap it in a good story to get people to read it." A good-doing preacher's daughter, she remains a storyteller.

I'm wondering if Tan has been spending too much time with her fellow Rock Bottom Remainder Barbara Kingsolver, absorbing Kingsolver's concern with the need for creating politically and morally relevant fiction. Still, Tan laughs hard when I bring up that *The Washington Post* reviewer said that her newest novel was too scatological and too sexual. "I was being playful in many ways. I wanted to look at all the reasons people read books—murder, mystery, travelogue . . . scatological."

When the tsunami hit, Tan got every major San Francisco Bay Area literary figure out for an impressive fund-raiser. Though she battled for and won creative control, the film of *The Kitchen God's Wife* never got made because she didn't want to give two years up to making a movie. Her devotion is to writing fiction and doing good. She now wants her fiction moral and political.

Maxine Hong Kingston

Whenever I see Maxine Hong Kingston I think about how vulnerable she appears. Small and shy, with iron-grey hair, a high halting voice and tentative speech, she seems fragile, venerably ancient. She is the older avatar of Little Dog, the tongue-tied girlchild of *The Woman Warrior*, not that mythic Fa Mu Lan who gave her first book its title. I hug her before we begin the hour, making small talk, reminding her of the time she surprised me by calling in during an hour spent with listeners discussing *The Woman Warrior*.

I led a discussion on California literature one evening at the U.C. Berkeley Bancroft library with an uber-PC black, brown and yellow trio of distinguished California writers—Al Young, Richard Rodriguez and Kingston, whom I had to prompt and pepper with questions to help her overcome her natural reticence. Though once Kingston starts to talk, she can drone. She may be a kind of steel lotus. Though she can seem naïve, there is a stubborn side to her. She has come for this morning's interview as a warrior of peace, telling me that her newest work, *The Fifth Book of Peace*, is all one text with her other work and claiming that art can be as strong as military weaponry. She is seeking a language of peace. She keeps asking herself if peace stories can be as dramatic as war stories and says, with what could easily be mistaken for overconfidence, "I do feel I am a pioneer in finding a peace language." This is who the great storyteller wants to become—a peace missionary. "There should be a peace member in the cabinet." "Why couldn't they have tried

bombing Afghanistan with butter, bread, cell phones and blankets?"
"Even Martin Luther King and Gandhi barely evolved."

What about anger, I ask? What about acts like the woman warrior
lopping off the head of the fat, greedy exploiter of the peasants? Kingston says she can communicate anger in words. "A lot of times I think
about picking up a gun and shooting a hateful person or people. The
more I write it or paint it, a transformation takes place in me. To be honest," she says, "I think of shooting myself when things go wrong. I have a
hard time blaming others."

Kingston works now with veterans of war, trying to help them heal
war wounds through writing. She has metamorphosed into a different consciousness—a serenity seeker, a dove of pacifism. The would-be
female Lao Tzu of peace.

 ## Ha Jin

National Book Award and Pen/Faulkner winner Ha
Jin is talking to me about the first time he saw the Charles River. A man
who was fishing there landed a huge carp, reeled it in and then threw it
back into the river. It surprised Ha Jin. He realized then how abundant
everything is in America.

Who would have thought of throwing back even a bottom-feeding
carp in China? When Ha Jin was living there, refrigerators were a luxury. Living like that and living in the cultural revolution remain in him.
So does Tiananmen Square. He came to America to study literature. He
decided to stay when he saw the AK-47s, the tanks and the blood on television. He couldn't believe what he saw, but he knew it was true, and he
decided he would not go back, since it would have meant serving in the
army. "I would not serve," he tells me. "I could not do it."

He is good humored. He laughs easily and frequently, a laugh hearty
enough to remind me of a hearty laughing Rinpoche I once interviewed,
but at times his laughter is nervous, more like a sigh. He has a humble,
scholarly and refined gentleness but underneath is fierce intellect and
drive and the Chinese industriousness Westerners marvel at. He tells
me he does thirty drafts of each novel he writes, and I think of Chinese
busboys and Chinese seamstresses who work hours beyond what most
Americans ever could. I remember inwardly gasping when the novelist

Mary Gordon told me she did half as many drafts. He talks to me about wanting to be a success in America, even though he already is. He speaks about how he wants to be an American writer.

Ha Jin would like his recent work to be read in China. *Waiting* is finally being read there, but his new novel *The Crazed*, is still unpublished there. He laughs as he tells me he would encourage more pirating of his work in his native land if he could be read there more. He is like Conrad and Nabokov in making English his own, and he feels connected to what he calls American tradition. He has a good life in the United States. He lives thirty miles outside Boston and has access to all kinds of libraries. He prepares for the classes he teaches at Boston University while riding in on the train.

Ha Jin is drawn to writers I am drawn to—Philip Roth and Alice Munro. We speak of the deep admiration both of us have for Henry Roth's *Call It Sleep*. I am talking to him like a colleague, like a fellow scholar and lover of literature, but what separates us more than East and West, or his lionization as a writer, is that what matters above all to him is the work. "In writing," he tells me, "I try not to appear."

Edna O'Brien

Did Edna O'Brien shtup Philip Roth? It's a question I won't ask her. But she does tell me she has always fancied Jewish men. And Roth called her the greatest woman writer of fiction in English. Maybe she is. And maybe it's sexist to wonder if there's a link between Roth being her former lover and the generous praise he has given her. I can't help noticing how he tempered the superlative by qualifying it with English.

Suffice it to say she is the kind of woman Roth would have loved to have loved. She talks to me of love—of its animal power and animal hunger, of the high-stakes game it often is. And she talks of writing, too, of the bleak and solitary life it is, in contrast to the kind of high Getty society feting she is getting while visiting San Francisco and staying as a guest at the Getty home. The writer's greatest fear, she says, is the fear of not being able to write again. All writers, like her hero James Joyce, write their way out of fear—in Joyce's case, fear of madness and fear of no money. Writers are all in exile because they have to remove themselves from the emotions they write about.

Like all great writers, O'Brien is in love with language. Madly.
Deeply. She tells me of working in a pharmacy in Dublin and coming
upon a T. S. Eliot edition of Joyce's *Portrait*, and she says it was for her
like Saul of Tarsus becoming Paul. O'Brien now lives in England and
pals around with Harold Pinter. She is a lot like the left-wing British
parliament member and former movie star Glenda Jackson; both hold
forth with brilliance and charm, serial monologists, but not with much
real connection to their interviewer. It is hard not to think also of famed
Irish memoirist and novelist Nuala O'Faolin, another passionate swirl
of old-sod garrulity who, by contrast to Jackson or O'Brien, performed
less on air but connected more with me. O'Brien claims she is off this
morning because of a cold, but her passion charms me and makes her
seem quite on. She is still raw and fierce, proud of having had her books
banned in Ireland and of having once been called a stain on Irish woman-
hood. More daring in her sexuality even than Roth, who turned mastur-
batory fantasies into onanism jokes and angered hordes of rabbis. The
fear and guilt engendered in her by the Catholic Church, O'Brien tells
me, are simply covered with a sheet. She feels passion still for Ireland to
be one country. There is a beautiful graveyard there that awaits her.

10   Cleveland Redux

IN 2002 Digger finally made it into the National Academy of Sciences, and I was pleased for him. He had received his bounty of glory in awards and honors, including being the recipient of UCLA's coveted Gold Shield award, given to only one professor each year for research and work with undergraduates. Drive and Cleveland and each others' influence conspired to bring us to where we were, and neither of us was likely to retire any time soon. Like Digger, I had lived a life pretty free of hobbies—just drive and ambition conjoined to a strong work ethic. Both of us had been lucky to find work we enjoyed, and both of us would keep on until illness, frailty, feebleness or death made work no longer possible.

I was being broadcast via NPR on the new Sirius satellite, and I could be streamed, too, via the Internet. Eventually I would be available as a podcast. My program remained the most successful local public radio program with the highest number of listeners in the country, and it continued to grow. But I seemed destined to stay mainly local and nonsyndicated, and that was okay, except for the embarrassment I sometimes felt when people asked why I wasn't syndicated on terrestrial radio—which was usually phrased as "Why aren't you national?"

Was the work we did good? For Digger, science was the answer to human ill and misfortune. For me, educating and elevating via content in talk had to be the measure of the work I did. Was there anything, any high, any activity apart from sex that came close? Writing used to bring me similar sensations, of course, and teaching could. In the classroom you saw the effects on students' faces, though it was easy to kid yourself. That happened one morning when I was teaching the great poem, "Sunday Morning," a paean to the secular and pagan by that Eisenhower Republican insurance executive Wallace Stevens, a sermon on the mount against believing in the eternal rather than that which is within our grasp or near our senses. I went deeper and deeper into the poem, drawing more and more out of it than I imagined, thinking to myself that the faces of my students were rapt from the passion that I felt. With the sense of an extraordinary high, I paused, took a breath and exhaled. "Any questions?" I asked. A young woman seated near the front of the class, who had been staring raptly, like the others, quickly shot up her hand. I nodded. "Yes," I said, waiting, anticipating her response to what I felt my inspired teaching might be evoking. Her question lurched out. "Could you please," she asked, "tell us more about the paper that's due?"

There was the rub. You never really knew what effect you were having. And there was no way to measure it. Ratings were simply numbers of listeners. Focus groups and student and colleague evaluations could reveal a good deal, but they also demonstrated how talk shows and classroom teaching both could be Rorschach tests. Real performers—and I was, I realized, a real performer—needed to be up. We needed to constantly prove ourselves, to make things work and to keep on doing it all over and over again and somehow, still, to make it new. And so we beat on. Striving. Performing. Filling the void between womb and tomb. My own parents seemed to lead a good life but did so with a kind of naiveté and lack of drive for anything but elemental needs. Neither became the person he or she could or might have been or, in my father's case, wanted to be. I thought inwardly with a laugh that what they needed was what we in the sixties celebrated as consciousness raising. How much did one need to raise consciousness in others or have one's own consciousness raised to live a good life? Or was it mainly about being trusted to show up, to be counted upon?

Leslie and I attended Amy Tan's fiftieth birthday party, an event redolent of Chinese motifs and Chinese cuisine, with an obese in-drag male pal of Amy's parodying her garb and the two Yorkshire terriers she always had with her, operatically singing, "Don't cry for me, all you round eyes." When we first walked in, a guy came up to me with a warm greeting and extended his hand. I had no idea who he was, and he must have realized it for he said quickly, "It's Scott, Michael. Scott Turow." And indeed it was Scott Turow, an author I had interviewed a number of times on air as well as on stage, who once studied writing at Stanford with Tillie Olsen, then went on to become an attorney, which allegedly caused Tillie to stop talking to him. He wrote a number of literate courtroom mysteries. The first, *Presumed Innocent*, became a major motion picture and was so successful it put him on the cover of *Time*. Many lawyers tried to follow his lead, and some far less talented, like John Grisham, had gone beyond Turow's success in sales and the Hollywoodization of his novels. I admired Scott's work and felt his ability to succeed with well-crafted, literate novels and still gain major national recognition put him in a rarefied category. Seeing Turow again and not recognizing him (he had a different hair style and had lost a good deal of weight) gave me pause—even his face hadn't been immediately recognizable to me. It reminded me of the on-stage interview we did a couple years back with a "disappointing house," as the impresario of the event characterized it. Turow was a fine, quality writer who had had his moment, and now it was dimming. It made me also remember the on-stage interview I did with Tony Kushner, lionized and lavishly adored after his ambitious, Pulitzer Prize-winning play about McCarthyism and AIDS, *Angels in America*. Within a swift and fame-depleting decade, and before Mike Nichols redid *Angels in America* on HBO, Kushner could barely fill half a house in Hayward—where, just a few weeks before, a standing-room-only crowd of many strongly identifying neurotic, ex-alcoholic and born-again women flocked to see Anne Lamott. Or the once-worshipped Alice Walker, author of *The Color Purple*, whom I agreed to interview on stage for a charitable event that I had to plug on air for lack of ticket sales. Then there was Gina Berriault, an exceptional San Francisco storyteller and former colleague of mine at San Francisco State, whom I tried unsuccessfully to coax past her shyness and get on the air with me, or another fine San Francisco writer, Alice Adams, who I did have on air and who spoke in short, clipped, nervous truncated sentences. Both gone now. Who was reading or remembering them? Who honored through memory the good work they had produced? The fleetingness of fame, especially literary fame, I understood. Alvah Bessie—former Communist novelist who fought with the Lincoln Brigade against Franco in Spain and was one of the writers blacklisted during the McCarthy era—wound up living in San Rafael in Marin County, and we became friends. Alvah had been working for Enrico Banducci in North Beach, doing the lighting at Banducci's famous club, The Hungry I. His writer's luster had dimmed and he was now dimming lights for Enrico. I arranged for him to speak at San Francisco State, generated the usual publicity for the talk, and then felt pain when only my friend and colleague Eric Solomon showed up.

And so I ask. What kind of guarantee of lasting recognition do writers have any more than the rest of us? Novelists like Norman Mailer or Robert Stone quickly admit, as they did to me, that they felt part of a dying breed, lamenting what was once the high and estimable peak the world's major novelists had once stood upon. "We were like rock stars," Bill Styron sighed to me. I related to famed editor and publisher Michael Korda on air the sentiments of Mailer and Stone and others, like Reynolds Price, who told me that Americans were far more interested in buying books on such things as how to groom their poodles than in buying novels. I suggested to Korda that perhaps the titan role of the novelist and the popularity of the quality novel were things of the past. Korda was quickly dismissive, suggesting that novelists who felt that way, like Mailer, hadn't had a hit novel in too long. Harold Bloom imperially denounced J. K. Rowling and the whole *Harry Potter* series on air with me as a bunch of sub-literate tripe. Had she, Bloom wondered, become the new iconized novelist in this age of, to alter Bloom's famous book title, post-anxiety that reeked to him of philistinism? All too many writers no longer remembered as the somebodies they once were or not remembered at all. Out of print. Out of memory. What kind of impact did their writing have? One could return as a different, more aged reader, but could the effect of literature be measured or quantified any more than teaching or broadcasting? Harold Bloom and all the bardophiles tell us that Shakespeare's work lives on, even though we know so little of the man. The man hardly matters, we are told, when the plays and sonnets confer his immortality. "No one remembers Shakespeare's daughter," Faulkner supposedly told his own daughter when she wanted his attention and he was too busy for her, holed up in his room creating his own literary Mississippi Grecian urn. I was glad Digger was in the Academy, but I was glad, too, that we both had work that provided for us and for others, even if, like literary art, it was ephemeral. I was glad, too, that I had a family and that I knew I would never keep the door shut on my daughters.

. . .

MICHAEL ONDAATJEE, who wrote *The English Patient*, was on with me in the studio. Walter Murch was on with us by phone from Bucharest, where he was working with Anthony Minghella—director of *The English Patient*—on a film of the novel, *Cold Mountain*. We were discussing a book Ondaatjee did of conversations with Walter Murch, all about the art of film editing—which, it turns out, was often similar, in Ondaatjee's view, to what went into writing a novel. A scene would be written, a character shown, and either or both might go from the cutting room floor back into the film or novel, in a different place. Murch, a sound and film editor, was a genius in many ways, the man Francis Ford Coppola called the film world's only real intellectual. He worked with Coppola on both *Godfather I* and *II* and with George Lucas on *American Graffiti* and won two academy awards for *The English Patient*. The first time I met him was at a creativity conference at Esalen, one that saw Amy Tan surprising the rest of us, even her husband Lou, by jumping into the baths without a bathing suit.

Murch's erudition surprised me, as did the ease and familiarity he had with theories about creativity, but he also impressed me with his bearing, self-possession, confidence. His wife, Aggie, an ebullient Brit, had worked across the bay for Berkeley-based station KPFA—the radical Pacifica station that I liked to refer to as Radio Havana, though I gave its supporters air time to defend the station when it looked as if infighting might cause it to go under. Murch's most famous sound editing was probably in *The Godfather*, in the scene where Michael Corleone was talking to the Turk in the Italian restaurant; we heard rocking subway noises, sounds Murch decided to include after the scene was shot. Many of Murch's touches were nuanced, keying us with sound or affecting us with an unseen hand, with a visual subtlety that triggered our senses. He had shown that film editors could do what great novelists did—inform us about a scene or a character and abruptly shift our attention, even our sensibility. Murch did not want to be involved with the real-life personalities of the actors in the films he worked on; he avoided contact with them while editing. Personal contact with actors only intruded and got in the way of the task.

Studious was the key word here. Both Murch and Ondaatjee were studious about their work. Murch got involved in a film. He read everything he could about it, including every draft of the script. In the case of *Cold Mountain*, he studied the historic backdrop, context and minutiae upon which the book was based. And Ondaatjee worked the same way—absorbing everything he could for the novels he wrote, putting everything he possibly could into each one of them without really knowing if the process was ever going to work for him again. I was probably as studious, as hard-working, maybe even as thorough in preparing for an interview or an hour of news discussion. But my work seemed so much less creative.

When I interviewed the author of *Cold Mountain*, Charles Frazier—who, like me, has a Ph.D. in English and was once a college literature teacher—I remembered thinking about all the years he put into writing the novel, a bestseller that came with much sacrifice and solitude. And when Murch and Ondaatjee discussed with me the solitary nature of their efforts, I was struck again by how the creation of high-quality work was unfailingly lonely and isolated. You do the work alone because you need to, and you don't do it for the glory. Hell, Balzac was likely driven to create mainly because he loved to shop. These two, Murch and Ondaatjee, deserved glory, but they were not driven by it. What drove both of them was art.

Now I was doing what old men often do—writing a look-back at an interesting life with interesting stories—though, as Moss Hart used to say, interesting usually closes the day after. Why did I want to write a memoir? Was it the need to write and the simple admission that fiction, or a worthy novel of literary merit, wasn't in me? I remembered again what Terry Gross had once said about wanting to write novels but not hearing the voices that novelists hear. I wanted them inside me but they weren't there. Many of the tales I wanted to meld into fiction came out of my own experiences and were about me. Robert Stone had told me that memoir writing, like fiction, requires a voice that becomes a character. "You find a voice and project a character, just as you do in fiction. It's close to the process of fiction." Were there simply stories, narratives, I needed to tell?

.   .   .

WHEN DIGGER AND I went to our fortieth-year Heights High reunion, the first person we saw was The Mole. He was with two girls who were best friends in high school. He had been engaged to one, DeeDee, who put off their engagement to go off to New York and to become a ballerina but failed; Kathy, the other girl, he married. Mole and Kathy now ran a couple of sub sandwich shops in Florida, and after some swift hugging and catching up, DeeDee turned to me and asked, "When did you become a *mensch?*" Good question. I was nothing like the big-mouthed wild boy I used to be—transformed over decades, like so many of us. We all spotted an obese, waddling, gray-haired guy who turned out to be Joey, once the most popular and best-looking boy in our grade in junior high. Joey was now "in moving and storage" and lived in Atlanta.

I enjoyed seeing all the old faces. Where I was philosophic and contemplative at my tenth, hearing T. S. Eliot's opening lines from "Burnt Norton" reverberating through my mind, I was now more at ease and disposed toward pleasant, even effusive greetings. Perhaps it was the age we had reached, but all was warm, fuzzy friendliness, even with those we had once made fun of, like one guy we called Buddha—whom Digger had chased for about a half hour one day, screaming like a mad banshee "BUDDHA, BUDDHA, BUDDHA," until a Phys Ed teacher stopped him and said, "Are you fucking crazy?" He came up to me with a huge grin and an extended hand and let me know who he was. "Stan Budin, Mike. Remember me?" I shook hands with him, grabbed Digger away from some people he was talking to and turned him around toward Buddha. "Do you know who this is? It's Buddha!" Buddha grinned widely. Then we saw another guy we used to make fun of whom we called The Puppet, another whom I called The Bear (and who called me The Beak, about the only words we exchanged throughout high school) and another guy Digger and I called "Falcon" and would crazily flap our arms at. A bestiary of nicknames. Even Baboon was there, whom our friend Jurinsky tormented for decades after high school by sending baboon photos from zoos all over the world. Baboon, now an IRS accountant living in Indiana, never knew who sent them, just as he never knew it was me who put itching powder all over his roll-on deodorant so he would scratch under his arms. They had all turned into nice, pleasant, respectable men who seemed, in every case, glad to see us and full of pleasant memories of us as fun, crazy guys. Where were those we thought had despised us? And where were the hoods, the bad guys whose names were all on the list of unfindables? Everyone seemed to know that I worked in radio and that Digger and I were the only two in our class who were in the school's hall of fame. I realized, even though Digger and I had both always wanted to go back and show THEM, the in kids, that we were now, in many ways, THEM.

Digger and I had always had our own way of communication, our instant ways of breaking each other up as only close friends can. We accepted each others' natures and fierce competition and drive. We welcomed each others' successes and hated each others' failures and developed an even closer and unimagined kind of friendship in the anomie soil of the Golden State. I came West as a humanities professor, and he as a scholar in genetics. I became what so many famous people or disgraced-by-scandal celebrities seem to become these days—a talk host—though I wanted a literary career. My friend became more famous in the world of science, covered with medals and honors and with the promise of biotech loot. But he never wanted either of us to forget the childhood we came from and our scurrilous but sacred rites of passage. I built a family. He stayed single. We would go back to Cleveland, prowl old haunts and old neighborhoods, and he would fantasize about how all his honors and awards and grants and fellowships would make "them," whoever they were, drop their jaws. Impressing them. Showing them. We had both become men far beyond the men we ever thought or imagined we would be, and there was both joy and pride as well as pyrrhic victory in that. We were bound to each other because of who we were and what we shared and who, in spite of who we had been, we turned out to be.

After the first evening's socializing at the high school, Digger said, "That's enough for me. I enjoyed myself, but one night is enough." One guy, the smartest kid in our class in high school, who broke state records on the SATs, came under Digger's fire. "He heads up a research group, and it isn't even a clinical research group. I'm much more successful." Digger was a member of the National Academy, and he was still proving himself to himself, still needing to persuade himself of his own accomplishments, even though no one would argue with him or contest that he was right. But high school shame can cling archaeologically. "Tell me, Michael. Who has done nearly half of what you or I have done? Who in this class can compete with either one of us?" I responded that one was an economics prof who'd worked for Bush Senior, another a political scientist who had published a scad of books. Another a millionaire in the junk business with a Vegas showgirl wife. Who knew what good or altruistic acts others had done or what all of them had accomplished? How, ultimately, do we or should we take measure?

There was a dinner and dancing night scheduled for the following evening at a Cleveland country club. Though Digger said why bother, I wanted to go. I found myself seated at a table with a classmate I hardly knew and his youngish, thirty-something second wife. I was talking animatedly with her while Ed Stephens, the emcee, was reciting items such as who had the most grandkids and who had come the farthest. Then I suddenly heard my name, followed by a lot of applause. Digger grabbed hold of me and pulled me away from the table, off into an alcove. "Those motherfuckers!" he yelped. "What? What's the matter?" I asked.

"Did you hear what they said about you?"

"No. No, I didn't. What did they say?

"They said Mike Krasny is the only member of the class in the Heights hall of fame. Those motherfuckers! I'm in there too, for Christ sakes!"

You want me to say something? I'll grab the microphone. I'll rectify it."

"No. Fuck 'em. The motherfuckers."

What was amusing and poignant was that it still mattered to Digger that he get the respect and recognition. I remembered Digger's mother, Leona, turning to us in a Cleveland deli and saying, in her blunt, no B.S. way—soon after both of us had established ourselves as university professors—"You know, you both were a couple of losers in high school." I wasn't sure then and was not now if she was right, because my memory of who we were in high school remained mercurial, subject to shifting narratives. As for Digger—if anyone had ever doubted his ability to become someone, there was no doubting it now.

"I just started out trying to compete with my brother," Saul Bellow quipped after winning the Nobel. Always one who identified with writers and what they had to say, especially Bellow, I thought that I, too, started out trying to compete with my soft-spoken, star athlete brother—and Digger, who had no brother, started out competing with me. It was one thing not to get mentioned as a member of the hall of fame, but another for them to mention me without mentioning him. Not long after the reunion, Digger would receive another major honor, a cool million over four years to spend on research as he saw fit. He had also, like me, been honored as an alumnus by Phi Beta Kappa at Ohio University. But high school was where things really mattered, where life gelled—perhaps because his mother had had it right.

When Leona died, I remember Digger telling me. "I went through all these things my mother had saved. A lot of clippings about me, about stuff I'd done and honors I'd won. And I wondered if any of that stuff had any meaning to anyone other than to my mother and me." I remembered the clippings I'd seen as a kid of Digger's father leading the fighting Methodists of Albion College. How cool I thought that back then. A Jew leading a pack of gentiles on the basketball court. Leslie's grandmother had pulled an old yellowed clipping from her purse and showed it to us as we drove her back after an outing we'd had with her to the home for the Jewish aged in New Jersey, where she was penned up. The article was about some Hadassah leadership work she had done decades before, but it was proof that she once had been a somebody; she had received recognition. I liked the story Ethan Canin once told me of a guy who came down in a paraglider to a mountain that Ethan and some friends of his had just hiked up. "You're Ethan Canin, right?" the guy asked. "Right," Ethan answered. "Love your work," the guy said, and then he went right back up and glided past the sight line, away from where Ethan and his friends were standing. You climb whatever mountain, like Sisyphus, and recognition or praise suddenly come, and then that's it. They're gone. Whoever you are. Whatever you do. And whoever you are or whatever you do, sooner or later, you're gone too.

My father still lived with my sister, Lois, and I was staying at her home while I was in Cleveland for the reunion. His life was the routine of the old and retired. He got up each morning, after my sister went to work, and made himself the identical breakfast of Cheerios, raisin bran and milk, topped with a banana, and a glass of prune juice, and then he moved on to the newspaper my sister left for him. The jumble word game and other puzzles on the comics page were part of his morning ritual, and he told me, "I've still got most of my marbles. Doing these puzzles helps me keep them. As long as I don't get Alzheimer's." He filled each of his days with reading material and small chores, with hours and hours of the television loudly blaring at top volume to accommodate his diminishing hearing. And he still played bridge two or three times a week. I called weekly and asked him how he was doing, and he would inevitably say, "Taking it easy," and then he'd talk about the last bridge game he played and how he did. You worked hard a lifetime, raised children, and this was the last act.

I heard the cliché frequently about parents, like mine, who managed to pass eight and, in my father's case, nine decades. How fortunate I was to have had them for so long though the longer they lived and the more they declined, the more I saw the shape of my own destiny, of growing old and losing both body and mind. In 1993, soon after I began working in public radio, *The Pacific Sun* did a cover story on me that observed:

Krasny chokes up when he speaks of his father. "I was lucky to have parents—and especially a father—who believed that success could come through education and who wanted me to succeed," he says in a quiet, reverential tone. "These are hard things to talk about, because they cut close to the bone, but my father had a hard life. He was a bright man who spent his life working in a factory and didn't feel the kind of pride he should have felt about his intelligence, his character, his decency."

Never in my life, even when my mother died, had I heard my father let out a sob as he did in 1993 when he read those words—though it was a muffled catch of a sob that he swiftly stifled. "I was born with a rectal thermometer in my mouth," he used to quip. He worked hard his entire life, and he managed to live longer than every one of his contemporaries, and now, as I stood beside his bed watching him asleep in my sister's home, he was looking helpless, curled up fetally beneath a framed photo of his three children as children—snoring, no teeth in his head, hardly a hair left on top of it. Had I been proving myself all these years mostly for his approval? Wanting to feel his love and pride, wanting to be like him but without a hard, frustrating life?

Though still alert, my father was becoming more feeble and, like many of the old who have problems hearing, he listened less because he heard less, even when his hearing aid was in. When he had come to California a few months before to visit my brother and me for a couple of weeks, I took him with me to the radio station and the university. During our time together in the car, I reminded him about all that he had done for me. I remembered, when I was a teen, accusing him of being the source of all my adolescent misery. "You're the reason I'm so unhappy," I nearly shouted at him, lashing out, from emotions for which I had no words, that he had not given me the attention or love that I hungered for from him; then I saw hurt flood his eyes, and I quickly vowed never to hurl hurtful words at him again. In my car in California, I enumerated his virtues and the good deeds he had done for all three of us as children. Why talk about his neglect or inattentiveness or his blunt and boorish peasant ways, his tactlessness, the strappings that he gave me, or the other woman we believed he had been involved with for many years—because in truth there was infinitely more good that he had done, and I could make him feel good about having been the father he had been. And it did give him pleasure, at least all the parts he could pick up with his diminished hearing.

My sister and I are the emotional progeny of our emotional mother who, unlike our quiet and stoic father, let her visceral, even hurtful words stream out at us as children. We had stood, Lois and I, next to our mother's bed as she lay mute and dying and poured out to her, with our eyes flowing, what a good, loving mother she had been. Was this, really, what children ultimately give the parents they love—words, just words, of gratitude, honor, tribute and love, at this end game, this downing of the shade? Words that fall from us do matter. Don't they?

Both my parents came with me one morning in the early seventies to a class I was teaching. I wanted them to see the film version I was showing of O'Neill's *Long Day's Journey into Night* and primed them that, though it was a tragic story of an Irish-American family, O'Neill's own family, they would see in it parallels to ours. I was thinking of the blame, guilt and accusations that haunt O'Neill's sad Tyrones—the failures and hurt they are unable to overcome—but also the deep love that they feel for each other. I wanted my mother and father to feel the emotion I felt as the play builds toward the unmasking of each member of the family, revealing their deepest terrors and resentments, the inescapable immediacy and presence of their past, but, too, the triumph of familial love. When the film ended, my dad was asleep and snoring. My mother simply said, "Honey, I don't know why you think those people are like us. No one in our family even drinks." On that visit we all drove down to Monterey for the weekend. I was still smoking then, and my mother was nagging me to give up cigarettes. But I didn't want to quit. I liked smoking. Then my father said, "Mike. I've never asked you to do anything for me. I may never again. But I'd like you to quit smoking. Quit for me." And so, that weekend in Monterey, I stopped smoking, cold turkey.

.   .   .

BEFORE LEAVING CLEVELAND, Digger and I drove through our old neighborhoods. We went past his house on Farland in University Heights, where mainly blacks lived now. "The houses are so frigging tiny," he exclaimed as we drove down his street and—once again measuring the distance life had taken him—he compared the home he grew up in to the stately home he had built for himself outside Los Angeles. Digger reminisced to me about guys in his neighborhood and on his block but, unlike much of the history we shared, they were part of his personal history that I hadn't known or grown up with. I barely knew Albert, the older car junkie who taught Digger about automotive mechanics, something that held no interest for me. We drove through the streets of our boyhood as we recalled incidents that occurred and who lived where, and we talked about how the neighborhoods had declined. The homes in his part of University Heights, which once seemed nearly affluent to me compared to the houses on my own more modest street in Cleveland Heights, now really did look small and humble. I especially remembered how, in my boy's mind, the houses on these streets were filled with the possibility of girls. Blocks and blocks of houses—from where I lived in Cleveland Heights up into the better homes in University Heights and beyond to Shaker and Beachwood Village and Pepper Pike and Gates Mills—any one of which could possibly have within it a teenage girl near or around my age whom I could romance, make out with, love or be loved by. I'd walk these streets with a cigarette cupped and hidden from sight, lest I be seen by someone who might report my smoking to my parents, and I would think to myself that a girl of my dreams might be in one of the houses I was walking past.

When we got to my old neighborhood on Beachwood Avenue, I urged Digger to park. The house looked pretty much the same to me, and I walked up, with Digger, to the front porch where we all would sit for hours on end—me and my brother, Pissy, Frog, Horse, the two Suctions, Sig the Sprayer. Only Sig had stayed in the old neighborhood, remaining with his mother, shackled to his schizophrenia, and I'd heard from my sister that he had recently died. I rang the bell of the house that had been my home and quickly told the white-haired, pleasant woman who came to the door that I had once lived there. I chatted with her a bit about the front porch and spoke of how it served as a kind of meeting ground for guys on the block. Her husband came up then and stood next to her, the two of them still behind the screened door, and then he introduced himself. "Would you like to come in and see the house?" he asked.

"This is very kind of you," I said as Digger and I stepped into the house I'd spent my life in through high school. I quickly learned that the man worked for a Cleveland chemical company, and he and his wife had four daughters, two married to missionaries. My home was now, I thought, a Christian home in a largely black neighborhood. The couple took us upstairs then guided us through the downstairs and into the backyard, patiently explaining changes they had made. As they showed us around, I was filled with emotion. Something unknowable, ineffably tender, prompted me to say to them, "I want you both to know that this house had a great deal of love in it."

"I'm reluctant to show you the basement," the man said to me. "It's really much too messy. But there is something down there you should see." He guided us down the steps, and what I first saw was an arsenal of tools. Our basement had been converted into a workshop, reminding me of those jokes by the Jewish comedian Jackie Mason about Jews trying to make their homes into museums, while gentiles made theirs into workshops. When Leslie and I were house hunting in Marin, a realtor who was showing us a home we were interested in kept excitedly saying to me, "Wait until you see what's in the garage, Michael. You'll be more excited than you can imagine." The garage turned out to have a workshop, and that incident turned into a running gag for Leslie and my daughters, given how uninterested I was in tasks or hobbies involving tools. If I had been handy mechanically—like my dad and my brother—or under the hood of a car like Digger and many of the guys on my block, perhaps I might have had a stronger certainty as a boy of my own masculinity. But at this stage of life I was glad for what I did have.

"Look at this, " the owner said to me, as we inched toward a door in the basement that was once a storage room for our family's accumulated junk. "It's been here since we moved in forty years ago." He was pointing to a slab of wood alongside the door of the former storage room, a wood board where we all had engraved our names in descending birth order. On the top my sister, who had carried a different last name than Krasny now for the past forty years, had carved LOIS KRASNY and the date, 5/31/57, which was, I quickly calculated, her twenty-first birthday. Under her name my brother had written, VARSITY VIC, which was the name he was known by back then after a comic book character. And under his name was the name, year and identity of Michael Krasny, then a member of a wild-guy high school fraternity:

MIKE KRASNY '60 PDG

Art Spiegelman

Art Spiegelman is wearing a peace sign button on his bohemian-looking sport jacket and fiddling with a small, white, tube-like surrogate cigarette that he keeps putting in and taking out of his mouth. He speaks in fits and starts, as if he is pulling threads into thoughts and knitting them to make sense, his consciousness clearly streaming. My mother would have called him a nervous boy, and he calls himself nervous and whiny. On the border of being downright frenetic, he talks quickly, and start-and-stoppishly, about what matters to him—comics, and how they take him a long time to draw and how they are difficult. He loved the Sunday comics as a kid, but they epitomized for him what workday, time-clock punchers had to turn out, with absolutely no potential for posterity like poetry or painting. Drawing daily comics was more like whistling or dancing, energized by the ephemeral.

The ephemeral matters to Art. His death camp-alumnus father told him he needed to remember always to keep his bags packed. The ultimate son of survivors, Art transmuted raw fear and the Shoa's shadow into manic energy and the shape and form of *Maus*. It took thirteen years, a bar or bat mitzvah, and after it succeeded wildly, they came from filmland and told him he could rake in big dough by having it become a movie. He wouldn't do it. There was no mandate to move *Maus* into another form. Maybe, he quipped, if they would use real mice. Errol Morris said he would.

Even though his French wife is the art editor of *The New Yorker*, it was the once all-Yiddish *Forward* that granted Art what he says was the law of return and published him on a regular basis after 9-11. He couldn't say that the sky was falling and keep his monocle in place. September 11 confirmed what he had connected to throughout his life and what matters to him—the umbilicus of his personal angst and Nazi-inspired fears of the horror politics and ideology can bring. September 11 once again saw humans up in smoke and the specter of annihilation.

Art subsumes and disperses the rawness of his fears with panels of comic strips, art, wit, family and friends and politics. "Don't call me a political cartoonist," he likes to say, but he can't stay away from the political. He tells me that we are in a war between heaven and heck. The Middle East is a zone of religious medievalism, but so is Washington, D.C. Both have their eyes on heaven, virgins and eternal rapture.

A caller tells him how much he loved the fact that the United States was represented in *Maus* as a dog. Then the caller asks if he would still use a dog to represent the G.I. Art tells him there are thoroughbreds and attack dogs, all kinds of canines, but the United States is a mutt. We are Hitler's nightmare. A mongrel race.

Larry David

Larry David is chomping on gum and saying, "Make me laugh." He says it over and over each time as flashbulbs pop, shifting from side to side with an arm slung around each of his daughters, his beauty of a political power broker wife on one side of his daughters and Julia Louis-Dreyfus, who played Elaine on Seinfeld, on the other side of them.

David and I are doing a benefit interview for the National Resources Defense Council, the group his wife has activist passion for. She has left behind booking comedians for the Letterman show and taken on motherhood and saving and sustaining the environment. She will later on win an Academy Award for producing *An Inconvenient Truth*. Larry is here for her. Julia is here for Larry and the cause. "There's nothing I wouldn't do to help the environment," Julia tells me.

Soon it's just the three of us backstage making small talk. David is answering my make-him-comfortable-and-establish-rapport questions, chomping his gum wad, a picture in attire and style of golf course casual. He asks me who I've interviewed at the theater. I tell him. Bellow. Rushdie. Atwood. Oates. "But," I assure him, "I've interviewed comedians on stage as well . . . though not here." I tell him I specialize in old Jewish comics for the Marin and San Francisco Jewish Community Centers.

Film clips go on from "Curb Your Enthusiasm." David and I watch them from behind the curtains. He is clearly amused by them and laughs hard at a few, though he has doubtless seen them many times. When we enter together, after the clips are shown, there is wild applause. We sit down, and right off I'm asking him a question mined from our backstage chatter—about how difficult it has been for him to add eight minutes more of writing than he had to do for "Seinfeld" to reach the required thirty minutes of ad-free time on HBO. The extra eight minutes, he says, add four months to his life. "But isn't it worth it since you have so much greater freedom?" I ask. He agrees, noting that it took three years before he even mentioned the idea to Jerry Seinfeld of doing the abstaining from masturbation contest episode.

David is full of ideas. Those who know anything about him know he jots them down in a funny-looking little spiral notebook and then plays Rumplestiltskin with them. Later on in the interview, when I mention the notebook, he will tell the audience that he just jotted an idea down in it the day before. He'll play them, telling them he can't reveal what the idea is lest it get stolen by somebody, then he'll lean back and say he will tell, then lean forward after a brief pause and say he won't. When he finally gives it to them, they are like a bunch of hungry seals eyeing a tossed fish.

David used to be terrible with audiences when he was trying to be a stand-up comic. He saw the audience as a monster that could turn on him and eat him alive. He played to conservative tourist audiences in New York. He went through hell, and no one knew who he was. He couldn't lie. Couldn't come out and glad hand and schmooze it up and act like Mr. Enthusiasm. That wasn't who he was. So he had to figure out an act where he wouldn't be lying and, he tells me, it was hard. He relishes telling the story of how he was getting nowhere with stand-up, looking for places in New York where he could hang out once he turned homeless. He used to take a Tropicana bottle filled with pennies to the grocery store.

Success and fame and riches came late for David. So did knowing he was funny. It wasn't, he claims, until after leaving Brooklyn and going to college in Maryland that he even began to know he was funny. In college, people started laughing at him, and he didn't know what the difference was. "I still don't," he adds.

David wanted to be a stand-up comedian. "Comedians," he tells me, "are the laziest people on earth." He says he is always prepared to quit whatever he is doing because it gets him out of working. "I'd like to quit and get out of here right now," he says. He wept when "Seinfeld" was picked up again because it meant working. Ten episodes of "Curb Your Enthusiasm" take all year for him to do, with no time off. He says this sounds like he's kvetching, but then he quickly resuscitates his inner comedian. "Yeah. Get out the violins. If you're rich, you need a terminal disease to complain."

David's biggest influence was Phil Silvers as Bilko. David loved the dark humor and he loved the character. Bilko did despicable things but was loveable. David tells me he likes the character he plays on "Curb Your Enthusiasm." The character does everything he'd like to do. He likes the character more than he likes himself. The character is not polite or nice, while David claims he is both. People curse the character and call him violent names, and it breaks David up. No one called him names in life. I ask: "Is playing the character therapeutic?" David: "Therapy didn't work for me in an office. Why should it work by me playing a character?"

"What about all the people who don't like the character or find him annoying?" I ask. "People who don't like the character shouldn't watch the show," he says. The show is silly, fun, dark, edgy, black, all he wants a show to be. But he didn't know he would take it to such an extreme. The most fun for him and for the actors is the improvising. It wouldn't be any fun if he had to write dialogue.

He could do the work on "Curb Your Enthusiasm" in half the time, he assures me, if he didn't have to follow the arc of the season's episodes, whether the arc is establishing a restaurant, starring in *The Producers* or finding a woman to screw just once to consummate the promise his wife made him to mark their ten-year anniversary. When I ask him why he made his wife gentile, he says, bemused and playing for laughs, that he wasn't necessarily looking for a gentile wife, but "after having a beautiful, wonderful Jewish wife for so many years . . . it was kind of refreshing."

David gets a lot of laughter and applause when I get him to talk about how his character couldn't perform sexually when he realized that the woman he wanted to have sex with had a framed picture of President George W. Bush. He compares it in real life to how he would feel if he discovered a woman he wanted to bed was a Holocaust denier. Then, after a pause, he muses. "Though maybe I could perform."

David claims he groveled a lot with women and that perhaps that led him, in not too hidden ways, toward success. A lot of Jewish comics were driven to succeed in part because of their desire to overcome shyness and win over women. Woody Allen and Howard Stern come rapidly to mind. David says he will probably go back to stand up after "Curb," and it will be so much easier now that people know him; though he also believes, like his character in one of the episodes of "Curb," that he could sell cars. He knows, of course, that he has enough that he need not ever worry about failure or the wolf at his or his children's doors.

Success, I think, has spoiled him. How could it not? People make a fuss about him now wherever he goes. He hangs out and golfs with the best actors and comics, though Richard Lewis—whom he met when they were boys at summer camp and despised at that time—is his closest friend. The wrestling, the fighting and the pettiness we see between the two on camera, he says, is identical off the air. He owns an *Architectural Digest*-featured home in Malibu and a place on Martha's Vineyard. He has his high-powered wife, Laurie, and two pretty and sweet daughters. And the adulation. After all the time without it, it's now constant.

I believe I know what pushes the humor. Self-flagellation. Aggravation. Oversensitivity to criticism and disapproval. He and Richard Lewis see themselves as mirror images, lost and frightened boys driven by aggression, self-loathing and the seals barking rampantly inside them for more and more laughter.

Harvey Pekar

I thought I might feel a small swatch of envy when I met up with Harvey Pekar. A Cleveland blue-collar Jew, he has an American Book Award and a movie, *American Splendor*, that was all about him. But right off, I start talking with him about his role in life and comics as being that of a *schlemiel*. He says: "I guess I was. I guess I could be called that." He says he still suffers every day of his life. But he adds that he's had "more luck than I'd let on."

Pekar met Robert Crumb in Cleveland in 1962 and ambled into a world of comics and alternative cultural fame. Then the other big break came with the movie. For years he had been trying to get a movie made just for the money, and then he got lucky. They came to him and gave him money and made a good movie. He went off to Cannes and Tokyo "to hustle," got contracts with Random House and DC Comics and started getting paid for speeches on college campuses. He also beat lymphoma twice. I tell him he has become an icon. "If you're going to be an icon," he says, "start with the movies." But he still has plenty to kvetch about. Terry Zwigoff wouldn't pay his way to New York. Letterman did him no good. Eight times he appeared on the Letterman show, including those two ugly, belligerent appearances when he called Dave a General Electric shill and told him he was full of shit. He had nothing to lose. Letterman was exploiting him. Trying to get him to do self-parody of a Cleveland working man. "Every man has his price, but he wasn't paying mine. He once offered me a cigar in a station break. He wouldn't even talk to me. He did nothing for me."

Pekar calls himself a quitter. He quit the Navy and college. He quit working at the post office. He says he is obsessive compulsive. He chews on his cheek and his tongue and wakes up in the middle of the night with" insane ruminations" on how to succeed and then about dying anyway and wondering what's the use. Early on his mother got him thinking that he was "a complete klutz." He shrugs. "So I am. It might have happened anyway."

Pekar laments "the shameful loss of interest in underground comics" since the war ended in Vietnam. He feels bad about John Kerry losing to Bush because of our home state Ohio vote. Bush, he says, "keeps screwing up," and is "one of the most incompetent public servants of all time. Yet he gets reelected. How is it that a lot of working-class people aspire to be rich, white people and let rich white people rob and cheat them and resent when anyone does anything for black people? It's terrible. People elect someone who does nothing for them."

Pekar is a *schlemiel*, a *kvetch*, a klutz and a loser, a prol icon and a man who has been lucky. A sweet head case and a rebel. A quitter who will not quit.

A. M. Homes

A. M. Homes teaches creative writing at Columbia and has had stories published in *The New Yorker*. She lives in her imagination and other people's heads—and will until she writes her memoir, *The Mistress's Daughter*, about being discovered by her biological parents.

A sexual predator. An icy woman physician with ovarian cancer. A woman with a broken neck who wears night goggles and collects used condoms at the beach to extract semen to inseminate herself. Ronald Reagan with Alzheimers. Nancy Reagan modestly changing clothes in her closet or furtively conversing on computer chat lines. Homes suspends herself and enjoys becoming the other. It clarifies, by contrast, what she thinks and feels. Her goal is to be true to the character regardless of what comes up, regardless of how frightening.

Characters, she says, come to her out of the ether. Grace Paley was her writing teacher, and Grace taught Homes to keep to being true to the character. Language and detail become clear, provided she stays true to the character. "If I was a painting," she tells me, "I'd be a Mark Rothko. If I was a song I'd be a Jimi Hendrix."

Homes says she thinks a lot about the American dream and the post-World War II American promise. Not just belief in getting things from working hard and keeping up with the Joneses—subjects that her writing mentors, John Cheever and Richard Yates, took on. "You often go into relationships wanting the best, with your most idealized self, and so often fail yourself or the other."

"The self-image versus who you really are?" I respond "Absolutely!" she says. "That's my turf!"

Homes thinks of herself as being funny in her fiction. Dark humor often but, yes, I agree, she is funny. "The funnier you are, the more serious you can be," she says.

She is a visual writer. "If I can't see it, I can't write it." At one point, she even talks to me of a "Homesian way" of writing. Her stories may be disturbing and dark, but they are meant to make the reader feel. "We aren't at ease or willing or comfortable to be made to feel." She also tells me how hard she researches, learning things she knows nothing about—as I often do for on-air work, but for facts not fiction. She makes up whatever she wants to make up. She invented a global tracking chip in one of her stories, that people told her did not exist, and then she read of one. Fiction is a more heightened experience. It comes from the culture—which she likes to read and crawl inside. "We live in a fact culture, but the best parts of this country are built on fantasy, hope, an idea or a dream."

11   Meetings with Remarkables

T HERE WAS A RECEPTION for Salman Rushdie thrown by the Friends of the San Francisco Library, before the two of us were to go on stage in front of a sold-out house. I was remembering the time I walked over to Margaret Atwood's home in Toronto, fearful that Shiite gunmen might be lurking behind trees or parked vehicles because she had sponsored Rushdie's appearance the night before. Rushdie and I are like old pals, and we greeted each other warmly, but I was wondering, despite all his public appearances and the supposed rescinding of the price on his head, if the Ayatollah's fatwa was still operative. I'd asked the event producer, Sydney Goldstein, about security—only to be told by her that there wasn't any that night. At Rushdie's last appearance at the Herbst Theater, two years before, she had to shell out, at the publisher's insistence, for bomb-sniffing dogs and security men. I was slightly nervous that there was no security and, at an appropriate moment's pause in our conversation at the reception, I asked Rushdie if the fatwa was still on. "Who knows," was his immediate response, after which he added, "But it's not stopping me from doing anything." "Good for you," I automatically replied, thinking of the hail of bullets that could easily blast their way up at us from the darkened audience.

Indeed, Rushdie seemed nearly indefatigable about appearing in public. A one-time aspiring actor, he even made a brief cameo appearance, playing himself, in the film *Bridget Jones's Diary*, and he explained to me, after I asked him about it at the reception, that it was odd having to act himself and utter words from a scriptwriter. I wondered if, like Howard

Stern, who frequently spoke about how well he felt he had performed as an actor playing himself in the movie *Private Parts*—Rushdie's subtext was a bit of a brag about being able to act, since he had frequently admitted to having long had actor's lust. I'd just the weekend before been to a screening of a film called *The Emperor's Club*, based on a story by Ethan Canin, who had a couple-of-words cameo in the film that brought howls of laughter from friends of his in the audience. It wasn't just seeing Ethan's familiar face on screen—it was watching poor Ethan trying to act.

I had heard Rushdie that morning talking on air with Ronn Owens. Ronn asked him the dopey question of whether he felt, all those years in hiding, a bit like Richard Kimble in *The Fugitive*. With great comic timing, Rushdie answered, "Well, I wasn't looking for a one-armed man." Rushdie talked to me about how, like his friend Gunter Grass—who spoke of his at-home self as Gunter and his public self as Grass—he felt there was a Salman who lounged at home reading the newspaper and drinking coffee and this other self, Rushdie, the figure the press wrote about, the public figure he had become.

Before we went on stage, Rushdie asked me if he could read a couple of pieces from his new collection of essays. Could I weave in two short readings by him at points in our conversation? He had already tried them on other audiences and knew they brought laughs. "Good," I quickly agreed. "People who don't know how funny you can be should."

Rushdie's lovely new Indian girlfriend, Lakshmi, was with us backstage. Since her field was culinary, we got to talking about food. "We have the same tastes," Rushdie said, nodding at Lakshmi. "It's quite remarkable. I mean that given a menu of whatever length we will inevitably order the same thing." I thought to myself that Rushdie and I had similar taste, too. We were both drawn to many of the same writers, we were both crazy for the music of our era, both of us had ties to the sixties and we had our political awakenings with Vietnam. We both skewed left politically, loved attention and knew how to present selves that were charming.

Though the reception was surprisingly small, many were asking for photo ops with Rushdie. Ronn Owens announced on air, that morning, that there would now be a photo of him on his website with Rushdie and the Forty Niners coach, Steve Mariucci. When I mentioned to Rushdie that I'd heard he'd posed for a photo with Mariucci, he said, "Yes. Pleasant fellow. I'm sure he had no idea who I was."

How could you not know who Rushdie was? Was there a writer on earth more famous? Of course, as he is quick to point out, his fame is not from the fact that people read his work but from the maelstrom *The Satanic Verses* caused and the attempts to censor the novel after the price Khomeini put on him. The public image that emerged from the fatwa made for strong associations in most people's minds of a serious and even grave fellow, instead of a man who often is comedic and stylishly funny. I recalled to him V. S. Naipaul's famous remark, after hearing of the fatwa, that it was "a most extreme form of literary criticism." I told him that I had asked Naipaul about it, and he had told me that it was said reflexively and without thought. "Well," Rushdie said, "I can believe that. It was a humorous remark. Our fights are over bigger political differences. We couldn't be further apart than we are on politics."

When I interviewed the sixties-singer-turned-Muslim-zealot Cat Stevens, I had to agree beforehand with the publicist that I would not bring up his alleged, enthusiastic words of support for the fatwa against Rushdie. Normally, I'm not inclined to make such agreements, but I knew it wouldn't matter because I was certain one of the callers would bring it up if I didn't—and, sure enough, the first caller did. The Islamic, new-named, bearded and robed Cat Stevens avoided answering directly, saying that the British newspapers had blown his statements out of proportion and that he wished no man harm, though he deplored the sacrilege that was heaped from Rushdie's poisonous pen onto the prophet Mohammed.

Once on stage I gave Rushdie a good, strong, laudatory introduction, and we started right off discussing literature, politics and the irony of how the two novels that preceded *The Satanic Verses*, *Midnight's Children* and *Shame*, were both highly political and meant to be. They both stirred up hornet's nests in India and Pakistan, but *The Satanic Verses* "was supposed to have been a non-political novel," Rushdie stated with his own well-timed sense of comedic irony.

Our talk flowed. Good conversation moves effortlessly with rhythms and cadences of its own and covers wide expanses of territory. Description can't grasp it; neither can transcription. It has a different potency than what the page in print delivers. It is, at its best, what Blake spoke of when he wrote of energy being pure delight, spontaneity, in-the-moment liveliness that the printed page, as much as I respect it, cannot capture. Too many rivulets and arbors and vistas along the way. Like a beautiful sporting event or, really, like great jazz or a piece of symphonic music it can move, unlike even poetry, into pure form.

Throughout our conversation, Rushdie spoke about writing in a musical language, of hitting the right notes or finding the proper chord. He told me that his son, at age eleven, read his children's book, *Haroun*, and gave Rushdie the best critical advice he ever received, announcing that the story "needs more jump." "That," says Rushdie "was precisely what the story needed. It needed jump. So I gave it jump."

"How do you generally respond to criticism?" I asked. "Not well," he answered, shaking his head, then hastened quickly to add, "But I'm getting better. I'm working at it, and I'm getting better." Another way that we were similar. "Sometimes you are the golden boy, and other times you are the donkey," he says. "It goes back and forth. I'm sort of in between right now. The golden ass perhaps." We talked about writing with music as its inspiration (he writes in solitude and without music), editors (he rarely uses them) and revisions (he does them). "I suppose I shouldn't mention who the writer is by name," he said, "but there is an author I know who never revises at all and looks at each sentence as being utterly beyond revision. As if those first strange jumbles of words that emerge must somehow be right. Oh, hell, it's Arundati Roy I'm talking about." How strange, I thought, as I recalled, years before, interviewing three Indian women writers, one of whom was Roy, author of *The God of Small Things*. She surprised me by speaking disparagingly of Rushdie, implying he was some sort of male chauvinist. This was at the height of Rushdie's hagiographic elevation over *The Satanic Verses*.

We spoke of the fatwa. It had taught him important existential lessons. Camus's words about how all of us are under a death sentence for the uncommitted crime of being born came to my mind but not out of my mouth. All of us, I thought, are subject to a kind of mortal fatwa that brought the uninvited cessation of life. Rushdie said he could not fictionalize his ordeal. He had to write about it in nonfiction form because it was real and actually happened. "Isn't there," I asked, "a greater truth in fiction, one that transcends the truth of experience?" Rushdie quickly agreed and expressed his hope that someone would one day write the great fictional work distilled from the zeitgeist of fatwas and jihads and the religious fanaticism behind terror attacks. " But, you know," he added musingly, "one must realize, too, that there are already too many books to read. I won't be able to read in my lifetime all the books I want to read. How much more fiction do we need? How many more books do we require? Unless they are great books, of course."

. . .

I SAT ON STAGE between two of the world's great scientists, a Nobel and two Pulitzers between them. E. O. Wilson, who gave us the word and concept of biodiversity, was on my right, while on my left sat the man Wilson once called the Caligula of biology, James Watson, who, with Francis Crick, is given the lion's share of credit for discovering the structure of DNA, the secret to this mysterious protoplasmic flesh we call life. I had interviewed both men before on the radio and found myself acting strangely protective with poor old Watson when a caller started in on him with accusations about how he stole the double helix out from under the brilliant and lovely brow of x-ray's dark lady, Rosalind Franklin. Watson singularly advanced the genome project. No doubt about who deserved credit on that. I'd once interviewed Watson's DNA double helix partner, Francis Crick, who was then on a neuron kick, connecting neural dots to show how we pitiful mammals are merely neuron impulses. And I'd talked on air with E. O. Wilson about ants and the earth's future. But this was different. I was on stage with both Watson and Wilson and we were before a large audience. *Star Trek* captain turned full-time commercial hustler and *Boston Legal* star William Shatner had begun the evening with a welcome, calling everyone's attention with a ribald sounding booming voice to the fact that "THERE IS SO MUCH MONEY IN THIS ROOM!"

The room was, in fact, filled with the well-heeled, and not even a room but rather a large, sprawling white tent, set up on the rolling, massive Woodside estate of Intel co-founder Gordon Moore, the billionaire who gave birth to the mantra that has come to be known and repeated with near reverence in the world of high tech as Moore's Law.

I was listening, and concentrating on what both men were saying, deciding what question would best serve the flow of discussion to offer up next and, like the former pool player I am, trying to think ahead to positioning, to other questions that would make the most of the time the three of us had. I was thinking, too, of what I might say to conclude this unrehearsed conversation, that would bring it to an end with dramatic weight. I'm not suggesting I was winging it. Like the former Boy Scout I am (though booted out for foul language), I was always prepared. It's just that, once on stage, I allow preparation to crystallize, to flow without notes, so the sense of movement from moment to moment can course its way through me like what I like to think of as a kind of zen mastery or, better and more humbly put, zen and the art of conversational maintenance.

Watson was making it easy by being funny. In his solid pink shirt, with his wrinkly, old neck bobbling up and down like a slightly inebriated goose and his voice both strong and staccato, Watson picked up on my question about extending longevity. Before I got to the question, I had started asking him about genetic engineering and concern expressed by recent guests who had been on my radio program, Bill McKibben and Margaret Atwood, that we were toying with and potentially endangering our own humanity with the brave new world fiddling of genetic engineering. Wilson mischievously quipped, "You're going to have to try harder if you want to get sparks of disagreement." Both men were in full agreement about having little concern over the risks of genetic tinkering, just as they were in agreement on not having ever been concerned over recombinant DNA, or just as they were in agreement over lack of risks genetically modifying food. This, of course, was because of their faith in science. We were then, soon enough, talking about gene substitution, and I mentioned to Watson that Stewart Brand, who founded *The Whole Earth Catalogue*, had told me at a recent event, that upon reaching age sixty he realized he had literally hit middle age since he believed most of us were likely headed for a one hundred and twenty year span. That's when Watson started being funny. "Talking about one hundred and twenty. That's silly," he declaimed in his intoxicated sounding voice. "We should be working on preventing dementia or senility because most people who reach one hundred . . . they aren't there. You'd be creating a large number of people who . . . the only thing they could read is *USA*

Today. You ought to withdraw life support if you see that." Watson got a lot of laughs, and Wilson quickly joined in with a comment about all the drool that would be on the enlarged print. I had a pair of brilliant biologists who were coming across like a comedic tag team.

The original phone call asking me to interview Watson and Wilson came months before from an event planner for Conservation International. They'd already had a big fund-raiser on the east coast with Charlie Rose interviewing both scientists, and they wanted to replicate the event on the west coast. "We were told repeatedly, by many people, that you are the best interviewer on the west coast," the contact person informed me. I quickly parried: "You've obviously been talking to all the wrong people." Before I could mention to my wife that the offer was a paying gig, she, once a biochemist, yelped, "Do it for free." Truth is I do too many fund raising events for free, but when they offer to pay me . . . well I'm not entirely a fool about money.

I was moving the conversation along. With a transition from me about extending individual longevity to probing how we can best extend the life of the planet and a few carefully chosen words about the necessity for new forms of energy and less consumption to attain sustainability, words Wilson called gospel, the old Southern born pismire lover was off on how we were running out of water and how the Chinese, too, would want U.S.-made SUV's. "Well at least the old people probably won't buy them," cracked Watson.

I tried being funny, earlier on, in my introductory remarks. After a generous introduction from Gordon and Betty Moore's daughter-in-law, I managed to jiggle in a story related by a friend of my wife's about their grandson. When asked if he knew the correct name for his "dangle," the family name for his genitals, the kid said, "penis" and was quickly told that, yes, that was what little boys have. Did he know what little girls had? He piped: "A brain." Well, sure, it got laughs, especially from the women, but Watson got bigger ones with his natural ironic tone and easy though broken delivery; picking up on Wilson's remarks about how we are an ingenious enough species to figure out sustainability and how our society needs to accept that we are stratified by genetic differences and then work to help those at or near the bottom, Watson sighed. "So many dreary Harvard students. I remember thinking if they only had better genes." I'm laughing with the audience at Watson's seeming disdain for those, to him, dreary and deficient in good genes students who went to a university I never would have dreamed of attending, wouldn't have been admitted to and never could have afforded.

There was, of course, serious talk going on in the midst of all this natural flow of conversation and humor, speculation by Wilson about windmills and hydrogen for alternative energy and by Watson about how bacterium culture could possibly serve to help us produce the hydrogen, and about genetically controlling depression and raising human potential, and then suddenly we were talking about the future and about the kind of hope both men had from their many years as scientists, hope tied to scientific exploration and pushing forward science frontiers, and I suddenly realized that I had my closing line. I thanked both for the knowledge they had given civilization, the contributions both had made to biology. Wilson interrupted me before I could get out my closer, "Are we done already? We were just getting started." I brought it back to the fact that Bill Shatner had opened the evening and then closed by thanking both men for taking us where no other men had gone before.

The applause was loud. I extended a hand toward Watson, gesturing to the audience for even more applause and saying his name with flourish, "Jim Watson," then followed quickly with the other hand extended toward Wilson. "Ed Wilson." Heavy applause followed. We shook hands all around and returned to the different dinner tables at which each of us had been seated. Then I looked down and realized that my fly was open. The whole time I had been on stage with perhaps the world's two greatest biologists and my fly had been wide open!

. . .

MICHAEL CRICHTON came ambling into the studio. He was a big man. Literally—he was huge. Six-seven. We talked, off air, about something I would not bring up on air—a robbery, recently reported in the news, in which he and his young teenage daughter had been tied up. Things were stolen from his home in a methodical, targeted way that suggested to him someone likely had provided the thieves with information.

Crichton comes across as low key, soft spoken. A handsome guy, he, like Michael Chabon, refused to be one of *People* magazine's most beautiful people—but the magazine, he told me before we went on air, dug up a photo of him and made him one anyway.

Here was someone who helped create the whole genre critics call the techno thriller. It was, he said, the situation that mattered, a situation like a lethal bacteria or a tornado or dinosaurs in our midst, or nanotechnology run wild, a situation that quickly overshadows everything—just as 9-11 did, as anthrax did. The nearing catastrophe of global warming, accepted as incontrovertible by most scientists, he would later derogate.

He has sold over one hundred million books. One hundred million! He, like Ethan Canin, was a Harvard doctor, the highest pedigree I could imagine as a kid. It brought together my father's aborted dream of medicine with the never realized, impossible dream of his sons becoming Harvard men, like the sons of his cousin Mike. Crichton was churning books out even before *The Andromeda Strain*, writing while at Harvard under a phony name so his profs wouldn't think he wasn't serious about medicine, even copping a Poe mystery award. And Crichton had made it in film, in the Hollywood world David Mamet called the big casino, with a scad of movies from his blockbuster books. He had written for the screen, and he had directed. He had made it in television, too, creating "E.R.," and in the-high tech world by designing software for film that won him an Academy Award for science and technology. He'd even written a book for Abrams, the fine arts publisher, on the artist Jasper Johns. Crichton was the only person to have had simultaneously the number-one best-selling novel, film and TV show. He had also been married four times, a fact that prompted comedian Steve Martin to ask him if he believed in premarital sex. But the guy was . . . well low-key. Charming and sweet but precise and deliberate in responses—quick to demystify early on any glamour I or others might associate with his life by describing how he spent most days utterly alone at the word processor. I asked him whether he, like many big cash-registering writers, was bothered by critics' lack of respect for his work; even mainstream reviewers seemed, after conceding the way he could hold readers, to lambaste his writing and deride it as commercial tripe. Did that irritate him?

Crichton replied that it didn't bother him in the least, that he found it a bizarre American perception that if you were popular, you couldn't be good. Since a young age he had felt the reverse, that if you were popular you were good. He valued success and named, to my surprise, Woody Allen as someone he admired, because Allen, Crichton said, had gone from being obscure to being increasingly popular. "Well," I remarked, "Woody Allen hasn't had any of the kind of success at the box office or at garnering readers or film audiences like you've had." "It's difficult to be widely read," Crichton said, as he gave serious thought to his words. "I can be complex and convoluted and read by eight thousand people. I can do that in a snap." I remembered the words of *Valley of the Dolls* schlock author Jacqueline Suzanne, who insisted that she must be as good a writer as Philip Roth or Vladimir Nabokov because she sold as many books.

. . .

SWAT CAME OUT TO SEE ME. He was in town for some kind of sales meeting related to the products he sells, bathroom and plumbing supplies. I'd called him Swat since we were fourteen, when I saw him slow dancing and furtively swatting at his erection so he wouldn't be embarrassed by it.

Swat now lived in Cherry Hill, New Jersey. He had missed the reunion, and I was surprised to see his head and beard flecked with gray. We shook hands, and then, awkwardly, each of us put one arm around the other in a half hug that signaled, in my mind, how we were kind of half pals and were still half in the past, when guys didn't hug, and half in the present, when they do. I wanted to kid Swat right off about being in the past, or at least out of vogue, with the gold chain he was wearing around his neck. But I brought him in the house and had him and Leslie say a few cordial words to each other, then steered him out for a sit-down in my backyard by the pool—which brought the predictable remark from him about who'd ever have believed that I'd own a house with a pool.

Swat related to me how he got to be big in bathroom fixtures and plumbing supplies, building a number of East Coast businesses and showrooms in different states. It was a success story that he wanted to tell me, so I listened as he detailed his rise, after flunking out of college and marrying two other women before he got it right with his present physician wife.

We caught up. Mostly I offered information about our friends, since he had been out of touch. "The hub. That's what you are," Digger used to tell me. "Why do these people from the past still call you and still come to see you? Who really cares about all that old stuff?" Well, it's true I did care about it, and I told Swat about Digger's successes, which caused Swat to shake his head. "Who would have ever thought Digger would do so well!" he exclaimed. I told him about Mole and his wife working like dogs with a few sub sandwich shops in Florida, Vampire turning to Jesus and being a principal up in New Hampshire and Lynx mysteriously leaving his D.C. law firm to live in some shack, like Ted Kaczynski, that he built in the wilds of Montana. "We were a kind of B group socially," Swat remarked. "Wouldn't you say? It was probably good that we were, don't you think?" Swat, like me, was trying to re-construct or at least provide order to the past.

Swat and Digger had gone to a whorehouse in downtown Cleveland when we were high school seniors, and Swat had left his wallet there, complete with three fake IDs. He was terrified the police would raid the joint, find his wallet and call his mother and his father, Sid, who was really the brother of his dead biological father. Or that Carol, the pros-titute he had screwed, would threaten to phone his mother unless he fed her cash. "It was Digger who saved your ass," I reminded him when we talked about the incident. "He went back down and got your wallet for you. Digger was always a stand-up guy for his friends. I was stranded out in the wilderness once outside Cleveland, and Digger came right out after I phoned him and fixed the car so I could get home."

"What happened to Jake?" Swat asked. I gave him the skinny. Told him how Jake had three marriages and a running battle with alcoholism, that he had ballooned to over three hundred pounds and had supposedly been dying of bladder cancer for the last decade. "He was a union bust-er, then he switched sides and wrote a tell-all book about the dreadful tactics of union busters. He got a lot of mileage out of all that because he consults now for a lot of the unions and lives pretty well, from what I hear, in Vegas." Chimp, a college pal, was my source of information on Jake. I told Swat a story Chimp related to me about Jake's mother and watched as Swat dissolved in laughter and tears. A few years back, I told him, Jake's mother supposedly married some Vegas guy, a rich gentile. The guy and Jake hated each other. So when Jake's mother died and Jake wanted to find out where she was buried, the new husband wouldn't tell him. Jake couldn't visit his own mother's grave. Swat found this hilarious.

The three of us, Swat and Leslie and I, went out to my local favorite Italian restaurant. Once we were seated, I told Leslie the story about Swat's purple pants. "He wore these purple pants day after day, and I kidded him about them constantly. Mercilessly. It wasn't mean kidding, like I used to do with a guy named Murray, who hung around Cain Park. I razzed Murray about wearing the same pants every day and got into a fist fight with him after he assured me the pants were washed every day by his family's maid, then came at me with knuckles flying when I called him a spoiled rich kid. Anyway," I went on, "I was relentless about those purple pants throughout high school. When I was in my last year at Ohio University, I got a package in the mail that I had to go down to the post office to get, and in it were Swat's purple pants. But here's the kicker. We always gave him a hard time about being cheap, and the package came with postage due. I had to pay postage for his goddamn purple pants!" Swat was laughing hard and so were Leslie and I. And soon after, Swat was telling me he was happy with his life. "I really mean it. Life is good. I'm really happy." Well, he had a pretty physician wife he was nuts about, five kids from three marriages and, I had discovered from our evening's conversation, a summer beach home, a Porsche and a country club membership. And I thought Murray and the kids who lived in University Heights were rich. But was Swat really happy, or was he just saying he was happy because what he was really saying was he'd done well and he liked his life, and he wanted me to know what he'd managed to achieve?

I ask myself the question all the time—Are you happy?—and it is a question that begs THE question, and THE question is can we ever really be . . . happy? Even now I say, "I want my wife and kids to be happy," or I tell them, "I'm happy if you're happy," and I mean it. But my more doleful, philosophical alter ego scoffs at the idea of happiness, thinks it somehow ontologically at odds with the human condition, with suffering, with privation and mortality. Can one be happy when the world, as Wordsworth said, is too much with us? Instead of happiness, I think of how life could always be worse. I told Swat that one of our more popular classmates lost his daughter to suicide. Now there was real tragedy, a life of heartache. "It can always be worse" isn't necessarily a bad way to think when things get upset, smashed or go to hell, as they often do, in spite of our certainty that we are happy, or believe in the moment that we are, as I did, over wine and pasta, with my wife and my old friend Swat.

.   .   .

WHEN THE GREAT PUBLIC TELEVISION CHEF, Jacques Pepin, came on air with me with Dorothy Hamilton, who headed up the French Culinary Institute in New York, she told me that walking with him either in New York or San Francisco was like walking with Elvis. But Jacques, like Michael Ondatjee and Walter Murch and Arundati Roy, does not seem seduced by any of that. If it swells Jacques' ego, he keeps it well concealed. I once joked with Tom Stoppard that his modest and humble demeanor with me was either a terrific act or true modesty and real humility—and that if he agreed that it was true modesty and real humility, he might be acting—though even if it was an act, it well might be derived from the real thing. How did one know?

I asked Pepin about all the work that went into preparing elaborate gourmet meals only to see his culinary feats consumed. "I realize you obviously enjoy seeing people eating whatever you cook. But when the food is eaten, what's in it for you?" I knew I was also asking for myself, for an answer that could help me better understand the value of all the preparation I did that then went into talk and out into the ether. Pepin, with his thick Gallic accent, thrust a forefinger up to the side of his head and pressed. "Memory," he said. "Memory for me . . . and memory for those who eat."

.   .   .

THE STATION'S RADIO ENGINEER warned me about Garrison Keillor. This stone-faced engineer was probably trying to compensate for the fact that I didn't like him, and the reason I didn't like him was that when I greeted him, he always stared back at me mutely, with a frozen, zombie-like countenance.

"Good luck with him," the engineer said with surprising warmth in his voice. "I hear he's really difficult." I'd heard this from others about Keillor.

One of the station's administrators spoke to me about how unpleasant and dismissive Keillor supposedly had been to a group of heavy donors. But he was also known to be full of kindness at book signings, and his newest book was dedicated to his readers, whom he called his darlings. I had interviewed Keillor when I was with KGO, and what struck me most at that time had nothing to do with him being difficult or sweet. It had to do with the fact that he never once made eye contact. He kept his eyeballs to the floor throughout the entire interview. I attributed it at the time to Midwestern shyness rather than rudeness.

Keillor lumbered into the studio looking older and more haggard than I remembered. It had been, after all, over a decade. There were large rings under his eyes, and he looked like a man who had gone for days without sleep. But he was friendly, as he slouched all of his tall lankiness down into the seat opposite me and said, in that mellifluous voice, "It's nice to see you, Mr. Krasny." I reminded him of our being together over a decade before, when I was on commercial radio. I told him that this time there would be no commercials, that we'd break at about the half hour, then take calls from listeners. "Please don't let on the adoring ones who just want to gush," he said. "It makes for bad radio." There was enough of a touch of weltschmerz in his voice that I wondered if fan adoration had truly become tiresome to him. I remembered listening to Ronn Owens doing a twenty-year anniversary show, and for three solid hours, minus the ads, fans told Ronn how much they appreciated him and recalled radio moments that they wanted, or felt moved, to mention. I asked myself if I would have liked that sort of tribute and truthfully answered that a part of me would have, but that that part was dimming. Everyone in this work wants appreciation, but for someone like Keillor, it was clear that it was too constant. "Beloved" was the word his press materials used to describe him, and Keillor cherished lines from a Raymond Carver poem—one that had always moved me and that now rests on Carver's gravestone—about getting what you want from life by feeling beloved on this earth. Must one be good to be beloved? Or to love? Perhaps, I thought, it had more to do with what my mother called *mazel*. Luck.

I spoke with Keillor about poetry. He was flogging a book of poems that he believed were memorable, and the lines from Carver were the words with which he ended the book's introduction. Carver, Kenneth Rexroth, Lawrence Ferlinghetti and Marin County's Kay Ryan, Keillor said, were not given their due as poets because of East Coast domination. Even Howard Nemerov, a poet both of us admired, was shut out because he lived mostly in St. Louis. Keillor had strong opinions that made for good radio—especially, in this case, if you were interested in poetry. Whitman, he said, begat "the gasbag" Allen Ginsberg, and T. S. Eliot was a "bloodless poet." Elizabeth Bishop was a much more exciting poet than Eliot, Keillor said, and what in creation did it mean to call her a woman poet or a confessional poet? What could one learn from such pidgeonholing—which is exactly what I had done while teaching her only a few days earlier? One of my graduate students, who had studied "The Waste Land" with me, sent an e-mail accusing Keillor of "canon envy" of Eliot. Another e-mail came from a former student of mine who thanked both Keillor and me for fostering in her a love of literature. I worried that reading that on air might sound self-serving, but I read it anyway. We talked about Lake Woebegone and his most recent memoir-type book of a concupiscent, Christ-loving boyhood—one he insisted was fiction and not memoir, and so I called it confessional fiction and got a hearty laugh from him.

I liked thinking of myself as a once-poor prol and lad of Midwest roots. Both were solid, well-fitting identities, but my family was never poor or hungry, and Keillor's and Fitzgerald's fictionalized and real Minnesota Midwest was a lot closer to the Midwest mark than the Cleveland that haunted my memories and imagination.

. . .

WHAT MAINLY INTERESTED ME about my interview with Angela Davis was, truthfully, her effect on me. She had been incarcerated in Marin County, after eluding capture for over a year as the top fugitive on the FBI's most wanted list. Free Huey. Free Leonard Peltier. Free Dennis Banks. Free Mumia Abu Jamal. At the time of her arrest for complicity in the attempted lethal jailbreak of George Jackson, some lefties were actually saying "free everybody," as if all perverts and felonious batterers and scary, violent gang members and serial murderers were all incarcerated victims of political oppression. But Angela was then, for me, a romantic revolutionary who seemed a victim of a racially oppressive system. Stately, noble and intellectual, soft but extremely well-spoken, aristocratic in her bearing and mien and crowned with the glory of that enormous, high Afro hairdo, she became an overnight symbol of the fight against racial injustice. Free Angela. I was not yet a journalist. Not yet in radio. I was an English professor. But I wanted to interview her while she was in prison. Longed to get to her as I had gotten to Saul Bellow, except with a tape recorder and a microphone. She had managed to become for me the incarnation of the clenched-fist struggle of blacks rebelling against and fighting the power. She was black is beautiful, and when I saw her walk into my radio studio nearly thirty years later, with a cell phone in hand and a white woman assistant trailing her, I was still smitten. She remembered me from a previous encounter and said so in that lilting seductive voice. Angela had changed but was still the same person—a real, live red commie, a lesbian, still talking with passion about freeing the incarcerated and stopping the boycott against Cuba, still following a revised but contiguous script, arousing tenderness in me about my youth.

The icons of our early days still have impact. When I interviewed Mickey Mantle, a couple of my New York-bred friends came down to meet him. He was a lecherous character who eyed every woman within eyeball range and murmured good-old-boy lustful appraisals of each, but to the guys who were there to meet him, he was their youth. I remembered a lecture I gave a number of years back to the local psychoanalytic society on the American playwright Clifford Odets. Margaret Brenman-Gibson, then a Harvard shrink and the wife of playwright William Gibson of *Miracle Worker* fame, had just written the first volume of an Odets biography. She spoke movingly of how Odets's death had touched her deeply because of what he had meant to her—how the effect he had on Margaret the girl had compelled Margaret the woman to become his biographer. His death awakened memories of her youth at the same time that it vivified its loss. Odets was her youth. And when I interviewed George McGovern, I felt the rush of all that had attracted me to him and his 1972 presidential campaign—the prairie preacher with the melodic Liberace-sounding voice evocative of decency, integrity, idealism and the bountiful heart. McGovern was on air with me to talk about his daughter Terry's death from alcoholism, speaking about her life as the father who had loved and lost. But he epitomized still the politician who cared about what I had cared about, a cruel Indochina war and economic and racial injustice; who had cared enough to make me go out and stump for him, even though I knew he was a lost cause with no chance of defeating the Quaker hawk from Whittier. McGovern spoke to me of his pride in being a liberal, how that maligned, derogated signifier and its ideology had given us civil rights, Social Security, Medicare. McGovern, like Angela Davis, put me back together with my former self, laid hands on nostalgia I neither entirely trusted nor exalted but welcomed.

.   .   .

WHEN DAVID ROCKEFELLER came on to talk about a memoir he spent over ten years writing, I thought, here is someone who should have a memoir. Rockefeller had the name, the family wealth, a history of power brokering and being on the world stage. An aristocrat of wealth—though his grandfather, John D., started out poor in Cleveland—David Rockefeller was a gentleman of the old school. He had charm and appeared charmed by my close reading of his tome and by the thoughts and facts I culled and brought to the table of our conversation. He struck me as a thoughtful man; although he was in his eighties, he was highly alert and self-possessed. Here was a man who helped build and shape New York— Rockefeller Center and the Twin Towers—as well as San Francisco's Embarcadero, and he was in my interlocutor's thrall for an hour.

I talked to him about his grandfather, the Standard Oil baron and religious zealot who was vilified by the radicals of his day and who made his grandson consume food slowly, even milk; and about his parents (his mother was Abby Aldrich), who insisted on formal wear at dinner every evening; about his roller skating to school each day and about his Harvard dissertation on the Fabians, as well as his time running the Chase Manhattan bank; and we talked, too, of the men he knew, The Shah, Khrushchev, Sadat, Mandela, Chou-En-Lai. How luxurious the ad-free talk time was on public radio, compared to the incessantly ad-riddled commercial airwaves!

I could not resist asking Rockefeller, at a point when it seemed right, what he felt about the proposal by Christopher Hitchens and others to prosecute Rockefeller's long-time friend, Henry Kissinger, as a war criminal. Rockefeller's response sprang from loyalty borne of friendship. How could people think to prosecute such an admirable and laudatory public servant as Henry the K.? I was tempted to trash his naiveté by going into specifics about Chile, Vietnam and East Timor, but I was more interested in being kind to him—and hearing his responses and what he had to say about the experiences and people he had written about—than I was in polemics, which can easily take over an entire hour and bore listeners. If it were Henry the K. himself, or commercial radio, it might have been different. But I preferred a full, wide-ranging hour that covered a broad expanse and didn't thrust me into the noxious role of angry, lefty broadcaster on a mission to "get" Kissinger through his pal, David Rockefeller. As Keillor said about gushing adoration, gotcha interviews, too, can make for bad radio.

I read an e-mail from a listener who said she had been prepared to dislike this man of such immense wealth and power, who was tied to petroleum and the ransacking of foreign corporate markets, but she found, instead, that the man she was listening to was decent and self-effacing. When the hour ended, two aides of Rockefeller's—a pair of secret-service-type, well-dressed characters—came into the studio with heaps of verbal praise for the interview and requested a hard copy of that listener's e-mail.

Was David Rockefeller a great man? He was a man of wealth, power and achievement. He was the first of the Rockefellers to write an auto-biography. But none of that necessarily meant his memoirs were worth reading, unless the writing was good and compelling and you happened to be interested in wanting to read about him and the life that he had led. The same, of course, could be said of you or me.

· · ·

WHEN I INTERVIEWED Alan King on stage, a man who had been a force in American comedy for half a century, he told me that he blanches at the adjective "great." He was not a great comedian or great actor, even though he had accomplished much in both fields, especially in comedy. He was a Jewish kid who was good with his fists and, for a while, a pro-fessional pugilist; he plugged away at everything he ever accomplished.

"None of it came to me," he confessed. "I just kept at it and kept at it. I had to work. But I loved it. Loved especially the challenge of working live. Loved winning over audiences or, as we say in comedy, killing them. I kept doing it and doing it. I think of myself as a working stiff who keeps on doing the job and doing the job, and eventually I've been at it so long that everyone knows me as the guy who does the job well and gets it done. Now they just announce me, and people start laughing. But that's not greatness."

King had written a memoir called *Name Dropping*, and he liked to mention names, like Sinatra, in my conversation with him. He also liked letting it be known that he had lectured at Oxford, Harvard and Vassar. I related to being not great, loving live work, to being hard-working and to being the Jewish prol. But Alan King, like Larry King, had become a regal performer—part of what Canadian sociologist Edgar Friedenberg once described as America's real aristocracy, based on fame.

I wanted to do a Jewish joke-off with King, who had published a Jewish joke book. But King demurred. "I'll do whatever you like, but I don't tell jokes. I tell stories." I managed, though, to get in a few good Jewish jokes. The zinger about a bunch of Jewish women eating in a restaurant, and the waiter comes up to the table and asks, "Is anything all right?" And the kugel joke. A father is dying, with his daughter at his deathbed holding his hand. They both know the final curtain is about to come down. He tells her he smells kugel coming from the kitchen, and he says he would like a last taste before he dies. She says, "Of course, Daddy," and jumps up and heads to the kitchen, but she is gone for quite a spell. By the time she returns, he is gasping his last breath. "Where's the kugel?" he manages to eke out as his death rattle begins. His daughter: "Mom says it's for after."

If you embark on a narrative of your life or experiences—when do you wind it up? Takeoffs and landings, I've always told creative writing majors, are the hardest parts of fiction writing. But this is not fiction. If it were fiction, I'd be eschewing summary narration and meditative self-reflection, showing not telling. I could keep on adding indefinitely to my own collection of recollections and musings as long as source material kept coming in, the people I have on, the news and topics that I cover. So when is it supposed to end? At whim? At death or at its door?

I remembered reading a book Ted Koppel wrote, which essentially went in memoir fashion from one news story to another. I was struck by the short shelf life of those news stories, something I realize from the day-to-day coverage of news stories I have done on air for years. Everything has speeded up. I was supposed to interview Koppel on television, but the interview was called off because he was called back East over the hanging-chad craziness in the Bush/Gore presidential election. I was disappointed. I had looked forward to spending the hour with him. Then, a few months later, I walked into an eating joint near the radio station, appropriately called The Slow Club, and there he was—triggering in me that strange sensation you get when you see an all too-recognizable-cathode or film screen face suddenly in front of you like some ectoplasm or emanation. Ted Koppel in Levis. I went up and introduced myself, asked him why he was in San Francisco. When he told me he was in town to promote his book, I told him I missed interviewing him about it a few months earlier but had read it. He asked me what I thought of it, and I made a few broad, kind remarks, then added that it was the kind of book he could have kept adding on to. I also thought, as I spoke with Koppel, of my old pipe dream about filling in for him on "Nightline." But I had changed, ambition tempered by time. I didn't daydream about that kind of perch now—any more now than I did of writing the great American novel that would do to the largely Jewish suburbs of Cleveland what Thomas Wolfe's *Look Homeward Angel* did for Ashville, North Carolina, or Roth's *Goodbye, Columbus* did for Newark and East Orange, New Jersey. I knew now, at last, that that was not what my life had been about. I realized, too, that honors and recognition lose even their fleeting pleasures as years pile on, and both have felt embarrassing and ill-deserved to me; like the brickbats and nastiness any public figure also gets, all of it comes and goes, often as mysteriously as rain.

Barbara Kingsolver

Barbara Kingsolver has a melodic voice. It sounds sexy to me, despite her habit of punctuating my words with nervous-sounding, repeated, jabbing utterances of ummm humm. Kingsolver is also a bit of a political naïf, though sincere in her desire to make litera-

ture political and the world more human. Why shouldn't literature be
political? Look at Soyenka or Gordimer. Kingsolver has established a
twenty-five-thousand-dollar writing prize for a first novel that has in it a
strong sense of social change. She has put her money where her convic-
tions are. She regrets that writing politically in America has come to
seem like crashing through literary picket fences. We need writers who
take social justice and social responsibility seriously.

Kingsolver lived a long time in Arizona and has published a book with
Cornell Press about the Arizona mine strike, but she has since moved
back to her native South with her family—to Virginia (where, for a year,
they ate only locally grown and produced food). She is, I tell her, still a
Kentucky populist at heart, as Molly Ivins is a Texas populist—though
Ivins sees, more than Kingsolver, the likelihood of humans being knaves,
rogues and reprobates. Kingsolver is certain that if people only knew how
their tax dollars were being used, they would do something, they would
do what was right. If people understood how immigrants contributed to
the economy and took jobs that no one else wanted, they wouldn't feel
that men and women from such places as Guatemala and Mexico were
taking jobs, and things would change. She remains, she tells me, unfash-
ionably optimistic about people. But we Americans have a frightful legacy.
Blood on our hands. We may not have made the decisions, but we have in-
herited them. What do we do with our guilt? There are people all across
the planet who are frustrated beyond repair by our government, people
who would rather die on their feet than on their knees.

Drugs aren't a problem, says Kingsolver. They are a solution for those
with economic problems. We need to provide alternatives, productive live-
lihoods for those who sell drugs. We need to own up and admit that we
are wrong and that the real problems are caused by a capitalism that de-
pends on growth at any cost and is concerned only with short-term profit.
Realizing how connected everything is keeps her from going nuts. "You
have to fight it," she says assertively. "You have to fight it day after day."

Kingsolver begins a novel by asking a question and settling on a
problem that she, still at heart like a scientist looking for a cure, wants
to eliminate. Novelists can bring change. There is more human tragedy
day-to-day than we can cope with. We become anesthetized to tragedy,
and victims of tragedy turn abstract to us. Novels can address large-scale

tragedy, make victims human and carve tragedy into our hearts. Film can do it too, but usually doesn't. Literature needs to be moral, and it needs to be manipulative. Any novel pulls you through an emotional knothole, and you live another person's life in real time in a place you never expected to go. It forces empathy on you and makes you be the other, and that is political. "I have a contract with my reader," Kingsolver says, and then she goes on to explain the transaction as if she is describing a chemical equation. "I take the history as a novelist and invent an intensely personal story . . . so much that you'll forget these people weren't real." Then she suddenly sounds a bit like the Madison Avenue she deplores. "I guarantee you a night's loss of sleep."

 Reynolds Price
Reynolds Price thinks novelists come by novel writing from their genes.

A Duke professor and celebrated novelist, Price is in a wheelchair from spinal cancer. Despite five operations, he characterizes himself to me as "a relatively happy man," though he adds that such self-characterization "may not be entirely sincere." He is a southern gentleman, warm and affable, and seeing him wheelchair-bound and listening to him speak of being disabled makes me think of an interview I did with Ram Dass soon after Ram Dass suffered a stroke and had to struggle to fetch words. I doubt I could keep my spirit up or my good nature in such adversity. Yes, Price admits, he struggled with depression. How could he not? Or not feel helpless with his full-time attendant caring for him. Yet strangely enough, he appreciates the way time has slowed now that he is an invalid. He tells me he now feels a far greater sense of his own humanity and the humanity of others with whom he shares being disabled.

Price assures me that he has taught many students through the years who had the talent to be novelists, who were truly hard-wired to be but did not become what they could have been. What, I want to know, about those of us who have wanted to become novelists but didn't have the hard wiring? Far more of us. Our numbers are legion.

Price talks about his writing schedule. Eight to ten hours a day, six days a week, years for each novel. Of course he is not read nearly as much as he would like to be. Few high-quality novelists are any more. His most recent novel is about ninety-four-year-old Roxanna Slade, the second novel he has done in a woman's voice.

I ask him how he is able to take on a woman's voice so well, and why he thinks two of the novels considered to be the best about women, *Anna Karenina* and *Madame Bovary*, were both written by men. "I can't think of any of the opposite," Price says. "No great novels about men written by women. I think it's perhaps because we were raised by women." My friend Eric Solomon responded after the interview: "Price should read George Eliot."

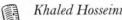 Khaled Hosseini

I first met Khaled Hosseini at a dinner party at Isabel Allende's home. He seemed sweet and self-effacing to me. Isabel and her husband Willy were rapturous about Khaled's novel. Effusive comments were what I kept hearing about *The Kite Runner.* When Hosseini and I did a charity fundraiser, there was so much flattery that I, alas, started to become suspicious. After all, it was a first novel. A steady diet of effusiveness was also what he got when he came on the air with me. It far exceeded anything I have ever heard for any writer. One caller after another was honored to talk to him, thrilled with the book, moved by it, in love with it. I viewed it with a more critical eye.

If 9-11 hadn't happened, the novel might not have seen print. The first version was so bleak, morose and grave that Hosseini had to create a note of hope for a different tomorrow, a better direction for the characters. He left Afghanistan at age eleven and has lived in the United States for twenty-five years. It is no surprise that a Judeo-Christian sense of redemption seeped into him, a Sunni Muslim, and into his novel. Afghans embrace him as their Homer, since he has managed to meld much of their history of the past three decades into a novel that has been read all over the world. But there is much more of the American in Hosseini, a Berkeley graduate and a rabid Cal Bears and Forty-Niners fan. I ask him which was the worse betrayal of the Afghan people—the Russians or the Taliban. "You mean which deadly poison?" he says. The real challenges for Afghanistan now, he remarks, are the separate identities and lack of central government control. "It's a teething democracy. But how do you impose law in tribal areas? The border is chaotic and porous and lawless. You don't know how strong the new Taliban insurgency is."

In 2003 Hosseini turned in his novel and went to Kabul. He saw a man on a donkey and felt like a tourist in his own country. He had the memories he invented for his character, Amir, struggling against his own personal memories. He realizes what an incredibly fortunate life he has had.

Writing was Hosseini's first love. Ever since childhood, he says, he could pick up a pen. A practicing M.D. who had for years been working at Kaiser Permanente, he has given up medicine to write another book. He describes it as a more challenging one to write than *The Kite Runner*. Set in Afghanistan, it is a mother-daughter story. *The Kite Runner* was "a quintessential American coming-of-age story about men in Afghanistan." Yet, Hosseini notes, the vast majority of his readership everywhere he goes is female. Writing female characters, as he is doing now, is the same as writing males, once you know the characters well enough. The aspect about *The Kite Runner* that seemed really to connect to readers was that it was a story of deeply flawed people who desperately want to be better. "A very brutal story, yet it is also tender, a love story of father and son, boy and servant, young man and his wife." A movie is being made. I ask if Brad Pitt has been cast as Amir, and Hosseini laughs.

A caller from Florida identifies himself as a former Marine who trained the Mujahadeen in Afghanistan. He had been proud of booting out the Russians but regretted it now, because it ultimately helped the Taliban after U.S. troops left and the country imploded. Jihad had been fine against the Soviets, the caller adds. Hosseini laughs at that and then cautiously adds that the United States did not fulfill its commitment to Afghanistan and was short-sighted in arming warlords to get to bin Laden. But there are encouraging signs. A constitution. Democratic participation. The problem remains. How to reconcile democratic sensibility with tribal laws.

I ask if there is a part of him that would like to go back to Afghanistan and perhaps practice medicine in a land deeply in need of skilled medical doctors. "I'm forty years old with children," he says. "There are some that can do that, but I'm not one of them." I also ask if he flies kites with his children. He says a PR person in Denmark got him to pose for photos flying a kite. "She talked me into it," he says. "There was no wind. It was a miserable experience."

Frances Mayes

Authentic charm may be an oxymoron, but Frances Mayes has it. We are long-time pals from teaching together at San Francisco State, and I will have a lifelong memory of a wonderful summer lunch with her at her villa in Cortona with Ed, her warm poet husband, and my wife and daughters. But the story I get her to tell me when we talk on air about *Bella Tuscany*, her sequel to *Under the Tuscan Sun*, is a tale that only dementia could cause me to forget.

With my prodding, Mayes tells it. It was awful—for her, "one of life's most mysterious psychological moments." She has no idea what Freud would have made of it. It was at her daughter Ashley's wedding at her home in San Francisco. She walks up to a wedding guest and introduces herself. "Hello. I'm Frances. I'm Ashley's mother." He responds: "I'm her father." Six years had passed, and she failed to recognize the man with whom she conceived her only child. And he had not physically changed that much.

We talk of Italy. To Mayes, rural Tuscany remains a paradise. Walled gardens. Cypress trees. Gentle green landscapes. Landscapes have power. They can change you, and you have no choice in the matter. That is how it was for Frances the young girl growing up in her small hometown in Georgia, with its landscape of black outer swamps with flowers on top and sinkholes in the ground. Landscape affected her poet's sensibility there, as does the peaceful and powerful landscape of Tuscany or the land under us in California that may shake at any time. The light in Italy is golden, almost a veil. The landscape connects with all of Italy's great art. "Everything is almost hyperreal there, more remote here. Beauty, art, history, food, the warmth of the people all set Italy apart."

Time in California, Mayes says, is "like a hula hoop." Italians own so much time. All the way back to the Etruscan walls. In California, it feels as if she is always working against time. As she so often does, Mayes offers food as the context. The Italians of Tuscany have a huge meal in the middle of the day and a much smaller meal at night, and then they are out in the piazza. A day equals two there and one half here. Frances no longer feels like an outsider there. She and Ed, despite being foreigners, are too involved in the real cycles of life, connected to the town and its people in ways she never would have expected. English is spoken. Italian is sung. "Maybe," she says, "by ninety I'll be fluent in Italian. I do use my hands a lot more."

A disagreeable caller phones in to say that perhaps his purpose in life is to point out the obvious. Most people own no homes. Here is talk of rich, bi-continental people who own two. "I find it nauseating," he says. Mayes's firm response: "Fine."

Norman Mailer once told me that if reincarnation exists, he would want to come back as a black athlete. Mayes says she would return as an Italian and as an architect. An architect because as a writer her house is the most important place to her, and the work it demands never seems to end. She and Ed will purchase another home in Tuscany for Ashley and Ashley's son to use, and Ed will put so much work and time into it that he will call it his epic poem. Francesca and Eduardo in *Bella Tuscany* have become part of the community and relish it. For Mayes, it is reconnecting to a town like Fitzgerald, the one she grew up in in Georgia, with an intense sense of community she didn't even know she had lost. Italy was a journey back. The locus remains for her the town and the piazza, like a large living room where everyone comes together. Mayes quotes Thoreau's line: "I have traveled much in Concord." She laughs and says, "You should have gone to Italy, Mister!"

THE MEMOIR OR AUTOBIOGRAPHY possesses much of the life of fiction. If I had had a worthy novel in me, I would have preferred pushing it out, but it just wasn't there. My imagination couldn't provide what I felt I needed, and I was struck by how that was at least a big part of my story, how the failure of an imagination to be ignited with the power it longed for and desired was in itself a story perhaps worth telling. So this is a memoir of failure? In part, yes. But success and failure, like winning and losing, I learned early on can easily collide, and one can sometimes imperceptibly produce or expunge the other. I have had successes as well as failures. Whatever drove me to be a novelist also drove me in other directions, both literary and nonliterary. Perhaps this text, all along, has been about the American fetish for finding and harnessing experience, catching fragments, unfurling minutiae and unheard melodies, ambitions, longings and the status of self from underneath the panoply, the caravan, the red, white and blue.

"No one writes without hope," Margaret Atwood once said. But what exactly was I hoping for? Where has all this knowledge—scholarly, arcane, general and trivial—led? What has all of it done for me? For my daughters, wife, extended family or friends? With all the books I've read, the knowledge I've absorbed through thousands of interviews, and the range of subjects I've managed to cover—where's the beef? The answers? The meaning of life? The meaning to this life of mine?

Spin this. I grew up with ordinary parents and went to ordinary schools and taught at an ordinary university and had an ordinary career as a broadcaster and married an extraordinary woman, met many extraordinary people, and lived a life both ordinary and extraordinary. "Who knows," as Ralph Ellison's *Invisible Man* says to us from his underground habitat, "but that on the lower frequencies I speak for you." I only know that I am driven by what sometimes seems like a relentless team of horses that feel tied to a carriage of identity and self-definition.

. . .

WHEN I HAD TOM BROKAW ON, I was keen to show him how thoughtfully I had read his memoir and to get from him as much as I could for listeners. There is a prairie decency to him, and he comes off as what we used to call a regular guy. He was looking older and more paunchy—ready, as he had announced, to pass his anchor torch to Brian Williams.

Brokaw had interviewed nearly every major world leader and a passel of presidents, but when we talked of interviews that meant the most to him, he spoke with near reverence, as David Halberstam once did to me, of the young people who displayed courage during the civil rights movement, who put their bodies on the line. He talked, too, of the admiration he had for people he'd interviewed on the front lines of war, or in the trenches of wars or who fought against epidemics and disease; those who risked their own lives to save others, who had neither power nor celebrity status, just everyday heroic mettle. What he said resonated with what I often felt. I told myself this could be rhetorical bilge, lines often uttered by a classic über anchor with blow-dried hair and a multimillion-dollar contract, who learned years ago how to dance with the big boys. Brokaw was one of the big boys—though, like George McGovern, with uncamouflaged South Dakota decency. "A talker" was how he described himself in his memoir, different than those sturdy, reticent, nonverbal South Dakotans of the generation he extolled, and yet one from their loins and ranks. Both of us were talkers. Both of us had spent most of our adult lives talking. But he was an institution and a guy who came across, or wanted to, as unpretentious. He had gone from being the big man on campus to becoming the big man in television, the biggest and most visible arena of our lives. Hadn't I wanted that? To become a big man, a *macher.* How and when does one become big enough? Iconic enough? How can we be so foolish to believe, by being the biggest of the big, or as rich as Rockefeller, that we can save ourselves from self-doubt, failure, loss, misery, suffering, calamity?

Especially when my own liberalism and moderation seemed incredibly yesterday. Rush's and Sean's demagogic right-wingery and the toxicity of Michael Savage—who heckled me at the commencement speech I delivered at his and my daughters' high school graduation—seemed to be winning the day, as well as hearts and minds and certainly ratings. I had chosen kindness rather than cruelty, civility rather than coarseness or kick-'em-in-the-groin sensationalism. Was mine a style whose time had gone? A small voice in a shrinking world—the world of ideas and civil discourse versus the world at large, the culture of rant and excoriation? I heard Howard Stern hyping a program he was doing on Sirius that featured a holocaust survivor and a former woman Nazi guard, separately mounting and riding a crotch-vibrating machine. That was apparently good radio! The bizarre. The profane. The extreme. A woman in Sacramento who literally drank herself to death with nearly two gallons of water on air to win a video game console. This brings in listeners! When did radio stop being a theater of the mind, a place of intimacy, a nearly sacred place for the exchange and airing of ideas rather than this multiplex of derogation, caterwauling, sexual sensation and dogmatic screeching?

 Umberto Eco
Eco and I are backstage. Geoff Nunberg, Terry Gross's language expert and a local linguistics prof, is chatting with him in a speedy, fluent, demotic-sounding Italian. Eco is full of spirit and zest in the ways that make many people love Italians. I think of British writers like E. M Forster or Doris Lessing, who had their characters escape the stiff-upper-lip, keep-emotions-in-check English ways to head south to the warmer, expansive, gesticulating ways of Eco and his tribe. We are drinking wine, eating cheese. Eco is telling Nunberg and me that we must visit him in Bologna when we take the summer trips that each of us is planning to Italy.

There, Eco, a scholar and an erudite leftist novelist, is a celebrity. Everyone knows Eco from his constant appearances on television. He

will tell me later on in our interview that he knows the contemporary
world only through the television screen, while he knows the medieval
world through experience.

When we begin to converse on stage, I ask Eco about his late start as
a novelist. Why did it happen after he had established himself as a semi-
oticist and scholar? He says he didn't play golf on weekends. He needed
to tell his children different kinds of stories because they were adults.
No; the truth, he says, is that it is the most difficult question because he
doesn't know the answer. He had conversations about a detection story
taking place in a medieval monastery and went home and wrote down a
list of monk names. He was excited. Something probably was already at
work in his upper or lower soul. An image flashed of a monk poisoned
while reading a manuscript at a lectern. At sixteen he had been in a
Benedictine monastery in Italy and discovered a library with stained
glass windows, aquariumlike, with a lectern. All those years later it was,
he realized, his last chance to be a novelist. His next step, after the image
of a monk falling down from a strange poison, was to design and set up
a world, an abbey, the labyrinth. How could he narrate unless he knew
where his characters were moving?

Movie makers came to him, and one was Marco Ferrari, who told
him his dialogues in *The Name of the Rose* lasted exactly the time they
should have. That was because, Eco says, his characters had to walk from
one place to another.

In *The Island of the Day Before* he designed the ship and the interiors.
He went to Fiji and cut his beard to accommodate the diving mask. He
was told he looked ten years younger but ten years more stupid, so he
grew the beard back. In *Foucault's Pendulum* he had images in his mind of
the pendulum he had seen in Paris thirty years before, the idea of being
under the only point that doesn't rotate like the rest of the universe. He
also had the image of a young boy playing a trumpet in a cemetery. From
the pendulum to the cemetery. He didn't know what to put in between.

It took him eight years. He would rather it had taken fifteen. Once you
have points of reference, the novel decides where to go and where to stop.
"A novel is a very private affair. You see a traffic light and pick up an idea
to put in a novel. But you're finished and there is no pleasure any more,
and you're obliged to present it to the publisher and to promote it. The

novel, at a certain point, says 'I am finished,' and you must obey. I'm convinced Tolstoy didn't want to kill Prince Andre, but he was obliged to."

Eco and I begin to talk about narrative structure. Even academic work, Eco says, has narrative structure. We define the world in narrative, beginning with the Bible. The narrative impulse is in all of his research. Roland Barthes, who was his good friend, claimed he was bitter his whole life because he wrote only essays and no novel or creative texts. "He was completely wrong," Eco says," because each of his texts were marvelous and creative, but he died with bitterness." Eco never had those kinds of feelings, because he felt all his writings were narrations. "So I didn't say I must write a novel. It was an unexpected impulse." If he had not become a novelist, he would likely be here for a presentation on his theoretical work, probably with the same audience, some less, some more, and he would be "equally happy." He then says, "It's what a logician calls a counterfactual statement. If my grandmother had wheels, she would have been a streetcar."

Though a symbol of Italy and Italian literature, Eco considers himself a European writer. For many years he knew much more French literature than Italian. He connected with the neo-avant-garde literary group known as the Sixty-Three. He saw how to arrive at the white canvas, silent music, the empty stage. Though a medievalist, he is identified with postmodernism because, he says, when people don't know how to define you, they place you in postmodernism. Many different meanings of the word exist, but one common feature of the great avant-garde movement of the twentieth century is how it succeeded in dismantling all our structures. "Avant garde represented purification of our culture on all its levels and then returns with double consciousness that it has already been told, and we visit it ironically." A lover has an expression for his beloved like, "I love you desperately," which may come from Barbara Cartland. The postmodern lover would say, "As Barbara Cartland would say 'I love you desperately.'" "In this way," Eco adds, "he is no longer innocent. He escapes the suspicion of ignoring the heritage that's overwhelming him, but succeeds in expressing his love."

Does the great literary eminence read Barbara Cartland? Of course. The breadth of his knowledge of popular culture is as wide as is its influence on his thinking—going back to his own childhood and a journalist in a Mickey Mouse cartoon who taught him for the first time, under Mussolini's reign, what freedom is. He loves Flash Gordon, who appears in *The Mysterious Flame of Queen Luana*. In 1962 he wrote an essay on Superman, critical of the myth but aware of the nostalgia. The fascist songs belong to his childhood, despite his criticism of their substance and ideology. We have to distinguish between trivial material that is part of memory and trivial popular culture. Different cultures have different perceptions. Comic books are read without ideology in America. Eco says he considers Charles Schultz and Art Spiegelman great artists of our time.

A dedicated collector of books, Eco is certain they will not disappear. He is confident his children will get some of his royalties after his death, despite all electronic technology. Preservation of a book is preservation of an object that is a piece of memory. Cinema has not destroyed theater. Photography has not destroyed painting. Airplanes have not destroyed ships.

V. S. Naipaul

V. S. Naipaul is telling me that the novel is no longer the preeminent literary form it was when Balzac, Flaubert and Gogol wrote. Things have to move. Forms play themselves out. He seems to feel that he, too, has played out. When I ask him if it is really true, as he reputedly has said, that he would like to divest himself of life, he says, "I'd like to go. Yes. One gets weary." When I challenge him with the argument that he still has creative juice as well as life, he simply snaps, "Let's see. Let's see what happens."

Some think Naipaul the greatest living English prose writer. A Nobel laureate, he began with no idea of what it meant to be a writer. He says he managed to make himself a writer and has kept it up all these years, and that it is almost impossible for him to judge his own work, even though he has the highest regard for it. He believes he has had a preternatural ability to read people and to see their flaws; "even though age makes one more tolerant and softer, one must remain hard." He saw vanity in the eyes of bin Laden. Many think Naipaul's portraits of Islam have been too harsh. He wrote what he saw. Islam, he tells me, has always been a political religion, and it has always been the duty of Muslims to engage in religious wars, an enduring fact about the Muslim world about

which there can be no fancifulness about moderation. When I mention
how the icon of postcolonial thinking, Edward Said, called Naipaul's
work insulting and idiotic, he says, "I never reply to any criticism." Still,
he bristles when an Indian woman caller tells him that his work needs to
show how imperialism damaged Islam in the thirteenth century. "If you
don't like my work, please stay away from it," he barks at her, with no attempt to mask his petulance. He likes speaking about himself in the third
person singular. "One doesn't want to analyze oneself," he says. He is
from the old T. S. Eliot school that argues that all one needs to know is
in the text. What Proust saw as the secret part of the soul and the secre-
tions of the heart that are in the work ought to have nothing to do with
the one who creates it.

Language, he says, has to dance above one in the air. The novel is the
most prolific form, but does not have the most weight any longer and
must be original. Those writing novels today aren't discovering much.
They're repeating programs laid out in the nineteenth century. The
novel has a brief, butterfly, seasonal life. The Shakespearean play ran its
course, too, and had to change, had to be replaced. His work, he says, is
not dishonest or tendentious, and serves no purpose except what is in the
writing. All his books are still alive and in print. He has had to live for
a half century in England with what he calls the narrowing of culture, a
plebeian culture, a culture that celebrates only itself. He doesn't need the
idea of a home. Trinidad is the place from which he escaped.

We shake hands as the interview concludes, and his young, handsome
wife enters the studio. "It's not true that he wants to die," she insists once
we are off the air. "Let's see," says Naipaul. "Let's see."

Amos Oz

Amos Oz is usually described as Israel's preemi-
nent writer. He founded Peace Now and personally knew every Israeli
leader. When I pictured him before I read his book about his life, I saw
an archetypal sabra, strong and virile, with the visage and stature of a
tall, visionary desert dweller. I knew he had lived for years in the desert
because of his son's asthma. I have had enough experience meeting icons
that I know they are never what I conjure. When I meet Oz before our
stage interview, I am somehow surprised—even after reading his book

and knowing better—at meeting an aging, short man who seems, despite his Israeli accent and strong, fluid speech, more like a shtetl Jew. That, I think, is the real Oz.

He tried for a long time to be someone he was not, as well as what his father was not. He wanted to be the opposite of the short, sweaty, bookish, scholarly and insecure diaspora Jew. He wanted to be like the heroic pioneers who toiled the land all day and fought Arabs and danced the hora at night. But the Jerusalem he grew up in was a shtetl of arguing, unheroic, insignificant Europeans. The same on the kibbutz. Ordinary people. He wanted, too, to be like Hemingway. A writer of the world who could punch men in the mouth and mount hundreds of women. He fought in the wars of sixty-seven and seventy-three, but only because he and his loved ones' lives were endangered. War, he says, is the consequence of aggression, and aggression is the real evil. He couldn't write about the battlefield because it was primarily stenches. It was so inhuman that even literature, even Hemingway or Tolstoy for that matter, couldn't contain it. He holds no sentimentality about war. He coined the phrase "peace not love" for Israel, instead of the American Vietnam war resisters' phrase, "love not war."

How to find peace between Israel and Palestine, both victims of Europe, who see in each other the cruel image, shadows and horrors of past oppression? Two refugee camps. Oz was one of the first to speak out strongly for a two-state solution. He thinks peace and a manageable divorce will happen. The house will be divided. Most people on both sides want it to happen. The patient is ready for the surgery, but the doctors are cowards. Only fanatics don't want compromise. To Oz, compromise is life. He smiles and says, with charm, "I know all about compromise from forty-five years of marriage."

Oz, the novelist and storyteller, has written a tale called *Of Love and Darkness*. It is his story and Israel's story. The English version subtitle is memoir, which he blames on the classification requirement of the Library of Congress. He insists that what he has written is narrative prose. Fiction—for which, he says, there is thankfully no word in Hebrew—has a ring of lying about it. His story is both fiction and nonfiction, the work of a novelist, not a memoirist. Imagination is required to reconstruct our past. There is no line between imagination and memory, just as there is none between tragedy and comedy. Everything we know of others, even those closest to us, is 20, maybe 30 percent data. All the rest is imagination, projection, wishful thinking, nightmare or a combination of all of them.

It was Sherwood Anderson who shaped Oz, who made him realize he could write about ordinary people and that where he sat, with a writing pad and a ballpoint pen, was the center of the universe. He learned from Anderson the ancient rule that the provincial and parochial can also be the universal. "Nothing is below the threshold of acceptance in literature," says Oz.

Oz tells me he uses two ballpoints of different colors to write—one for angry essays, when he is in agreement with himself, and another for stories or novels when he is not. When he is in disagreement with himself he becomes pregnant with a story, a novel, a tale. Telling stories, he says, is a primeval need, like breathing or sleeping. He wanted to keep the storyteller locked up. First, as a boy, he actually wanted to be a book. Then he wanted to be nonbookish, to be a tractor driver or a farmer. But he could not not write.

Diaspora Jews, Oz says, were viewed as parasites, ruthless intellectuals, cosmopolitans. The Europeans wanted to murder them. In the western Ukraine, where his mother lived, twenty-five thousand were murdered in two weeks, more than have died in all the Israeli conflicts. Before the Second World War, there were graffiti in Europe that told the Jews to go back to Palestine. Now there are graffiti, on the same European wall, telling Jews to get out of Palestine. Israel, Oz says, was a life raft for those who survived. Oz loves Israel, even though he hates it, too, and often has to tell its leaders where to go. But he loves it for its argumentativeness, its moral and intellectual restlessness, its "anarchistic gene." Everyone in Israel argues. It is a nation of tireless talkers and fiery arguers. "Everyone talks, and no one listens. Except me, sometimes, since I need to make a living." The Jews couldn't have a Pope, he says, because too many would be explaining to the Pope what God really means.

Despite the claim by Oz that Sherwood Anderson shaped him as a writer, what really shaped him was the kibbutz and, before that, the mother he adored—who took her life when he was still the boy wunderkind—and the father he rebelled against at fourteen, only to go back, like many rebels do, to what he was trying to rebel against. He was shaped, too, by his mother's having been a wonderful, scary storyteller, and by his librarian father's love of books and by language. "Hebrew," he says, like a true chauvinist, "is the most marvelous musical instrument in the whole world."

Oz started out to write his book of his life with the idea that he would solve the lifetime enigma of why his "good, gentle, kind parents, who had invested so much in him, their only son, had created such tragedy." He was angry for decades at his mother for killing herself, because she made him feel there was something wrong with him. He was angry, too, at his father, who seemed responsible for his mother's walking off to embrace death. In the course of writing the book, though, he lost interest. There were no clear villains. With many tragic conflicts it is easy to take sides. Colonialism. Apartheid. World War II. Vietnam. But not with the Palestinian-Israeli conflict, and not with Oz and his parents. Writing one's life can make ancestors of ghosts and peace with the past. It can make one see.

Epilogue

I AM SPEAKING from what that old-time religion of mine would have called the end of my line. My father gave me a good deal of wisdom, but not enough heritable DNA neurotransmitter power from his gene pool, combined with my mother's, to reach greatness. What if I had moved to the center stage of the national spotlight? Then it might have made sense for me to write a paean praising the virtues that my parents or in-laws lived their lives by. They were people who worked hard, provided and cared for each other and their children, helped neighbors, gave to their community—the virtues of droves of the anonymous and ordinary. Tolstoy, as Philip Roth said to me, was too harsh in calling ordinary terrible.

My father asked for one other thing from me, aside from his wish that I quit smoking. That was that I would say the *kaddish*, the Jewish mourner's prayer, for him on his death. "You and your brother will say my *kaddish*," he used to tell me. When I went to Israel, on a foundation fellowship, I wanted some kind of mystical or spiritual experience, but all I got was a surge of ephemeral emotion at the Wailing Wall while I watched a father walking hand-in-hand with his skull-capped son. I suddenly felt an unexpected sensation of wanting a son of my own—a throwback, I think, from hearing my father tell me that only sons can say *kaddish*—and some quickening recognition of my own mortality. A self-proclaimed feminist and agnostic with two wonderful and incomparable daughters, I was involuntarily and momentarily lured by ancient Jewish tribal notions of primogeniture and patriarchy, the anachronistic faith of fathers and sons, of Abraham, Isaac and Jacob. The only male in my father's line, from his own sons, who will carry on his name is my brother Vic's son, my nephew Max, whose mother isn't Jewish. When Max married, his bride wanted a wedding in her family's huge Baltimore Episcopal church. After my gentle urging, they settled instead for one in a Baltimore country club. I was worried that a church wedding would hurt or disturb my father. "What's the difference?" Dad muttered. "Max is a goy." According to Jewish law, my father was right. Max's mother wasn't Jewish, so neither was Max. The Krasny name would go on with Max, but the male umbilicus to Jewishness would be lost. How much should I care? Max had grown into an exceptional man, a radio executive with a family of his own.

Strange that sons, and especially Judiasm, should still resonate for me in the holy land, as the religion of my father and my father's fathers wanes in America through assimilation. I thought Jewish fiction writers were becoming extinct in America except for their DNA, and then along came Ethan Canin, Michael Chabon, Nathan Englander, Jonathan Safron Foer and Rebecca Goldstein. And what kind of Jew was my father, really? His father played pinochle on Rosh Hashanah, a heresy to my Uncle Joe who, with his own rigid notions of piety and adherence to Jewish law, never forgot or forgave. Now Joe's grandchildren and great-grandchildren are all celebrating Christmas every year.

The last time I saw my cousin Howard, Joe's son, I told him that I had good news. His mother, Marie—who had died years before—had been, according to my dad, visiting with him just that afternoon. Dad was confusing Marie, his older sister, with Lois, my sister. Cleveland's Jewish home for the aged was a place where nearly all memories and what-ifs dissolved. The place where both my parents wound up, the place for final filial endings. How could my brother, sister and I go the assisted living route or hire full-time help to care for my non-ambulatory father, who didn't even realize that he couldn't walk? At least here at the Menorah Park old home, he received custodial warehouse care—dutifully though sporadically responsive to alarms set off when he tried to get up to walk—along with desultory attempts to provide recreational, rehab and walker activities, and where aides took him to the toilet.

It was cold in snow-laden Cleveland as 2003 had begun, and here at Menorah Park, where my mother expired, my father now sat surrounded by his daughter and his younger son, grandchildren and great-grandchildren. Lauren and Alexa hovered over him, their last living grandparent. There had been great excitement throughout the city over yesterday's overtime gridiron victory of the national champion Ohio State Buckeyes. Like the old joke about Jewish Alzheimers being the forgetting of everything but the grudges, my father remarked that he did not take any pleasure in the OSU victory, because this was the alma mater that had turned him down for medical school over seventy years before. "You know why they turned me down, don't you?" he asked, as if putting us all through a test. Then he answered his own question: "Because I'm a Jew." Still, the what-ifs were implicit even now, crystallized into his old man's momentary bitterness at how life somehow had cheated him out of his dream of being a doctor—a loss he seemed more resigned to for most of the years of his life. What if he hadn't been turned down, and what if he had become a physician . . . or . . . what if he hadn't been Jewish? What if I had written the great American novel? But here at Menorah Park, all what-ifs really did end, because this was the end before the grave.

If life was really that ongoing transmutation of Oedipal struggle, as Freud believed, then what did it mean to see one's father come to this? In the place he had come every day to visit his wife, sitting for hours by himself—usually with a dog-eared, worn book in his hands, always the same book, or with a television screen in front of him spewing transitory images and sounds loud enough for most to hear but not for him. Now it was a program on plastic surgery that was on "Entertainment Tonight," disclosing who among the stars had had a facelift, lipo, lip enlargement, botox and rhinoplasty. One of the women attendants came up and asked us if we wanted to move "with Hyman" to another, larger room and watch the Browns and the Steelers in the playoff game. All his life and since childhood my father had been called Zaz, a nickname he preferred to the maidenhead-and-too-Jewish-sounding Hyman. But here he was Hyman once again to the women who cared for him.

The social worker talked of my father's frustration at being bridled and unable to walk. "He was trying to get up and said something about wanting to go home, and the next thing we knew he was cursing and saying he couldn't take it anymore." That's it, Daddy. Do not go gentle. I watched as a few of the other patients gazed with slack jaws, staring blankly as the Browns lost to the Steelers. What can celebrities, facial aesthetics, attempts to preserve youth or football playoffs possibly mean here, in this nursing home, where the news was incontinence, steadfast decline and memory loss?

I stood by my father's bedside routinely answering the same questions he asked over and over of me. "Where do you live now, Mike?" "What is it you do, Mike?" "What is your wife's name again, Mike?" "How many kids do you have?" I also talked to him about old friends of his—some of whom he remembered but most he had forgotten—about relatives and the home we lived in and the neighbors on our block. I talked about the subjects he loved, Judaism and bridge and medicine and philosophy. I talked about my brother and sister and our lives as children and adults and his and my mother's lives and his grandchildren, whom he could no longer name or recognize. I talked and I talked as I sifted through memories, which are really old identities, and brought forth words and stories while my father listened but remembered nothing of what I said. My words were offerings at the bedsides of both the parents I loved as they drew their final breaths.

The masters of prose, the writers for whom I have had a lifetime's admiration, they were the ones who provided, through language, the solace and understanding we need. That was one reason why I had wanted to be of them, to fuse my identity, irretrievably, to theirs. I thought of Faulkner writing about how the old confuse time with its mathematical progression and for whom "all the past is not a diminishing road but, instead, a huge meadow which no winter ever quite touches." That was where my father was now, in a mostly muted discontent of his life's winter, where memory could barely reside. That, too, was the kind of language—never-to-be written, the words of the novelist—I had wished I could summon. I saw my own road diminishing as I sat with the residue of life that my father once had.

I thought of the last interview I did with Norman Mailer, nearly six decades after the publication of *The Naked and the Dead.* He compared being old to being a battleship looking for port and said the self is a land of confusion. "We live," he told me, "with our truths and the truths of others." Novelists, he said, need distance from the self, which memoir writers can ill afford. I remembered, too, my first interview with his one-time nemesis Gore Vidal, and the young man I was then, hungry for literary identity. My gambit as a neophyte interviewer before we went on air was to try engaging Vidal by talking about Saul Bellow's beloved friend Delmore Schwartz—who once asked what there is besides the memory and the photograph. That seems a foolish question to the man I have become because there is, for me, the life I have written here, a life poured into teaching, broadcasting, family and friendships archived in memories and on tape for years to come—a good man's life, I hope; that is the real oeuvre.

I will say *kaddish* for my father as I did for my mother. And I know, somehow, that at his grave I will find words, my words.